A CONCISE
INTRODUCTION
TO PHILOSOPHY

A CONCISE INTRODUCTION TO PHILOSOPHY

Third Edition

WILLIAM H. HALVERSON
The Ohio State University

 Random House · New York

Third Edition

9876

Library of Congress Cataloging in Publication Data

Halverson, William H
  A concise introduction to philosophy.

  Includes bibliographies and index.
  1. Philosophy—Introductions. I. Title.
BD21.H23 1976   100   75-38807
ISBN 0–394–31985–0

Manufactured in the United States of America

Excerpts from *Summa Theologica* by St. Thomas Aquinas. Reprinted from *Basic Writings of Saint Thomas Aquinas*, edited by Anton C. Pegis. Copyright 1945 and renewed 1973 by Random House, Inc.

Limerick by Ronald Knox on pp. 102–103 reprinted by permission of Lord Oxford.

To Lynn, Kay, Beth, Sue, and Carol . . .
a string of pearls of very great price!

PREFACE

One of the good things about the occurrence of our nation's bicentennial is that it has given us the opportunity to put the problems of the present into some kind of historical perspective. The political crisis of Watergate, the worldwide energy shortage, the erratic behavior of an economy that once appeared robust and secure somehow seem less cataclysmic when viewed against the background of two full centuries of national life. Every era poses unique problems for those destined to live through it. A nation's history is the story of how its people have responded to the problems thrust upon them in each succeeding era.

The problems with which philosophy deals are, to be sure, less "dated" than the problems that occupy the headlines of *The New York Times*. This does not mean, however, that philosophy is unconcerned with the issues considered most important during any particular period of history. Philosophy is timeless in the sense that it deals with the most fundamental problems posed by man's life in the world. But philosophy is also timely, for, to some extent, the life experiences of a given period determine which of those fundamental problems most urgently demand our attention and the particular forms in which those problems are conceived. Vietnam and Watergate and the energy crisis have not created any new philosophical problems, but our way of thinking about various philosophical problems is almost certainly different than it would have been had these events not occurred.

This edition of *A Concise Introduction to Philosophy* incorporates several changes that, I think, will greatly enhance its value as an introductory text. Two new sections are included—one on the Problem of Evil, and a concluding section on Philosophies of Life. The section on metaethics (The Language of Morals) has been abbreviated somewhat, and the sequence of topics has been changed in response to suggestions from many users of the previous edition. Every chapter has been carefully reviewed, and where revisions seemed appropriate they have been made.

The *dialogue form* that is used throughout this book calls for a few words of explanation. Each topic is introduced in an introductory chapter in which I attempt to clarify the problem that is to be discussed, define the principal alternatives, and introduce any technical terms that may be necessary for the discussion that is to follow. Each succeeding chapter on that topic is then written *from the point of view of a convinced advocate of the view in question.* Only in Part I (Chapters 1–5) and in the introductory chapters of each succeeding part do I write, so to speak, "in my own name." The remaining chapters should be read as if they had been written by many different authors.

What is gained by this somewhat unusual format is a combination of the principal advantages of an anthology and of a single-author text. Like an anthology, *A Concise Introduction to Philosophy* keeps the discussion in the first person. The various writers are not merely talking *about* something: they are advocating a point of view, trying to secure agreement. Also like an anthology, *A Concise Introduction to Philosophy* is able to give a fair hearing to a variety of philosophical views: it does not bias the argument in favor of any one philosophical tendency or school. But it is also like a single-author text in certain respects: it has the coherence and, most important, the terminological consistency that cannot be expected in a book that is the product of many different authors.

It is both a duty and a pleasure to express my sincere thanks to the many individuals who have had a part in the making of this book. A number of users of earlier editions who have offered suggestions will, I trust, see the results of their proposals in these pages. Donald Walhout of Rockford College has again made many helpful comments that have made this a much better book than it would otherwise have been. Special thanks are due to Professor Oscar Schmiege of United States International University, who has not only read and commented on the entire manuscript, but has also been most helpful in updating the bibliographies. My colleagues at Random House have, as usual, been merciless in holding me to deadlines, and I thank them for it. Those deadlines would not have been met were it not for the patient and careful efforts of Doris Coon, who typed the final manuscript.

Columbus, Ohio   W.H.H.
January, 1976

CONTENTS

PART I

A PROLOGUE TO PHILOSOPHY

1

THE STUDY
OF PHILOSOPHY

You are, I assume, a beginning student in philosophy. You do not claim to know very much about what the so-called great philosophers thought or said, and more than likely you have never taken a philosophy course in your life. Yet the fundamental issues of philosophy are issues that all of us think about at one time or another, and for many years you undoubtedly have been "doing" philosophy—that is, asking philosophical questions, engaging in philosophical arguments, and adopting philosophical views.

The new element in the picture for you, then, is that you are now going to *study* philosophy. You are going to try to get a handle on it, to find out what it is all about, and maybe even find the answers to some important questions that have been bothering you. The philosophizing you have done up to this point has probably been fairly tentative and unsystematic. You know that the questions you have been asking are important ones, but you have not quite known how to go about finding the answers. The study of philosophy, you have been told, will help you in your search.

The first step in such a study is to develop a clear conception of just what philosophy is. Let us approach that task by taking a brief look at some of the most common beliefs that people often bring to their first study of philosophy.

Common Impressions

Many people understand the term "philosophy" to mean a general theory about something, particularly about how to approach some broad undertaking. It may be said, for example, that liberals and conservatives have some fundamental disagreements in *political philosophy*, or that public education has recently had to come to terms with a radically different *educational philosophy*. In both these cases, however, we could substitute the term "theory" for "philosophy" without changing the meaning. Hence, it is clear that in these instances, "philosophy" simply means "theory." Since this is one of the most common ways in which people who are not professional philosophers hear and use the term, it is one of the strongest impressions that people have of philosophy.

It may be of some importance to note in this connection that the term "philosophy," when used in this way, always has a very practical orientation: it is a theory about how to *do* something in a given area of human concern. Indeed, the broader the area, the more appropriate it seems to speak about activity in that area as being guided by some "philosophy." Whereas we do not hesitate to talk about a person's "political philosophy" or "educational philosophy," it would seem very odd to talk about one's theories regarding gardening or house painting as "gardening philosophy" or "house-painting philosophy."

Not too far removed from this impression of philosophy as functional theory is the idea that "philosophy" means a general view of life, or a general theory about how we ought to conduct our lives. Here, too, philosophy is understood to have a very practical orientation. The activity envisioned in this case, however, is not restricted to this or that area, but includes the whole of life. People can live for gain, or they can live to serve: it depends, we sometimes say, on their "philosophy of life." And a "philosophy of life" would presumably include views on such things as the nature of man and man's place in the universe, some convictions about what things are worth living for, and so on. When the term "philosophy" is used without a qualifying adjective ("political," "educational," "economic"), most people probably understand it to mean "philosophy of life."

It also seems to be a common notion that philosophy has to do with matters that are profound and usually very abstract. Philosophers accordingly are thought to be wise and learned (though it may not be very clear just what they are so learned about, or how they acquired their peculiar wisdom). Consequently, when students approach their first course in philosophy, they are sometimes apprehensive about their ability to master such an apparently forbidding field.

Perhaps another reason that philosophy is often regarded as difficult derives from the understanding of "philosophy" as "general theory." People do know in a general way what is meant by "political philosophy," or "philosophy of education," or "philosophy of life," but few have detailed knowledge in any of these areas. Indeed, it is almost axiomatic that a theory must be somewhat mystifying before we are willing to dignify it with the name "philosophy." Hence, we readily accept the view that someone who has worked out the details of a "philosophy" of something must be a person of superior wisdom. Learning how to paint a house or raise a garden does not strike us as being very difficult; thus it seems ridiculous to call views on these things "philosophy." But a theory about how to organize an economic system, or about the purposes of education, or about the correct way to live, is a different matter. Here the perspectives are so broad, the content so vast, the categories so obscure, that people automatically conclude, "This must be philosophy."

Another possible reason for the impression that philosophy is difficult to understand is that often when someone makes a general or vague statement about something, we hear it said that he is "getting philosophical." It is not always clear in such cases whether it is broad generality or vagueness that makes the statement "philosophical," but "philosophical" is what it is called. And so, many people get the impression that philosophy is, at best, concerned with matters that are profound, beyond the understanding of most men, or, at worst, simply vague and imprecise.

Then, too, there are those who regard philosophy as dangerous. Well-meaning people sometimes warn college students (in the words of St. Paul) to "see to it that no one makes a prey of you by philosophy and empty deceit" [1]—the inference being that all philosophy is nothing but "empty deceit" that will "make a prey" of the unwary. Not uncommonly, perhaps, philosophy is seen as a threat to religious faith, to morality, and perhaps to citizenship; the conclusion is drawn that for this reason it ought to be avoided by anyone who values these things.

It is interesting to note that this impression regarding philosophy dates from the earliest days of the Western philosophical tradition. The most notable example of the "bad press" from which philosophy has long suffered is, of course, the trial and conviction of Socrates, the great Greek philosopher of the fifth century B.C., who was charged with "impiety" and "corrupting the youth." Socrates, in making his defense to the Athenian court, was quite explicit about the fact that the court's opinion of him was prejudiced because of the prevailing negative opinion of philosophy. He told the court:

> I have had many accusers complaining to you, and for a long time, for many years now, and with not a word of truth to say. . . . These . . . got hold of most of you while you were boys, and persuaded you, and accused me falsely. . . . These, gentlemen, who have broadcast this reputation, these are my dangerous accusers; for those who hear believe that anyone who is a student of that sort of lore must be an atheist as well.[2]

Whether or not philosophy really is dangerous, or potentially dangerous, to the generally accepted values of society is a question that the student will ultimately have to decide for himself. It is indisputable, however, that philosophy is regarded as dangerous by many people, with the result that students who register for their first course in philosophy

---

[1] Colossians, 2:8.

[2] Plato, *Apology*, in W. H. D. Rouse (ed.), *Great Dialogues of Plato* (New York: New American Library, 1956), p. 424.

often do so with the feeling that what they are about to study is mildly subversive.

Finally, it is not unusual to hear it suggested that philosophy is a waste of time. The indictment might read like this: "Scientists and technicians do things that help to provide the necessities and comforts of life; doctors and dentists work to alleviate human suffering; athletes and musicians provide enjoyable entertainment—but what do philosophers do for their fellow-men? They speculate and dream and talk nonsense and undermine the faith of men. Anybody who wants to amount to anything will do well to leave philosophy alone."

In some respects, perhaps, negative attitudes toward philosophy derive from the actual character of the philosophical enterprise; in other respects, they show a total misunderstanding of that enterprise. The student will be able to assess their accuracy for himself as soon as he has developed some understanding of what the philosophical enterprise is about. For the present, it may be of some value to make a few generalizations about philosophy that relate to the popular views we have just discussed.

A Preliminary Characterization

Acquiring competence in philosophy is not primarily a means to a vocational goal. In this respect, the study of philosophy is similar to the study of literature: an appreciation of it is presumed to be valuable in and of itself, and this is the justification for spending time on it. You can, of course, teach philosophy, just as you can teach literature; but it would be quite pointless to do so if the study and appreciation of either were not worthwhile in itself.

It must be admitted that the values of our society in recent years have not been conducive to the flowering of philosophy, literature, or the arts. Our society tends to value what pays and to devalue what does not pay. Painting and sculpting, for example, are considered worthwhile activities only if the painter or sculptor is able to "make a living" at it. Music is considered a truly appropriate field of study only if the student is believed to have the talent to become a successful performer, composer, or teacher of music. And the study of literature, sad to say, is often regarded as a time-wasting diversion for people who should have more important and "practical" things to do.

What is missing in this very commercialized view, of course, is any recognition of the intrinsic and nonsalable value of developing a genuine appreciation of art or music or literature. But if the cultivation of such an appreciation is not worthwhile in itself—if it is not justified simply on the ground that it makes life richer and broader and more human—then the teaching or promotion of these things is wholly unjustified.

Because of the commercialization of values in our society, it is necessary to remind ourselves from time to time that there is a difference between education and job training. Education is concerned with the development of our capacities for creative participation in life. Job training is concerned with preparation for some particular kind of employment. To forget this distinction, and to think only in terms of the latter, is to render irrelevant a considerable part of what is typically included in a baccalaureate program.

Do not, then, approach the study of philosophy—or, for that matter, of history, music, literature, or art—with the expectation that you will acquire some salable knowledge or skill. Chances are that you will not. Approach it rather with the hope that it will increase your self-awareness and enrich your appreciation of the powers as well as the limits of the human mind; then you will not be disappointed.

Also bear in mind that philosophy is by its very nature critical of the status quo, unwilling to accept as unquestionable even the most widely held beliefs. It was Socrates who provided philosophy with its central cue when he declared that "the unexamined life is not worth living." [3] Do not be surprised, therefore, if you encounter, as you undoubtedly will, views that seem preposterous. The beliefs that are called into question may indeed be true; the philosopher's point is simply that their truth ought not to be taken for granted.

We shall have more to say on this point in a moment (see pp. 12–13). For the present it is enough to note that a good deal of the suspicion with which many people regard philosophy derives, understandably, from the fact that philosophers almost invariably stand in a critical, questioning relation to prevailing modes of thought.

Philosophy and Liberal Education

John Henry Newman once said:

> A University training is the great ordinary means to a great but ordinary end. . . . It is the education which gives a man a clear conscious view of his own opinions and judgments, a truth in developing them, and a force in urging them. It teaches him to see things as they are, to go right to the point, to disentangle a skein of thought, to detect what is sophistical, and to discard what is irrelevant. It prepares him to fill any post with credit, and to master any subject with facility.[4]

Those words were written in 1852. At the time, they summed up beautifully and accurately the ideal end product of liberal education: a man of broad learning and culture, a conscious heir of the cultural riches of the past, an expert in the exercise of reason, a master of the art of conversation, a gentleman. Such a man, said Newman, is "at home in

[3] *Ibid.,* p. 445.

[4] John Henry Newman, *The Idea of a University,* in Henry Tristram (ed.), *Newman's Idea of a Liberal Education* (New York: Barnes & Noble, 1952), pp. 104–105.

any society." He has "the repose of a mind which lives in itself, while it lives in the world, and which has resources for its happiness at home when it cannot go abroad." [5] He is, in short, a liberally educated man.

Much has happened since 1852 to make the university a very different place from that described by Cardinal Newman. The educated man of Newman's ideal was a generalist; the university graduate of today (man or woman) is expected to be a specialist. Higher education, as Newman conceived it, was supposed to be available only to the privileged few; today it is regarded as the right of the many. The university, as Newman described it, was aloof from society, a sanctuary of the mind well removed from the cacophony of the marketplace; the university of today is a mirror of society, highly solicitous of its support and responsive to its needs. The university of Newman's day functioned chiefly as conservator of the old; the modern university places a far higher priority on the discovery of the new. The "university" whose idea Newman so eloquently proclaimed has all but disappeared; in its place has appeared what Clark Kerr has aptly called the "multiversity." [6]

For a student, the multiversity can be a very confusing place. One's courses all seem to be "specialty" courses: one hour is history, the next chemistry, then sociology, and so on through the day. But there are times when the student must wonder, "Don't these various fields of study relate to each other in some way? Does education really consist in nothing more than the acquisition of information in isolated compartments? Surely there must be *some* context in which I can comprehend these various bits of information as somehow hanging together."

An important function of philosophy is to provide a context in which such integration can be realized. The great questions of philosophical controversy, such as those we shall be discussing, are by no means the special preoccupations of just one more group of specialists called philosophers. They are questions that cut across the artificial barriers of our academic specialities and compel us to *relate* our little pockets of specialized knowledge (and opinion, and conjecture, and even feeling) in some coherent way. "Philosophy," said René Descartes, "is like a tree, of which metaphysics is the root, physics the trunk, and all the other sciences the branches that grow out of this trunk . . ." [7] The study of philosophy should be approached as a context within which to relate and integrate what is learned in the various specialized fields. If this intent is realized, the study of philosophy can yield one of the choicest fruits of a liberal education: the capacity "to see life steady and to see it whole."

---

[5] *Ibid.*

[6] Clark Kerr, *The Uses of the University* (Cambridge, Mass: Harvard University Press, 1964), chap. 1.

[7] René Descartes, *The Principles of Philosophy*, in *A Discourse on Method and Selected Writings*, tr. John Veitch. (New York: Dutton, 1951), p. 174.

STUDY QUESTIONS

1. Are there any questions that you have thought about or discussed that might qualify as philosophical questions? Is it true that you have been "doing" philosophy even though you may never have taken a course in philosophy?
2. What prior impressions about philosophy do you bring with you to this study? How have you acquired these impressions?
3. Write four or five sentences in which it seems natural to you to use the term "philosophy." In what sense or senses are you using it?
4. How widespread, in your judgment, is the view that philosophy is "dangerous" and "a waste of time"? As far as you can judge, do the people who hold these views know enough about philosophy to be entitled to an opinion?
5. Do you think it is fair to say that our society is consistently "commercial" in its values? With what sort of evidence could you support your answer?
6. Can you see any possible value in questioning beliefs that most people take for granted? Would it not be better to leave such matters alone and to concentrate all our efforts on attempting to find solutions to the social, economic, and political problems that plague mankind today?

2

THE TWO SIDES OF
THE PHILOSOPHICAL TASK

There was a time when people who called themselves philosophers were generally in accord about the definition of the philosophical task. At the present time, however, there is substantial disagreement among philosophers concerning what they are, or are supposed to be, doing. Before we proceed to outline our own proposal for a definition of the philosopher's task, it may be helpful to look briefly at a few of the reasons for this lack of consensus.

One development that contributed to the present uncertainty in philosophy was the progressive takeover by the special sciences of areas of inquiry formerly belonging to philosophy. Aristotle, for example, included in his philosophical inquiries a large number of matters that are now customarily carried out by biologists, physicists, psychologists, zoologists, political scientists, literary critics, and so on. For Aristotle, "philosophy" was virtually a collective name for the quest for knowledge, in whatever area, by whatever means. But since the time of Aristotle, and particularly during the past three or four hundred years, this quest has been carried on with increasingly sophisticated techniques by a wide variety of specialists.

For some time after the advent of modern science, the general view among philosophers was that their peculiar domain (as distinguished from that of the natural scientists) was *metaphysics*.[1] The relation of metaphysics to the special sciences was a matter of some dispute, but for a time everyone seemed happy with the arrangement whereby philosophers concentrated on metaphysics and scientists claimed the various kinds of merely "factual" inquiries as their own.

---

[1] For the definition of this and other technical terms used in this book see the Glossary, pp. 445–452.

During the eighteenth century, however, questions were raised about the validity of the whole idea of metaphysical knowledge. David Hume and Immanuel Kant, in very different ways, both asked, in effect, "Is there anything to the claims of philosophers, or are their speculations really empty?" Hume recommended consigning all metaphysical treatises to the flames. Kant called upon metaphysicians to suspend their labors until they could give a satisfactory account of the methodology upon which they based their assertions. In both cases, however, the enterprise that had become the central business of the philosopher was radically questioned, and it could only be a matter of time until philosophers would have to give some kind of answer to this challenge.

After a century or more, the strictures of Hume and Kant had their effect. Here and there—in England, in Austria (the "Vienna Circle"), in America—some philosophers began to question the validity of the philosophical enterprise as it was being pursued by most of their contemporaries. Gradually a loosely organized movement became discernible, the most obvious features of which were an abandonment of metaphysics and an affinity for the empirical methods of the natural sciences. A principal goal of its adherents was to define the philosophical task in such a way as to relinquish all claims to a special kind of knowledge transcending that of natural science.

But if the several natural sciences have taken over the empirical inquiries that were once a part of the philosophical domain, and if metaphysics is abandoned as unwarranted or empty speculation, does there remain anything at all for the philosopher to do? This question haunts present-day philosophers, and the many conflicting statements they make about "what philosophy is" give some idea of how far the discussion remains from anything like a consensus.

There is general agreement among philosophers on one point, however: that at least one part of the traditional philosophical enterprise remains an important responsibility of the philosopher, namely *logic*. Some philosophers are of the opinion that logical studies, broadly conceived, constitute the whole of philosophy. Others believe there must be something more to philosophy, but are uncertain what that "something more" might be. And still others, of course, continue to believe that metaphysics is possible.

The Nature of the Question

What are we actually asking when we pose the question, What is the proper task of the philosopher?

Note that our question is not an arbitrary verbal one, a matter of simply assigning some useful meaning to the phrase "the philosophical task." This is why it is not helpful to say, as it sometimes has been, that "philosophy is what philosophers do." We could, of course, assign to a group of people some random function—basket weaving, for example—

and say, "That is what we shall hereafter call 'philosophy.' The task of the philosopher is to weave baskets." But this would obviously be pointless.

Our question is, rather, a very special kind of historical question. Philosophy is an academic discipline that emerged (as have all academic disciplines) out of the long sorting-out process whereby Western man has tried to organize his knowledge and inquiry. Its present status is in doubt, as we have said, because many of the inquiries that once were a part of philosophy have become independent disciplines (biology, physics, etc.), and because a major part of what was once regarded as the philosophical task has been rejected by many philosophers as being beyond the limits of human knowledge. Our question, therefore, is this: Is there not some task that (a) has traditionally been performed by men who have called themselves philosophers, (b) has not been taken over by any of the special sciences, and (c) is still performable? If such a task can be identified, it is that task that is most appropriately designated "the task of the philosopher."

The Critical Task

As we saw in the previous chapter, Socrates was convicted by the Athenian court of "impiety" and "corrupting the youth" and was condemned to die.[2] What led to the charges against Socrates? Evidently it was not his deliberate intention to promote impiety or to corrupt youth. Rather, according to Plato's Apology, which is considered to be a fairly accurate account of the historical Socrates, the facts are these. A friend of Socrates, Chairephon, inquired of the oracle at Delphi whether anyone was wiser than Socrates and received the reply that no one was. Hearing this, Socrates—who, as he says, knew in his conscience that he was not wise—proceeded to test the oracle's statement by interrogating some of his fellow citizens who were generally regarded to be wise and learned. Socrates comments on his interrogation as follows:

> I approached one of those who had the reputation of being wise for there, I thought, if anywhere, I should test the revelation and prove that the oracle was wrong . . . But when I examined him . . . and when I conversed with him, I thought this man seemed to be wise both to many others and especially to himself, but that he was not . . . After that I tried another, one of those reputed to be wiser than that man, and I thought just the same; then he and many others took a dislike to me.[3]

Socrates took it to be his unique task to interrogate his fellow citizens to see whether or not their opinions could stand up under close scrutiny. Wherever he found people holding opinions, or making truth claims,

---

[2] A moving description of Socrates' death is given in Plato's Phaedo.

[3] Plato, Apology, in W. H. D. Rouse (ed.), Great Dialogues of Plato (New York: New American Library, 1956), p. 427.

there he went to work. Does Meno claim to know whether or not virtue can be taught? "Meno," asks Socrates, "what is virtue? Do you really know what virtue is? And if you do not know what virtue is, how can you possibly know whether or not it can be taught?" Does Euthyphro claim to know that his father is guilty of impiety? "Euthyphro," says Socrates, "I do not even know for sure what piety and impiety are. Could you instruct me in this?"

This picture of Socrates going about questioning the men of Athens to test the soundness of their opinions represents what we may call the *critical* side of the philosophical enterprise. We all take many things for granted; indeed, everything we do is determined by or at least affected by our assumptions, even though very often—perhaps most of the time—we are scarcely aware of them. It is in the assumptions that underlie supposed knowledge that the philosopher is chiefly interested. He wants to know what those assumptions are and whether or not they are reasonable; so, like Socrates, he examines them.

Socrates, of course, went about his business in a very informal and personal way. Since his time, however, philosophy has become more or less institutionalized. The questions that philosophers raise today are directed not so much at individuals as at fields of learning. The philosopher questions not the scientist, but the assumptions and the truth claims of science; not the religious person, but the assumptions and the truth claims of religion; and so on. Philosophy is, so to speak, the gadfly in the curriculum of a modern college or university, just as Socrates was a gadfly to his fellow citizens in ancient Athens.

The Constructive Task

Philosophers, however, do not engage in this critical task merely to make a nuisance of themselves. Indeed, a careful scrutiny of the work of many generations of practicing philosophers suggests that the principal aim of the philosopher is to construct a picture of the whole of reality, in which every element of man's knowledge and every aspect of man's experience will find its proper place. Philosophy, in short, is man's quest for the unity of knowledge, a perpetual struggle to create the concepts that allow the universe to be seen as unified rather than fragmented. The history of philosophy is the history of this attempt. The problems of philosophy are the problems that arise when one attempts to grasp this total unity.

The theoretical goal of the natural sciences is to produce a description of the universe so complete that everything that occurs—every phenomenon from the behavior of the tiniest particle within the simplest atom to the most complex biological processes—can be understood as instances of regularities that we call laws. Let us suppose, for the sake of argument, that this goal were to be reached: our "picture of the whole of reality" would still be incomplete. We would still want to ask questions such as the following: What are good and evil? What is their place in the universe whose physical workings we now understand so completely? Does this complete description of the universe describe the universe as it is, or is it, wholly or in part, merely a description of the universe as we perceive it? Is beauty a quality in objects that we call beautiful? Is it something "in the eye of the beholder"? Or is it something else? Does the physical universe exist as a self-subsistent entity, or is it dependent for its being on some reality beyond itself? Is the consciousness that we ourselves experience a merely physical phenomenon, or is it something else? The fact is, our awareness of suffering, of tragedy, of injustice, of good and evil, of beauty and ugliness, of meanness and nobility, leaves us dissatisfied with a merely physical description of the universe. We cannot be content until the truths about these and other dimensions of our experience have also been understood and brought into some coherent relationship with what we know about the universe as a system of purely physical phenomena.

The attempt to achieve this total understanding stands without rival as the most audacious enterprise in which the human mind has ever engaged. Just reflect for a moment: Man is surrounded by the vastness of a universe in which he is only a tiny and perhaps insignificant part—and he wants to *understand* it, to conceive the whole thing in his mind, in such a way that no reality that confronts him, no event that occurs, no fact that he discovers, nothing that he experiences, is beyond the categories of his understanding. Audacious indeed; but what are the alternatives?

One alternative would be to attempt no understanding at all. Perhaps, if he tried hard enough, man could learn to accept the world unquestion- ingly, responding to it in terms of self-preservation only. Apparently other species do no more and survive rather well in the struggle for life.

In all seriousness, however, it does not appear likely that man ever could or would do this, even if it were desirable. As Aristotle said long ago, it seems that by his very nature man desires to know.[4] Not only does he seek to know in order that he may more effectively manipulate his environment; he also seeks to know purely for the sake of knowing. The total abandonment of the quest for understanding, then, is not a promising alternative to constructive philosophy.

Another alternative would be for man to be content with piecemeal knowledge—to establish what he can in each of the special sciences and to make no attempt to see the "total picture" of which each of these fragments is presumably a part. Such an approach is expressed in statements like "It is better to know one thing well than to know a little bit about everything" or "It is better to be a good chemist than a poor philosopher."

---

[4] Aristotle, *Metaphysics*, I, i, in Richard McKeon (ed.), *The Basic Works of Aristotle* (New York: Random House, 1941), p. 689.

But here, too, there is a problem, one that makes it impossible to hold such a view except in the half-jesting mood reflected above. For as we focus our attention on first one area, then another, we are sometimes driven to conclusions that appear to be in conflict with one another. They are the by-products of compartmentalized thinking, what we may call apparent incompatibles, and not easily accepted by a healthy mind. How, we insist on asking, for example, can man be free in the sense that ethics seems to require, if, as appears to be the case, the whole universe is subject without exception to causal law? If all knowledge comes to us through experience, and if experience yields only probability, how is it that in mathematics we appear to be able to establish our conclusions with absolute certainty? These and other questions thrust themselves upon us, almost in spite of ourselves. It is out of such tension among the various elements of our piecemeal knowledge that much philosophical thinking arises. For to ask such questions is precisely to ask for the wider concept, the total picture, in which what is legitimate in each of these competing truth claims can be given its due.

It was the desire to arrive at just such a total picture that motivated the great philosophers of the past. And since it is apparent that the task of unifying human knowledge has not been taken over by any of the special sciences, it might appear self-evident that this is still an important part of the philosophical enterprise. Some philosophers would say, however, that this task is simply not performable, and that it therefore cannot be a part of the philosopher's present concern.

How are we to understand such an objection? If, as we have already argued, the only alternatives to such a quest are either to abandon altogether the search for knowledge or to be content with piecemeal knowledge, and if neither of these is a practicable course to follow, then it would appear that somebody must continue to pursue this task within the household of learning. Who should it be if not the philosopher? On what grounds, or for what reason, could a present-day philosopher forswear this task as being "unperformable" in the modern world?

The answer to the puzzle is something like this: Those philosophers who decline the traditional philosophical quest for the unity of man's knowledge recognize that any proposals they might make with respect to the total picture cannot have the empirical probability of a scientific hypothesis, and they are reluctant to commit themselves to any proposals that do not meet this qualification. Their objection, in effect, is that the traditional philosophical task is not performable *with the same degree of certainty* as are the several tasks of the special sciences. This is indisputably true, and its truth should be a warning to any philosopher to make his proposals with considerable caution if he nonetheless elects to pursue this quest. But if our previous reasoning was sound, this consideration ought not prevent pursuit of this quest with such probability as the nature of the inquiry will allow.

One thing, at least, seems clear: the quest for the total picture, the struggle to discern the unity that we instinctively believe lies behind the apparent inconsistencies of our little fragments of knowledge—in short, the constructive philosophical quest—will go on, with or without the cooperation of professional philosophers. The student who undertakes the study of philosophy because he finds himself involved in a similar quest will discover that he is in the company of many great philosophers from Plato to the present, and he may legitimately expect to find a new and exciting challenge as he considers the answers that philosophers have given to the profoundest questions that man has dared to ask.

STUDY QUESTIONS

1. What do you understand to be the "critical" task of philosophy? What are some of the questions that a philosopher might ask in attempting to pursue this task?
2. Are you convinced that the *only* alternatives to "constructive philosophy" are (a) giving up the quest for understanding altogether, or (b) settling for "piecemeal" knowledge? How might one go about trying to refute this claim?
3. Are you inclined to agree or to disagree with the following statement: "The constructive task of philosophy is a task that cannot be avoided: the only question is whether it is to be pursued carefully and systematically or informally and haphazardly"?

3

PHILOSOPHICAL PROBLEMS AND PHILOSOPHICAL SYSTEMS

The history of philosophy, we have observed, is the history of man's quest for a comprehensive picture of reality, in which every element of knowledge and every aspect of experience finds its proper place. The problems of philosophy, we suggested, are the problems that arise when one pursues this end. But when is a problem a philosophical problem? How does an answer to a philosophical problem relate to this quest for the total picture? And how does all of this relate to the so-called philosophical systems?

Characteristics of a Philosophical Question

Consider the following questions:

1. At what temperature does pure water freeze, assuming sea-level barometric pressure?
2. What is the name of the capital of India?
3. Who held the office of president of the United States in 1797?
4. Is the atomic theory helpful in explaining the process of photosynthesis?
5. What is religion?
6. Is moral responsibility compatible with the determinism assumed in most scientific inquiries?

Of the six questions, the first three are obviously not philosophical. Nearly everyone will readily recognize that question 1 belongs to physics, question 2 to geography, and question 3 to history. If we wanted an answer to any of these questions we would turn, respectively, to the physicist, the geographer, and the historian.

Question 4 may puzzle us for a moment. Is it a question for the botanist to answer, or is it one for the physicist? We are not sure. But note this: we do recognize it to be a scientific question, our reason for hesitation being only that we are uncertain which of the sciences is competent to handle it. We shall call such questions intrascientific; they arise because of the particular ways in which the natural sciences have marked out the boundaries of their inquiries.

Questions 5 and 6 present some new features. First, there is evidently no existing science that is competent to handle either question. Consider, for example, question 5, What is religion? We could imagine a number of scientists having opinions about the correct answer. Sigmund Freud, for example, felt strongly enough about his opinion regarding this question to write a book about it. But it is not, strictly speaking, within the competence of a psychologist *as a psychologist* to answer this question. The same must be said about the sociologist, the anthropologist, and the archaeologist: each of these scientists, pursuing his own proper inquiries, may discover some important facts about religion (such discovery *is* within his competence), and each may go on to form an opinion concerning "what religion really is." But in forming such an opinion the scientist is no longer speaking *as a scientist*. The same holds true for question 6.

Thus, one of the defining characteristics of philosophical questions is that they do not fall within the competence of any of the special sciences, or even within the competence of any combination of the special sciences. Philosophical questions, in short, are neither straightforwardly scientific nor intrascientific.

A second feature of questions 5 and 6, and a second defining characteristic of philosophical questions, is that we cannot readily imagine what kinds of evidence, if any, would be relevant to answering them. With respect to question 5, for example, we suppose that some of the findings of psychologists, sociologists, archaeologists, anthropologists, and historians would be relevant. But which? And how would we go about gathering the relevant data? These are puzzling questions, and it is characteristic of philosophical questions that they puzzle us in just this way.

Third, philosophical questions are questions whose possible answers appear to have far-reaching consequences for our whole world-view: any answer that is given has implications that touch many areas of human concern. If on question 6, for example, we decide that determinism is not compatible with moral freedom and that determinism is true, we must then ask what the consequences are for our view of man's moral responsibility, for our understanding of the penal system, for the status of law, for the conduct of international diplomacy, for our estimate of our own conduct and that of our fellow-men. We could go on and on finding areas of human concern to which any answer to this question would be directly or indirectly relevant, and we could make the same point by using as an illustration any one of dozens of philosophical problems that have been discussed over the centuries. But let our single example suffice. A philosophical question is one whose possible answers have profound consequences for a total world-view, consequences of which we may be only vaguely aware or even totally unaware when the problem is initially raised.

Another way of putting the same point would be to say that philosophical questions are questions that are logically fundamental; that is, the answers to them determine to some extent the questions that can reasonably be asked at other (less fundamental) logical levels, and determine also what kinds of answers can be reasonably given. If, for example, we hold in reply to question 5 that religion consists, first, of illusory beliefs invented to enable human beings to cope with their fear of the unknown and, second, of a group of practices based upon those beliefs, we can no longer reasonably ask the theological question, Is God omnipotent, or is His power, however great, limited in some way? Philosophical questions are questions about the most fundamental—that is, logically fundamental—beliefs and assumptions that people hold. This is why the answers that we adopt, whatever those answers may be, have the far-reaching consequences of which we spoke earlier.

Finally, philosophical questions are typically questions of very broad generality. The philosophical question, Is man free in the sense required to render him morally responsible? is not a question about the freedom of a particular individual (such as a psychoanalyst might ask), or of a particular group of citizens (such as a political scientist might ask); it is a question about the freedom of man as such. To answer this question we do not study the case histories of individuals or the political fortunes of groups of people. Rather, we attempt to analyze carefully the *concept* of freedom as it relates to the ascription of moral responsibility to man, and then we consider whether this quality or power (or whatever "freedom" turns out to be) is ascribable to man, and if so, under what circumstances.

These characteristics of philosophical questions all derive from the fact that the overall goal of the philosophical quest is, as we have said, to achieve a picture of the whole, an all-inclusive concept of reality in which no truth fails to receive its proper due. Every philosophical problem is an integral part of this broader project; it is only because (or perhaps insofar as) we are interested in the larger project that we find ourselves interested in the particular problems. We shall have occasion to return to this point when—after having studied a number of philosophical problems—we focus explicitly on the issue of alternative world-views.

Types of Philosophical Questions

Any question exhibiting the above characteristics is, then, a philosophical question. During the long span of time in which Western philosophers have been discussing questions of this sort, however, philosophical inquiry has come to assume a fairly well-defined structure. As a result, it is possible to speak of various "departments" of philosophical inquiry and, accordingly, of various "types" of philosophical questions. There is nothing final or definitive about this typology, but it has value as a system of points of reference when one is attempting to get one's bearings in this field.

Many philosophical questions are what may be called logical questions. That is to say, they are questions that arise in that department of philosophical inquiry known as *logic*. It is not easy to define logic in a way that does justice to the wide range of problems that concern logicians. However, a definition of logic as an inquiry concerning the principles by which one may distinguish between correct and incorrect reasoning would probably be acceptable to most logicians. Some representative problems of this type would be, What does it mean to say that an argument is "valid"? How does one test the validity of an argument?

Some philosophical questions are what may be called ontological (or metaphysical) questions. These are questions that arise in that department of philosophical inquiry known as *ontology* (or *metaphysics*). Again, it is difficult to give a definition that would be acceptable to everyone concerned. Ontology has been defined as "[the science of] being *qua* being" [1] and as "[an investigation concerning] the character of everything that is insofar as it is." [2] It is assumed that simply to *be*—not to be a man or a house or a tree, but simply to *be*—a thing must have a certain "structure." Ontology is the attempt to ascertain what that structure is. The question "Do some entities exist even though they are unperceived?" is an ontological question. The statement "Every object is a substance having at least one property" is an ontological statement. Some philosophers, though they allow that the metaphysical proposals of the past are appropriate subjects of historical study, would maintain that it is not possible to pose an intelligible question of this type, much less to give an intelligible or, at any rate, a defensible answer. (The student may wish to reserve judgment on this until he has had an opportunity to reflect on some of the questions dealt with in later portions of this text.)

A third general type of philosophical question is commonly called epistemological. *Epistemology* is that department of philosophy which attempts to ascertain the nature and limits of human knowledge. Under what conditions may we properly be said to "know" such and such? Does all knowledge of the real world arise out of experience, or do we have knowledge that is in some degree independent of experience? If all

---

[1] Aristotle, *Metaphysics*, IV, i, in Richard McKeon (ed.), *The Basic Works of Aristotle* (New York: Random House, 1941), p. 731.

[2] Paul Tillich, *Systematic Theology* (Chicago: University of Chicago Press, 1951), vol. I, p. 163.

knowledge does arise out of experience, and if experience can yield only varying degrees of probability, how is it possible to achieve the absolute certainty that we seem to achieve in logic and in mathematics? These are representative of the epistemological questions in which some philosophers are interested.

A fourth type of philosophical question is technically called axiological, although the terms *axiology* and *axiological* are not very commonly used among philosophers at the present time. Instead, philosophers speak of theory of value and of questions that arise in this context as questions concerning the nature of value. Some typical examples of this type would be, Are beauty and goodness qualities that are objectively present or absent in things? If so, how is their presence or absence ascertained? If not, are they simply sentiments in the mind of the person who judges that something is good or bad, beautiful or ugly? And if this is not the case, what *is* the status of beauty and goodness? That branch of axiology that is principally concerned with the values of special relevance for the arts is called *aesthetics*. The branch of axiology that deals with the nature of (and fundamental principles governing) good and evil, right and wrong, is known as *ethics*, or *moral philosophy*.

Philosophical Systems

In view of the fact that the philosophical quest has been going on for a very long time, it is not surprising that by now a considerable number of proposals have been made suggesting that this and that are the key elements in the total picture of reality, in terms of which every element of reality can be understood. To make such a proposal is to offer a philosophical system, that is, a view of the whole that purports to do justice to every element of human knowledge and every aspect of human experience.

There is some hesitation among philosophers today to talk about philosophical systems, just as there is a certain reluctance to accept as the central task of the philosophical enterprise the quest for unity as we have described it. The day of system-building, in the view of many philosophers, is past; it came to an end when—within the memory of some philosophers still living—it was concluded that constructive metaphysics is an impossible undertaking, a building of castles in the air.

In actuality, however, we do not need to be convinced of the possibility of metaphysics in order to hold that philosophical systems are not only possible but necessary—any more than we need to hold to the possibility of constructive metaphysics in order to acknowledge that the proper business of philosophy is to seek the total view. The truth is that every human being (including philosophers who do not like systems) carries on his thinking within some kind of philosophical system. To say that someone's philosophy constitutes a system is a perfectly innocuous statement: it is to say only that (a) his views on various matters (whatever matters he *has* views on) are logically consistent with each other and that (*b*) they are logically interdependent. Not everyone, of course, is explicitly aware of the system with which he operates, and even fewer people are sufficiently confident of the superiority of their system to recommend its adoption by others. But an intelligent being with no philosophical system whatsoever is unthinkable.

Types of Philosophical Systems

To avoid being overwhelmed by the number of philosophical systems encountered in the study of philosophy, it is helpful to think of these systems as belonging to one or the other of two families of systems, that is, the *naturalist* family and the *transcendentalist* family. A philosophical system may be said to be naturalistic if it affirms that (*a*) there is only one order of reality, that (*b*) this one order of reality consists entirely of objects and events occurring in space and time, and that (*c*) this one order of reality is completely self-dependent and self-operating. A system may be said to be transcendentalistic if it asserts that (*a*) the world of space and time depends for its existence on a reality that transcends space and time, that (*b*) reality is therefore *not* limited to objects and events occurring in space and time (i.e., some realities transcend space and time), and that (*c*) explanations of even spatiotemporal phenomena may, therefore, take thought beyond the spatiotemporal world to the dimensions of reality that transcend it. As a matter of historical fact, the dialogue between proponents of these two great types of systems has provided much of the impetus for philosophical discussion all through the long and sometimes tortuous history of Western philosophy. Many philosophical controversies that would otherwise be insignificant take on profound importance when viewed in the context of this dialogue.

All philosophical thinking is implicitly systematic in character. This is why philosophers passionately defend their views on what sometimes appear to be relatively trivial matters. Indeed, it is because of the systematic character of all philosophical thinking, because of the multidimensional relevance of all philosophical questions, that no philosophical question is trivial. Every philosophical problem is, so to speak, a test case: our whole world-view (the entire system in the context of which we attempt to understand the complex array of data coming before our consciousness) is at stake. The position we adopt with respect to a given philosophical problem inevitably limits the options available on other problems that we may encounter.

Would it not be advisable, then, simply to suspend judgment? Should we not refuse to commit ourselves on any point until its relevance to all others is known? Ah, but we are fogetting: *as rational beings we cannot help philosophizing.* We can, of course, suspend judgment on some points some of the time, but not on all. At the very least, we must think and act *as if* we had decided about a vast number of things. The alternative of not philosophizing at all is not available to us. We can decide only whether we will do it carelessly and poorly or deliberately and with care.

STUDY QUESTIONS

1. Review the characteristics of philosophical questions suggested in this chapter. Can you think of any questions that may have puzzled you that are philosophical according to these criteria? What are they?
2. Consider carefully the questions you have formulated in response to the previous question. Can you identify them as belonging to one or another of the four types (logical, ontological, epistemological, and theory of value) discussed in this chapter?
3. If it is true that "an intelligent being with no philosophical system whatsoever is unthinkable," then (presumably) every reader of this book has such a system. What are some of the elements of your system? What are some of the ways that your philosophical system is different from that of, say, a member of a society other than your own?
4. As far as you understand these matters at present, does it seem to you that the philosophical system with which you operate is naturalistic or transcendental-istic? Does this question strike you as being important? Why or why not?

4

FIRST STEPS
IN PHILOSOPHY

Getting one's bearings in philosophy, as in any new field, requires a bit of disciplined effort. The purpose of the present chapter is to suggest a method of study that will enable the beginning student to make maximum progress toward a mastery of philosophy.

Students should take encouragement from the fact that they have on many occasions, probably without knowing it, concerned themselves with philosophical problems. Very often in the study of philosophy we find ourselves involved in a rigorous and systematic discussion of a problem that we have encountered before but have not pursued because of lack of direction. The fact that everyone who comes to the point of studying philosophy has already been introduced to it in this informal way makes it much easier to establish a "beachhead" in the field than would otherwise be the case.

Alternative Approaches to Philosophy

One way to become acquainted with philosophy is to study its history, an approach that has two unique advantages and two serious disadvantages. On the positive side, the student becomes familiar, perhaps to some extent firsthand, with the thought of the greatest philosophers, and he also comes to recognize the intimate relation that always obtains between the philosophical reflection of a given period and other elements of the culture of that day. The disadvantages of making a first approach to philosophy by the historical route, however, are extremely serious. It is very confusing to spend several weeks or months studying the history of something whose essential nature is not understood. (What is the history of philosophy the history of?) Second, there is a semantic problem that is not readily resolvable through a purely historical approach. Unfortunately, different philosophers frequently use different terms to express the same idea. The student who lacks any prior systematic orientation is often bewildered by the profusion of terms used to discuss the new ideas that he is attempting to understand.

Many teachers of philosophy, therefore, prefer a *systematic* approach, which has three distinct advantages over the historical. The first is that it greatly minimizes the semantic problem by allowing the student to build up his philosophical vocabulary step by step in the context of philosophical discussions that, with reasonable effort, he is able to clearly understand. The second advantage is that it provides the novice in philosophy with a more familiar starting point, namely, problems and concerns that he has already encountered and that do not seem so strange and unfamiliar as would, for example, those addressed by Thales and Heraclitus (two early Greek philosophers). Third, the systematic approach enables the student to identify with the philosophical enterprise and to participate in philosophical discussion far more readily than does the historical approach. To really understand a philosophical problem—almost any philosophical problem—is to see its relevance for many areas of concern that previously may not have seemed at all related.

These remarks are not meant in any way to disparage the study of the history of philosophy. The point is rather that as a first introduction to philosophy the systematic approach has a great deal to commend it, and that the study of the history of philosophy is considerably enriched if it is begun with the kind of prior understanding and equipment that the systematic approach is intended to provide. There is no substitute, however, for an actual encounter with the writings of the great philosophers. Students who do not go on to participate in this encounter are depriving themselves of one of the most enriching experiences a liberal education has to offer.

The present book, in any case, uses the systematic approach. We shall therefore be considering, in succession, a number of philosophical problems, and with each of them we shall attempt to understand the possible solutions. We shall, of course, refer from time to time to philosophers, past and present, who have addressed themselves in one way or another to these same problems. But our purpose is not, except perhaps incidentally, to provide historical information; it is to lead students to the kind of understanding that will enable them to enter into the philosophical arena as participants rather than as mere spectators. The suggestions that follow are intended to help students focus their efforts in order to make maximum progress toward such understanding.

Three Steps Toward Understanding

There are three distinct determinations to be made when dealing with any given philosophical problem. First, attempt to understand precisely *what the problem is.* Note well: Understanding a problem is not the same as memorizing some approved formulation of it. There are undoubtedly some things that must be learned by rote, but there is very little in philosophy that can profitably be learned in this way. To understand a philosophical problem is to know what question you are asking, and what kind of assertion would count as an answer to the question. If you do not know this—if you cannot imagine anything that would qualify as a possible answer to your question—then you have not really asked a question; you have only made a little interrogative noise.

Most of us, unfortunately, are so much in the habit of deceiving ourselves (and others) about what we really understand and what we understand only in a general, hazy way, that it is necessary to apply some very strict self-discipline if we are to overcome this deception in our struggles with the philosophical problems that follow. The deception is rendered all the more difficult to get rid of because there is no sure method for determining when we are guilty of it. The following may, however, be offered as a general rule: If you really understand something, it should be possible for you to vary the expression of it without altering the meaning. If you cannot express an idea in more than one way, then you have not understood that idea.

It is impossible to overemphasize the importance of *understanding* in philosophical learning. Facts and words can be memorized, but meanings and relations must be understood; and philosophy is concerned with meanings and relations. I know the *meaning* of the question "Is New York City more populous than London?" Thus, I can ask the same question in a variety of ways: "Is the population of New York City greater than that of London?" "Do more people live in New York City than in London?" "Does New York City have a greater population than the capital of England?" But I am not at all sure what people mean when they ask "What is the meaning of life?" I cannot hope to make any progress in my reflections on this question until I understand precisely what is being asked; then, and only then, can I imagine what sort of assertion might count as a possible answer to the question.

The second step is to make a conscious and determined effort to ascertain *all* the alternative ways of answering the question with which we are dealing. Then, and only then, can we weigh the arguments for and against the various positions and perhaps make up our minds on the matter, confident that we have not simply neglected to consider some position that, if examined carefully, might commend itself more strongly than any of those under consideration.

Some philosophical problems allow as few as two possible alternative answers. An example is the epistemological problem discussed in Chapters 6–10 of this book. More commonly a problem will allow three or four possible solutions. Sometimes, however, it is not possible to state with certainty that such and such are the *only* possible positions to take with respect to a given problem. Even in such a case, however, it is extremely important to make the attempt to define the alternatives, since in so doing we may discover why a limit to the number of possible solutions cannot be set. And we may, of course, be reasonably confident that we have considered all of the plausible alternatives, even though we have not surveyed all those that may be logically possible.

If we demand precision in understanding the problem, and precision and completeness in understanding the alternative possible answers, we have in hand a powerful instrument for organizing subsequent philosophical inquiry. Consider: If I have understood a given problem P, and if I have determined that positions A, B, and C are the only possible positions to take with respect to it, then nothing that anyone can say with respect to P can be completely novel to me. If Plato, or Aristotle, or Kant, or Bertrand Russell, or anyone else addresses himself to this problem, he must do so in behalf of (or in opposition to) position A, or position B, or position C, no matter what terminology he may employ. Hence, I can attend carefully to his arguments and can enter into the discussion with a clear understanding of what it is all about.

The third step toward philosophical understanding is a consideration of the arguments for and against the various alternative positions. To the making of arguments there is no end, and it is impossible to state with respect to any philosophical position that thus and so are *the* arguments for or against such a position. Practically all philosophical discussion consists in presenting arguments either (*a*) in favor of some position in an attempt to establish it or (*b*) in opposition to some position in an attempt to refute it. Step three is never completed: it is the arena of philosophical discussion into which we are qualified to enter as soon as steps one and two have been mastered (with respect to any given problem).

Again, there is no great value in memorizing a list of "approved" philosophical arguments—for example, three or four arguments in favor of one theory and three or four arguments in favor of another. Rather, you should ask, What kinds of considerations would tend to support the first theory? What kinds of considerations would tend to refute it? What kinds of considerations would tend to support or to refute the second theory? Then you will be in a position to assess any arguments that you may encounter, and perhaps to devise a few of your own.

The Importance of Terminology

At each step along the route to philosophical understanding it is important to observe one cardinal rule: Maximum care must be taken at all times to establish the exact meaning of terms, and terms once defined must be used appropriately.

For the purposes of ordinary discourse we can often get along without demanding absolute precision in language. We can, for example, discuss the weather, and even agree that it is a "nice day," without being too fussy about exactly what qualities a day must have before it qualifies as a "nice" day. Anyone who doubts that we do operate with relatively inexact language in our everyday conversation might try giving precise definitions to such phrases as "a nice day," "a good ball game," "a boring speaker," or "a snap course."

For some purposes, however, it is important that language be used with as near-perfect precision as possible. In mathematical computation, for example, it is obviously important that the symbols employed have precise meanings and that those meanings remain constant throughout the course of computation. The ideas of force, mass, velocity, and many others have been given similarly precise meanings in physics; calculations involving these concepts would not be possible were it not for this precision.

In philosophy, however, it is seldom possible to define terms mathematically. Nevertheless, a technical and semitechnical language of philosophy has been developed for the express purpose of enabling philosophers to discourse with greater precision than would otherwise be possible. The serious student of philosophy will make every effort to master this terminology as he goes along, for, however esoteric it may sound at first, its real and valid function is to enable us to think and speak precisely about matters that in everyday language remain obscure and imprecise.

More than this, however, we must learn to be on the lookout for ambiguities in everyday language that, if not detected, may mislead and confuse. If, knowing that Socrates died in prison, we hear someone say, "Socrates was a freer man on the day he died than those who brought about his imprisonment," the chances are that we shall find the statement confusing. In one sense of "free," Socrates clearly was *not* as free as his accusers. They were free to walk the streets of Athens and to spend time with their families; he was not. What, then, does the speaker mean? Is he talking about some "inner state," which Socrates supposedly had on the day of his death in a greater degree than his accusers? Or is the speaker suggesting that in dying, Socrates was somehow freed from his body, and in this way became "freer" than his accusers—or what? Some careful analysis of the term "free" is needed if we are to dispel the bewilderment that such a statement can create. To think critically, carefully, analytically about the exact meanings of terms is to observe the rule stated above.

Being What We Are

Finally, it is important that we develop the habit of intellectual honesty in our consideration of philosophical problems. Very often in the study of philosophy we discover that we already have an opinion on the question under discussion, in spite of the fact that we have never consciously considered the question before and have certainly never given careful consideration to the arguments for or against that opinion. We have, as we say, simply "taken it for granted." It is easy to become embarrassed about the fact that we have opinions we have never examined, or did not even know we had, and to try to conceal them from those with whom we are discussing the question. It is this concealment that we must attempt to avoid, for it is precisely *our opinions* that must be put to the test. If we approach philosophy as a body of knowledge that can be kept at arm's length—something to be memorized and, after a time, largely forgotten—we shall miss the whole point. Philosophy is about us, our beliefs, our opinions. We progress in philosophical study only insofar as we clarify and either reinforce or alter the beliefs and opinions with which we begin.

An excellent way to clarify one's thinking about an issue is to try to express one's ideas *in writing.* Many students find it helpful, for example, to keep a journal in which they record ideas and questions that occur to them in the course of their reading and study. Some of this material may later find its way into essays and term papers in which one presents a carefully reasoned argument on some philosophical position. It is a fortunate student of philosophy whose teachers require him to put his thoughts in writing from time to time.

STUDY QUESTIONS

1. What is the history of philosophy the history of? In short, what is philosophy?
2. What is the difference between asking a question and merely uttering an interrogative sentence?
3. Has your education thus far tended to obscure the difference between understanding something and memorizing some recommended or official verbal formulation about it? What kinds of behavior by parents and teachers might tend to obscure this distinction? What steps might you take to overcome whatever unfortunate habits of this kind you may have developed?
4. State something that you *remember* from this chapter. Now state something that you *understand.* How would you explain the difference between the two?
5. This chapter makes a number of specific suggestions about how best to study philosophy. Summarize those suggestions.

5

PHILOSOPHICAL ARGUMENTS

Philosophy, we have said, is a dialogue, a conversation expressing varying points of view about the questions that force themselves upon us when we try to conceive of the whole of reality in a way that allows for every element of human knowledge and experience. The vehicle of this dialogue is, of course, language; and the dialogue consists, for the most part, of *arguments* put forward in support of or in opposition to a given position. In philosophical study it is important, therefore, that we pay close attention to how language is being used and to the arguments intended to lead us to certain conclusions.

Real Disputes and Verbal Disputes

Interesting philosophical questions are always controversial: they have at least two more or less plausible answers, both (or all) of which cannot be correct. Philosophical questions are the occasion for disputes among the proponents of opposing positions. However, the fact that two parties appear to be in disagreement—one assenting to a given statement and the other denying it—does not necessarily mean that their dispute is *real;* it may be merely *verbal.* In order to have a real dispute, the parties involved must be in genuine disagreement concerning what is the case. If they are in agreement about the facts and are simply using certain terms with different meanings, then their dispute is not real but verbal. A real dispute can be settled only by determining what really is the case. A verbal dispute can be resolved only by securing agreement on the meanings of the terms that are being used differently by the disputants.

Suppose, for example, that two people are arguing about the question, Are all men created equal? A says, "All men are created equal. No one has a right to any special privileges by virtue of his race, religion, or social status. All men have an equal right to life, liberty, and the pursuit of happiness." B says, "I disagree with you: it is not the case that all men are created equal. They differ in their physical and intellectual endowments by virtue of their differing heredity, and in their privileges and opportunities by virtue of their birth into either wealth or poverty. To deny this is simply to ignore the facts."

Although A and B are talking as if they were in genuine disagreement, their dispute is verbal only. A is arguing that all men have equal rights; B is arguing that they have unequal endowments and opportunities. What A is asserting, therefore, is not at all incompatible with what B is asserting, but this fact is obscured by the apparent incompatibility of the two statements "All men are created equal" and "It is not the case that all men are created equal."

Unfortunately, it is not always as easy as it is in this example to determine whether or not a given dispute is merely verbal. Language is extremely complex, and it is quite possible for intelligent, able people to debate long and hard over a question that, as they later discover, posed a strictly verbal issue. Only if there is agreement on the meanings of the key terms of the discussion can it be determined whether or not there is genuine disagreement on a substantive issue.

There is no method that can guarantee the detection of verbal disputes. Indeed, there have even been philosophers who have maintained that all philosophical questions are merely verbal in character, although in the judgment of most philosophers this does not seem very likely to be the case. Undoubtedly, however, the discussion of many philosophical questions of substance is frequently obscured by issues that are only verbal, and one should always be on the alert for such confusion-producing issues.

Fallacies

Once disputants have satisfied themselves that a problem they are considering is a substantive one—that what separates them is not differing understandings of certain terms but a genuine disagreement concerning what is the case—then they may enter into a serious discussion of the issue, with each party to the dispute presenting arguments intended to persuade others to agree with his position.

An argument is a piece of rational discourse in which some propositions (the premises) are offered as grounds for assenting to some other proposition (the conclusion). If the premises are said to offer conclusive evidence for the truth of the conclusion—that is, if it is claimed that the conclusion follows necessarily from the stated premises—the argument is termed *deductive*. If it is claimed only that the premises offer some evidence in support of the conclusion—thereby allowing that the conclusion might be false even if the premises are true—the argument is termed *inductive*.

In the case of deductive arguments, if the conclusion does follow necessarily from the premises—if the truth of the premises does guarantee the truth of the conclusion—the argument is said to be *valid*. If, instead, it is logically possible (in the case of a deductive argument) for the conclusion to be false even if the premises are true, the argument is said to be *invalid*.

That a given deductive argument is valid does not, of course, establish that the conclusion of that argument is true; it establishes only that the conclusion is true *if the premises are true*. If you agree that a given deductive argument is valid, you cannot reasonably accept the premises and reject the conclusion. You can reasonably point out, however, that the truth of the premises remains to be determined. The claim that an argument is *sound* involves the dual claim that it is valid and that its premises are true.

To say that an argument is invalid is to say that it is "logically incorrect" in one of several specifiable ways: it contains, as logicians say, a *fallacy,* a logical error. The argument may be incorrect in form, in which case it contains what is called a *formal* fallacy. Normally, such fallacies are fairly easy to detect, however, and so are unlikely to confuse the discussion of an issue for very long. The troublesome fallacies are the *informal* fallacies, logical mistakes that occur in the course of reasoning and that cannot be detected by the purely mechanical methods that suffice for the detection of formal fallacies. It is customary among logicians to distinguish two general classes of informal fallacies: *fallacies of relevance* and *fallacies of ambiguity.*

A fallacy of relevance occurs whenever the premises of an argument are logically irrelevant to the conclusion. Suppose, for example, that someone argues for the existence of God on the grounds that millions of people believe in the existence of God, and those millions of people cannot be mistaken. The fact that millions of people believe a proposition to be true is logically irrelevant to the truth of that proposition: millions of people were for many years mistaken, for example, in their belief that the earth is flat. But to some people this argument is psychologically persuasive (perhaps because they hesitate to go against the judgment of millions of people), and they fail to notice that the belief of those millions is quite irrelevant to the truth of the proposition in question.

There is, as we have said, no certain method for detecting such fallacies. They deceive us because they are psychologically persuasive: they make us want to—or at least feel that somehow we ought to—accept the conclusion, and thus they divert our attention from their irrelevancy. All that we can do if we suspect that we are being deceived in this way is to ask whether or not the premises provide logical grounds for accepting the proposition in question. If we conclude that they do not, but still find the argument psychologically persuasive, the likelihood is that we are dealing with an argument containing a fallacy of relevance.[1]

A fallacy of ambiguity is a logical mistake that occurs as a result of ambiguity in the language in which an argument is framed. Many words have a variety of meanings. Sometimes in the course of an extended argument the same term will be used in more than one sense, whereas the logical persuasiveness of the argument presupposes that each term is used in the same sense throughout. Sentences, too, or parts of sentences, can sometimes be construed in more than one way, depending, for example, on which terms are emphasized, or on how one understands the grammatical construction of the sentence or phrase. If in the course of an argument a term, a sentence, or a phrase undergoes a subtle shift of meaning, the result may be a fallacy of ambiguity.[2]

Suppose, for example, that someone asserts that human beings have never been morally responsible for any of their actions, because (*a*) in order to be morally responsible one must be free, and (*b*) no one has ever been truly free, for everyone is in some degree a slave of fear, passion, prejudice, ignorance, and a host of other weaknesses. We may sense that something is wrong with this argument, but it may not be immediately apparent that what is wrong is that it contains a fallacy of ambiguity. It uses the term "free" (a very tricky term, by the way) in two rather different senses. The first premise asserts that in order to be morally responsible one must be free in some unspecified sense; the second premise asserts that in fact no one has ever been free in the sense of being *free from*—that is, wholly without—fear, passion, prejudice, and so forth. The argument, therefore, is fallacious by virtue of a fallacy of ambiguity.

There is, happily, a fairly reliable method for eliminating such fallacies: the substitution of a more precise formulation for the term, phrase, or sentence suspected of being ambiguous. For example, we would substitute for an offending term a precise definition of that term (a definition, one hopes, that is not itself ambiguous). If the argument does contain a fallacy of ambiguity, and if we have correctly identified the ambiguous term (or phrase, or sentence), the result of the reformulation should be a patently unconvincing argument. Note how this works out in the argument we considered a moment ago. We define "free" in the sense required by the second premise: "wholly without fear, passion, prejudice, ignorance, and other human weaknesses." Using this definition in both premises, the argument becomes

In order to be morally responsible one must be wholly without fear, passion, prejudice, ignorance, and other human weaknesses.

---

[1] Several distinct types of such fallacies have been identified and given special names. A helpful discussion of the most common of these may be found in Irving M. Copi, *Introduction to Logic*, 4th ed. (New York: Macmillan, 1972), pp. 73–87.

[2] See *ibid.*, pp. 92–99, for a discussion of several types of fallacies of ambiguity.

No one has ever been wholly without fear, passion, prejudice, ignorance, and other human weaknesses.

Therefore no one has ever been morally responsible.

Thus stated, the argument is highly unconvincing because the first premise no longer strikes us as plausible. Arguments of this type deceive us by concealing implausible assertions in a haze of ambiguity. A precise reformulation removes the haze and enables us to judge each assertion on its own merits. Reformulation, if we are careful to avoid new ambiguities, is therefore an effective method for the detection and elimination of fallacy-producing ambiguities.

The Reductio Ad Absurdum *Argument*

The *reductio ad absurdum* is a powerful form of argument for refuting the position of an opponent, and it appears with such frequency in philosophical discussion that the student should become familiar with it as soon as possible. It consists in showing that the position attacked implies absurd consequences. Suppose that I wish to attack position A: if I I can show that A implies X, Y, and Z, and that X or Y or Z is absurd or contrary to fact, then I have shown that A is absurd; for from a true proposition you cannot validly deduce false consequences. This type of argument may also be used constructively in situations where there are only two possible positions on a given problem: if either A or B must be the case, and if A is shown (by a *reductio ad absurdum* argument) to be untenable, then B must be the case. If there is more than one alternative to the position, then separate arguments must, of course, be constructed against each of the alternative positions.

In attempting to assess such an argument, two questions must always be asked: Do the alleged consequences really follow from the position in question? Are they really absurd? If the answer to either of these questions is negative, the attempted *reductio* is not successful.

Learning by Doing

Thus far we have been talking *about* philosophy. Such talk is appropriate when one is introducing philosophy to the uninitiated, but it is now time to stop talking *about* philosophy and to begin engaging in philosophical discussion. And here, philosophy being what it is, the student must be prepared to play his or her appropriate role.

"Philosophy being what it is"—what do we mean by this? We mean that philosophy is an activity to be engaged in, not a body of information to be committed to memory. As with any skill, there are some points of information that must be mastered. In learning to ski, for example, we have to find out where we should put our weight, what to do with the poles, how to use the edges of the skis, and so on, if we are to be able to execute the various maneuvers that constitute skiing. But the point of all this learning is to do something, not simply to acquire some information. And this is true also for philosophy. The point in studying it is to learn to philosophize, to "do" philosophy.

Thus, students should approach the discussions that follow not simply as spectators but as participants. The first chapter in each part will provide a "ticket" to the arena: a statement of the problem and a description of the alternatives. These must, of course, be carefully studied and thoroughly understood. Beyond that, it is altogether a matter of arguments: each position is allowed to speak for itself, to marshal whatever arguments it can in support of itself and in refutation of all others. Not all the arguments used are good ones, obviously, since most philosophical problems allow only one "correct" position, and the arguments that allegedly prove some other position must, therefore, be unsound. But which position is "correct" in each case? And which arguments are unsound? Those, obviously, are questions that can rarely be answered with finality. Within the living dialogue that is philosophy there is room for differences of opinion on these matters. Indeed, it is these differences of opinion—differences that must occur when honest thinkers seek answers to questions that have long puzzled the greatest minds—that keep the dialogue alive.

And now, to the dialogue itself.

STUDY QUESTIONS

1. Consider the questions that follow. In each case decide whether you think differing answers to the questions would represent a *real* dispute or a *verbal* dispute:
   a. If the events that produce a clap of thunder occur in a place where no one is around to hear, is there or is there not a sound in that place?
   b. A cow is at position X. A dog goes in a complete circle around position X, but the cow turns in such a way that it is always facing the dog. Is the dog going around the cow?
   c. Does Telstar go around the earth? Is it stationary?
   d. Is *Gone with the Wind* one of the ten greatest movies of all time?
   e. Is a Buick a better car than a Chrysler?
   f. Are some people naturally brighter than others?
   g. Are some teachers better teachers than others?
   h. Do people sometimes act freely, or is their behavior always the result of antecedent causes over which they have no control?
2. Write definitions for the following terms: argument, inductive, deductive, valid, invalid, sound, fallacy, formal fallacy, informal fallacy, fallacy of relevance, fallacy of ambiguity.
3. True or False:
   a. All arguments are either inductive or deductive.
   b. All arguments are either valid or invalid.
   c. If an argument is valid, it is sound.
   d. If an argument is sound, it is valid.
   e. If the conclusion of an argument is true, its premises must be true.

  f. If the premises of a sound argument are true, the conclusion must be true.

  g. If an argument contains a fallacy, its conclusion must be false.

  h. If an argument contains no fallacies, its conclusion must be true.

  i. If the conclusion of an argument is true, it is a sound argument.

  j. If an argument is sound, it contains no fallacies.

4. Give an example of a *reductio ad absurdum* argument (not necessarily relating to a philosophical question). On the basis of what has been said about this type of argument in the present chapter, what uses do you anticipate will be made of arguments of this sort in the discussions that follow?

FOR FURTHER READING

Ayer, A. J. *Philosophy and Language.* New York: Oxford University Press, 1960.

Hahn, Lewis E. "Philosophy as Comprehensive Vision," *Philosophy and Phenomenological Research,* 22 (1961), 1–25.

Hamblin, Charles L. *Fallacies.* London: Methuen, 1970.

Jaspers, Karl. *Way to Wisdom,* tr. by Ralph Manheim. New Haven, Conn.: Yale University Press, 1951 (paperbound). See especially Chapters 1–3.

Körner, Stephen. *What is Philosophy? One Philosopher's Answer.* Baltimore: Penguin Books, 1969.

Krikorian, Yervant H. (ed.). *Naturalism and the Human Spirit.* New York: Columbia University Press, 1944. See especially Chapter 15, "The Nature of Naturalism," by John Herman Randall, Jr.

Loewenberg, Jacob. *Reason and the Nature of Things.* LaSalle, Ill.: Open Court, 1959.

Merleau-Ponty, Maurice. *In Praise of Philosophy,* tr. by John Wild and James M. Edie. Evanston, Ill.: Northwestern University Press, 1963. See especially pages 33–64.

Nagel, Ernest. *Logic Without Metaphysics.* New York: Free Press, 1956. See Part I, Chapter I, "Naturalism Reconsidered."

Newell, R. W. *The Concept of Philosophy.* London: Methuen, 1967.

Passmore, John. *Philosophical Reasoning.* London: Gerald Duckworth, 1969 (paperbound). An examination of some common forms of philosophical argument.

Plato. *Apology.* Many editions. Plato's moving account of Socrates' defense—of himself and of philosophy—before the Athenian court.

Russell, Bertrand. *The Problems of Philosophy.* New York: Oxford University Press, 1959. See especially Chapter 15, "The Value of Philosophy."

Ryle, G. "Systematically Misleading Expressions," in Antony Flew (ed.). *Essays on Logic and Language,* First Series. New York: Philosophical Library, 1951.

Sheldon, W. H. "Critique of Naturalism," *The Journal of Philosophy,* 42 (1945), 253–270.

Smart, J. J. C. *Philosophy and Scientific Realism.* New York: Humanities Press, 1963. See especially Chapter 1, "The Province of Philosophy."

Supek, Ivan. "The Task of Philosophy Today," *Philosophy and Phenomenological Research,* 24 (1963), 117–124.

Waismann, Friedrich. "How I See Philosophy," in H. D. Lewis (ed.). *Contemporary British Philosophy,* Third Series. New York: Macmillan, 1956.

White, Morton. *Toward Reunion in Philosophy.* Cambridge, Mass.: Harvard University Press, 1956.

PART II

RATIONALISTS AND EMPIRICISTS

6

THE ISSUE BETWEEN RATIONALISTS AND EMPIRICISTS

It is a commonplace but nonetheless remarkable fact that we human beings have the ability to acquire some knowledge of the world in which we live. This ability is certainly not infallible, for time and again something that we had believed to be true turns out to be false, and what we had believed to be false turns out to be true. Nonetheless, prone to error though we may be, each of us has come to know quite a few things about the world, and we would have little difficulty in writing down a long list of statements that we know to be true. Indeed, knowledge appears to be so plentiful today, and its acquisition so common an occurrence, that most of us have probably never paused to consider that this capacity to acquire knowledge is a truly remarkable human fact.

Philosophers, whose business it is to ask questions about certain things that many people simply take for granted, have long been interested in the phenomenon of human knowledge. There is, in fact (as was noted in Chapter 3), a division of philosophical inquiry called epistemology (from the Greek *episteme,* meaning "to know"), which is devoted exclusively to a study of the nature and limits of human knowledge. The problem with which we shall be dealing in this section is one of the central problems in epistemology.

Knowledge

What does it mean to "know" something about the world? Suppose, for example, that we say, "Johnny *knows* that if you put your hand into a flame, you will get burned." Just what does this mean? It appears to mean three things: (1) it is the case that if you put your hand into a flame, you will get burned; (2) Johnny believes that if you put your hand into a flame, you will get burned; and (3) Johnny has reasonable grounds

Pn post
Knowledge

for so believing. Let P be any statement about the real world, and let A be any person whatsoever. When A knows P, then (1) what P asserts is the case, (2) A believes that P is the case, and (3) A has reasonable grounds for believing that P is the case. If any one of these conditions were not present, we would not say that A *knows* P. If (1) were absent, we would say that A mistakenly believes P. If (2) were absent, we would say that although P is true, and A ought to know it (since he has reasonable grounds), he does not. And if (3) were absent, we would probably say that A just had a hunch or made a lucky guess.

It is important to note that what we are talking about at present is knowledge of the real world, which accordingly is expressed in a statement about the real world, that is, a statement that asserts that something is the case, that some state of affairs exists. If what it asserts really is the case, then it is a true statement; if not, it is false. Some philosophers speak of such statements as "statements asserting some matter of fact." Another common name for them is *empirical* statements.

Statements about the real world should be clearly distinguished, however, from statements that tell us something only about the meaning of some word or phrase. The statement "All bachelors are bald" is a statement about the real world: it asserts that something is the case, and it can be shown to be false by producing the appropriate evidence: a bachelor who is not bald. But the statement "All bachelors are unmarried" is not a statement about the real world: it is simply an elucidation of a part of the meaning of the term "bachelor." We do not have to produce a single spouseless adult male human being in order to support the statement that all bachelors are unmarried, for it is not a statement about human beings at all; it is a statement about the meaning of a word. Construed as a statement about the real world, it is redundant: it says that all unmarried adult male human beings are unmarried. Hence, we know better than to construe it in this way.

The Sources of Knowledge

It is evident that there are many statements about the real world that we know to be true; that is to say, we have a good deal of knowledge about the real world. How did we acquire this knowledge? What are the ways by which we come to know something about the world?

One source of our knowledge, obviously, is our own experience. We have, in the course of our lives, seen and heard and touched and tasted many things; on this basis we can say a good deal about the world. We know, in this way, many *simple facts* about ourselves, for example, that we have two arms, two legs, eyes, ears, and so on. Moreover, we know on the basis of our own experience many *general truths* about the world, for example, that unsupported objects fall, that fire produces heat, that rain makes things wet. The list of things that each of us knows by direct experience would be very long indeed, and since every person's experience is in some ways unique, no two lists would be exactly alike.

But if each of us knew only what we ourselves had directly experienced, our knowledge would be vastly more limited than in fact it is. By far the greater part of what we know we have learned from others. Through listening and reading we have learned many things about history, geography, literature, and the sciences, things that in all probability we would never have been able to discover for ourselves.

In reality, however, there is not much difference between these two sources of knowledge. It is as if ten people set out together to inspect a ten-room house, and in order to save time and effort agreed to inspect just one room each and report to the rest. Each person, then, would know about one room by direct experience and about the other nine by indirect experience. The information that we get from teachers and from books is what we might call secondhand experience. If we trace this information to its source, we will inevitably find someone whose experience has taught him what he is now teaching us.

Rationalists and Empiricists

Apart from a minor quibble over whether or not what we have been talking about really deserves to be called knowledge (Plato, for example, called it mere opinion), most philosophers would have no quarrel with what has been stated so far. It is obvious that we have some kind of cognitive rapport with the world by means of direct and indirect experience, and it is perfectly consistent with ordinary usage to say that what we acquire in this way is *knowledge* of the real world.

At this point there arises, however, one of the most controversial and important issues in philosophy: Do we or do we not have any knowledge of the real world that is in any degree *independent* of experience? Is there or is there not such a thing as "direct apprehension" of empirical truths? Is experience the whole and only source of our knowledge of the real world, or is the human mind capable of grasping some truths about the world "on its own," with experience serving merely as the occasion for this insight?

Some philosophers hold that the human mind is capable of a direct apprehension of certain empirical truths and that we in fact have some knowledge of the real world that is in a specific way independent of experience. This view is called *rationalism,* and a person who holds this view is called a *rationalist.* Other philosophers deny this possibility and maintain that our knowledge of the real world arises entirely out of experience. They are called *empiricists,* and the position that they represent is called *empiricism.* With respect to this question, rationalism and empiricism are the only alternatives, and they are mutually exclusive. You can be a rationalist or you can be an empiricist, but you cannot be both and you cannot avoid being one or the other.

In order to discuss this issue with maximum precision, however, we need a vocabulary that is somewhat more technical than the language we have been using thus far. Let us pause, therefore, to define a few terms and then attempt to state our problem in a more precise way.

Analytic and Synthetic Statements

We may begin by making a distinction between *analytic* and *synthetic* statements. An analytic statement is one in which what is affirmed in the predicate is already contained in the concept of the subject. An example of such a statement would be "All circles are round." In order to test the truth of such a statement, it is not necessary to examine any circles to see whether in fact they are all round. Being round is part of what is meant by the term "circle"; consequently, we know without making any inspection that all circles are round, that if anything is a circle it must be round. We need only analyze the subject of the statement, and there we shall find the notion of roundness. To call something a circle and to deny that it is round would be a contradiction: it would be equivalent to saying that some round things are not round.

A synthetic statement is one in which what is affirmed in the predicate adds something to the concept of the subject. A house, for example, may be defined as an enclosure within which human beings live and find shelter. If, then, I say, "Some houses have pink shutters," I am uttering a synthetic statement, because the idea of having pink shutters is not contained in the idea of a house. I cannot produce my statement simply by analyzing the subject (house); rather, I must make a synthesis of two different concepts (house and pink shutters), in short, a synthetic statement.

Strictly speaking, the definitions of "analytic" and "synthetic" given here apply only to analytic and synthetic statements of the subject-predicate type. But if the distinction is understood, it can be easily generalized to apply to statements of other types. An alternative, and broader, definition of "analytic statement" would be "a statement whose truth is determined solely by the meaning of its terms"; and of "synthetic statement," "a statement whose truth or falsehood is not determined solely by the meaning of its terms." A statement whose *falsehood* is determined solely by the meaning of its terms is said to be analytically false.

A Priori and A Posteriori Knowledge

Two additional terms for which we shall shortly have use are *a priori* and *a posteriori*. Something is said to be known a posteriori if it is known on the basis of experience. How do we know that lemons are sour? We know it a posteriori; we have tasted them. How do we know that too long an exposure of skin to the sun causes sunburn? We know it a posteriori; we have been sunburned, or we have seen others who have been sunburned. All the things we know by direct or by indirect experience we know a posteriori. Experience (either our own or someone else's) is the whole and only source of such knowledge, and if such knowledge is challenged, it is to experience, and experience alone, that we must appeal for confirmation. A posteriori knowledge is only as secure as the factual evidence upon which it rests.

With a priori knowledge the situation is different. Here factual evidence is not relevant, though some philosophers would say that many a priori truths are constantly exhibited in experience. What, then, is an a priori truth? It is a statement the truth of which is evident apart from the facts of experience. To know something a priori is to know it immediately, directly, without recourse to factual evidence. In a certain sense, it is to know something prior to experience—in the sense, namely, that all subsequent experience must conform to what is thus known. What is known a priori is seen, as Immanuel Kant said, to be necessary and universal. Once grasped, its untruth is inconceivable, and it is then immediately evident that it must be true at all times and in all places.[1]

The Problem Restated

It is perfectly evident that we know a great many synthetic truths a posteriori. No one, not even the most enthusiastic of rationalists, denies this, and it is a caricature of Rationalist's position to say that he does.

It is equally evident that all analytic truths are known a priori. No one, not even the most incorrigible of empiricists, denies this, and it is a caricature of Empiricist's position to say that he does.

The question is, however (and this is where the rationalist and the empiricist part company), Do we or do we not have any a priori knowledge of synthetic truths? The rationalist says we do, the empiricist says we do not. It is upon this one issue that we must focus our whole attention in the chapters that follow. The controversy might be represented as follows:

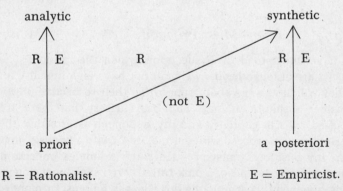

R = Rationalist.   E = Empiricist.

[1] Immanuel Kant, *Critique of Pure Reason*, Intro., II, tr. Norman Kemp Smith (New York: St. Martin's, 1965), pp. 43–44.

It should be apparent that we now have before us a rather more precise statement of the problem posed earlier. We talked previously about "knowledge of the real world," and we asked whether we can have such knowledge in a way that is to any degree independent of experience. Now we are asking whether we can have any a priori knowledge of synthetic truths. To know a synthetic truth is to know something about the real world; to know something in a way that is to any degree independent of experience is to know it a priori. We have before us, therefore, a nontechnical and a technical formulation of the same problem. The technical formulation, however, permits us to talk about the problem with greater precision than the other does.

The Issue Behind the Issue

It may be well to say a few words at this point about what is at stake in this celebrated controversy. If empiricism is right in affirming that all knowledge of reality (as opposed to knowledge of analytic truths) is a posteriori, then it is clear that our knowledge of reality is limited to that which falls within or can be definitely inferred from the realm of experience. If such is the case, it seems clear to most philosophers that speculative metaphysics is impossible, for metaphysics consists precisely in the attempt to acquire knowledge of things that are beyond (the Greek *meta* means "beyond" or "behind") the world of experience. Any talk about God, or the soul, or a transcendent good is thus ruled out as meaningless.

Bear in mind, then, that when Rationalist offers examples drawn from such sources as geometry and logic to build his case, what he is basically trying to do is establish the principle that an a priori knowledge of synthetic truths is possible. If he can establish this principle, then he may hope to employ it in his metaphysical inquiries; if not, his whole procedure—the very possibility of metaphysics—is highly suspect.

How the Argument Must Proceed

If we have understood the issue upon which the rationalist and the empiricist are at loggerheads, we shall not have any difficulty in seeing how they will have to go about supporting their respective positions.

Consider a simply analogy. Suppose I assert that there are some pink-tufted owls in captivity and my opponent asserts that there are none. How can we proceed with our dispute? Quite obviously, in order to support my position I must produce some examples. Indeed, if I can produce just one example of a pink-tufted owl, I shall have won my case. And my opponent, what must he do? Clearly, he must attempt to show that any example that I bring forth is not really a pink-tufted owl. This he may do in either of two ways. He may show that (a) although the bird

I am offering as an example of a pink-tufted owl is indeed pink-tufted, it is not an owl, or that (*b*) although it appears to be an owl, it is not pink-tufted. If he can make good his claim to either of these points, my example ceases to be an example.

Likewise, it is up to the rationalist to bring forward examples of synthetic truths that, as he believes, we know a priori. If he can produce a single convincing example of such a truth, he will have won his case.

The empiricist, on the other hand, must show that the examples offered by the rationalist are not, after all, examples of synthetic truths known a priori. This he may do in either of two ways. He may attempt to show that although a particular example is a synthetic truth, it is not known a priori; or, alternatively, he may attempt to show that what is offered as an example of an a priori synthetic truth is not synthetic. For the empiricist is convinced of two things: that all statements that are synthetic are known a posteriori and that all statements that are known a priori are analytic. Empiricists may disagree among themselves as to which of these two categories a given statement belongs in, but they are agreed that every statement whose truth is knowable by us belongs in one or the other.

The empiricist, it should be noted, cannot fairly be expected to produce an independent argument to prove his contention that all synthetic truths (all truths about the real world) are known a posteriori. In the very nature of the case, this is not possible. The burden of proof lies, as in a formal debate, with the party making the affirmative claim. In the present instance, therefore, the burden of proof rests with the rationalist. All that we have a right to expect of an empiricist is that he present a convincing refutation of anything that a rationalist may offer as an example of a synthetic truth known a priori.

In attempting to enter into the discussion of this issue, therefore, we must reflect carefully on the examples that are offered by the rationalist. Concerning each example that is given, we must ask ourselves two simple questions: Is this a synthetic truth? Is it known a priori? If with respect to any example that is given we answer both questions in the affirmative, then we are agreeing with the rationalist. If we find no example that, after due reflection, seems to be both synthetic and a priori, then we are agreeing with the empiricist.

STUDY QUESTIONS

1. Are you satisfied with the analysis of "knowing" suggested in this chapter? Can you think of any instance that fails to meet the criteria suggested here that you would be inclined to call an instance of knowing? Or an instance that satisfies these criteria that you would not be inclined to call an instance of knowing?
2. List the several ways the problem of a priori knowledge is stated in this chapter. Then check your understanding of the problem by restating it in your own words.
3. Are you convinced that rationalism and empiricism are the only possible

positions to take with respect to the question of knowledge of the real world? Is it true that "you cannot be both and you cannot avoid being one or the other"? Explain.

4. What is the difference in meaning between "analytic" and "a priori"? between "synthetic" and "a posteriori"? As you understand these terms, is it correct usage to speak of a statement as being a priori or a posteriori? Is it correct to speak of a statement as being known analytically or synthetically?

5. Why must the argument between rationalists and empiricists proceed by way of considering examples brought forward by the rationalist? Why is it impossible for the empiricist to construct an independent proof of his position?

7

THE RATIONALIST THESIS

The introductory chapter has presented an excellent statement of the problem about which my empiricist friends and I are in such complete disagreement.[1] It is now my turn to present what I consider to be the correct answer to the problem there stated, that is, the rationalist answer. I believe that we do have some a priori knowledge of synthetic truths, and I propose to offer a number of examples that I think will prove convincing to any fair and open-minded reader.

Before I do that, however, there is one point that I should like to make clearer than it has been made thus far. The point is, I admit, somewhat subtle, but a full comprehension of it is absolutely essential to an understanding of my position.

The Two Roles of Experience

Let me state unequivocally, then, that I am not maintaining that we have knowledge of any kind (of either analytic or synthetic truths) in a way that is *totally* independent of experience. It seems obvious that if we know something, there must have been some time at which we learned it, and that the occasion on which we learned it was for us an experience of some kind. I am not, therefore, a proponent of "innate knowledge"; I do not think, as some philosophers have, that there are some bits of knowledge that we are born with and therefore have prior to all experience.

What I wish to maintain, rather, is that experience does not always play the same role in learning. For much of our knowledge, experience is

---

[1] The reader is reminded that the "I" of this and of subsequent chapters is in each case a hypothetical advocate of the view in question. See the Preface, p. vii.

the whole *source* of what we come to know. In this case knowledge is a posteriori. But sometimes experience functions in another way. Sometimes it is merely the *occasion* for our coming to know, and what we come to know on that occasion vastly transcends the particular learning situation. We consider some statement about the world, we ponder it, and then we "see," directly, immediately, that it is, and indeed *must be*, true. It is when we come to know something in this way—when experience is only, so to speak, a window through which we look—that we have a case of a priori knowledge.

Perhaps the difference can be clarified by the use of a pair of contrasting examples. Let us first consider a case of something that is known a posteriori. A teacher is talking to her class about various kinds of birds, particularly crows. "What color are crows?" she asks; and the little boy in the fourth row who always likes to be the first to answer a question pipes up, "They're black." Little Suzie is not convinced, so she asks, "Is that right, Miss Twaddle? Are all crows black?" And Miss Twaddle says, "That's right, Suzie. All crows are black." But Suzie still is doubtful, so she presses a little further. "Miss Twaddle," she asks, "how do you *know* that? How do you know for sure that some place, some time, there may not have been a white crow? How do you know that *all* crows are black?"

How could our poor hard-pressed teacher go about answering Suzie's question? One way, of course, would be to play a little trick on Suzie. She could say, "Suzie, if you come across a bird that is just like a crow except that it is white instead of black, it won't be a crow. You'll just have to invent some other name for it." But if Miss Twaddle wants to deal fairly with Suzie, she will have to proceed in a rather different way. She might ask, for example, whether anyone in class had ever seen a crow that was not black. She might report that she herself had seen thousands of crows in her lifetime and that each and every one was black. She might send the class to the library to see if they could find any reports of nonblack crows. She might consult a bird expert and report to the class that as far as he knew there had never been an authenticated case of a nonblack crow.

The point is that the statement "All crows are black" is only as secure as the factual evidence on which it rests. The statement is a summary of the experience of many people, and if it is called in question, the only way that it can be supported is to point to that evidence. Suzie, if she is wise, will not be completely convinced. It is still possible, she may point out, that somewhere, sometime, a nonblack crow, perhaps an albino, will hatch from the egg of a normal crow. And in this, of course, Suzie would be right.

But now let us consider a second example. Our class is a few years older and has graduated from a study of birds to a study of geometry. A Mr. Twiddle is their instructor. "Class," he begins, "let us briefly review yesterday's lesson. What is a triangle?" And the young man in the fourth row, who still likes to be the first to answer any question, replies, "A triangle is a closed plane figure having three straight sides." "All triangles?" asks Mr. Twiddle. "All *Euclidean* triangles," our hero replies. "How big must the angles be?" asks Mr. Twiddle. "They can be any size you like," comes the reply, "provided only that you have a closed plane figure with just three straight sides. That, and that alone, is enough to make it a triangle, no matter how big it is or how big the angles are or anything else."

"Very well," says Mr. Twiddle, "but today I want to show you something else about triangles." Whereupon he demonstrates the theorem that the interior angles of a Euclidean triangle total 180 degrees. The class struggles briefly with the theorem. One by one they catch on, and by the time the hour is half over they have all apparently gotten the point and are able without difficulty to prove the theorem for themselves.

But Suzie is still with us, and she still wants to make sure that she is getting the straight information. So she asks, "Mr. Twiddle, how do you know that *all* Euclidean triangles have interior angles that total 180 degrees?" Now in this instance it would be pointless for Mr. Twiddle to collect evidence to show that of all the Euclidean triangles that he or anybody else had ever seen, none had ever been found to have interior angles that totaled either more or less than 180 degrees. He can only return to the proof of the theorem and try to help Suzie see that the very nature of triangularity is such that anything that is a Euclidean triangle *must* have interior angles totaling 180 degrees. Furthermore, once Suzie really "sees" this, once she really has hold of this truth about triangles, nothing in the world can ever dissuade her from assenting to it. To know something a priori is to know it with a directness and with a certainty that experience alone can never give.

Kant once put the matter as follows:[2] All knowledge clearly *begins* with experience—both knowledge a priori and knowledge a posteriori—but not all knowledge *arises out of* experience. It is only a posteriori knowledge (as in the case of the example about crows) that arises out of experience. Accordingly, it is to experience alone that we can turn if a statement that is affirmed on that basis is called in question. But there is also an a priori knowledge of the world (as in the example about triangles). And it is characteristic of such knowledge that if a statement whose truth is known in this way is called in question, we must turn for support not to empirical evidence but rather to an inspection of the nature of the thing about which the statement is made. You may parade before my eyes as many black crows as you like. I shall still retain some doubt about whether in fact all crows are black. But I know beyond the shadow of a doubt that if anything is a Euclidean triangle, its interior angles total 180 degrees. What is the difference? The difference is that in

---

[2] Immanuel Kant, *Critique of Pure Reason*, Intro., II, tr. Norman Kemp Smith (New York: St. Martin's, 1965), p. 41.

the one case we are dealing with a posteriori knowledge and in the other with a priori knowledge. In the former the knowledge arises out of experience; in the latter, experience is simply the occasion for my coming to know.

Examples of Truths Known A Priori

I hope that these few remarks will have clarified what we rationalists mean when we talk about knowledge that is in some degree independent of experience. The point is so important to a fair appraisal of my position, and so easily and so often misunderstood, that I want to urge my readers to ponder it very carefully—until they are absolutely sure they grasp it—before considering the rest of the discussion.

That settled, I now want to offer a few instances of synthetic truths that all of us know a priori. This is not difficult, for there are countless examples at hand.

One large class of such truths is *arithmetical* truths. Any true arithmetical statement will do. Let us consider the statement, $7 + 5 = 12$. This expression, of course, is simply a brief and convenient way of saying what could be said in ordinary language: seven things added to five things yield a combined total of twelve things.

The first fact to notice about this statement is that it is synthetic: it is a statement about the real world. It is, of course, a very general statement about the world, applicable to apples and oranges and pennies and kittens and anything else that we might have occasion to count and add together.

Consider what would have to be the case, however, if this statement were analytic. We would then have to say that by simply analyzing the subject ("seven things added to five things") we could find the predicate ("twelve things") already present. But we cannot do this. What we find when we analyze the subject is this: (a) the concept seven, (b) the concept five, and (c) a direction to perform the intellectual operation involved in combining seven and five into a single total ("added to"). To get our predicate we have to perform the prescribed intellectual operation. We must therefore leave off analysis and consider the nature of "seven" in conjunction with "five" and then perform the intellectual act of combining them. In order to do this, we must add to our subject the quite different concept "twelve" in the synthetic statement "seven things plus five things are twelve things." Arithmetical statements are one and all synthetic.

The second fact to notice about this statement is that its truth is not known a posteriori. It is not like the example of the crows: our confidence that seven things added to five things equal twelve things is not relative to the number of times we may have added seven and five. We *know*—absolutely—that any time seven things are added to five things the total will be twelve things. There is a necessity, a universality, a self-evidence, that is to say, an unshakable certainty about this statement that no statement whose truth depends upon the facts of experience can ever have. The statement may be illustrated by experience, but experience can never contradict it. Its truth is known a priori. We learned it, indeed, through experience, but not by way of summarizing the facts of experience.

Here, then, are as many examples of synthetic truths that are known a priori as anyone could ever ask for. What is true of 7 + 5 is equally true of 8 + 9 and 4 − 2 and 6 × 7 and every true arithmetical statement that ever has been or will be made. Each of them, it will be seen, is a synthetic truth which, if it is to be known at all, must be known a priori.

A second large class of synthetic truths known a priori consists of the truths of geometry. We have already had an illustration about the triangle. Let us consider that example more closely.

Geometry is what we might call the science of physical space. Since any object that could ever appear to us must appear in space, we know a priori that it must conform to the truths of geometry. If, therefore, someone tries to tell us that one time—perhaps, say, in the jungles of Africa—he saw a Euclidean triangle whose interior angles totaled only 160 degrees, we are simply not going to believe him. We may suggest that he made an incorrect measurement, or that the sides of what he thought was a Euclidean triangle were not straight, or even that he is lying. In any case we know that his report cannot be true, because we know a priori that Euclid's theorem is true. And because this is so, experience—wherever, whenever, and to whomever it occurs—must conform to it. Geometrical knowledge is knowledge a priori.

A third class of synthetic truths that are known a priori consists of what, for lack of a better name, we shall call *logical* truths. An example of such a truth is the statement "Anything that has shape has size." Another example would be the statement "A thing cannot both have and not have the same characteristic at the same time."

Consider, for example, the statement that anything that has shape has size. Surely it is evident that this is a synthetic statement. It asserts a fact about the world that we know to be true, namely, that in each and every instance in which there is an object that has shape there is also an object that has size. Now shape and size are not the same thing: I can know that something is round, for example, without having the slightest idea how big it is. Shape and size are diverse characteristics that an object may have. But—and this is the point—the nature of shape is such and the nature of size is such that whenever one characteristic is present, the other must be also. There is, we might say, a necessary connection between the characteristic that we designate by the term "shape" and the characteristic that we designate by the term "size," and it is this connection that we are affirming when we say that anything that has shape has size.

We "see" this necessary connection directly, and know without the slightest doubt that the statement concerning shape and size is universally true. We know, with a certainty that empirical evidence could never give us, that there never has been and never will be an instance of shape without size, or of size without shape. In knowing this, we know a priori a logical truth which no experience can contradict.

Now consider the statement "A thing cannot both have and not have the same characteristic at the same time." It is true, of course, that we have empirically observed that an object is not simultaneously hot and cold, or colored and uncolored, or big and small. But our statement goes beyond this. It affirms not merely that as a matter of observable fact things *do* not simultaneously have and not have a given characteristic; it asserts that they *cannot*. The rational mind perceives a necessity and a universality in this truth that experience could never provide, thus certifying it as a truth that is known a priori. And yet it is a truth about the world, a truth that has been exhibited in our experience countless times. It is on the basis of our certainty regarding this statement that we know with equal certainty that contradictory statements (one affirming and another denying that a certain object has a given characteristic) cannot be simultaneously true. Logical truths are synthetic truths that are known a priori.

The fourth class of synthetic truths known a priori that I should like to mention is general *ethical* truths. Numerous examples come to mind, but let us confine our attention to the statement "The infliction of needless pain is evil."

There can be no question, it seems to me, that this statement is synthetic. The notion involved in the infliction of needless pain is undoubtedly highly complex, but this much at least is clear: we can analyze that notion as thoroughly as we please, but we will never find that the idea of evil is part of it. By "the infliction of needless pain" we mean such things as a boy's torturing an animal "just for the fun of it" or someone's mauling a younger and weaker person in order "to show how tough he is." What we are saying about such instances is that, in addition to being instances of animal or human suffering wilfully caused by some responsible agent, they have the additional character of being evil. In so saying we are adding to the concept of the subject something not a part of that concept; we are connecting them in our synthetic judgment "The infliction of needless pain is evil."

What evidence could possibly be adduced in support of such a statement? All kinds of evidence could, of course, heighten our awareness of how painful such acts can be, or how absurd and pointless they are, but that is beside the point. What we are affirming is not only that the infliction of needless pain is needless and painful (that *is* analytically true) but that it is also something else, namely, evil, reprehensible, morally blameworthy. Not all the evidence in the world could either confirm or disconfirm our judgment; if its truth is known at all, it is known a priori.

And its truth is known, is it not? We are not moral ignoramuses, though we may not always act in accordance with the moral truths we do perceive. We know, even if it is we ourselves who inflict needless pain, that such an act is evil. We see directly, with an immediacy and a certainty that empirical evidence could never give us, that this act has the moral quality of being evil. All ethical truths are apprehended in this direct way.

Arithmetical truths, geometric truths, logical truths, general ethical truths: here are four classes of truths that seem to me to be clear and irrefutable examples of synthetic truths that are known a priori. But there are many others as well. Consider the following examples:

Every event has a cause.
If anything is red all over then it is not blue all over.
If anything has happened, it cannot be made to not have happened (i.e.,
    the past cannot be undone).
Everyone ought to do good and not evil.
Time moves ever forward.

I assume that it is evident to everyone that these are synthetic statements. If anyone is in doubt about the a priori character of our knowledge of any of these statements, however, I suggest the following question: How would you go about defending the statement if it were challenged? Would you assemble evidence? I say that you would not. Rather, you would ask the challenger to consider the statement more carefully to see exactly what is being said. You would proceed on the assumption that if the challenger really understood the statement, he would certainly cease to challenge it; for in the case of a truth that is known a priori, to understand it is at the same time to see that it is true. When we are dealing with truths known a priori we are involved not with empirical evidence but with direct insight. Our knowledge of the world would be much the poorer if we lacked the capacity for such insight.

Let me conclude by presenting a small but important disclaimer. In arguing as I have for the possibility and the reality of an a priori knowledge of synthetic truths, I have not meant to disparage in any way the importance of a posteriori knowledge. There are things that can be known only a posteriori, and due credit should be given to the scientists, historians, and others who, through careful observation and experimentation, have contributed so greatly to the sum of human knowledge. The point of my remarks is simply this: However great the quantity of knowledge gained in this way, it does not constitute the whole of our knowledge of reality. We have, as I have shown above, countless examples of truths about the real world that are known a priori. It may or may not be important for us to be aware of this; that is another matter. But important or not, it is the case, and that is all that I have tried to show.

STUDY QUESTIONS

1. What difference or differences do you see between the theory of "innate knowledge" and the theory that Rationalist attempts to defend in this chapter?
2. Is there a difference between the role that experience plays in our knowledge about crows and that which it plays in our knowledge of geometrical truths? Has Rationalist succeeded in identifying a real difference here, however one might wish to account for it?
3. List the several classes of truths that Rationalist offers as examples of synthetic truths that are known a priori. What evidence does he offer that these truths are synthetic truths? that they are known a priori?
4. Can you think of any examples in addition to those offered by Rationalist that might plausibly be considered as examples of synthetic truths that are known a priori? Which of Rationalist's own examples do you find most convincing? which least?
5. Suppose that you become convinced that arithmetical truths are not synthetic. Would this by itself make it reasonable for you to reject rationalism? Why or why not?

8

AN EMPIRICIST RETORT

There is some danger, I think, that readers of Rationalist's account may have come away with a view of empiricists as rather stubborn and close-minded individuals who are so enamored of empirical methods that they simply refuse to recognize that knowledge can be acquired in another way.

This impression of empiricists is quite mistaken, and I shall attempt to dispel it immediately. Let me state plainly that I am an empiricist for this reason only: I have never encountered a single example of an alleged a priori synthetic truth that did not prove upon closer inspection to be either analytic (hence not a truth about the real world at all) or a posteriori. I am, however, willing to be shown, and if I ever do encounter an example of such a truth, I will concede immediately to the rationalists. Until then I must honestly state that every synthetic truth known to me is known a posteriori, and every statement that I have ever seen that could with any degree of certainty be said to be known a priori is clearly analytic. Pending evidence to the contrary I must, therefore, continue to maintain that as far as I can make out, all our knowledge of the real world is a posteriori.

This much, however, I will grant the rationalists: I think it would be very nice if it were possible to acquire some knowledge of the world a priori, as they say we all can and do. The empirical method of observing, measuring, and testing one hypothesis and then another is painfully slow and laborious. It would be most pleasant if instead we could, by merely thinking, "see" truths about the world in the way that Rationalist says we can. But we have no right to demand that things be the way we want them to be. We have to take things the way they are. Unfortunately, they are not the way Rationalist says they are, as I shall now attempt to show.

Arithmetical Truths

Let us begin by reconsidering Rationalist's account of arithmetical truths. Such truths have long been the rationalists' favorite examples whenever challenged to defend their position. If we are successful in refuting these examples, we may be reasonably confident that the others will prove no more difficult. If it can be shown that arithmetical truths are not a priori synthetic, then the chief citadel of rationalism will have been destroyed.

It is my belief that arithmetical truths are synthetic truths known a posteriori. I am, therefore, in agreement with Rationalist in affirming that the truths of arithmetic are synthetic truths, but I am disputing his claim that they are known a priori.

My reasons for concurring with Rationalist on the first point are the same as those given by him. It seems evident that when we know an arithmetical truth—for example, that $7 + 5 = 12$, or $4 - 2 = 2$, or $6 \times 7 = 42$—we know something about the real world. We know that whenever you add seven things to five things, you will get a total of twelve things; that whenever you subtract two things from a group of four things you will have a remainder of two things; that whenever you combine six groups of seven things each, or seven groups of six things each, you will have a total of forty-two things. It also seems evident to me that, as Rationalist maintains, the notion "twelve" cannot be found by analyzing the subject term "$7 + 5$." If I know that $7 + 5 = 12$, as I do, then what I know is a synthetic truth.

The crucial question, then, is *how* do I know this arithmetical truth? My answer is that I know it by experience. I did not know it when I was born. I did not learn it in some ecstatic moment of insight, when the eternal truth of this statement suddenly flashed into my mind. I learned it in the way I have learned everything else that I know about the world: by experience and nothing else. First I learned to count. In so doing, of course, I was simply learning the meanings of the words "one," "two," "three," and so on. Then I began to notice certain relationships—for example, that I have five fingers on each hand, and that five fingers plus five fingers makes ten fingers; that I have five toes on each foot, and that five toes plus five toes makes ten toes; that if I had one penny, and my father gave me another one, I then had two pennies, and so on. Everywhere I turned, no matter what objects I had to deal with (fingers, toes, pennies, playmates, apples, kittens, everything), certain numerical relationships impressed themselves upon me. My experience, your experience, everyone's experience has been thoroughly pervaded by numerical facts since the moment we began to be aware of the world around us. It is this experience that has given us our knowledge of arithmetical truths.

What makes some people think that there must be something unique and wonderful about arithmetical truths is, I suppose, the remarkable certainty that such truths seem to have. We are, as Rationalist says, sure about these truths in a way that we are not sure about the statement "All crows are black," no matter how many crows we may have seen. So much is this the case that "mathematical certainty" is for most people, as it was for the philosopher Descartes, a model of the highest degree of certainty possible. How are we to account for this certainty?

The answer, I believe, is very simple. We are supremely sure of the truth of arithmetical truths because of the overwhelming amount of supporting evidence. Every day of our lives, in thousands and thousands of different ways, experience has exhibited the truths that we express in our arithmetical equations. With all of this corroborating evidence, and never a scrap to the contrary, we at length become convinced. We *know* that $7 + 5 = 12$ (and $4 - 2 = 2$, etc.); our certainty reflects the unbroken uniformity of our experience.

Why, then, are we less certain about crows, even if we have never seen a crow that was not black? There are, I think, two reasons. The first is that the quantity of experience upon which this inference is based is infinitesimal in comparison with that upon which our inferences regarding arithmetical truths are based. Practically everything that we experience exhibits arithmetical truths, whereas it is only on relatively rare occasions that we happen to see crows. Furthermore, experience has taught us that in many species, color is a variable characteristic. Perhaps we have seen a black sheep in a flock of white sheep, or an albino mouse, and so we find it easy to conjecture that there might be an exception with respect to color among crows as well. Hence, it is not surprising that we are less than certain that the statement "All crows are black" will stand the test of all future experience.

It may be noted that there are other empirical truths, which everyone agrees are known a posteriori, about which we are much more certain than we are about the color of crows. We can state with a high degree of certainty, for example, that at sea-level barometric pressure, pure water freezes at a temperature of 32° Fahrenheit. We know this by experience. Countless individuals, in many different parts of the world and at many different times, have had an opportunity to observe this phenomenon, and never has a case been reported in which the stated conditions failed to bring about the same result. With all this supporting evidence, and none to the contrary, we make the statement confident that all future cases will conform to those of the past.

If we imagine an example having even more supporting evidence, it is not difficult to see that the result would be knowledge that is so certain as to amount to "absolute certainty." The evidence in the case of freezing water is so great that it is virtually inconceivable that there should ever occur an exception to it. But the evidence in support of arithmetical truths is greater yet—so great, that for most of us an exception to one of these truths is, in fact, totally inconceivable, leading us to say that we know these truths with absolute certainty.

Note, however, that this inconceivability of an exception expresses nothing more than a psychological fact about ourselves. The falsification of an arithmetical truth is inconceivable to us in the same way that it is inconceivable to us that an object should defy the law of gravity, the principal difference being that in the former case the evidence is truly overwhelming. Our inability to conceive of an exception, however, does not mean that an exception is not logically possible.

Geometrical Truths

The account that I should be inclined to give of geometrical truths is identical to the one I have given of arithmetical truths. They are, as Rationalist says, synthetic truths; but like the truths of arithmetic, they are known a posteriori, not a priori.

Consider, for example, the statement "Two straight lines cannot enclose a space." This, presumably, would qualify as one of the truths that Rationalist says we know a priori. I shall argue, on the contrary, that we know it a posteriori.

In the first place (and I think Rationalist would agree with me), it is clear that we learn the meanings of the words of this statement by experience. We learn the meaning of "straight line" in the same way that we learn the meanings of words like "table" and "chair": by hearing the words applied to certain kinds of objects—"straight", for example, to matches, knitting needles, a pencil, the edge of a ruler, but "curved" to barrel staves, the edge of a dish, a dog's nose, or a cat's ear. If we did not have any experience of this kind to tell us the meanings of certain words, those words would be nothing to us but nonsense sounds.

The question, then, is this: Once we know the meanings of the words in the statement in question, how do we come to know that the statement is true? I hold that we learn this by experience.

What kind of experience is it that teaches us that two straight lines cannot enclose a space? The question need not puzzle us long, for our experience is replete with evidence to support this general truth. We may have noticed that the two lines of a roof that intersect to form the peak never (by themselves) enclose a space. We have observed the parallel sides of a road, the parallel tracks of a railroad, the intersecting lines of a leg and rung of a chair, and so on. And never—not once—have we seen an instance in which two straight lines have by themselves enclosed a space. We do not, perhaps, consciously formulate the *statement* at first, but the statement is, nonetheless, a true generalization about our experience. When, therefore, we study geometry and come upon this axiom (as it is called), it may strike us as being obviously or self-evidently true. Indeed, we may be so impressed with its obviousness that we are tempted to say with Plato that it is not a case of learning but rather one of "recollecting" an "eternal truth" that has been present within our soul ever since its creation. But is it really surprising that a truth so lavishly exhibited in our everyday experience should seem obvious when we see it formally stated for the first time? It does not seem so to me.

What is true of this particular example is equally true of all other geometrical truths—with one proviso. Many of the more complex and unobvious theorems of geometry are not directly exhibited in our experience, but they are deducible from those that are. If proposition A and proposition B are learned from experience, and proposition C can be validly deduced from propositions A and B, then proposition C has ipso facto been learned from experience as well. Geometry is a science wherein the more complex and remote truths are deduced from those that are simpler and closer at hand; the latter, as I hope I have made clear, are gathered from the vast data of our everyday experience.

The certainty of geometrical truths, as of arithmetical truths, rests upon the immense quantity of evidence that supports the foundational truths of the science of geometry. It is not necessary, therefore, to repeat what has already been said on this point in connection with arithmetical truths.

Logical Truths

If I have succeeded in showing that the truths of arithmetic and geometry are a posteriori synthetic truths, my readers should have no difficulty in seeing that the truths of logic have the same status. Rationalist's first example—the statement that anything that has shape has size—is a perfect instance of a fact about the world that has been exhibited in our experience so many times that it is now inconceivable that there could ever occur an exception to it. With all this experience upon which to base our statement, what need have we for a special theory about a remarkable human capacity that supposedly enables us to "immediately apprehend" this homely, everyday truth? The same may be said with respect to his second example, that an object cannot both have and not have the same characteristic at the same time. The "necessity" that Rationalist finds in this statement is nothing more than our psychological certainty that a truth so consistently and lavishly exhibited in our experience will continue to be exhibited without exception.

One type of logical truth, which might pardonably be taken as a priori, would be one that states a set of circumstances in which a particular conclusion may be drawn from certain premises, for example, any statement of the form "If all As are Bs, and all Bs are Cs, then all As are Cs." There is, admittedly, a certain self-evidence about such a statement. We certainly cannot imagine the possibility of going wrong in asserting the conclusion if we are granted the premises, no matter what meanings may be assigned to A, B, and C.

Nonetheless, the explanation of this certainty is the same as in the previous examples. When Aristotle set about the task of formulating and systematizing the rules of logic, he did not just sit down and think, waiting for "direct apprehensions" to occur. Rather, he paid attention to the actual arguments that people used, and he noted the conditions under which arguments either succeeded or failed in establishing their conclusions. The conditions under which they did succeed he called "rules of inference"; the conditions under which they failed he called "logical fallacies." But the data from which he began, and the data on the basis of which other logicians have modified and augmented his work, are the actual arguments, successful or unsuccessful, that people employ. Logical truths are derived from the data of experience. The certainty of these truths is due to the large quantity of evidence upon which they are based.

Ethical Truths

I admit that there is something unusual about ethical statements, and it is understandable that Rationalist would appeal to this class of statements in support of his position. I am not sure that I understand just what makes ethical statements so unique, but I am quite sure that it is not (as Rationalist claims) that they are synthetic truths known a priori.

For one thing, we do not know "ethical truths" with the kind of certainty that is supposedly characteristic of a priori knowledge. To affirm an ethical statement is to affirm a belief, a conviction. It is as if we were saying, for example, "I don't know for sure what is right or wrong in this matter (perhaps no one does), but I will take my stand on this, that the infliction of needless pain is evil." What is affirmed as an ethical statement is not something that we know; it is something that we believe, something that we venture. And if it is not known at all, it is obviously not known a priori.

There are, it seems to me, two features of ethical statements that might explain their unusual character. First, they are typically affirmed in this venturing, convictional way. An ethical statement is not a report; it is a statement recording an intention to act in certain ways and encouraging others to do the same. Second, such statements, unlike all the others we have been considering, speak not of what *is* the case but of what *ought to be* the case. It may be the connotation of "oughtness" that makes ethical statements seem so different from all other statements.

There are, as a matter of fact, numerous ways in which an empiricist can construe ethical utterances without compromising his empiricism. The subject is a complex one, however, and will be discussed in detail at another time (see Chapters 43–48). For the present, we leave the status of ethical statements an open question. What is quite clear is that they are not synthetic truths known a priori; and this, so far as the refutation of rationalism is concerned, is the only point of importance.

Other Alleged Examples

Rationalist offers as a parting gift a miscellaneous group of examples of synthetic truths that we allegedly know a priori, and he asks, "How would you go about defending [one of these statements] if it were challenged?" My answer is that I would point to the evidence upon which my confidence in the truth of these statements clearly rests. I have seen millions of examples of events having a cause, but no examples of uncaused events. I have seen tens of thousands of objects of one color, but none that were simultaneously totally another color as well. I have seen countless examples of events happening, but never an example of an event "unhappening." I have seen—but is it really necessary to go on like this, refuting example after tedious example? The point that I am urging certainly should by now be abundantly clear: Our knowledge of the real world arises out of our experience, and in no other way. The function of reason is not to invent truths to which experience must somehow conform, but to generalize from the data of experience and to refine those generalizations by testing them against further experience. Such is the origin of every truth about the real world that we shall ever know.

STUDY QUESTIONS

1. Empiricist has argued that our knowledge of arithmetical truths, like our knowledge about crows, is a posteriori. How does he explain the fact that we are much more certain about the former kind of truths than about the latter? Are you satisfied with his explanation?
2. What evidence does Empiricist offer in support of his claim that geometrical truths are known a posteriori? Do you think he is right on this point?
3. Suppose that Aristotle worked out the "rules of logical inference" in the way that Empiricst says he did. Would this fact be sufficient to establish that they are truths known a posteriori? Could Rationalist allow this account and still claim that they are truths known a priori?
4. Is there something unusual about ethical statements, as Empiricist says there is? If so, does it seem plausible to you that this is because ethical truths are synthetic truths known a priori? Do you find Empiricist's explanation of this alleged uniqueness more or less persuasive than Rationalist's?

9

ANOTHER ALTERNATIVE FOR EMPIRICISTS

I wish to begin by asserting that on the main issue of the present controversy, the author of the last chapter and I are in perfect agreement: all knowledge of synthetic truths arises out of experience. We are, therefore, united in our opposition to rationalism, since we cannot allow the claim that there are some synthetic truths—some truths about the real world—that are known a priori. It is our contention that whatever is known about the real world has been learned from experience, one's own and others', and that whatever is known apart from experience (a priori) is not a truth about the real world at all but merely an analytic truth.

Nevertheless, we do share a disagreement common among empiricists, that of whether certain classes of statements are to be construed as analytic a priori or as synthetic a posteriori. My colleague has argued that arithmetical, geometrical, and logical truths are all synthetic a posteriori. However, in my opinion they are, except for logical truths, actually analytic a priori truths, and I shall attempt to show this. I shall also have something further to say about ethical truths, not so much in disagreement with as in addition to what was said about them in the last chapter.

Arithmetical Truths

Statements about the real world—synthetic statements—have one distinguishing feature in common: it is always possible to specify some state of affairs which, if it were the case, would make the statement in question false. The statement "All crows are black" is made false by the supposition that there exists a white crow; hence, it is evident that in this case we have a synthetic statement. This test, carefully applied, should enable us to distinguish without difficulty between synthetic and analytic statements.

Our test, it should be noted, is not an arbitrary one. It follows from the definition of a synthetic statement as a statement about the real world. A synthetic statement asserts that the world is thus and so; it asserts that something really is the case. Consequently, it must be possible to specify a state of affairs in which this would not be the case—in which, accordingly, our statement would be falsified.

Let us now apply our test to an arithmetical statement. What would have to be the case for the statement "7 + 5 = 12" to be false? Let us suppose that I put what I believe to be seven objects (oranges, say) into a bag, and then I put in what I believe to be five more. I bring them to the grocery clerk to be priced. He counts them and finds, to my surprise, that the bag contains only eleven oranges. I count them again, he counts them again, and finally I am convinced: there are only eleven oranges in the bag.

Does this state of affairs falsify the statement "7 + 5 = 12"? Obviously not. We might adopt any one of several explanations of what happened. Perhaps I miscounted the first time; perhaps one of the oranges that I counted did not get into the bag; or perhaps someone removed one of the oranges after I had put it in the bag. But note that we would not think of adopting the explanation that this was a remarkable exception to the statement "7 + 5 = 12." The case just described does not, then, falsify our arithmetical statement.

What state of affairs would falsify our statement? None. The only way the statement "7 + 5 = 12" could be rendered false would be to change the meaning of one or more of the symbols that comprise the statement. If the symbol 7 were defined to mean what is ordinarily meant by the symbol 8, the statement would, of course, become false. But then we would no longer be describing a state of affairs in the real world to which the statement in question refers. We would be altering the meaning of the statement itself.

The truth about arithmetical statements is that they are, one and all, *analytic truths*. What tends to mislead us is the fact that a number has meaning only in the context of the whole number system. The meaning of a number consists, partly, in its relation to every other number in the system. Part of the meaning of the number 7, for example, is that it is one more than 6 and one less than 8, that it is two more than 5 and two less than 9, and so on. Hence, it is a part of the meaning of 7 that it is five less than 12. Consequently, when we affirm that 7 + 5 = 12, we are merely stating explicitly some of the meaning relations that obtain in the system between the numbers 7, 5, and 12. Were this not the case, mathematical reasoning would not have the certainty that it has.

If we look at the reasons that the previous two writers have given for holding that arithmetical truths are synthetic, it is not difficult to see where and why they have gone wrong. First, they have failed to note that the concept of a number is exceedingly complex, involving the relations of that number to every other number in the number system. If we make the mistake of thinking of 7 and 5 as simple concepts—visualizing seven dots and five dots, or some such thing—then it seems very natural to conclude that we cannot get the predicate 12 by analyzing the complex symbol 7 + 5, that we can get it only by "performing the prescribed intellectual operation." But as soon as we realize the complexity of the concept of a number—as soon as we realize that its meaning includes its relations to the other numbers in the number system—the error becomes apparent.

Second, these writers have been misled by what I shall call the quasi-empirical character of arithmetical truths—a character they share with many analytic truths. At first glance, analytic truths often appear to be "about the real world"; that is why we cannot decide on the status of a given statement simply on the basis of whether or not it "seems" to be about the real world. The statement "All bachelors are unmarried," for example, seems to be a statement about real bachelors. It is only when we apply the test—when we try to specify a state of affairs which, if it were the case, would falsify the statement—that it becomes evident that the statement is not really about bachelors at all, but only about the meaning of the word "bachelor."

So it is with arithmetical truths. They seem, admittedly, to be about the real world—about "apples and oranges and pennies and kittens and anything else that we might have occasion to count and add together," as Rationalist says. But this appearance is deceptive, as we have already shown. When the crucial test of *falsifiability by empirical facts* is applied, it becomes obvious that arithmetical statements are purely analytic. No state of affairs can be imagined which, if it were the case, would render an arithmetical truth untrue, for the very good reason that an arithmetical truth is not a statement about the world; it is a statement about the relations between numbers in a number system. Arithmetical truths are analytic truths known a priori by anyone who understands adequately the meanings of the symbols. Such truths have certainty because, as Rationalist asserts, they are known a priori; but because they are analytic truths, our knowledge of them does not constitute an a priori knowledge of the real world.

Geometrical Truths

It is not surprising that many philosophers have believed that the truths of geometry are synthetic truths known a priori. It seems plausible to hold, as Rationalist does, that geometry is "the science of physical space" and that a geometrical statement is therefore about the real world. If we hold this and then reflect on the peculiar certainty with which we are able to demonstrate the theorems of geometry, it is also natural to conclude that geometry consists of a remarkable collection of a priori truths about the real world.

It must be said, however, that this conclusion is less tenable today than in the time of Plato, or Descartes, of even Kant. Today we know that Euclidean geometry is not the only possible geometry; we know that what can be demonstrated in any geometry depends, not on a correspondence to the real world, but on the definitions with which we begin. We may or may not be able to use a given geometry to explain physical space: that is an empirical question to be decided only by trial and error. What is known, therefore, when we have demonstrated a geometrical theorem, is not anything about the real world at all but only some consequence implicit in the definitions with which the demonstration began.

One reason so many people have been persuaded that the truths of geometry are synthetic rather than analytic is that in studying geometry they have the impression that with each demonstration of a new theorem, they are discovering (or "grasping") a new truth. They learn, for example, that a triangle is a closed plane figure having three straight sides, and subsequently they "discover" a truth that does not seem to be contained in this definition (for example, that the interior angles total 180 degrees). But the fact is that this latter theorem *is* implicit in the definition of a triangle together with the other definitions (some of which are called axioms) of Euclid's system. If this were not the case, it would not be possible to construct a valid proof of the theorem. Were it not for the fact that our intellects are limited, we would never have a sense of discovery when we first succeed in proving a complex geometrical theorem. We would immediately see all of the logical consequences of our definitions and would have no need for a formal demonstration. But this human limitation should not be allowed to obscure the fact that geometrical reasoning always begins with gratuitously assumed definitions and concludes with theorems having the same gratuitous character. Geometrical truths, without exception, are analytic.

Logical Truths

I am uncertain what Rationalist intends to include in the class of logical truths. It may be that some of the truths he has in mind would require one explanation, whereas others would require somewhat different ones. I shall, however, deal briefly with his two examples and shall add a few remarks that I hope will eliminate any possible misunderstanding on this point.

One example that Rationalist discusses in some detail is the statement "Anything that has shape has size." To me this is rather obviously an analytic statement. The concept of a "thing"—or of an "object," as Rationalist says later—includes both the idea of shape and the idea of size. Shape and size are, indeed, diverse characteristics, but both are implicit in the idea of a spatial object, which is what Rationalist has in mind. Fully stated, Rationalist's statement should read, "Anything that occupies space has both shape and size." Rationalist has been misled by the elliptical character of his own statement.

Rationalist's second example is a rather confused statement of the Principle of Noncontradiction, which asserts merely that a statement and its contradictory cannot both be true. There is, to be sure, something very puzzling about the status of this principle. Let us try to make it less so.

The Principle of Noncontradiction, in my opinion, is nothing more than a linguistic convention: it plays the same role in language that rules play in a game. There are, in fact, many such rules in any language "game," one of which is that every simple proposition is either true or false. Another rule is that if a proposition is true, then it is not false; and if it is false, then it is not true—the Principle of Noncontradiction. As linguistic conventions these rules are neither analytic nor synthetic, since they are not statements at all. They are merely rules that we must follow if we are to use language intelligibly.

Much the same can be said of rules of inference. It has been argued that rules of inference are empirical generalizations based upon analyses of the actual arguments used, successfully or unsuccessfully, to establish conclusions based on certain kinds of premises. This position contains some truth, but on the fundamental question of the logical status of the rules of inference I think it is incorrect. It rightly asserts that these rules were determined by Aristotle and others through a process of inductive reasoning. But what Aristotle discovered by this method was not truths about the real world (in any significant meaning of that phrase) but rather the rules by which we reason successfully from premises to conclusions. Aristotle might be compared to a person who, knowing nothing about the rules of baseball, figures them out by watching how the game is actually played. What would be discovered in this way, however, would be not a group of synthetic truths but a system of rules prescribing what players may and may not do in the game of baseball. Just so with the rules of inference. They are not synthetic truths, since they are not truths at all; they are rules governing logical inferences in our language. To know these rules is not to know some truths about the real world. It is to know how to speak intelligibly when playing the remarkable game of human discourse.

Ethical "Truths"

I have already indicated that I am quite in agreement with the remarks about ethical truths made by the author of the last chapter, and I have no wish to discuss at this time the many ways in which an empiricist might handle such utterances. I would like, however, to make just one suggestion as a kind of footnote to those remarks.

We found in the case of what are commonly called logical truths that, properly speaking, they are not "truths" at all, but simply rules, linguistic conventions governing the use of language. Once this is recognized, the question whether they are synthetic or analytic disappears: since they are not truths at all, they are neither synthetic nor analytic. Perhaps an analogous account can be given of ethical truths. Perhaps they are not "truths" at all, and hence neither analytic nor synthetic. I suggest that they might be linguistic expressions of a quite different type. Three possibilities come to mind: (*a*) statements of intention, (*b*) veiled commands, or (*c*) expressions of feeling. Since the logical status of ethical discourse is still a controversial issue, I do not wish to attempt a defense of any one of these options. I would suggest, however, that in view of this controversy it seems extremely hazardous to rest any part of the case for rationalism on an appeal to examples drawn from this source.

Other Truths

Of the miscellaneous statements that Rationalist offers as his final examples of synthetic truths known a priori, there is one on which I should particularly like to comment. That is the statement "If anything is red all over then it is not blue all over." I would suggest that our confidence in the truth of this statement rests on exactly the same basis as our confidence that if something is round then it is not square, that is, on our aforementioned decision not to violate the Principle of Noncontradiction. Note that it is impossible to form the *concept* of an object that is at one and the same time red all over and blue all over. It is clear also from this that we are dealing here not with a truth about the real world but rather with a statement whose truth depends upon the definitions and the linguistic rules of our language.

Without discussing in detail Rationalist's remaining examples, let me conclude by saying that I believe that any fair-minded person who carefully considers the statements offered by rationalists as examples of synthetic truths known a priori will find that every such example can be convincingly shown to be one of the following: (*a*) an analytic truth, (*b*) an empirical generalization (a synthetic truth known a posteriori), or (*c*) not a statement at all—that is, a sentence that *appears* to assert something but does not in fact do so. To be sure, we may sometimes be in doubt about the correct status of a given sentence, but I believe that is only because the precise meaning of the sentence is not clear (as in the case, for example, of the sentence "Time moves ever forward," which sounds more like poetry than a straightforward assertion). Once we have settled on the exact meaning of the sentence, however, I am confident that we will find that it can always be construed in one of the three ways I have indicated. Unless and until we find an example that clearly cannot be so construed, we must remain empiricists.

STUDY QUESTIONS

1. At what point or points does the author of this chapter (Empiricist B) claim to be in agreement with the author of the previous chapter (Empiricist A), and at what point or points does he claim to be in disagreement? Would it be inconsistent for someone to agree with Empiricist A's account of some of Rationalist's examples and Empiricist B's account of others?
2. What is the "falsifiability test" that Empiricist B proposes as a method for distinguishing between analytic and synthetic truths? Does this seem to you to be a valid test? What use does Empiricist B make of this test in his subsequent discussion?
3. What account does Empiricist B give of "rules of inference"? Do you think he is right? In your judgment, would it be plausible for Rationalist to argue that these are examples of synthetic truths that are known a priori?
4. What do you think of the suggestion that what Rationalist calls "ethical truths" are not "truths" at all? Is Empiricist B right in saying that if this is the case, it is not proper to ask whether they are analytic or synthetic? Why or why not?
5. Summarize the case for empiricism as you now understand it, drawing upon both this chapter and the preceding one.
6. Is it possible in principle to finally "prove" empiricism? Why or why not?

10

A RATIONALIST REPLY

I suppose it would be excessively unkind to whisper the suggestion that our two empiricist friends, in their respective efforts to defend an embattled empiricism, rather effectively cancel each other out. Empiricist A allows that most of my examples of synthetic a priori truths (all except ethical truths) are indeed synthetic, but then he attempts to show that the certainty with which we hold these truths is due to the vast amount of experience upon which they are based. Empiricist B recognizes that A's attempt is a failure, and he tries the other alternative of interpreting these statements as analytic a priori. I cannot resist the temptation to play peacemaker in the present dispute. I think each of our empiricist friends is half right: Empiricist A is right in holding that the truths in question are synthetic, and Empiricist B is right in holding that they are known a priori. It is scarcely necessary to point out that in addition to being half right, each is also half wrong.

There would be little point in rehashing all the arguments in support of the view that arithmetical, geometrical, logical, and ethical truths are all synthetic a priori. I have already stated what I consider to be the most convincing reasons for so regarding them, and I have little to add to what I consider to be a strong positive case. Our empiricist friends have raised a number of interesting points, however, and since I have been given the last word, I should like to use the opportunity to counter their criticisms.

The Status of the Argument

There is always some danger, when arguments become numerous, that the main point at issue will become obscured, so perhaps we should begin by stating once again the status of the argument.

The question at issue is this: Do we or do we not have any a priori knowledge of synthetic truths? I have argued that we do and have offered several classes of examples in support of my view. Our two empiricists have argued that we do not and have attempted to show that my examples can all be interpreted in some other way than mine.

Some readers may have come to the conclusion that my account of ethical truths, for example, is not correct. If it were not, what effect would this have on the argument? It would remove one group of examples of synthetic a priori truths, leaving the others intact. Nothing more. The case would still be that we have some a priori knowledge of synthetic truths, and my basic position would remain unscathed. *Only if every plausible example of synthetic truths known a priori has been shown to have some other status has rationalism been shown to be mistaken.*

I do not mean by the above to withdraw my claim that ethical truths are in fact synthetic truths known a priori. I stand by all the examples I offered earlier. My point is simply that if someone were to disagree with me about the correct interpretation of some of my examples, while agreeing with me with respect to others, he would still be on my side on the fundamental issue in the rationalist-empiricist controversy. Rationalists have some differences, too. But it takes only a single example of an a priori synthetic truth to clinch the case for rationalism. I turn now to a consideration of some of the points raised by my opponents.

Necessary Truths and Empirical Generalizations

Empiricist A has argued that arithmetical, geometrical, and logical truths are synthetic a posteriori, and he has attempted to account for the certainty with which we hold these truths by saying that they are based on a very large quantity of experiential data. I think he is mistaken on this point, and I want to present one final argument in support of this opinion.

An empirical generalization is only as strong as the evidence on which it rests. Indeed, there seems to be a perfect parallel between the quantity of evidence upon which a generalization is based and the degree of certainty with which it is held to be true. But surely it is evident that the certainty with which we hold arithmetical, geometrical, and logical truths to be true is out of all proportion to the quantity of "evidence" upon which, if they were empirical generalizations, they would have to be based. There are, admittedly, some simple truths of this sort that are confirmed by our experience almost every day of our lives (simple combinations of numbers up to ten or so, for example, and simple geometrical axioms such as the one about the impossibility of two straight lines enclosing a space). But consider for a moment some more complex examples. How many times in your life have you multiplied 762 by 316? Perhaps never. Yet you know, *with absolute certainty,* once you work the problem, what the answer is. How many triangles have you measured to find the sum of the interior angles? How many triangles have you inscribed in a semicircle? Yet you know, once you have understood the proof of the relevant theorems, that the interior angles of a Euclidean triangle total 180 degrees and that any triangle inscribed within a semicircle must be a right triangle.

There are, on the other hand, many truths that are really empirical generalizations for which there is a great deal of supporting evidence but to which we can readily conceive exceptions, though we may never in fact encounter an exception. I can imagine, for example, that on some occasion pure water at sea-level barometric pressure might fail to crystallize at 32° Fahrenheit as the law says it will. I am highly confident that this will not happen, but as with even the best-documented empirical generalizations, I do not have the absolute certainty that I have about a priori truths. If, then, I encounter a truth that I see to be necessarily true, and therefore know to be true with absolute certainty, I know that it is an a priori truth. And if, in addition, this truth is about the real world, so that in knowing it I know not just the meanings of certain terms but something about reality, then I know that it is a synthetic a priori truth. Those in doubt on this point should compare any one of the examples I have given with the best-documented empirical generalization that they can think of. I am confident that they will not fail to see the difference. There is much, very much, that we know by observation and experimentation, but such knowledge we do not possess with the absolute certainty that is the hallmark of a priori knowledge.

The Falsifiability Test

Recognizing that the truths we have been discussing cannot be accounted for by Empiricist A's approach, Empiricist B tries to account for them in another way. Contrary to what may seem to be the case, he argues, arithmetical and geometrical truths are not synthetic truths at all: they are analytic. And the proof of this, he goes on to say, is that it is not possible to describe a state of affairs that, if it were the case, would render one of these statements false. This "falsifiability test," as he calls it, is the big weapon in his attack on synthetic a priori truths. Just how lethal is it, really?

Admittedly, the falsifiability test may be of some occasional value in helping us decide whether a given statement is analytic or synthetic; but it is not the infallible test that Empiricist B thinks it is. The reason is that a *logically impossible* state of affairs cannot be consistently described. If, therefore, we find ourselves unable in some instance to describe a state of affairs that, if the case, would falsify the statement in question, there are two possibilities: the statement may be, as Empiricist B says it must be, an analytic statement, or it may be a synthetic truth to which there are no logically possible alternatives.

Consider once again the statement "Anything that has shape has size." I grant that neither I nor anyone else can imagine or describe a state of affairs that, if it were the case, would falsify this statement. (I can, of course, construct a sentence that appears to contradict the statement. I can say, "Some things that have shape do not have size," but Empiricist B and I both know that in saying this I would not be describing a possible state of affairs.) The reason that I cannot describe a state of affairs that, if true, would falsify the statement in question is not, however, that my statement is analytic, but rather that there is no logically possible alternative to the synthetic truth it expresses. We can see that although size and shape are different characteristics of spatial objects, they are, nonetheless, related in such a way that where one is present the other must be also.

Even if the falsifiability test were taken at face value, however, it would not do the job that Empiricist B wants it to do. I noted with great interest that he himself, as a matter of fact, did not make use of the test in his discussion of geometrical truths. And with good reason. Even by this measure geometrical truths turn out to be synthetic truths. For it is not at all difficult to describe a state of affairs that, if true, would falsify almost any geometrical theorem we can think of. It is perfectly conceivable to a nonmathematician that the interior angles of a Euclidean triangle, for example, might have totaled 160 or 190 degrees instead of 180, or that a triangle inscribed within a semicircle might always have had one obtuse angle instead of one 90° angle. It just happens that Euclid's theorems with respect to these matters are true, and if we have studied a little geometry, we know they are. But to know that they are true is not, in this case, to render the alternatives inconceivable.

Even the one application that Empiricist B does make of the falsifiability test—to arithmetical truths—is not very convincing. Obviously we would not, in the example of the oranges, adopt the explanation that there were only eleven oranges in the bag due to a remarkable exception to the general rule that $7 + 5 = 12$. But surely the reason we would not adopt this explanation is that we know a priori that $7 + 5 = 12$. Because we know this, and know it with absolute certainty, we quite naturally seek some other explanation for the fact that the bag does not contain as many oranges as we expected it to; for to know something a priori is to know also that experience must conform to what is thus known.

Let us suppose, however, that (in spite of his unfortunate reliance on what has turned out to be a faulty weapon) Empiricist B were right in his interpretation of mathematical truths. What would be the consequences?

In the first place, it would remain a gigantic puzzle that we are able to use arithmetical and geometrical reasoning to draw conclusions about the world at all. It is a remarkable fact that we are able to calculate all sorts of things—budget deficits and satellite orbits and a million other things—by applying the appropriate mathematical formulas to the data with which we begin. Remarkable though this is, it is, nonetheless, a fact. On Empiricist B's account, however, this fact is not only remarkable, it is inexplicable. By his view, mathematical truths are not truths about the world at all. They are purely vacuous statements that do nothing more than make explicit some of the meaning relations that have, apparently quite arbitrarily, been assigned to the various symbols in our number system. It is difficult to take seriously a theory that forces us to the conclusion that the applicability of mathematical reasoning to the real world is nothing but a happy coincidence.

In the second place, if the applicability of mathematical reasoning to the real world were, as Empiricist B holds, a matter of simply "trying it out to see if it works," then we ought to question whether it will work when it is applied to phenomena with which we have had no previous experience—whether, for example, the arithmetical and geometrical truths with which we are familiar on earth will hold on the moon or on Mars. But we do not in fact entertain such doubts (that is *not* one of the things we worried about when we sent men to the moon), and the reason we do not is that we know that the truths that we express in our equations are necessarily and universally true.

Logical Truths

I am delighted that Empiricist B has seen fit to explore the status of the so-called rules of inference, because they constitute some of the most convincing examples in support of my position. I hold, of course, that the rules of inference are synthetic a priori truths. It seems to me that whatever plausibility my opponent's account of these truths has depends on the unargued assumption that speaking a language is very much like playing a game, and that the rules governing the use of language are, like the rules in a game, altogether a matter of convention. This is hardly the place for a full-length discussion of the relation of language to reality, but we should be aware that the account of logical truths with which we are now dealing presupposes an extremely implausible view of the status of language.

My own view is that language has evolved out of the encounter of the human mind with reality, and that it therefore incorporates a certain logical structure that corresponds to the structure of reality. The rules of inference, in this view, are not at all a matter of convention. They are grounded in the very structure of reality, are, in fact, universal and synthetic truths about reality. They may be ignored at the cost not simply of speaking unintelligibly but of speaking falsely. If I were to attempt to ignore the Principle of Noncontradiction—to say, that is, that some simple propositions are both true and false—I would be guilty not merely of breaking one of the rules of the language game; I would be guilty of uttering a statement that is not true. A proposition cannot be simultaneously true and false, for the reason that a given state of affairs cannot both be the case and not be the case at one and the same time. It is reality, not merely conventional rules, that determines the truth or falsity of what we say. A so-called language that did not mirror the structure of reality in its own logical structure would be no language at all.

A Word About Ethics

Perhaps it was unwise to bring ethical truths into the present discussion, since I might have anticipated that it would lead only to confusion. So much has been written of late on the status of these truths, and so many theories have been propounded, that some philosophers hesitate even to mention the matter for fear that they will be compelled to defend their position against a vast number of opposing theories.

It is interesting to note, however, that this question did not become a matter of serious controversy until early in the present century, when British and American philosophers began to rally in large numbers around the banner of empiricism. Since then, the question of what to do with ethical truths has remained one of the thorniest problems for an empiricist to handle. If there are, as Empiricist A has said, "numerous ways in which an empiricist can construe ethical utterances without compromising his empiricism," it is not because these various ways are all so plausible, but rather because no one of them is sufficiently plausible to win very many adherents. But this is a matter that is to be discussed elsewhere at some length (see Chapters 43–48), so we need not enter into it here.

My position, in any case, remains unchanged and, for that matter, virtually unchallenged by the few remarks my opponents have made on the subject of ethical truths. If anyone is absolutely determined to be an empiricist, I have no doubt that he will be able to find among the many empiricist accounts of ethical truths one that is to his liking. If, however, I have succeeded in persuading some of my readers that we do in fact have some a priori knowledge of synthetic truths, I think they will have little difficulty in agreeing that ethical truths are among those known in this way.

STUDY QUESTIONS

1. Is Rationalist right in saying that "it takes only a single example of an a priori synthetic truth to clinch the case for rationalism"? Explain.
2. Is Rationalist right in saying that (a) our certainty of the truth of an empirical generalization varies according to the amount of evidence on which it rests, and that (b) the certainty with which we hold arithmetical, geometrical, and logical truths is out of all proportion to the quantity of evidence upon which, if they were empirical generalizations, they would be based? If so, how does this affect Empiricist A's position? Empiricist B's?
3. What considerations does Rationalist bring forward in his attempt to show

that the falsifiability test is not capable of doing the job that Empiricist B wants it to do? How might Empiricist B answer Rationalist on this point?
4. State briefly Rationalist's attempted *reductio ad absurdum* of Empiricist B's account of mathematical truths. Does it succeed? Explain.

FOR FURTHER READING

Aune, Bruce. *Rationalism, Empiricism, and Pragmatism.* New York: Random House, 1970 (paperbound).

Blanshard, Brand. *The Nature of Thought,* vol. 1. New York: Humanities Press, 1939, chaps. 28–30.

———. *Reason and Analysis.* LaSalle, Ill.: Open Court, 1962, chaps. 6 and 10.

Cassirer, Ernst. *The Problem of Knowledge,* tr. by W. H. Woglom and C. W. Hendel. New Haven, Conn.: Yale University Press, 1950, chaps. 1–4.

Hamlyn, D. W. *The Theory of Knowledge.* Garden City, N.Y.: Doubleday, 1970 (paperbound).

Harris, James F., and Richard H. Stevens (eds.). *Analyticity.* New York: Quadrangle Books, 1970.

Kant, Immanuel. *Critique of Pure Reason,* tr. by Norman Kemp Smith. New York: St. Martin's Press, 1965 (paperbound). See Introduction, Sections 1–5.

Leibnitz, G. W. *New Essays Concerning Human Understanding.* Many editions. See especially Book I and Book IV, Chapters 1–9.

Lewis, C. I. *An Analysis of Knowledge and Valuation.* LaSalle, Ill.: Open Court, 1947, chaps. 1–6.

———. *Mind and the World Order.* New York: Scribner, 1929, chaps. 7–9.

Locke, John. *An Essay Concerning Human Understanding.* Many editions. See especially Book I and Book IV, Chapters 1–9.

Monsat, Stanley (ed.). *The Analytic-Synthetic Distinction.* Belmont, Calif.: Wadsworth, 1971. Both classical and contemporary selections.

Morick, H. (ed.). *Challenges to Empiricism.* Belmont, Calif.: Wadsworth, 1972. Contemporary papers.

Pap, Arthur. "Are All Necessary Propositions Analytic?" *The Philosophical Review,* 58 (1949), 229–320.

Pears, David. *What Is Knowledge?* New York: Harper & Row, 1971.

Plato. *Meno.* Many editions.

Quine, W. van Orman. *From a Logical Point of View,* 2nd. ed., rev. New York: Harper & Row, 1961 (paperbound). See especially "Two Dogmas of Empiricism."

Reichenbach, Hans. *The Rise of Scientific Philosophy.* Berkeley and Los Angeles: University of California Press, 1958 (paperbound).

Russell, Bertrand. *Introduction to Mathematical Philosophy.* New York: Humanities Press, 1960, chaps. 1, 2, 13, and 14.

Ryle, G., K. Popper, and C. Lewy. "Why Are the Calculuses of Logic and Mathematics Applicable to Reality?" *Proceedings of the Aristotelian Society,* Supplementary 20 (1946), 20–60.

Sleigh, R. C., Jr. (ed.). *Necessary Truth.* Englewood Cliffs, N.J.: Prentice-Hall, 1972.

Sumner, L. W., and John Woods (eds.). *Necessary Truth: A Book of Readings.* New York: Random House, 1969.

PART III

REALISTS AND PHENOMENALISTS

11

COMMONSENSE REALISM AND ITS CRITICS

We turn now to the consideration of a problem that is closely related to the epistemological problem with which we were concerned in the preceding section. It is the so-called problem of the *ontological status* of the physical world. Now "ontological status" is a phrase that is not used in ordinary conversation; it is, rather, a part of the technical vocabulary of philosophers. Let us begin our discussion of the problem, then, by trying to make clear what philosophers are talking about when they use this rather forbidding-sounding combination of words.

To talk about the ontological status of something is to talk about the kind of being that it has. To say that the ontological status of X is this or that is to say something about X's *mode of existence*: it is to state in precisely what sense it is true to say that there *are* Xs. Let us consider a few examples.

It makes sense to say that there are such things as dreams. The word "dream" does not denote a nonentity. It denotes something real, some real occurrence. But what sort of occurrence? What really are dreams? What is their ontological status? Someone might reply that a dream is an experience that a person has in his astral body while his physical body is asleep. Most of us would probably say that a dream is a series of occurrences that takes place in our imagination while we are asleep. To reply in either of these ways is to say something about the *kind* of reality that a dream has. The disagreement that is apparent in these two answers is a disagreement about the ontological status of dreams, a disagreement about what sort of thing the item in question is.

Consider the case of angels. What are angels, really? Someone might say that angels are rational, sexless, winged creatures existing in heaven and serving God in a variety of ways. Someone else might say that angels are mythical beings imagined to exist in a mythical heaven, no more real than the elves and fairies of children's tales. Once again, the disagreement is over the ontological status of angels. To affirm either position is to hold a particular view regarding the kind of being or mode of existence of whatever it is that is denoted by the term "angels."

Let us consider a third example. Someone remarks, "I was at the theater last night and saw Othello kill Desdemona. What a bloody sight!" A bystander exclaims (not in jest), "How terrible! Did they catch the murderer? Is he in jail now? Will you have to be a witness at his trial?" The bystander, in this example, has mistaken the ontological status of the event in question. He has interpreted a murder in a play as if it were an actual murder; he has treated Othello and Desdemona as if they were real people instead of fictitious characters in a dramatic production.

Three observations may be made at this point. The first is that what we are prepared to regard as live options with respect to questions of ontological status depends in part on our world-view, on the picture of reality we have. The astral-body theory of dreams is not a live option unless this picture includes a theory about astral bodies that are able to leave their physical counterparts on occasion, have adventures with other wandering astral bodies, and so on. The same is true of the theory that angels are real inhabitants in a real heaven. Some disputes about ontological status, therefore, resolve themselves into disputes about the credibility or incredibility of this or that world-view.

The second observation is that within any given world-view there can be genuine disagreement as to the ontological status of this or that particular class of phenomena. Indeed, for the most part it is only insofar as people share a relatively common world-view that they can fruitfully discuss questions of ontological status; otherwise some of the parties to the dispute will be proposing answers that are not considered by the others to be live options.

The third observation is that the number of ontological categories available within the context of any given world-view is fairly large and not capable of exhaustive enumeration. There are, to take some fairly noncontroversial examples, bodies and properties of bodies; minds and their ideas; living creatures and their behavior; and so on. To "place" something ontologically is to assign it to its proper place in a world-view, to interpret it as belonging to such and such a kind of being. To ask about the ontological status of something is to ask what its proper "place" is.

Ontological Dependence

Some things could not exist without other things, upon which they may accordingly be said to be "dependent" for their existence. Dreams, for example, could not exist without dreamers. It is ridiculous to talk of dreams as if they went about on their own looking for someone to "have" them.

To say that something A is dependent on something else B for its existence is to affirm a relation of onotological dependence: it is to say that A is ontologically dependent on B. Thoughts are ontologically dependent on thinkers, dreams on dreamers, actions on actors, and so on. If the ontological status of B is assumed to be known, the question of the ontological status of A may be satisfactorily answered by pointing out its ontological dependence on B. If the ontological status of B is itself in question, then the ontological status of everything held to be ontologically dependent on it is also in question.

The Physical World

The question considered in this section concerns the ontological status of a very large class of objects that we designate by the collective phrase "the physical world." It includes everything we perceive by means of our five senses.

There is no serious disagreement, either among philosophers or among nonphilosophers, about what we perceive the physical world to be. It appears to consist of a vast number of individual objects—trees, stones, birds, animals, human beings—that exhibit a wide variety of colors, shapes, sounds, smells, temperatures, tastes, textures, and so on. Were anyone to deny that this is how the physical world appears, we would be inclined to think that either that person was not being honest with us or else was lacking some of the normal faculties of sense perception.

But is the physical world *as we perceive it* an exact copy of the physical world *as it really is*, or is the reality "out there" different in some ways from our perception of it? To ask such a question is not to ask about the ontological status of the physical world; it is only to call in question the trustworthiness of our perceptions. Nevertheless, it is a very short step from this question to the ontological one: Is the physical world to any degree dependent on a perceiver for its existence? Does this varicolored, varishaped, varisounding reality that we perceive exist even when someone is not perceiving it, or is it in some sense constituted by and therefore dependent on perception? The point of the question may be made clearer by a brief preliminary survey of the possible answers.

Four Alternatives

The commonsense answer to this queston, and certainly the view held by most people prior to any sophisticated reflection on it, goes something like this: There is a real physical world that causes us to have the perceptions that we have, and our perceptions are more or less exact copies of the qualities that are really present in those objects. An object that appears to be brown really is brown; one that is perceived to be hard or cold or smooth really is hard or cold or smooth; and so on. In short, the physical world *exists* and is in no way dependent on our perception for its existence. If all perceivers were annihilated, the varicolored, varishaped, varisounding world that they had formerly perceived would still be there, though there would not, of course, be anyone around to perceive that it was there.

The view that we have just stated is often called "naïve realism" by philosophers who address themselves to this problem. The name is somewhat unfortunate, however, since the term "naïve" might seem to suggest that the position is obviously not worthy of serious consideration. In the discussion that follows, therefore, we shall refer to this position as *commonsense*, or *direct*, *realism* and to someone who holds it as a *commonsense*, or *direct*, *realist*.

A second position that may be taken with respect to this question is the view known as subjective idealism, or phenomenalism. (The former name is rather closely associated with George Berkeley, an early-eighteenth-century Irish philosopher, and is not in general use at the present time. Nevertheless, although it now goes by the name of phenomenalism, and the grounds upon which it is commonly held are somewhat different from those upon which Berkeley first maintained it, the position is essentially Berkeley's.)

In the scale of possible answers concerning the ontological status of the physical world, phenomenalism stands at the opposite extreme from commonsense realism. It explicitly rejects the "copy" theory of perception and asserts that the being of a physical object *consists in* its being perceived, that the physical world is accordingly *completely dependent* on the perceptions of a perceiver for its existence. Berkeley's classical formula for this view was *Esse est percipi*, "to be (a physical object) is to be perceived." Strange as this position may seem initially, it can be supported by a number of very powerful arguments, and it is held by many philosophers at the present time.

In addition to commonsense realism and phenomenalism there is only one other approach to this question, and that is to say that the physical world is partly dependent on a perceiver for its existence and partly independent of a perceiver. What is perceived is in some ways like and in some ways unlike what is really "out there." There is both similarity and dissimiliarity between the world as we perceive it and the world as it really is. This view is called *critical realism*.

Within this view, however, there are significant differences, depending upon whether the emphasis is on the similarity between our perceptions and the real world (thus being fairly close to the realist end of the scale) or on the dissimiliarity between the two (thus coming closer to the phenomenalist view). We shall, in the discussion that follows, make a semantic distinction to mark these two forms of critical realism, calling the more mild form *critical realism* and the more radical form *hypercritical realism*. The difference between them, it must be remembered, is one of degree only.

In philosophical writings on this problem, the term *sense datum* (plural, *sense data*) occurs rather frequently. Sense data are what we immediately perceive whenever we are ordinarily said to be perceiving something, without regard to whether there is anything "out there" corresponding to our perception. Thus a person who is hallucinating, for example, and who "sees" a pink elephant is said to have the same kind of sense data as people who are not hallucinating and who see a real pink elephant.

Employing this term, we can distinguish the four positions defined above in the following way. Commonsense realism is the view that the sense data that people have when their senses are not impaired are accurate copies of the physical world, and that, accordingly, the physical world is not constituted by sense data in any way whatsoever. Phenomenalism is the view that what we call the physical world is simply the inferred totality of our actual and possible sense data (except when we are hallucinating, etc.) and does not exist apart from these sense data. Critical realism (in any form) is the view that the sense data that we directly have when we are perceiving the physical world are in some respects similar to the characteristics objectively present in the physical world and in other respects dissimilar. Hypercritical realism, which is simply a variant of this view, claims that the dissimilarity between the two is significantly greater than most critical realists recognize.

There is a special form of phenomenalism—some philosophers would say it is a logical implication of phenomenalism—known as *solipsism*. This view is difficult to state with precision, but a fair approximation is the following: *I* alone exist in the primary or fundamental sense of "exist" and everything else that exists does so only in the secondary sense of being my perception or thought. Just as my dreams do not exist unless I am dreaming them, so nothing exists unless I am having the perceptions or thoughts that constitute the existence of something. This view, though difficult to refute, is universally considered highly implausible. To the best of my knowledge it has not been seriously advocated by any major thinker in the whole history of Western philosophy. Solipsism stands, however, as the fantastic limit to which skepticism regarding the inferences made from the data of sense experience can be carried, and it does come up occasionally in discussions of the problem of the ontological status of the physical world.

It is possible to discuss many of the matters in this section in terms of a slightly different question: Can our senses be trusted to give us accurate information about the world? Actually, many philosophers prefer this question, partly because discussions of ontological status have been more or less out of style in recent years. However, the classical examinations of perception—those of John Locke, George

Berkeley, David Hume, Immanuel Kant, and others—were quite openly directed toward a determination of the ontological status of the physical world. Moreover, it seems evident that any view we might adopt with respect to the veracity of our perceptions would have important implications for our view of the ontological status of the physical world. For these reasons we shall focus our discussion on the ontological question.

Chapters 12–14 may be viewed as three successive critiques of commonsense realism, each one progressively rejecting more of what commonsense realism affirms concerning the ontological status of the physical world. The discussion moves from a mild form of critical realism to hypercritical realism and then to phenomenalism. Finally, a defender of direct realism is given an opportunity to show what, if anything, can be salvaged of the commonsense view.

STUDY QUESTIONS

1. What ontological status would you be inclined to assign to each of the following: a hunch, a plan, redness, temperature, weight, Huckleberry Finn, Abraham Lincoln, a headache?
2. What precisely is the main question posed for consideration in this chapter? Restate it in at least three different ways (without changing the point of the question!).
3. In brief summary, what answers do the four alternatives defined in this chapter offer to this question? As you understand the problem, do these four alternatives exhaust the logical possibilities?
4. Do you find anything odd about the following statement? "The arguments in favor of solipsism are so convincing that I find myself compelled to adopt the position; I am surprised that more people do not come to the same conclusion."

12

CRITICAL REALISM

It is obvious that most people trust their sense perceptions and accordingly believe that the world is really very much as they perceive it to be. Most people would also grant, I suppose, that they can err in *judgment*: for example, that they might mistake a stone in the distance for a dog. But they would not, on this account, mistrust their senses; they would realize that they had judged too hastily and perhaps resolve to suspend judgment on some future occasion until they have made a closer inspection. Once they had identified the object in question as a stone, however, they would not doubt that the stone really is hard, rough, heavy, porous, and gray, as it appears to be. And if one were to ask them how they *know* that the stone really has these characteristics, they would reply with some indignation: "Because I have seen it with my own eyes, and felt it with my own hands!"

However accustomed we may be to thinking of the world in this way, the view that the world really is as we perceive it to be, that it really has all the characteristics we perceive it to have, is one that cannot survive critical reflection, as will be evident from the following considerations.

Critique of Commonsense Realism

That commonsense realism is not a defensible position is evident, in the first place, from the fact that we sometimes have illusory perceptions. A straight stick immersed in water, for example, looks as though it is bent; there is no point of view we could adopt that would make it look any other way. It is only because such a stick does not feel bent and again looks straight when removed from the water that we have learned not to rely on our visual sense data in this instance. Or consider a mirage that taunts a traveler in the desert. He sees it just as surely as we can see real water and real trees; it is only because the mirage recedes or disappears as he "approaches" it—only because he can never reach it, drink its water, be cooled by the shade of its trees—that he calls it an illusion. The phantom pains of persons who have suffered the loss of a limb may also be mentioned as a case in point.

There is no reason to conclude that because our senses deceive us at times, they deceive us all the time. Indeed, it is only on the assumption that they do not deceive us all the time that we can identify our perceptions of the bent stick, the mirage, and the phantom pains as illusory. But in view of these examples of illusory perception, we cannot reasonably maintain that the physical world *exactly corresponds* to our perception of it. The most that can be maintained is that the world is like the majority of our perceptions.

The same conclusion may be reinforced by a second consideration, namely, that certain changes in a perceiver produce changes in his perceptions of the physical world. Suppose, for example, that a quantity of water is kept at a constant temperature. On one occasion I come from a hot bath, immerse my hand in the water, and pronounce it cold. On another occasion I come from having handled ice, immerse my hand in the water, and pronounce it warm. The water is not really cold in the first instance and warm in the second, but the same temperature. It is my perception that varies, not the water itself.

As another example, consider what happens when we wear colored glasses—pink, brown, green, or what have you. The world, as we all know, then appears more pink, more brown, more green, than otherwise. How can we be sure that the colored glasses do not enable us to see more clearly what the world is really like? Another example: Persons under the influence of certain drugs perceive the world differently than they do when not under their influence. Which set of perceptions provides an "accurate copy" of the real world?

A particularly interesting phenomenon to consider with regard to this question is color blindness. Two observers, A and B, look at patches of color. A perceives some patches to be red and others to be green; B perceives them to be all the same color. B, accordingly, is said to be color blind. But note that it is only because, like A, most people are able to make the distinction between "red" and "green" that the few unable to do so are said to be color blind. Were the statistics reversed, persons who perceive a distinction would perhaps be regarded by the majority as subject to a strange illusion. Whose perception is to be regarded as an accurate copy of the real world? We cannot say, "Those who are normal," since normalcy is here defined in terms of the perceptions of the majority. It is not reasonable to decide a question of this sort by means of a referendum.

We could, of course, save some vestiges of the commonsense view by making a number of arbitrary decisions. For example, we could say that what tells us about the world as it is really is the majority of the perceptions of people who have normal perception—people who suffer no impairment of sensory responses, who are not color blind, who are not wearing colored glasses, who have been for some time in a room whose temperature is exactly 68° Fahrenheit, and so on. However, since such decisions are purely arbitrary, each new difficulty that appeared would require a new condition to be introduced. To realize this is to realize that something other than commonsense realism must be adopted.

The Case for Critical Realism

The principle that should guide us in determining what is real about what we perceive is the one enuciated by Locke: qualities that are utterly inseparable from a physical object, such that a particle of matter however small could not be conceived to exist without it, are real qualities of that object; everything else that we perceive, though it indeed may appear to us to be a real quality in the object, is in truth nothing but a modification of our faculty of perception.[1] We shall, following Locke, call these *primary qualities* and *secondary qualities*, respectively. We shall say, accordingly, that primary qualities are really in the object and, in respect to these, the object is as we perceive it to be. Secondary qualities, however, are not in the object at all, but are only modifications of our faculty of perception caused by the object through its primary qualities. Let us see what account of the physical world can be given on the basis of this distinction.

Every object that we perceive appears to have the following qualities: color, shape, size, temperature, solidity, texture, and either rest or motion; some objects also have some odor, some taste, and some sound. These are the qualities that our various senses perceive to be present or absent in the objects that come before us.

Which of these qualities really are present in the object? Applying Locke's principle, we see that if we take any object and divide it up into as many tiny parts as we please, each part will still have some shape, some size, some temperature, some degree of solidity, and some texture, and it will be either in motion or at rest. These, therefore, are the primary qualities of an object.

What remain to be accounted the secondary qualities of an object are, therefore, its color, odor, taste, sound, its apparent degree of warmth or coldness. These, it is clear, depend on the sense apparatus of the perceiver and consist of nothing more than a modification of that apparatus by the object. Were the senses associated with our eyes, our ears, and our nose capable of being affected differently, things would appear to have different colors, different sounds, different odors than

---

[1] See John Locke, *An Essay Concerning Human Understanding*, II, xxiii (New York: Dover, 1959), pp. 390–423.

they now appear to have. Were our body temperature higher or lower than it is, things would not be perceived to be warm or cold in the proportions that they now are.

The qualities that are objectively present in an object—shape, size, temperature, texture, solidity, and either rest or motion—cause, via the mechanism of our sense apparatus, (*a*) impressions that are like the qualities themselves, which we call impressions of primary qualities, and (*b*) impressions unlike the qualities, which we call impressions of secondary qualities.

There is one further point that must be made to complete our account. It is impossible to conceive of an object as being made up simply of its several qualities randomly thrown together. An object has a certain unity for which our account thus far has made no provision. Formerly it was possible to posit a "substance" or a "substratum" that underlay and supported the object's qualities—an admittedly vague concept that Locke, for example, disparaged as merely "the supposed but unknown support of those qualities we find existing, which we imagine cannot subsist . . . without something to support them."[2] With the more sophisticated knowledge of matter that we have now, however, it is impossible to account for the unity of objects in this way. We say, therefore, that this unity is simply the natural consequence of the laws of nature acting upon the particular piece of matter in question. In the case of inanimate objects the relevant laws are physical and chemical laws, and the resultant unity is merely structural. In the case of living things this account must be supplemented by citing certain relevant biological laws, and the resultant unity (so long as the organism is alive) is organic as well as structural.

To come to a decision about the physical world's ontological status, we may safely ignore the more recondite facts about matter that have been reported by modern science. Whatever science may conclude concerning the nature of the physical world at the atomic and subatomic level, at the macroscopic level this world exhibits real qualities of shape, size, temperature, texture, solidity, and either rest or motion. These are real, and although they may indeed be dependent on atomic and subatomic processes for their reality, they are in no way dependent on us as human perceivers.

But critical realism does hold that color, sound, taste, smell, apparent degree of warmness and coldness—the secondary qualities of objects— are indeed dependent on a perceiver, that they are, in fact, nothing but modifications that occur within the perceiver. If there were no perceivers capable of being modified in this way, there would be no color, sound, taste, odor, warmness or coldness, in the world (whereas primary qualities would continue to exist even in the total absence of perceivers).

The chief reason for adopting critical realism is that it enables us to

---

[2] *Ibid.*, p. 391.

solve the puzzles about perception that originally caused us to question the commonsense view. It enables us to explain the fact that alterations in a perceiver result in certain changes in that person's perception—to see, for instance, that what is perceived to be cold at one time may, without itself changing, be perceived to be warm at another time (or even simultaneously, if one of the perceiver's hands is warm and the other is cold). Similarly, the puzzles that arise in connection with our perception of color are easily solved: things appear to be colored differently to persons who are color blind, under the influence of certain drugs, or wearing colored glasses, because such conditions alter the visual sense apparatus and because color is nothing but a modification of this apparatus.

There are other puzzles in connection with perception that can also be solved in the context of this view. For example, some people are able to hear high-pitched signals that are completely inaudible to others. From the point of view of commonsense theory, this fact immediately poses a question: Is a signal that is inaudible to all but a few people a sound or is it not? For critical realists, this phenomenon causes no difficulty. Sound is nothing but a modification of the audial apparatus of a perceiver, and any such modification is a sound. It is simply the case that some people are capable of being affected by air vibrations of a higher frequency than others; hence, the difference. Individual differences with respect to taste and smell can be accounted for in the same manner.

Some Remarks About Perception

It is evident that we must reject the commonsense view regarding the ontological status of the physical world, along with the "copy" theory of perception. The real world is not exactly as it appears to be; if our sense impressions are a "copy" of the real world, they are a very poor copy indeed. What, then, shall we say of the status of our sense impressions? How are sense data related to the objects in the real world that are their causes?

The answer implied in the position I am advocating is that the sense data *represent* the real objects before our minds. We directly perceive the sense data, and we make certain inferences about the objects that they represent. What we see, hear, taste, touch, and smell, we *really do* see, hear, taste, touch, and smell. But what we infer about the objects that are represented to us by these various kinds of sense data may be in error. Commonsense realism is thus seen to consist in the view that for every sense datum that appears in our perceptual field there is something *just like it* in the physical world. And this view, as we have seen, is one that is not consistent with the facts.

We must take care, however, not to reject more of the commonsense view than the facts require us to, which, so far as I can see, is no more than already we have rejected. There are, I am aware, certain considerations that seem to favor the phenomenalist view on this matter, and these obviously are worthy of being considered on their own merits. That view, however, involves certain difficulties that I do not think can be resolved without returning to something like the view here proposed. It seems to me that every argument that tends to support the phenomenalist position is equally valid, if it is valid at all, as an argument in support of solipsism—a view so patently absurd that the arguments in its support must be regarded as highly suspect. That we must depart as far from the commonsense theory as I have proposed seems obvious; but it seems equally obvious that to depart any further would be neither wise nor prudent.

STUDY QUESTIONS

1. What considerations does Critical Realist bring forward to support the view that commonsense realism is not a defensible position? Can you think of any way to defend commonsense realism against this critique?
2. What is the criterion by which Critical Realist proposes to distinguish between primary and secondary qualities? Does he apply it consistently in drawing up his two lists? In your opinion, is the criterion itself a valid one?
3. What, according to Critical Realist's account, are the primary and secondary qualities, respectively, of each of the following: a red brick? a book? a bowling ball? a siren? a mirage?
4. What reasons does Critical Realist give for adopting his theory regarding the status of the physical world? Do you find his reasons convincing? Can you think of any way that his case might be strengthened?

13

HYPERCRITICAL REALISM

I think my readers should know that "hypercritical realism" is a term they are not apt to find in any philosophical writings prior to the early 1960s. It was originally coined by Herbert Feigl, obviously in jest. However, it is remarkably suggestive of what I hold concerning the relation of our percepts (what we perceive) to the physical world, and I would not object if it were to come into general use as a descriptive title for the position that I represent.

Anyone who is at all familiar with the advances that have been made in the science of physics during the past few decades will recognize immediately, I think, that we cannot stay as close to commonsense realism as Critical Realist has urged us to do. This rough-and-ready description of the world in terms of primary and secondary qualities may have deserved some credence a century or two ago, but certainly not today. We have learned a good deal since the time of Locke. It is now a matter of common knowledge that the particles of which material objects are composed are not little nuggets of matter, each retaining the "primary qualities" of which Critical Realist speaks—shape, size, motion, and all the rest. We know, or at least we think we know, that everything in the physical world is a compound of some few basic elements; every element is reducible to molecules; every molecule to atoms; every atom to protons, neutrons, electrons, and numerous other even smaller particles. To try to understand the relation of our percepts to a world thus conceived in terms of Critical Realist's theory is like trying to do fine etching with a pickax: the tool is simply too unrefined for the task.

There is no need to plunge into the complexities of modern physics, however, in order to see that so minimal a departure from the common-sense theory as Critical Realist has proposed will not do. A number of far less recondite facts are as evidently fatal to his theory as the facts he does mention are to the commonsense theory. Let us consider in some detail the damaging facts that Critical Realist has overlooked.

Some Paradoxes of Perception

Critical Realist has pointed out a number of rather unusual perceptual phenomena—the refraction of light as it passes through a transparent liquid (the example of the bent stick), mirages, phantom pains, and the like—and has rested the case for his view on the claim that he is able to account for them. However, a number of paradoxes arise in connection with some far less unusual perceptual phenomena that cannot be easily accounted for in the context of his theory.

The first such group of paradoxes have to do with what I shall call the "perspectification" that accompanies all visual perception. Consider, first, the quality that we call shape. The shape that an object *appears* to have depends entirely on the point of view from which it is viewed. A sheet of typing paper, for example, appears to be a rectangle if you view it from a point directly above its center; each of its four corners, accordingly, appears to be a right angle or very nearly so. Turn it at a slight angle, however, step away from it a few feet, and two of the corners will appear to be acute angles and two obtuse. The same phenomenon occurs in all cases of visual perception: the apparent shape varies depending on the point of view of the observer and is constantly changing as the observer moves in relation to the object being viewed (or vice versa). A lake that looks round when viewed from the air (directly above its center) looks like a wide oval when viewed from the top of a nearby mountain and like a very long and thin oval when viewed from any point along its shore. A penny looks round from one point of view, oval from another, and rectangular from yet another, and so on.

Which of the many shapes that every object appears to have is supposed to be really present in the object? Why should the topside view of a printed page, or the air view of a lake, or the front-and-center view of a penny be granted a privileged status? Such selectiveness is obviously arbitrary. To say that something is round, for example, is only to say that it will appear to be round if it is looked at from such and such a point of view. No reason can be given, however, for saying that this point of view rather than some other is the one from which the "real" shape of the object can be seen. In the case of three-dimensional objects there is, in fact, no point of view from which an object appears to have the shape that it is usually said to "really" have.

Consequently, if we wish to maintain Critical Realist's position, we must be prepared to do one of two things. Either we must say that an object has many shapes and that the one seen depends on the point of view from which the object is observed; or, quite arbitrarily, that this or that point of view puts us in a position to see the object's "real" shape. If we are not willing to accept one or the other of these alternatives—and I for one am not—then we must give up the view that objects have a "real" shape that corresponds to some shape we perceive.

The same perplexities arise in connection with size. From a long distance, a tractor-trailer may seem the size of a child's toy, but as it speeds closer, its size may become disproportionately large. So it is with all visual perception: the size that an object appears to have depends on how close you are to it. I have yet to meet a person to whom the moon, when viewed from earth with the naked eye, does not *appear* to be about the size of a basketball. Through a telescope, of course, or from a spaceship near its surface, it looks much larger.

Which of the apparent sizes of an object is to be accounted its "real" size? Is it the close-up view? How close? We are faced, evidently, with alternatives comparable to those that we had to contend with in connection with shape. Either we must hold that an object really has many sizes, and that the one perceived depends on how far away the observer is from the object; or we must claim to know that there is some precise distance from which the "real" size can be perceived. Or we must give up the view that objects have a "real" size to which some perception of ours exactly corresponds.

What, then, can be retained of Critical Realist's account? Is temperature a real quality in an object? Perhaps. But we do not perceive temperature; we merely infer it from what we see on a thermometer. What we perceive is only impressions of warmness and coldness, and these even Critical Realist admits to be modifications in the perceiver. Can texture be retained as a real quality in objects? Here, too, difficulties arise. What feels smooth to the touch looks rough when viewed under a microscope, a terrain of hills and valleys that previously seemed perfectly even. Which is it "really," rough or smooth? Or is it both? We are back in our old dilemma.

It is scarcely necessary to discuss the paradoxes that arise if we try to regard rest and motion as real qualities objectively present in objects. Since motion is relative, it is obvious that whether a thing is to be regarded as being in motion or at rest depends entirely on what is assumed to be at rest in making the judgment. If the earth is assumed to be at rest, then a boulder lying on a mountainside is also at rest; if the sun is assumed to be at rest, then the earth and everything on it, including the boulder, are in motion. To an observer on earth, the earth appears to be at rest, and the sun, the moon, and the stars appear to revolve around it. To an observer on the moon, or on Mars, the surface on which he stood would appear to be at rest, and everything else would appear to be in motion in relation to himself. Since whether a thing is perceived to be in motion or at rest depends on the point of view of the observer, our alternatives are (a) to say that every object in the universe really has many motions, (b) to say that only one of these is its "real" motion and give some reason for so saying, or (c) to concede that rest and motion are not real qualities of objects at all but merely "appearances" perceived by an observer.

There remains of Critical Realist's list of primary qualities only solidity, and by this time I suspect we are prepared to concede that it, too, is unlikely to stand up under close scrutiny. It seems evident, in the first place, that "solidity" can only mean the resistance of one object to another and that this resistance must vary depending on the size and strength of the invading object. To a fly a piece of balsa wood must appear quite solid; to a human being it does not. To a small child a piece of stiff paper appears quite solid; to an adult it appears soft and malleable. What is the case "really"? Any answer that we might give would be completely arbitrary.

In point of fact, we know that nothing in the whole world is "really" solid. The desk upon which I am writing appears to be solid, to have such and such a color and texture, and to stand absolutely motionless here in the center of my study. In reality it has none of these qualities. They are all relative to the particular senses with which I happen to be equipped and the particular point of view from which I happen to observe the desk. What really is "out there" is quite different, radically different, from what I perceive to be out there. What, then, are we justified in believing about the real qualities of physical objects?

Appearance and Reality

In order to solve these paradoxes, we must make a clear distinction between the world of our percepts and the world as it really is, between appearance and reality. The world appears to us to consist of a multiplicity of objects of various sizes, shapes, colors, textures, temperatures, and so on. On the basis of these appearances, common sense constructs a theory of a real three-dimensional space in which all these objects are believed to exist and to possess the various characteristics that they appear to have. When subjected to close scrutiny, this whole commonsense theory collapses.

What is really "out there"—the physical world as it really is—is being discovered with greater and greater accuracy by the natural sciences, especially physics. This is hardly the place to begin to summarize all that we now know about the constitution of the universe, but a brief sketch may indicate how we ought to think about an object if we want to conform in some degree to what physics tells us about it.

Take the above-mentioned desk, for example. According to modern physics, it is not, as it appears to be, a solid block of "matter" that occupies some particular position or series of positions in a fixed three-dimensional space. It consists, rather, of several series of events occurring in a four-dimensional manifold that physicists call *space-time,* these several series being interrelated in a vast variety of ways. What I refer to as "my desk" is, in short, something that happens; it is, in fact, a vast conglomeration of happenings that occur in the particular region of space-time that it occupies. None of the particles involved in the events constituting my desk—the protons, neutrons, electrons, and so forth—is solid, or colored, or warm, or cold, or anything else that we perceive when we perceive the desk. The language that is appropriate to the desk as I perceive it is totally inappropriate for a description of the atomic events of which it is really composed.

It is logically possible, of course, that the atomic events comprising my desk should be occurring without my being aware of them in any way, just as radio waves are constantly passing through the region of space-time that I occupy without my being aware of them in any way. It happens to be the case, however, that as a result of the atomic events that constitute my desk, and as a result of certain other atomic events that are related in various ways to the atomic events that constitute my desk, radiations are emitted that, when I am properly situated, cause a series of occurrences in my brain that I call "perceiving the desk."

Consider, for example, the perception of solidity. I perform the activity that I call "pressing my hand against the desk" and say that the desk is "hard," or "solid." In reality, however, no particle that is involved in the events of which my hand is composed comes in contact with the particles involved in the events of which the desk is composed. What really happens is that an electrical force is created by the nearness of the former to the latter, and this force, through a complicated process involving my nerves and my brain, causes the event that I call perceiving the "hardness" or "solidity" of the desk.

Or consider color. My desk looks brown; according to the common-sense view, it really is brown. Physics, however, tells us otherwise. What is really happening when I am "perceiving brown" is that electromagnetic waves of various frequencies are being emitted from the sun and (after a journey requiring roughly eight minutes) are streaming through my window and striking my desk. Some of these waves enter the desk, causing certain changes in it that we describe as an increase in its temperature. Others are scattered by the particles that constitute the surface of the desk, and some of these (by way of my eyes, optic nerve, and brain) create the event in me that I call "perceiving brown." And so on for all sensible qualities.

Thus, hypercritical realism holds that the physical world is dependent on a perceiver for the existence of all of what we may call its commonsense qualities: color, sound, taste, odor, shape, size, solidity, and all the rest. It is only because of the constitution of our faculty of sensation—the particular modifications of which it happens to be capable—that the world appears to us to have these qualities. If we, or beings having a faculty of sensation like ours, were to be annihilated, all such qualities would accordingly disappear. What would not disappear, however, are the atomic and subatomic events that constitute the physical world and cause us to have the particular perceptions we do have. To that extent, the physical world has a real existence of its own and is in no way dependent on a perceiver for its existence.

Perception

I find myself, therefore, in agreement with old-fashioned critical realism on two important points: (a) there is something "out there" that constitutes the real world, and (b) it is what is "out there" that causes us to have the perceptions we have. Perceptions do represent realities in the external world, but they do not represent them as they really are. To infer that the physical world is just like, or somewhat like, the world as it appears to us is to ignore most of what science has taught us and to become involved in endless paradoxes. The way to resolve these paradoxes is to make the distinction we have made between appearance and reality, and to allow that the perceptions that represent physical realities to us are in no way like the realities they represent.

In conclusion I should like to state that I am well aware that it is not easy for any of us to relinquish the idea that the physical world really is as we perceive it to be. Looking now at the desk that I have recently been so busy dissolving into atomic and subatomic events, I am as powerfully tempted as the most unconvinced commonsense realist to think that it really has the solidity, the color, the smoothness, that I perceive it to have. It is only when I attend carefully to the arguments, only when I consider the difficulties involved in maintaining the commonsense view, that I know it cannot be so. As a *theory*, commonsense realism or anything very close to it simply will not do. But as a way of looking at the world, as an attitude that governs our everyday commerce with the world, it is very much with us; none of us is able to divest ourselves of it. For the world that we must take account of in most of our affairs is the world of appearance, not the world of reality.

STUDY QUESTIONS

1. What paradoxes does Hypercritical Realist mention which, according to him, cannot be explained in the context of a mild form of critical realism? Can you think of any way that Critical Realist might be able to defend his position against this attack?
2. What is Hypercritical Realist's general answer to the question posed in this section? What, if anything, makes his position a form of "realism"?
3. What, according to this theory, is the ontological status of color? of sound? of temperature? of electrons? of atoms? of molecules?
4. What criterion does Hypercritical Realist use in distinguishing between "appearance" and "reality"? Is it, in your opinion, a sounder criterion than that employed by Critical Realist?

14

PHENOMENALISM

Phenomenalism is the view that the existence of a physical object is dependent upon its being perceived, that a physical object is a construct made up of the percepts that are the immediate objects of perception. It follows directly from this that the physical world is completely dependent on some perceiver(s) for its existence and that, if all perceivers were to be annihilated, the physical world would accordingly cease to exist.

The task of explaining and defending this view is rendered easier than it might otherwise be, because much of what I ordinarily would have to say in order to build my case has already been said by the two writers who have preceded me in this discussion. The latter has, indeed, left us at the very borders of phenomenalism, and I propose to show that precisely the considerations that have brought the argument to this point require us to take a further step that leads to the phenomenalist position.

The Inconsistency of Hypercritical Realism

Hypercritical Realist has argued, quite rightly, that we cannot validly infer from the fact that the world appears to us as a multiplicity of objects of various colors, shapes, sizes, textures, and so forth, that it really is so. If we try to say this, a host of puzzles arise that we cannot solve without departing rather far from the commonsense view. He also suggests that we know, nonetheless, that there is something "out there" that causes us to have these sensations, and that what this something is can be learned by studying physics. He then proceeds to give us a short course in atomic physics and supposes thereby that he has persuaded us that so much at least can be retained of the realist view.

But surely it is fair to ask how we know that the atomic events that we *do not* see are objectively real, when we evidently do not know that the physical phenomena that we *do* see are objectively real. How have the physicists come by this esoteric knowledge of what is supposed to lie behind the appearances?

We know the answer, of course. They have inferred it from certain observed phenomena. Commonsense realism is the consequence of an unsophisticated inference from some more or less obvious facts of observation; hypercritical realism is the consequence of a sophisticated inference from some less obvious facts of observation. But if the inference is not justified in the first instance, neither is it justified in the second. There is no more reason to say that the latest theory of the physicists is an accurate description of something real "behind the appearances" than there is to say that the description of a commonsense realist is accurate. The two differ considerably in their respective degrees of sophistication, but so far as validity is concerned, they are on the same ground. Realism is equally naïve, whether it is maintained in a commonsense or in a scientific version.

It is worthy of note that Hypercritical Realist's mistake of regarding scientific theories as descriptive is not made by scientists themselves. What Andreas Osiander said in his preface to Nicolaus Copernicus' treatise *On the Revolutions of the Heavenly Bodies* may be said of all scientific theories: There is no need for these hypotheses to be true, or even to be at all like the truth; one thing is sufficient—that they should yield a calculus that agrees with the observations. Scientific hypotheses are, in short, nothing more than instruments useful for purposes of calculation. Their function is not to tell us what the world is really like but to aid us in controlling the world as it appears to us.

It seems clear, therefore, that the very arguments that have been used in the preceding chapters to establish some form of critical realism actually tend to support the phenomenalist view instead. We have no basis for inferring a universe of signaling stations beyond or behind the perceptual signals that we constantly receive. The only world of which we have or can have any knowledge is the world of our perception. This is precisely what we mean by the phrase "the physical world"; hence, it is clear that the physical world is altogether dependent on perceivers for its existence.

A Commonsense Argument for Phenomenalism

Let us return again to the example of the desk. If I want to teach a child the meaning of the word "desk," I have to show one to him and let him see it and touch it, and I have to say the word "desk" so that he will associate that word with the sense data he is receiving. After he has learned this word, what can he possibly understand it to mean but the impressions of hardness, brownness, flatness, and so on, that he has been taught to associate with it? Surely all of us learned the names of such familiar objects as desks, chairs, tables, stones, trees, and so on, in just this way.

What does it mean, then, to say that a thing *exists*? It can mean only that if you go to a place where, say, a desk is said to exist, you will, if the statement is true, have percepts of the sort that you have learned to associate with the word "desk"; if the statement is false, you will not. A statement affirming the existence of something is always a statement about percepts.

Do things exist, then, when nobody is perceiving them? Yes they do. But to say that something exists when nobody is perceiving it is still to say something about percepts, namely, that if someone were to go to the place where a particular thing is said to exist, he would have particular kinds of percepts. Every statement to the effect that something exists is a statement about actual or possible percepts. Any meaning that we try to ascribe to the word "existence" in addition to this is simply unintelligible.

Consequently, if someone says that something exists behind percepts that is the cause of our having them, he is saying something that has no meaning. It makes sense to say that there are real actors in a real studio that cause us to have the particular percepts we have when we look at television, because we know what it is like to have the percepts that constitute the set of events we call "actors in a studio." Here we can "go behind the scenes," so to speak, without forsaking the realm of percepts. But to talk about a reality behind the appearances, a nonperceptual something that causes us to have percepts, is to talk nonsense. The appearance *is* the reality. If there is anything beyond the world as it appears to us (whatever that might mean), we must remain forever in ignorance of what it is.

The physical world, therefore, exists only in our percepts. If there were no perceivers, there would be no percepts and hence no physical world. Berkeley was right: To be a physical object is to be perceived.

I do not think that the phenomenalist view of the ontological status of the physical world is really very vulnerable to attack. The various forms of critical realism that have been proposed are, I am convinced, nothing more than temporary stopping places for "backsliding realists." Philosophers who have failed to complete the route to phenomenalism have done so more by default than by acute philosophical argument. There are, however, a few commonsense objections that are sometimes raised against the phenomenalist view. To demonstrate just how strong the case for phenomenalism really is, I should like to state these objections and show how easily they can be met.

It is sometimes objected, for example, that it is silly to say things like "I had some Wheatieslike percepts for breakfast this morning," or "Help! Someone has stolen my carlike percepts," but that according to the phenomenalist view this ought to be a perfectly proper way of speaking. However, the phenomenalist theory does not sanction talk of this sort. Indeed, it is never proper to mix ordinary language and technical theory in this way. It would be equally absurd to say, "I had a bowl of Wheatieslike protons, neutrons, and electrons for breakfast," or "Someone stole my carlike atoms." The objection is quite beside the point.

A second objection is that phenomenalism provides no basis for distinguishing between valid and illusory percepts. If to be is to be perceived, then mirages and other things that even common sense regards as illusions must be as real as anything else, for these illusory phenomena are obviously perceived. Because we can distinguish between illusory and nonillusory perceptions, it is sometimes concluded that phenomenalism must be in error.

To answer this objection it is necessary only to point out that the difference between illusory and nonillusory perceptions is a difference among perceptions. The reason that we call some perceptions illusory is that they lead us to have certain expectations that are not subsequently fulfilled. We regard a mirage as illusory, for example, precisely because it leads us to expect certain other perceptions—those constituting what we call "drinking water" and "resting in the shade of a tree"—that are not forthcoming. To say that a thing is real is not to posit an unperceived metaphysical reality "behind" our percepts of the thing; it is to say that the expectations created in us by our percepts of the thing can be fulfilled. Try as we will, I do not think we shall find any further reason for making the distinction between illusory and nonillusory percepts. If the water-and-shade percepts that we anticipate when we see a mirage were forthcoming, we would not call it a mirage; it would then be identical with what we call an oasis.

It is sometimes argued that according to the phenomenalist account, physical objects—trees, stones, freight trains, skyscrapers, and other such apparently solid and substantial things—are constantly popping in and out of existence. When someone is perceiving them, they exist; when nobody is perceiving them, they cease to exist. And this, it is said, is absurd. Even Berkeley, it may be pointed out, found this idea so preposterous that he advanced the idea that things exist continually in the omniscient perception of God—a view that is wittily parodied in this often quoted limerick:

> There was a young man who said, "God
> Must think it exceedingly odd
>   If he finds that this tree
>   Continues to be
> When there's no one about in the Quad."

> Reply

> Dear Sir:
>   Your astonishment's odd:
> *I* am always about in the Quad.

> And that's why the tree
> Will continue to be,
> Since observed by
> Yours faithfully,
> God.[1]

My form of phenomenalism, however, can easily account for the continued existence of objects during those times when they are not being perceived—and I do not have to invoke a "perpetual perceiver" in order to accomplish this. According to my view, to say that something continues to exist even when it is not being perceived is simply to say that *if* someone were to fulfill such and such conditions, he would have such and such perceptions. Physical objects, as John Stuart Mill once said, are permanent possibilities of sensation. A physical object consists of percepts, actual and possible; the intervals of time during which the object is not being perceived are filled in by the continuing "possibilities of sensation" that remain.

Even after hearing this explanation, however, we may be inclined to ask how it is that common sense comes to take it for granted that objects when they are not perceived continue to exist in exactly the same way that they do when they are perceived. Where does the commonsense idea of an objectively real, ontologically independent physical world come from? The answer, I think, is that certain features of our perceptual experience induce us to posit such a world. The most important of these features are (*a*) the resemblance between the various percepts that we call percepts of the "same thing," (*b*) the occurrence of these similar groups of percepts in the context of a relatively stable perceptual environment, (*c*) the fact that we can, within certain limits, predict what kinds of percepts we shall have under such and such conditions, and (*d*) the fact that the perceptions we have can be varied in a more or less systematic way depending on our own movements. The idea of an independently existing world of physical objects, which appear to us in the vast variety of ways evident in our actual perceptions, is an ingenious hypothesis that common sense has erected to account for these features of our perceptual experience; but it is, as we have seen, a hypothesis that does not stand up under close scrutiny.

How are we to account for the consistency and the order that obtain among our percepts, if there is no independent physical world that is the cause of them all? Phenomenalism cannot satisfactorily answer this question, but neither can the realist theory. The realist theory only pushes the problem one step back. It accounts for order among our percepts by positing an ordered world and either takes the order of the world for granted or leaves it unexplained. Phenomenalists say that the order that evidently obtains among our percepts *is* the order in the

---

[1] Ronald Knox, as quoted by Bertrand Russell, in *A History of Western Philosophy* (New York: Simon and Schuster, 1945), p. 648.

world, because the only world of which we have any knowledge is the world of our percepts. If there is some explanation of why there is order in the world, then that is why there is order among our percepts; if there is no explanation, then there is none for the order among percepts either. The discussion about order, in any case, in no way favors the realist view.

Therefore, it is not to the point to argue that the phenomenalist view is refuted by the fact that people in the same general vicinity possess more or less the same kinds of sense data. Of course they do; if they did not, they would not be able to speak and act as if they lived in a common world. That our percepts are more or less alike and systematically related in a wide variety of ways is simply an ultimate fact that has to be taken for granted. To try to explain it by positing an ordered world "behind" the percepts is like trying to explain the sleep-producing effect of some drugs by saying they have a "soporific power." Not only is such a statement an inadequate explanation; it is not even a meaningful combination of words.

The final objection with which I should like to deal is that if phenomenalism were true, we could never know that other minds exist. If to say that something exists is to say that we are having, or could have, such and such percepts, then other minds do not exist, since no actual or possible percepts can warrant our saying that they do. By this argument it is concluded that phenomenalism must lead to skepticism regarding the existence of any mind other than one's own, and in the end, to solipsism.

This question has always been a difficult one for empiricists, and I shall not pretend to give a definitive answer to it. I may say, however, that neither I nor any other phenomenalist known to me is a solipsist; therefore it is evident that being a phenomenalist does not entail accepting the solipsist position. But it is not easy to say how we know of the existence of other minds.

Much of the difficulty results from the obscurity of the very notion of a "mind." In some senses that have been given to that word, I do not think we know of the existence of any minds, including our own. What we really want to know when we ask if other minds exist is whether other conscious and sentient beings exist. It seems to me that the phenomenalist can answer as follows: (a) our own existence as conscious and sentient beings is immediately evident to us (our existence consists, as Berkeley said, in perceiving, not in being perceived); (b) we perceive beings that look, talk, and act much the way we do; and (c) by analogy we infer that they, too, are conscious and sentient beings. Common sense, in my opinion, can do no better.

Phenomenalism and Empiricism

In conclusion I want to state briefly what I consider to be the relation of phenomenalism to the epistemological question discussed in the preceding section of this book. Anyone who intends to be absolutely consistent in his adherence to empiricism must adopt the phenomenalist view with respect to the ontological status of the physical world. If we are serious about the view that all we know is what comes to us in experience, then it is clear that all we know is our percepts. To posit an unseen world "behind" the world of our percepts is to claim that by means of experience we can go beyond experience, and this is just what an absolutely consistent empiricism will not permit us to do. The point, briefly put, is this: Phenomenalism is the ontology of empiricism. Let phenomenalism be overthrown and rationalism will have won the day.

STUDY QUESTIONS

1. What argument does Phenomenalist use to enforce his conclusion that hypercritical realism is no more tenable then commonsense realism? Is his argument sound? Can you think of any way to defend Hypercritical Realist's view against this argument?
2. How does Phenomenalist attempt to establish his position? Is this a sound argument in your opinion?
3. Summarize the "commonsense objections" to his position that Phenomenalist mentions, and his reply to each. Are you satisfied with his replies? Can you think of any other difficulties with this theory that Phenomenalist may have neglected to mention?
4. Phenomenalist says: "Neither I nor any other phenomenalist known to me is a solipsist; therefore it is evident that being a phenomenalist does not entail accepting the solipsist position." Is this a good argument?

15

RETURN TO REALISM

A wise old professor of mine once said, "There are times in the study of philosophy when you must listen very carefully to that still, small voice that whispers insistently in your ear, 'Poppycock!' " Surely this is one of those times. From the simple commonsense view that we live in a world that exists whether or not it is perceived—a world whose features we are able to discern (to some extent, at least) by means of our five senses—we have been led step by step to the preposterous view (a) that the physical world "exists only in our percepts," (b) that "to be is to be perceived," and (c) that the idea of an independently existing world is nothing but a mistaken hypothesis for which there is no evidence at all. Now this conclusion is utterly senseless, and I propose to begin by pointing out some of the most glaring absurdities inherent in the phenomenalist position.

Critique of Phenomenalism

First, let us take another look at the "commonsense objections" that Phenomenalist attempts to refute. He states five such supposed objections to his position and offers answers to each. The first two of these—the semantic absurdities to which phenomenalism allegedly leads, and the problem of distinguishing valid and illusory percepts—are not valid objections to phenomenalism, in my opinion, so I shall say no more about them. The other three arguments, however, are quite decisive, and I want to show how inadequate Phenomenalist's replies are.

To begin with, it is absurd to say, as Phenomenalist does, that physical objects are forever hopping back and forth between the status of "possible percepts" and "actual percepts," depending on whether or not someone is perceiving them. Phenomenalist dismisses Berkeley's view that the world is saved from an intermittent existence because it is perceived at all times by God, and takes obvious delight in reciting Ronald Knox's famous mocking limerick about the tree that, thanks to God's perpetual observation, "Continues to be/When there's no one about in the Quad." I offer the following bit of verse to show that Phenomenalist's position lends itself to ridicule no less than Berkeley's:

> "I wish," said a possible tree
> "That someone would come *stare* at me;
>   For to be very factual,
>   I'd like to be actual:
> I am tired of mere possibility."

> "Be patient," replied an old stone,
> "You trees really ought not to moan;
>   Why, for billions of years
>   There were no eyes or ears:
> We survived on possibility alone."

Let me put my point very plainly. When I say that a physical object exists even when I am not perceiving it, I do not mean that it exists because God is perceiving it, nor do I mean merely that if someone were to fulfill such and such conditions, he would have percepts of a certain kind. I mean, quite simply, that it *exists.* Now, it is true that if something exists, it will be perceived by a person who gets himself into a position to perceive it. The existence of the object is a factual precondition of its being perceived. But the statement that it exists is not logically identical with the statement that it is being perceived.

Note that in order to sustain his view Phenomenalist must hold that prior to the evolution of sentient life, nothing at all existed except, of course, potentially. The generally accepted view that the universe existed—really existed—for billions of years prior to the emergence of life becomes unintelligible on this view. Yet in studying the rock samples recently brought back from the moon, we obviously are not trying to determine what kinds of "percepts" an observer might have had four and a half billion years ago if he had been on the moon: we are trying to determine what really happened there (and elsewhere in the solar system) during those eons of time prior to the emergence of life.

Phenomenalist argues, further, that the realist theory is no more capable of explaining order in the world than is the phenomenalist theory; hence, he says, the fact that phenomenalism has no explanation for "the consistency and order that obtain among our percepts" ought not to count against it. I think, on the contrary, that the consistency and order of what we perceive does count, decisively, against Phenomenalist's view. There are two facts that have to be explained. First, each individual perceives the world as being relatively ordered: objects appear to be more or less permanent, change usually occurs in an orderly and intelligible way, and so on. Second, people in the same general vicinity perceive the same world—to use Phenomenalist's language, they perceive similar sense data. Now, it is totally unconvincing to say that the order and consistency that are thus perceived are ultimate facts to be taken for granted. These facts are easily explained within the context of a realist ontology; they become inexplicable only from the phenomenalist position.

Consider a simple analogy. Most of us occasionally have the experience of standing in a television showroom and observing a number of sets that all display what we call "the same picture" and emit what we call "the same sounds." Suppose that someone who knows nothing at all about television were introduced into this situation. What hypothesis would he be justified in forming to explain these identical pictures? He could, of course, hypothesize that for no reason at all the sets just happen to be displaying the same pictures, but that would hardly satisfy him, no matter how primitive he might be. Surely, he would be inclined to say, there must be some *common source* of these pictures. And in so saying he would, of course, be right. Just so with respect to the present point, except that in the present case it is the consistency of the perceptions of hundreds of millions of people that has to be explained. Phenomenalism has no explanation for this, whereas realism does. I consider this a decisive argument against phenomenalism.

The last objection that Phenomenalist attempts to refute is that a completely consistent phenomenalist ought to be a solipsist, since no actual or possible percepts warrant our saying that another mind exists. What is Phenomenalist's reply to this objection? That "neither I nor any other phenomenalist known to me is a solipsist; therefore it is evident that being a phenomenalist does not entail accepting the solipsist position." Now I submit that the fact that Phenomenalist and his friends are not solipsists in no way demonstrates that solipsism does not follow logically from their position. It proves only that they do not have the courage to draw this particular logical inference. It is not by logical argument but by mere fiat that Phenomenalist rejects the solipsist dilemma. Phenomenalism implies solipsism: this is the ultimate *reductio ad absurdum* of phenomenalism. Phenomenalist acknowledges the absurdity of solipsism and attempts to escape the *reductio* by pleading that his position does not really commit him to solipsism. But the question crucial to phenomenalism remains unanswered: If on the basis of our percepts we are not justified in affirming the existence of a real world that is the cause of those percepts, how on the basis of those same percepts can we be justified in affirming the existence of minds other than our own? Until Phenomenalist answers this question, we must hold that he is saved from solipsism not by rational argument but by a small residuum of common sense.

Further absurdities, which Phenomenalist does not mention, follow if we adopt his position. If phenomenalism is true then it follows, for example, that some merely *possible* things are the causes of some *actual* things. The collisions that are believed to have created the craters on the moon were (so far as we know) observed by no one. The supposed collisions, on the phenomenalist theory, are nothing but some possible percepts that were not actualized. Their existence is purely hypothetical and nonactual. But the craters on the moon are actual (at least part of the time), since they are frequently observed by astronomers, astronauts, and people who visit observatories. Now according to the phenomenalist theory, the statement that "the craters on the moon were caused by the impact of meteors that strayed into the moon's gravitational field" means, roughly, "the actual crater percepts that you get when you look at the moon through a sufficiently powerful telescope are the result of some possible collision percepts, the conditions for which existed some billions of years ago when, unfortunately, there were no perceivers to actualize them." To say the least, this statement is more than a little difficult to swallow. I am not even sure that it makes sense to say that one set of actual percepts (rain percepts) causes another set of actual percepts (wet-pavement percepts); but I am completely convinced that it makes no sense at all to say that some actual percepts are caused by some merely hypothetical possible percepts. Phenomenalism reduces the notion of causality to utter nonsense.

One final objection. Phenomenalism implies that if there were no perceivers, nothing would actually exist, since all that exists is minds and their perceptions. The annihilation of all sentient life is, however, logically conceivable and is, in fact, a ghastly empirical possibility that we have been forced to think about since the advent of the atomic age. But surely it is absurd to say that the annihilation of all sentient life would terminate the actual existence of the whole physical universe. I think it makes more sense to say that in the event of such a tragedy the sun, the moon, the stars, and the planets would continue to exhibit the motions they now exhibit; that on this sad old planet we call Earth the winds would still blow, the snow and the rain would still fall, and perhaps in time grass would grow and flowers would bloom once more; only no one would be here to observe these occurrences. Still, phenomenalism would insist that such a statement makes no sense, or that it makes a kind of sense (the possible-percepts story) that is about as close as you can come to no sense at all. Thus we may add one more item to the long list of reasons for rejecting the phenomenalist position.

Realism Reconsidered

Where, then, has Phenomenalist gone wrong? If phenomenalism is really as vulnerable as the preceding argument has shown it to be, how can so many able philosophers be persuaded of its truth? Most important of all, what view are we warranted in holding about the ontological status of the physical world?

I suggest that the initial error that has sent so many philosophers down the slippery slope to phenomenalism is the innocent-looking claim that the immediate objects of perception are sense data. I shall argue, on the contrary, that the immediate objects of perception are sights, sounds, tastes, smells, tactual qualities. I shall, in short, defend the view known as *direct realism*. In order to do this, I must refute the argument from illusion, which is the principal basis for the erroneous claim that the immediate objects of perception are sense data.

What, exactly, is an illusory perception? It is nothing more than a combination of the mistaken belief that something exists and the mistaken belief that one is immediately perceiving it. A mirage, for example, is the mistaken belief that at a certain place in the desert there is an oasis, combined with the mistaken belief that one is immediately perceiving the oasis he mistakenly believes to exist. Were these two beliefs not mistaken, one would not be the victim of a mirage but would instead be having the experience called "seeing an oasis."

What, then, is a person perceiving when he is "seeing a mirage"? Nothing at all. Normal perception is the true belief that an object exists together with the true belief that we are immediately perceiving it. Illusory perception is the false belief of these same propositions. The immediate object of normal perception is the object that we believe we are perceiving—sounds, color patches, shapes, and so on. Since in the case of illusory perception there is no real object, it follows that nothing is being perceived. Illusory perception is *not* the perception of sense data to which nothing corresponds in reality, but the holding of certain *beliefs* that happen to be false. Sense data are mere phantoms, introduced to provide an object for perception in those cases in which someone is said to "see" something that does not really exist. My analysis of illusory perception shows that no such object is required; thus we can simply dispense with the whole concept of sense data.

The immediate objects of perception, *when perception is actually occurring,* are the colors, shapes, sounds, tastes, odors and so forth that we perceive by means of our senses. The term "immediate" here means simply that these are the phenomena that appear directly in our perceptual field: they present themselves to us, and under appropriate conditions we perceive them. In a derivative sense, however, we may say that what we perceive are not colors, shapes, sounds, tastes, odors, but trees, stones, automobiles, steaks, perfumes. That is, we may add to the immediate perception the *judgment* that the sound we just heard was from an approaching automobile, or that the object we see in the distance is a tree—and in this we may be mistaken. It seems perfectly proper to say, however, "I hear an automobile," "I see a tree," or "I smell perfume"; in such cases we are expressing what I should call *mediate* or *indirect perception*. The immediate objects of perception are colors, shapes, sounds, tastes, odors, and the *mediate* objects of perception are the objects that have those colors, shapes, sounds, tastes, odors.

Is the physical world, then, in any degree dependent on a perceiver for its existence? No. The physical world is altogether independent of the perceptions of any perceiver. It existed for billions of years before the emergence of sentient life and may well exist for billions of years after all such life has vanished from the scene. In the meantime, however, our unaided senses reveal to us some of the shapes, colors, sounds, and so forth, that are really there; by the use of various instruments that magnify the powers of our senses—microscopes, telescopes, amplifiers, and what not—we are able to perceive features of the world that are not discernible to the unaided eye or ear. The account of the physicist does not conflict with but supplements the account of common sense. To say that the observations of physicists are valid whereas those of ordinary people are not (hypercritical realism) is purely arbitrary.

I would observe in conclusion that there is no need to develop a constructive argument in support of direct realism. Commonsense realism is the position from which everyone sets out in this controversy: people become critical realists or phenomenalists (or even solipsists) only because they are persuaded by some argument or other that they must abandon their "naïve" or "commonsense" realism. In order to reestablish the realist position, we have only to refute the arguments that led to its abandonment in the first place. Direct realism is merely commonsense realism that has become sure of itself through having defended itself against its critics. Hence the arguments of direct realists are typically directed not toward the positive fortification of their position but rather toward the refutation of the arguments commonly leveled against it.

STUDY QUESTIONS

1. "The existence of the object is a factual precondition of its being perceived. But the statement that it exists is not logically identical with the statement that it is being perceived." Explain.
2. Does the fact that "people in the same general vicinity perceive the same world" count against the phenomenalist position? Defend your answer.
3. "Phenomenalist is saved from solipsism not by rational argument but by a small residuum of common sense." Do you agree? Explain.
4. What, according to Direct Realist, is an illusory perception? Do you agree with his analysis?
5. "Sense data are mere phantoms introduced in order to provide an object for perception in those cases in which someone is said to 'see' something that does not really exist." Does this seem plausible to you?
6. "There is no need to develop a constructive argument in support of direct realism." Attack or defend this statement.
7. Has Direct Realist answered all the objections to commonsense realism raised by the previous writers? List the objections, and show how he has or has not replied to them.

Adams, E. M. "The Nature of the Sense-Datum Theory," *Mind*, 67 (1958), 216–226.

Alexander, Peter. "Curley on Locke and Boyle," *Philosophical Review*, 83 (1974), 229–237.

Armstrong, D. M. *Perception and the Physical World*. New York: Humanities Press, 1961.

Austin, J. L. *Sense and Sensibilia*. London: Oxford University Press, 1962 (paperbound).

Ayer, A. J. *The Foundations of Empirical Knowledge*. New York: St. Martin's Press, 1958 (paperbound), chaps. 1, 2, and 5.

————. *The Problem of Knowledge*. New York: St. Martin's Press, 1956, chap. 3.

Barnes, W. H. F. "The Myth of Sense-Data," *Proceedings of the Aristotelian Society*, 45 (1944–1945), 89–117.

Bergmann, Gustav. *Logic and Reality*. Madison, Wis.: University of Wisconsin Press, 1964, chap. 14.

Chisholm, R. M. "The Problem of Empiricism," *The Journal of Philosophy*, 45 (1948), 512–517.

Curley, E. M. "Locke, Boyle and the Distinction Between Primary and Secondary Qualities," *Philosophical Review*, 81 (1972), 438–464.

Dewey, John. *Essays in Experimental Logic*. New York: Dover, 1960 (paperbound), pp. 1–74, 250–302.

Dretske, Fred I. *Seeing and Knowing*. Chicago: University of Chicago Press, 1969.

Eddington, A. S. *The Nature of the Physical World*. Ann Arbor, Mich.: University of Michigan Press, 1958 (paperbound).

Ewing, A. C. *The Fundamental Questions of Philosophy*. New York: Macmillan, 1951, chap. 4.

Garnett, A. C. *The Perceptual Process*. London: G. Allen & Unwin, 1965. Short, highly readable, critical realist view.

Gibson, James J. *The Senses Considered as Perceptual Systems*. London: G. Allen & Unwin, 1968.

Hinton, J. M. *Experiences: An Inquiry into Some Ambiguities*. New York: Oxford University Press, 1973.

Joske, W. D. *Material Objects*. New York: Macmillan, 1967.

Lewis, C. I. *An Analysis of Knowledge and Valuation*. LaSalle, Ill.: Open Court, 1947 (paperbound), chap. 7.

Locke, D. *Perception and Our Knowledge of the External World*. London: G. Allen & Unwin, 1967.

Mandelbaum, M. *Philosophy, Science, and Sense Perception*. Baltimore, Md.: Johns Hopkins Press, 1964. Defends critical realism.

Mundle, C. W. K. *Perception: Facts and Theories*. New York: Oxford University Press, 1971 (paperbound).

Pitcher, George. *A Theory of Perception*. Princeton, N.J.: Princeton University Press, 1971.

Price, H. H. "The Argument from Illusion," in H. D. Lewis (ed.). *Contemporary British Philosophy*, Third Series. New York: Macmillan, 1956, pp. 391–400.

————. *Perception*, 2nd ed. New York: Dover, 1950.

Russell, Bertrand. *Human Knowledge*. New York: Simon and Schuster, 1962 (paperbound). See Part III, "Science and Perception."

————. *The Problems of Philosophy*. New York: Oxford University Press, 1959 (paperbound), chaps. 1–4.

Warnock, G. J. *Berkeley*. Baltimore, Md.: Penguin Books, 1969 (paperbound).

PART IV

THE EXISTENCE OF GOD

16

ON PROVING
GOD'S EXISTENCE

There are a number of questions about God that philosophers have asked at various times in the history of Western philosophy. Many of these have been concerned with the *nature* of God. Is God rightly described as a "person"? Is God absolutely eternal and immutable, or does He in some sense change? If God does not change, how is it possible for Him to experience love, or solicitude, or compassion? These, and dozens of other questions of this kind, figure prominently in the writings of such Christian philosophers as St. Augustine, St. Anselm, St. Thomas Aquinas, and Duns Scotus. To modern ears, such questions often sound exceedingly strange, even insignificant; but to the philosophers of the Middle Ages they were questions of the first importance. Indeed, one measure of the distance that modern thought has traveled from that of the Middle Ages is the infrequency with which such questions are discussed today.

There is another question, however, that has been of interest to at least some philosophers in every age. That is the question, Does God exist? Some philosophers, for example, St. Augustine, thought the existence of God so self-evident that it did not even require proving (though he does offer one such proof in his treatise *On the Free Will*). Others, like St. Albert the Great, St. Thomas Aquinas, and René Descartes, thought the existence of God required proof but they considered the task a relatively simple matter. Aquinas, for example, offers no less than five "proofs" in the space of just two or three pages. Most philosophers today are at least in agreement on this, that the proof of the existence of God, if it is possible at all, is no easy matter; and it is probably true to say that the majority of them regard it as impossible.

The Problem of Definition

Before we can intelligently discuss the various arguments that have been offered as proofs of the existence of God, it is necessary that we consider carefully a prior question, namely, What is the meaning of the term "God"? But, first, let us see why, in connection with the arguments concerning the existence of God, this is such an important question.

Suppose that someone proposed for discussion the question, Do *snergs* exist? Now, it would be obviously futile to begin to construct arguments for or against the existence of snergs until some agreement had been reached as to what was *meant* by the term "snergs." Indeed, confusion would most surely occur, for those who affirm the existence of snergs might have one thing in mind, and those who deny their existence might have another. As a result, their disagreement would be merely verbal rather than real (see Chapter 5). Unless there is agreement on this key point, and thus agreement on what is the point of the question, the question itself cannot be intelligently discussed.

Even philosophers, unfortunately, have not always understood clearly the crucial importance of this prior question, and as a consequence a good deal of confusion has been created in the discussion of God's existence. Some philosophers have supposed, for example, that the question, Does God exist? is equivalent to, Does there exist, some place beyond the reach of even our most powerful telescopes, a very wise and powerful being who once upon a time brought the world into existence, who occasionally even now interferes in its orderly operations, and who will some day reward the righteous and punish the wicked? They have supposed, that is to say, that it is God *as conceived by popular unsophisticated Christian piety* whose existence is in question; and they have relatively little difficulty in showing that none of the arguments that have been offered in proof of "the existence of God" succeed in proving the existence of such a being. But, then, no philosopher who has seriously proposed an argument for the existence of God has ever intended to prove the existence of a being so conceived.

What, then, have those philosophers who have attempted to prove the existence of God meant by the term "God"? It is very difficult to answer this question with the precision that might be desired. Those philosophers who have entered most seriously and profoundly into the discussion of this question—philosophers such as St. Anselm, Aquinas, Descartes, and Immanuel Kant (who are far from agreeing on the soundness of the various arguments for the existence of God)—appear to have meant by the term "God" at least the following:

1. A reality that transcends space and time
2. The ground of being and value
3. A reality worthy of man's worship

The question, Does God exist? means, therefore, Is there a reality that transcends space and time, is the ground of being and value, and is worthy of man's worship? To answer this question in the affirmative is to affirm that God exists. To answer it negatively is to deny that God exists. To affirm or deny the existence of any other sort of being is to miss the point of the question, Does God exist?

However, certain terms in this formulation of the question are unclear, notably "reality" and "ground." Let us try to clarify them. Perhaps the best way to get at the meaning of "reality" as used in this context is to note the reasons for using this term instead of "being." To speak of God as "a being" would not do justice to what philosophers who have attempted to prove the existence of God have meant by the term "God." Why? Because our notion of "a being" is one of a spatiotemporal something that exists alongside other spatiotemporal somethings. To speak of "a being" is to speak of something that exists in some places but not in others, at some times but not at others. Philosophers who have believed that God exists, and that His existence could be proved, have not intended to assert the existence of a *being* occupying some particular region of space-time. They have meant to assert, rather, the existence of a reality that is not subject to the categories of space and time, a reality, in other words, that transcends space and time. Hence, we must speak of God not as a being but as a reality.

To say that God is to be conceived as a reality that transcends space and time is to say that God is not to be conceived simply as a natural object, as one of the many objects that we might encounter within the realm of nature. No telescope will ever be constructed, no space journey ever undertaken, that will reveal God's habitation—not because the distance is too great, but because the question of God's existence does not concern distance at all. If we cannot attach some meaning to the phrase "a reality that transcends space and time" (and many philosophers today insist that they cannot), then we simply cannot enter into the discussion of the question, Does God exist?

The same reasoning obtains in the use of the term "ground" rather than "cause." "Cause" is (in contemporary usage) too closely tied up with the notions of space and time. A cause is a spatiotemporal something that stands in a certain relation to something else that we call its effect. But the notion of God, we have said, is the notion of a reality that transcends space and time; hence, we must not speak of God in a way that suggests "a spatiotemporal something." We want, however, to affirm something like the relation of cause and effect between God and being and value. How shall we do this? Philosophical usage has given us the term "ground," which means roughly (in philosophical usage) "nonspatiotemporal cause." Let us say, then, that God is the ground of being and value.

What, finally, does it mean to say that the idea of God is the idea of a reality "worthy of man's worship"? This is in many ways the most puzzling of the three statements. Yet something like this must be said to take account of the fact that the term "God" is in the first instance a *religious* term—so much so that we would not be too far from the truth if we were simply to define "God" as "the object of the act of worship." The supposition is, however, that the object of worship is somehow worthy of man's devotion, which in our philosophical tradition at least has meant that God is conceived to be holy, just, good, merciful, and so on. Many philosophers (Aquinas, once again, is an excellent example) have attempted to construct proofs of a number of such attributes of God, but it seems clear that the very notion of God includes in embryonic form the idea that He possesses in an eminent degree those virtues that we normally admire in one another. It is this notion that we are including in the idea of God when we say that God is to be conceived as "a reality that is worthy of man's worship."

The question whether God exists—whether there exists a reality that transcends space and time, is the ground of being and value, and is worthy of man's worship—is no trivial question. I think most people would agree with the sentiments of the philosopher who said (though he himself rejected all the arguments for the existence of God):

> If we found that any of the traditional arguments for the existence of God were sound, we should get out of our one hour this . . . afternoon something of inestimable value, such as one never got out of any hour's work in our lives before. For we should have got out of one hour's work the answer to that question about which, above all, we want to know the answer.[1]

Many philosophers who believe that none of the traditional arguments for the existence of God is sound believe, nonetheless, that the question of the existence of God is an exceedingly important question. In fact, some of those who hold that God does not exist (for example, Friedrich Nietzsche and Jean Paul Sartre) have recognized that such a conclusion must profoundly alter one's understanding of oneself, one's fellows, and one's world. It is probably safe to say that anyone who does not regard the question of the existence of God as a serious and important question has not really understood the point of the question.

A Related Question

To the question, Does God exist? there are just three possible answers: Yes (theism), No (atheism), I don't know (agnosticism). Philosophers, however, are not interested just in people's opinions on this matter; they are interested primarily in the reasons that might be given in support of

---

[1] J. J. C. Smart, "The Existence of God," a public lecture given at the University of Adelaide in 1951, published in Antony Flew and Alasdair MacIntyre (eds.), *New Essays in Philosophical Theology* (London: SCM Press; and New York: Macmillan, 1955), pp. 28–46; see p. 28.

an opinion. Therefore, let us for the moment approach the question of the existence of God by asking whether there are any *rational grounds* for believing in the existence of God, whether there are any *good reasons* for believing that the proposition "God exists" is true. Such a question may be answered in a number of ways.

First of all we could assert that there are some rational grounds for believing in the existence of God—in which case we ought to be prepared to say what those grounds are. In practice this means that an *argument* for the existence of God is put forward and an attempt is made to show that the argument succeeds. (Chapters 17–19 attempt to do this in terms of three of the traditional arguments for the existence of God.) It should be noted at this point that what is to be allowed to count as "rational grounds" in this connection depends very much on one's epistemological persuasion. If one is an empiricist, for example, one cannot agree with the proponent of the cosmological argument when he makes an appeal to "rational insight" (Chapter 18). If, on the other hand, someone is persuaded by the cosmological argument, then he must be prepared to draw the epistemological consequences. Here, as with every philosophical problem, intricate and important interrelationships with other philosophical issues are evident.

A second way of answering this question is to say that none of the arguments offered in support of the existence of God is sound and to draw the conclusion that God does not exist. Since philosophical naturalism cannot allow the existence of God (as defined above), it is incumbent upon a naturalist to take this second position. A critique of the arguments from this perspective is offered in Chapter 20.

Not all those who deny the soundness of the traditional arguments for the existence of God are philosophical naturalists, however. Some theologians, for example, deny that the existence of God can be established by rational argument; yet they obviously do not draw the conclusion that God does not exist. This view that there are no sound arguments by which the existence of God can be proved, but that God nonetheless exists and His existence is certified in certain (presumably) nonargumentative ways represents a third response to the question posed in this section. Chapter 21 attempts to build the case for such a view.

A Preliminary Look at the Arguments

Since the question of the existence of God is one in which many people have been extremely interested, it is not surprising that a rather large number of arguments have been constructed in an attempt to prove that the proposition "God exists" is true. No less than five types of arguments have been put forward. Let us survey them briefly before proceeding to a more detailed consideration of three such arguments.

It is possible to argue, first, that the *existence* of God can be correctly inferred from the *idea* of God. Such an argument is termed an *ontological* argument for the existence of God. This type of argument, the most famous example of which was formulated by St. Anselm of Canterbury (1033–1109), is considered in some detail in Chapter 17.

Second, it is possible to argue that the existence of the world presupposes, implies, or points to the existence of God. This type of argument is called a *cosmological* argument for the existence of God. Among the best-known arguments of this type are those of Avicenna (980–1037) and St. Thomas Aquinas (1225–1274).

A third type of argument attempts to reason from the assertion that there is order in the world to the conclusion that God exists. An argument of this type, advocated by such men as William Paley (1743–1805) and F. R. Tennant (1866–1957), is called a *teleological* argument.

The *moral* argument for the existence of God attempts to reason from certain features of moral experience to the conclusion that God exists. Immanuel Kant (1724–1804) defended a version of this argument, as did the British philosophers W. R. Sorley (1855–1935) and A. E. Taylor (1869–1945).

A fifth type of argument is the *argument from religious experience,* which begins with certain features of religious experience and attempts to reason from these to the conclusion that God exists. It is rarely encountered in serious philosophical discussion, but it is attacked from time to time—apparently on the supposition that there are people who endorse some version of it.

Few areas of philosophical inquiry evidence the poverty of language more plainly than does discussion of the arguments for the existence of God. The "five ways" of Aquinas, for example, are stated in the language of Aristotelian metaphysics and are quite unintelligible apart from an understanding of that metaphysical system. Since Aristotelian metaphysics is not part of the conceptual vocabulary of most people today, an intelligent appraisal of Aquinas' arguments is simply impossible for them. It will be evident in the essays that follow that the advocates of the various arguments for the existence of God are groping for a terminology that is both adequate to express their ideas and intelligible to modern ears.

STUDY QUESTIONS

1. Why is it necessary to come to some agreement about the meaning of the term "God" before engaging in a discussion of arguments purporting to prove the existence of God?
2. Does the definition of God here proposed agree with what you have ordinarily understood the term to mean? If not, how would the definition have to be altered to do so?
3. What are the reasons given for using the terms "reality" and "ground" rather than "being" and "cause" in the definition of God? Do these strike you as being

sound reasons? What difference would it make in the discussion if the terms "being" and "cause" were substituted for "reality" and "ground"?
4. What is an ontological argument for the existence of God? a cosmological argument? a teleological argument? a moral argument? an argument from religious experience?

17

THE ONTOLOGICAL ARGUMENT

The history of Western man's struggles with the problem of the existence of God during the past sixteen hundred years provides an interesting commentary on the development of Western thought during this period of time. Initially, in the work of St. Augustine especially, the existence of God is simply taken for granted. It is regarded as a matter so self-evident that a proof of God's existence would be utterly superfluous. At the present stage of this development (I do not say the last), the nonexistence of God is so commonly taken for granted that any attempt to prove the existence of God would be viewed by many of our contemporaries as anachronistic and futile. The intervening chapters in this history, marked by the explicit formulation of the ontological argument (St. Anselm), the rejection of the ontological argument in favor of the cosmological argument (Aquinas), and the rejection of both of these in favor of the teleological argument (deism), indicate the course by which our culture generally has moved from an implicit belief in the existence of God to an implicit disbelief. An advocate of any argument for the existence of God today has little reason to be hopeful of winning many adherents.

Moreover, the task is rendered even more difficult by the widespread ignorance regarding what is actually to be proved. A reasonably well educated person should know that philosophers who believe it is possible to demonstrate that God exists emphatically do not believe in the existence of "the Old Man in the Sky" of primitive supernaturalism. Even St. Augustine, who might have been excused for holding what we would regard as "primitive" ideas, knew better. If our only alternatives were naturalism and supernaturalism, it is clear that the honest choice would have to be naturalism. Supernaturalism, with its demons and its angels, its throne in the heavens, and its Old Man in the Sky, belongs to the childhood of our culture. These things may survive indefinitely in the symbolism of religious communities and as the picture language of simple religious faith, but they have no place in serious discussion of the existence of God. It would be better if the question were not discussed at all than to have it reduced to such childish and superficial terms.

There is, happily, an alternative, and that is to enter earnestly and passionately into a consideration of what it means to affirm that God exists, to try to grasp this great affirmation so profoundly and so intimately as to understand how some of the intellectual giants of our culture could have regarded it as unthinkable that anyone *who knew what he was doing* could refuse to affirm it. Let this question be our point of departure: How could intelligent and learned thinkers such as St. Augustine and St. Anselm have been persuaded, as almost nobody is today, that the existence of God is self-evident? What did they see, or think, or feel, or understand that most people today apparently do not? Perhaps by considering this question we may begin to understand what a twentieth-century version of the ontological argument would be, and why, even today, it deserves our attention and respect.

St. Anselm

St. Anselm of Canterbury (1033–1109) was one of the few truly original thinkers who appeared during the long interval between St. Augustine (354–430) and St. Thomas Aquinas (1225–1274). Like St. Augustine, whom he sought to emulate, St. Anselm conceived his role to be that of an apologist for Christian orthodoxy. All his writings reflect his theological and apologetic concerns; indeed, he did not make a hard and fast distinction between theology and philosophy. However, in two of his writings, the *Monologium* and the *Proslogium*, he advanced a number of arguments for the existence of God. These are worthy of study in themselves, quite apart from the apologetic context out of which they arose.

The ontological argument was the product of St. Anselm's quest for

a single argument which would require no other for its proof than itself alone; and alone would suffice to demonstrate that God truly exists, and that there is a supreme good requiring nothing else, which all other things require for their existence and well-being.[1]

The arguments that he had previously offered (in the *Monologium*) were, St. Anselm realized, extremely complex and, therefore, unconvincing to many readers. The argument he sought and believed he now had found was to be so simple and so cogent that no one could fail to understand it and be convinced by it.

Unfortunately, the argument as developed by St. Anselm is far from simple, at least to modern ears. The crucial passage reads as follows:

[1] St. Anselm, *Proslogium and Other Writings*, tr. S. N. Deane (LaSalle, Ill.: Open Court, 1962), p. 1.

Even the fool is convinced that something exists in the understanding, at least, than which nothing greater can be conceived. For, when he hears of this, he understands it. And whatever is understood, exists in the understanding. And assuredly that, than which nothing greater can be conceived, cannot exist in the understanding alone. For, suppose it exists in the understanding alone: then it can be conceived to exist in reality; which is greater. Therefore, if that, than which nothing greater can be conceived, exists in the understanding alone, the very being, than which nothing greater can be conceived, is one, than which a greater can be conceived. But obviously this is impossible. Hence, there is no doubt that there exists a being, than which nothing greater can be conceived, and it exists both in the understanding and in reality . . . There is, then, so truly a being than which nothing greater can be conceived to exist, that it cannot even be conceived not to exist.[2]

This is a far more forceful argument than most of St. Anselm's critics have realized. In order to appreciate its cogency, however, it is first necessary to understand it, and this is not easy. Perhaps the following restatement will help.

Proposition 1. By the term "God" is meant a being than which none greater can be conceived.

Proposition 2. Whether we affirm or deny the existence of God, a being than which none greater can be conceived exists in the understanding.

Proposition 3. It is possible to conceive of a being than which none greater can be conceived existing not only in the understanding but in reality as well; and this is greater.

Proposition 4. If, therefore, a being than which none greater can be conceived exists *only* in the understanding, it is not a being than which none greater can be conceived.

Proposition 5. Therefore, a being than which none greater can be conceived exists also in reality.

I do not think that anyone would deny that if Propositions 1–4 are allowed to stand, Proposition 5 (the conclusion) would follow from them. Let us consider what may be said in defense of Propositions 1–4.

Proposition 1 simply asserts a minimal definition of the term "God." St. Anselm is saying, in effect, that people who believe in the existence of God believe in the existence of a being than which none greater can be conceived, that the only way to deny the existence of God is to deny the existence of a being than which none greater can be conceived. Thus far, it seems to me, St. Anselm's opponents have no reason to object. At most, they could only quibble over terms, since it is this definition that determines the substance of what St. Anselm means when he affirms that God exists.

---

[2] *Ibid.,* pp. 8–9.

Proposition 2 points out the obvious fact that anyone who affirms or denies the existence of God must, first, understand the meaning of the term "God." If anyone says the words "God does not exist" but means something other than "a being than which none greater can be conceived does not exist," he is only denying the existence of something else to which he incorrectly gives the name "God." In order to really affirm or deny the existence of *God*—in order, that is, to be a party to this debate at all—we must understand what the term "God" means. And since, as St. Anselm says, "whatever is understood, exists in the understanding," Proposition 2 must be affirmed.

This brings us to Proposition 3, which is surely the crux of St. Anselm's famous argument. It states that it is possible for us to distinguish in thought between (a) a being that exists only in our concept and (b) a being that exists in our concept and in reality, and that a being of the latter sort is greater than one of the former. Let us consider this matter very carefully in terms of two important questions: Can we make the distinction St. Anselm says we can make? Is it self-evidently true that a being existing in concept and in reality is on that ground alone greater than a being existing only in concept?

Concerning the first question, it seems evident that in at least some cases we have no difficulty making the distinction that St. Anselm asks us to make. We can distinguish without difficulty, for example, between an imaginary dog and a real dog, the proof being that we have certain expectations in connection with the one that we do not have with the other. I am thinking at this moment, for example, of a particular Dalmatian. I expect to see him occasionally as I drive by the yard where he usually is kept, I expect to observe him playing with the neighborhood children, and so on. But I can also form the concept of a dog identical with him in every respect save one: this dog exists only in my concept, not in reality. This dog, I know, will never be lying in the yard as I drive by, will never play with the neighborhood children, will never chase my car—unless, of course, I provide some *imaginary* children and cars for him to frolic with. Thus, if Kant's often quoted statement that existence is not a predicate means, as it is usually supposed to mean, that it is not possible for us to make this distinction between real and merely conceptual existents, then I think we must conclude that on this point Kant was simply mistaken. We can and do make the distinction that St. Anselm is asking us to make.

Is it self-evidently true, then, that a being existing in reality is on that ground alone greater (more perfect) than an otherwise identical being existing only in concept? Here, it seems to me, we must choose among three alternatives: either (a) whatever order of excellence may be attributed to a thing in concept, some additional excellence accrues to that thing if, in addition, it is conceived to exist in reality; or (b) whatever order of excellence may be attributed to a thing in concept, that excellence is totally unaffected if, in addition, it is conceived to exist in reality; or (c) whatever order of excellence may be attributed to a thing in concept, that excellence is diminished if, in addition, it is conceived to exist in reality. I know of no way to *prove* that the first of these alternatives is to be preferred. For myself, however, I have no doubt that St. Anselm's assumption on this point is correct, and I think that the burden of proof must lie with those who would adopt either of the other two alternatives.

I urge my readers to ponder very carefully what St. Anselm is saying at this point, for if they can understand and accept Proposition 3, they should have no difficulty in agreeing with the remainder of the argument. Can we distinguish between a being that exists only in concept and a being that exists both in concept and in reality? The answer certainly is that we can. Then it makes sense to say that existence in concept and in reality is better than existence in concept alone. Peace in the world is certainly better than a mere concept of peace. That God should exist in reality is certainly better than that we should merely have a concept of Him. We can and do distinguish between mere conceptual existence and real existence, and we do regard the latter as superior. It *is* possible to conceive of a being than which none greater can be conceived existing not only in the understanding but in reality as well: and this *is* greater.

It follows (Proposition 4) that if a being than which none greater can be conceived exists in the understanding only, that being is not a being than which none greater can be conceived. As has already been shown (Proposition 3), a being existing in concept *and* in reality is superior to an otherwise identical being existing in concept only. If, therefore, you say that this being exists in concept only, you are contradicting yourself; for you are saying that a being than which none greater can be conceived is not in fact a being than which none greater can be conceived. Such a statement is contradictory in the same way that the statement "Some round figures are not round" is contradictory: it asserts something in the subject that is denied in the predicate.

Thus *you cannot deny the existence in reality of a being than which none greater can be conceived without contradicting yourself.* Since by the term "God" we mean a being than which none greater can be conceived, it follows that the statement "God exists" is necessarily true. God, as St. Anselm says, "cannot even be conceived not to exist."

Some who reject this argument reason that if it were a sound argument, it should be possible to prove in the same way the existence of many things—for example, an island than which a more beautiful one could not be conceived. The reasoning is not parallel, however, so the conclusion does not follow. There is no logical necessity in the existence of an island than which a more beautiful one could not be conceived, for the concept of existence is not implicit in the concept of maximum beauty. The reasoning applies only in the unique case of a being than which a greater cannot be conceived, for existence *is* implicit in the concept of such a being (Proposition 3). In this one case, and only in this one case, real existence follows necessarily from the mere concept of such a being.

We began with the question, Are there any rational grounds for believing in the existence of God, and if so, what are those grounds? I have argued that the very concept of God as a being than which none greater can be conceived makes it logically necessary that God exists, that is, that our belief in the existence of God rests on the very secure rational ground of logical necessity. It follows, then, that to deny the existence of God is not only to make an error of fact; it is also to be involved in a self-contradiction, to make a logical error. Thus we ask with St. Anselm:

> Why, then, has the fool said in his heart, there is no God (Psalms 14:1), since it is so evident, to a rational mind, that [God] dost exist in the highest degree of all? Why, except that he is dull and a fool? [3]

STUDY QUESTIONS

1. The author of this chapter seems to be rather pessimistic about the prospects for convincing many of his readers of the soundness of his (or any other) argument for the existence of God. Why? What factors in our culture does he cite as obstacles that an advocate of any such argument must try to overcome?
2. Does the restatement offered here accurately reproduce St. Anselm's argument? If not, how should it be revised in order to do so?
3. We are advised in this chapter that we ought to accept the first two premises of St. Anselm's argument without question. Do you agree? Defend your answer.
4. "It is possible for us to distinguish in thought between (a) a being that exists only in our concept, and (b) a being that exists in our concept and in reality." Do you agree or disagree? Defend your position.
5. "A being that exists in our concept *and* in reality is superior to an otherwise identical being existing in concept only." Do you agree or disagree? Defend your position.
6. In your opinion, is the ontological argument a sound argument? If not, where do you think it goes wrong?

---

[3] *Ibid.*, p. 19.

18

THE COSMOLOGICAL ARGUMENT

Anyone seriously involved with the problem of the existence of God—or, more specifically, the problem of assessing the cogency of the several arguments for the existence of God that have been put forward—is painfully aware that the present-day advocate of any such argument faces a number of difficult obstacles. Chief among these are the following: (a) the apparently inescapable vagueness of the concept "God," (b) the antimetaphysical bias of much modern thought, and, as a corollary, (c) the absence of a vocabulary acceptable to the modern mind that is suitable for the construction of a proof of the existence of God. I am not sanguine about the prospects for overcoming these obstacles in what follows, but I do think the existence of God is capable of strict demonstration and I shall try to state my proof in a form that will not require a modern reader to stretch his ordinary categories of thought too far.

It is not surprising that the concept of God is less precise than most of the concepts that we customarily employ. Most of our concepts are of objects that exist in space and time—objects concerning which it is appropriate to ask questions like, Where is it? How big is it? What color is it? and so on. If the concept of God were to be given that kind of precision, we would no longer be talking about *God* at all; for whatever we do mean by "God," it is clear that we do not mean "one object (or being) among others in the world of space and time."

The question concerning the existence of God is, therefore, unique. It would be silly to try to prove the existence of a spatiotemporal object. The existence of any such object is a purely contingent fact: to convince anyone of its existence you must produce not an argument but *the object itself*. Only if it presents itself in some way to at least one of our senses are we willing to say that it "exists." And rightly so.

But we cannot know of God's existence in the same way that we know of the existence of spatiotemporal objects. If we are to know of the existence of God, therefore, it must—in this one, unique case—be by way of argument, or demonstration. The question we must ask is this: Is there any feature of the world of space and time that points to a reality that *transcends* space and time, is the ground of the being and value of this world, and is worthy of man's worship? To answer this question in the affirmative is to construct (or at least to affirm that it is possible to construct) a cosmological argument for the existence of God.

St. Thomas Aquinas

"The existence of God," said Aquinas, "can be proved in five ways." [1] Thereupon, in a scant three pages, the great Angelic Doctor gave to the world five of the most famous arguments for the existence of God that have ever been formulated.

None of the "five ways" is original with Aquinas (nor, of course, did he claim that they were), and they are not equally persuasive. The first three, in particular, are very similar, and differ markedly from both the fourth and the fifth arguments. There are reasons for regarding the third way as the fundamental, or centrally important, one. The complete text of this argument reads as follows:

> The third way is taken from possibility and necessity, and runs thus. We find in nature things that are possible to be or not to be, since they are found to be generated, and to be corrupted, and consequently, it is possible for them to be and not to be. But it is impossible for these always to exist, for that which can not-be at some time is not. Therefore, if anything can not-be, then at one time there was nothing in existence, because that which does not exist begins to exist only through something already existing. Therefore, if at one time nothing was in existence, it would have been impossible for anything to have begun to exist; and thus even now nothing would be in existence—which is absurd. Therefore, not all beings are merely possible, but there must exist something the existence of which is necessary. But every necessary thing either has its necessity caused by another, or not. Now it is impossible to go on to infinity in necessary things which have their necessity caused by another, as has already been proved in regard to efficient causes. Therefore we cannot but admit the existence of some being having of itself its own necessity, and not receiving it from another, but rather causing in others their necessity. *This all men speak of as God.*[2] [Italics, which are mine, are explained below.]

Although I hold this to be a sound argument, I do think it suffers from one serious defect. It is more complicated than it needs to be because of Aquinas' inclusion of a multiplicity of "necessary things which have

[1] St. Thomas Aquinas, *Summa Theologica*, I, ques. 2, art. 3, in Anton C. Pegis (ed.), *Basic Writings of St. Thomas Aquinas* (New York: Random House, 1945), vol. I, p. 22.

[2] *Ibid.*, pp. 22–23.

their necessity caused by another." This may have served some polemical purpose at the time that Aquinas was writing, but to a modern reader it appears as excess baggage that only clutters up the argument. Nothing essential to the argument is lost, I think, if we simply omit this reference to a series of hypothetical "necessary beings" (everything *not* in italics above) and conclude directly from the existence of "beings [that] are merely possible" to the existence of "something the existence of which is necessary . . . [that] all men speak of as God."

Both defenders and critics sometimes assert that the starting point of the argument is a fairly obvious feature of the world, namely, that something exists. I think this assertion indicates a serious misunderstanding of the argument. The starting point of the argument is not that something exists (that *is* obvious) but that some *contingent beings* exist, and that is not nearly so obvious. It is precisely at this point that we determine whether or not we are going to go along with Aquinas' argument; either we share his insight into *the contingency of finite beings,* or we remain unconvinced by his argument.

Two Common Criticisms

It will be convenient to deal here with two criticisms that are frequently made of this argument. The words "necessary" and "contingent," it is sometimes said, are words that apply not to *things* but to *propositions.* To speak of God as a "necessary being," or "something the existence of which is necessary," must mean (if it means anything at all) "The proposition 'God exists' is a necessary proposition." But this is precisely the claim of the ontological argument. Therefore, the cosmological argument reduces ultimately to the ontological argument, and if the ontological argument is not sound, then neither, obviously, is the cosmological.

It is easy to show, however, that this is a superficial criticism. It starts with purely arbitrary definitions of the terms "necessary" and "contingent" and then attempts to employ these definitions to make Aquinas—or anyone else who advocates this form of the cosmological argument—say something he clearly did not say and did not mean to say. Granted that in logic the terms "necessary" and "contingent" apply only to propositions, not to terms or to arguments. In logic a necessary proposition is one the negation of which involves a self-contradiction, a contingent proposition is one the negation of which does *not* involve a self-contradiction. Does this exclude the possibility that *outside* the realm of logic—in metaphysics, for example—these same terms may have a somewhat different meaning? Of course not.

The cosmological argument, in whatever form, always moves from the *ontological contingency* of finite being to the *ontological necessity* of the ground of being. Aquinas does not, in the argument quoted above, use the term "contingent"; he speaks instead about "things that are possible to be or not to be." But that is precisely what "ontological contingency" means.

A second very common—and, in my view, mistaken—objection to Aquinas' argument concerns his claim that "it is impossible to go on to infinity," which is essential to the argument in each of the first three ways. Why can you not go on to infinity? some critics have asked. Mathematicians regularly employ the notion of an infinite series. Why should we regard it as self-evident that a series of "contingent beings" or "causes" cannot proceed to infinity?

This objection, like the first, rests on a misunderstanding of the cosmological argument. Aquinas' point is not that a particular being—a man, let us say—is dependent on his parents for his existence, and they on their parents, and they on theirs, and so on, all the way back to God. The cosmological argument has nothing to do with the relation between parents and children. It has to do with the *present* ontological contingency of some being and its *present* dependence for its existence on some noncontingent ground. The possibility of an infinite mathematical series is, therefore, totally irrelevant to the argument.

That the cosmological argument has nothing to do with this story of one generation's succeeding another may also be seen in the fact that if the argument is construed in this way, it can at best prove that *at some time in the past* there was a remote ancestor of this presently existing contingent being. It is not the purpose of the cosmological argument to prove the present existence of somebody's great-great-great-great . . . grandfather. Therefore, it should be evident that to construe the argument in this way is to *mis*construe it, indeed to render it altogether ludicrous.

I have dwelt briefly on these two objections to the cosmological argument for two reasons: first, because they are frequently accepted as sound, and second, because they reveal some of the most common misunderstandings of the cosmological argument. Discussion of them affords an opportunity to point out and attempt to remove these misunderstandings. I may be wrong in my view that the cosmological argument is a convincing proof of the existence of God, but I am surely not wrong in insisting that any opinion of this argument should be based on a serious effort to understand the argument as it is understood and intended by those who support it.

A Restatement

So that the truly persuasive character of the cosmological argument will be abundantly clear, I should like to offer a restatement of it in what I take to be its simplest possible form. I propose to state it in terms of two premises and a conclusion and to indicate the grounds on which each of the premises rests. I hope that some of my readers may then find it possible to join me in affirming the conclusion.

Reduced to its simplest possible form, the cosmological argument may be stated as follows:

Some contingent beings exist.
Contingent beings require a noncontingent ground of being in order to exist.

A noncontingent ground of being exists.

The crucial step in this argument, as I have already indicated, is the first premise. The question that must be asked, then, is, *On what basis* is it affirmed that "some contingent beings exist"? And the answer that must be given will, I fear, be disappointing to many, for I am obliged to reply that the ontological contingency of finite beings cannot be demonstrated on the basis of some other more evident truths: it must be grasped directly. I know only too well that the notion of "rational insight" is distinctly out of favor at present; but if we do not have such direct insight into the ontological contingency of finite things, we cannot know it at all.

Even though this truth cannot be demonstrated, it may be possible to suggest a few things that will help to "elicit the insight." Aquinas does this, for example, when he calls attention to the fact that things in nature are subject to "generation and corruption"—they come into being and pass away. "My days," says the Psalmist, "are like a shadow that declineth, and I am withered like grass." [3] The coming into being and the passing away of individuals is, of course, an observable fact, one that often gives rise to the feeling of the transitoriness of all things, of the tenuous and precarious character of finite existence. From this awareness it is but a step to the rational insight into the ontological contingency of finite being upon which the cosmological argument rests.

Or we may take a slightly different approach. At the present moment you are, of course, existing, a fact which, like most people, you probably take for granted. Concerning the future (tomorrow, for example), you ask not, Will I *be?* but, What will I be *doing?* Yet in all seriousness, how can you simply take your own existence for granted? Is not existence a gift received anew moment by moment? It is certainly conceivable that at any second, we could simply cease to exist, that individually or collectively we and our world could be annihilated—in short, that the gift of existence could be withdrawn, and in our place, nothing. To ponder our own existence in this way is to feel the uncertainty, the precariousness, the gratuitousness of all finite existence, including our own. To conceptualize this feeling is to grasp the ontological contingency of finite being, the rational insight with which the cosmological argument begins.

The second premise of the argument—that contingent beings require (presuppose) a noncontingent ground of being in order to exist—is

---

[3] Psalms, 102:11.

analytically true. To say that something is "contingent" is to say that it is "ontologically dependent"; it is to affirm a relation and therefore implicitly to posit that to which the relation refers. If we understand what we have said when we have affirmed the contingency of finite being, there is no difficulty in affirming this second premise. Its function is simply to spell out what is implied in the initial insight into the contingency of finite being, and this in such a way as to make it evident that this insight does indeed imply the existence of God.

The Object of Worship

Although in my discussion thus far I have had in mind chiefly those critics of the cosmological argument who think it tries to prove too much (that God exists), I know there are other critics who object that the argument proves too little. A deeply religious person may respond to the cosmological argument with profound indignation because the "ground of being" who appears at the conclusion of the argument—this "God of the philosophers," as Blaise Pascal said—bears little or no resemblance to the loving Heavenly Father of living religious faith. "Away with these abstractions!" is the cry of such well-meaning people. What is to be said in answer to such an objection?

The only answer I shall attempt to give is that it is not the business of the philosopher to attempt to prove everything about God that is of importance for religious faith. Faith simply presupposes the reality of God and by means of a rich symbolism seeks to worship Him in a way that is worthy of Him. Faith lives in symbolism and imagery, not primarily in concepts; this is why all *conceptions* of God—even those formulated by theologians—seem, from the point of view of faith, woefully inadequate.

But philosophers *qua* philosophers are not entitled to such a presupposition. For philosophy the question whether God exists is a legitimate and, indeed, inescapable question. As I have indicated, I believe that we are entitled to answer this question in the affirmative. I believe, further, that the conception of God that emerges at the conclusion of the cosmological argument is capable of considerable enrichment, when the argument is applied to a wide variety of contingent existents (as Aquinas does, for example, in the first three of his five ways). But the God whose existence is thus established, though surely worthy of mankind's worship, can never acquire by philosophical argument the rich (but profoundly anthropomorphic) connotations that religious faith ascribes to Him in poetry, prayer, and song. In comparison with the God of living faith, the God of the cosmological argument must appear highly abstract, austere, and remote. Philosophical argument is limited to concepts, which it must strive to make as precise as it possibly can. It cannot deal in imagery. It cannot disclose to us the richer reality that is the object of religious faith. But it can and does disclose to us the reality of God as the ground of the being of finite things. We must not expect of it more than this.

STUDY QUESTIONS

1. What is meant by the statement that the question concerning the existence of God is "a unique question"? Is it? What assumptions is one making if one holds that it is? If one holds that it is not?
2. Restate St. Thomas Aquinas' third way premise by premise, just as St. Anselm's argument was restated in the previous chapter.
3. What are the "two common criticisms" of the cosmological argument that our author attempts to refute? Does he succeed?
4. What is the difference between attempting to "prove a proposition" and attempting to "elicit an insight"? Why does the author of this chapter resort to the latter?
5. Who would be apt to criticize the cosmological argument on the ground that it proves too much? on the ground that it proves too little? What is your own opinion of the argument?

19

THE TELEOLOGICAL
ARGUMENT

Like the two writers who are to succeed me in this discussion, I am not at all persuaded by either the ontological or the cosmological argument for the existence of God. I have never been impressed with them in their "classical" formulations—those of St. Anselm and Aquinas, respectively—and I am equally unimpressed after reading the explanations offered by the preceding two writers. Both these arguments are vulnerable to a really devastating and, I think, decisive critique, which I assume will be forthcoming in the chapters that follow. I shall be content, therefore, to simply state my rejection of these arguments, leaving the detailed criticism to others, and shall proceed directly to the formulation and defense of a third argument that in my estimation is far more persuasive.

The argument of which I speak is commonly called the teleological argument (from the Greek word *télos,* meaning "end" or "goal"). Aquinas' fifth way is a version of this argument, but the "classical" statement of the argument is in William Paley's *Evidences of the Existence and Attributes of the Deity.*[1] It is an argument that deserves to be studied with great care.

The Sense of Wonder

We shall be better prepared both to understand and to appreciate the teleological argument if we first consider briefly the kind of human experience out of which the argument has come to be formulated.

All but the most pedestrian human beings must, at times, be

---

[1] William Paley, *Natural Theology,* ed. Frederick Ferré, (Indianapolis: Bobbs-Merrill, 1963).

impressed by the vastness, the grandeur, the beauty, and the order of the universe. There is a feeling of awe and wonder when we stand upon the shore of a stormy sea, gaze upward on a starry night, or survey the rugged beauty of a range of mountains. Here is power, restless and profound; here is vastness, staggering in magnitude; yet here is order, beautiful to behold.

Scientists in whom the sense of poetry is still alive tell us of a similar experience when they have penetrated some of the less obvious wonders of nature. To understand the structure of the atom is to marvel at its ordered complexity; to survey the course of evolution is to view a magnificent process unfolding through millenniums of time; to grasp the genetic code is to possess a key that may unlock yet further mysteries of nature. Here are phenomena capable of inspiring awe of which our ancient predecessors could not even dream. How very much there is, in the world as we perceive it, to inspire that sense of awe of which we have been speaking.

It seems very natural, when some feature or other of the universe impresses us in this way, to say that it could not be by chance that the universe is the way it is. A beautiful poem, a great symphony, a particularly inspiring work of architecture, a remarkable engineering achievement—these are impressive, and rightly cause us to give honor to their creators. But more wonderful still is the poetry, the harmony, the power, the beauty, the structure of the universe itself. Surely it, too, has an Author, an Architect, a magnificent Craftsman, whose wisdom and power are commensurate with the mighty work that He has wrought. Every person living, at some time in his life, must have entertained sentiments such as these.

The teleological argument is simply an attempt to extract and to render conceptually precise the argument that is implicit in the natural reflections inspired by this experience of wonder.

The Argument

Paley's formulation of the argument in *Evidences of the Existence and Attributes of the Deity* does not, unfortunately, lend itself to a brief summary statement. It is, as he says, cumulative; his whole book is the argument. However, I shall try to indicate the general course Paley takes.

He begins by noting that whenever we observe of something that "its several parts are framed and put together for a purpose"—a watch, for example—we conclude without hesitation that it has been devised for this purpose by some intelligent designer. Nothing that we may subsequently learn about the watch (that it sometimes fails to work perfectly, that it is capable of reproducing itself, or anything else) can dissuade us from this belief. Paley states:

> There cannot be design without a designer; contrivance, without a contriver; order, without choice; arrangement, without anything capable of

arranging; subserviency and relation to a purpose, without that which could intend a purpose; means suitable to an end, and executing their office in accomplishing that end, without the end ever having been contemplated, or the means accommodated to it. Arrangement, disposition of parts, subserviency of means to an end, relation of instruments to a use, imply the presence of intelligence and mind.[2]

So much for the first part of Paley's argument. The second part attempts to show that the universe abounds with phenomena that, like the watch, exhibit teleological order:

> Every indication of contrivance, every manifestation of design, which existed in the watch, exists in the works of nature; with the difference, on the side of nature, of being greater and more, and that in a degree which exceeds all computation . . . The contrivances of nature surpass the contrivances of art, in the complexity, subtlety, and curiosity of the mechanism; and still more, if possible, do they go beyond them in number and variety: yet, in a multitude of cases, are not less evidently mechanical, not less evidently contrivances, not less evidently accommodated to their end, or suited to their office, than are the most perfect productions of human ingenuity.[3]

Paley's favorite example of design in nature is the eye, whose delicate and intricate mechanism he discusses in great detail. But countless other examples are to be found.

The conclusion, Paley suggests, must therefore be drawn: Design in nature points to the existence of an intelligent Designer of nature, just as design in a watch or other machine points to the existence of its designer.

> Were there no example in the world of contrivance except that of the eye, it would be alone sufficient to support the conclusion which we draw from it, as to the necessity of an intelligent Creator. It could never be got rid of because it could not be accounted for by any other supposition, which did not contradict all the principles we possess of knowledge.[4]

I think that this argument is sound and convincing, and I propose to reduce it to its barest essentials and to add a few comments by way of elucidating its fundamental structure.

Elucidation and Defense of the Argument

The teleological argument contains two premises. One, straightforwardly factual, is that nature exhibits a number of instances of means ordered to ends. The other, a general principle, is that the ordering of means to ends presupposes the existence of a designer whose intelligence and power are sufficient to account for the product he has wrought. The whole argument, therefore, is as follows:

---

[2] *Ibid.*, p. 10.
[3] *Ibid.*, p. 13.
[4] *Ibid.*, p. 44.

Nature exhibits a number of instances of means ordered to ends.

The ordering of means to ends presupposes the existence of a designer whose intelligence and power are sufficient to account for the product he has wrought.

The ordering of means to ends in nature presupposes the existence of a designer whose intelligence and power are commensurate with the magnitude of his product.

It is important to note, in attempting to assess this argument, that it does not say, or presuppose, that the whole universe is cooperating to achieve some single ultimate purpose. This may or may not be the case: the argument is neutral with respect to this question. Unfortunately some critics of the teleological argument have failed to grasp this point.

It should also be observed that the argument does not say, or presuppose, that the several "ends" toward which the various means are ordered are necessarily good, or are what human beings would always approve of, or tend to serve our needs. For example, the various endowments that make the tiger a very dangerous animal serve the end of the *tiger's own* self-preservation—sometimes, at man's expense. This is an "end" in the sense in which that term is used in this argument, human preferences in the matter notwithstanding. Numerous other examples could be given.

The factual premise in this argument seems to me beyond dispute. The evidence is all around us, and it is overwhelming. Animals have eyes in order to see, ears in order to hear, teeth in order to chew their food, digestive organs in order to utilize their food, lungs in order to breathe, and so on. In the plant world, too, we observe the adaptation of means to ends: root systems in order to draw nourishment from the soil, leaves in order to derive the benefits of the sunlight, and so on. Look where we will, the evidence is the same. Every species of living thing known to us, every plant, every insect, every fish, every mammal, is endowed with those characteristics necessary to its existence and way of life.

We know, of course—as Paley did not—that this remarkable state of affairs has come about through a long process of evolution in which the forms of life now found in nature have developed from other forms no longer extant. But this alters the argument not at all. Consider this process at any point you will, the kind of evidence we are now considering abounds there. However far we press our inquiry into the remote past, we find not chaos but order: means subservient to ends, processes conducive to the emergence of life, circumstances conducive to the proliferation of life, powers adapted to the preservation of life. So much for the factual premise.

The second premise—that the ordering of means to ends presupposes the existence of some intelligent designer to "do the ordering"—is an inductive generalization well substantiated by experience. It is beyond dispute that in every such instance of which we have any reasonably certain knowledge, the principle holds true. We know of no watches without watchmakers, ships without shipbuilders, or planes without plane-builders. We would never allow, if we were to be shown one of these objects, that without the intelligent direction of any mind what-soever the object in question just "happened to happen." Where we find *means ordered to ends*, "chance" is as good as no answer at all; for in every such instance of which we do have knowledge, we find mind—intelligence—behind it. Every day we observe countless examples of this principle; we have never observed, or been offered, a counterexample. The principle would seem to be as secure, therefore, as it is possible for any inductive generalization to be.

If the argument is to be attacked, then, it must be on the ground that the order that we find in nature is not sufficiently similar to the order that we find in human contrivances to justify applying the principle. David Hume saw this clearly and in his *Dialogues Concerning Natural Religion* (published posthumously in 1779) he exercised, as he says, "all [his] sceptical and metaphysical subtilty" in an attempt to weaken the analogy. But after doing his best, or rather his worst, to find some alternative to intelligent design as a principle of explanation, even Hume was forced to conclude (in the words of Philo, his chief spokesman in the *Dialogues*):

> In many views of the universe and of its parts, particularly the latter, the beauty and fitness of final causes strike us with such irresistible force that all objections appear (what I believe they really are) mere cavils and sophisms; nor can we then imagine how it was ever possible for us to repose any weight on them.[5]

The order that we find in nature calls for *some* explanation. The analogy between it and the order found in contrivances known to be the product of intelligent purpose is infinitely stronger than any other analogy so far suggested. Against this objection, therefore, the teleological argument stands secure.

The Wider Teleological Argument

We have, of course, learned a great deal about the world since the days of Paley and Hume, and I can well imagine a reader acknowledging that such an argument had some persuasive power prior to the work of Charles Darwin but pointing out that the adaption of means to ends as we find it in nature is adequately explained by the principle of natural selection. In this opinion, there is no need for explanation through "divine intelligence." Since this objection appears serious to many people, it deserves to be treated with respect, though it is by no means

---

[5] David Hume, *Dialogues Concerning Natural Religion*, ed. Norman Kemp Smith, 2d ed. (New York: Social Sciences, 1948), p. 202.

fatal to the teleological argument. What it does is to force us to broaden the scope of the field within which we may discern the workings of the divine intelligence.

Consider the following remarkable facts about the world as we know it:

1. The world is intelligible in a very high degree. The world, somehow or other, is capable of being understood by means of the logical and mathematical categories of the human mind.
2. The evolutionary process, which posits "chance" mutations whose survival depends on their suitability to enhance the organism in its struggle for life, has operated *as if* it were intended to produce variety, beauty, mind, and intelligence.
3. The inorganic world, which according to current theory existed for hundreds of millions of years before life emerged on our planet, is remarkably well adapted—physically, chemically, thermally, and so on—to the maintenance of life.
4. Nature has developed in such a way that there are numerous phenomena that elicit in man a sense of beauty.
5. The conditions of human life have developed in such a way that man is able to postulate, pursue, and to a high degree achieve moral ideals.

How are we to account for these remarkable facts? What hypothesis will do justice to the truly astonishing fact that out of a mass of inorganic matter there has emerged, through a process that might have worked in countless other directions, not only life (which is remarkable enough in itself) but a being possessing intelligence, morality, and a sense of beauty? Say, if you will, that it is all a matter of chance, that the laws of nature had to produce *some* kind of world, and that this just happens to be the one that developed. I for one do not believe it. If this world evolved by "a throw of the dice," then I cannot escape the conclusion that the dice were loaded. There is, as Sir Arthur Eddington once remarked, a "cheater" some place in the vicinity. The hypothesis that the world is the way it is because God so arranged it is, I think, strongly supported by facts such as those enumerated above. Evolution, far from destroying the teleological argument, provides new evidence of adaptation of means to ends and thus supports the God hypothesis that it is the purpose of the teleological argument to establish.

The Limits of Philosophical Argument

The teleological argument by itself does not and cannot be expected to give us a rich, "full-blown theology," such as would satisfy a religious community. For that is needed the images evoked and provided by religious literature, the sentiments that are nourished in various rites of worship, and the vocabulary and ideas that have life and meaning only in the context and the tradition of this or that worshiping community. Any philosophical attempt to "fill out" the concept of God in these essentially religious ways would be rightly resisted both by philosophers and by nonphilosophical adherents of religion.

The God whose existence is proved by the teleological argument is not the Brahman of Hindu faith, the Yahweh of Jewish faith, or the Heavenly Father of Christian faith. The God of the teleological argument, strictly speaking, is simply an unknown Mind and Power, by virtue of whose workings we find order in the world about us. About this austere notion cluster the sentiments of awe and wonder at the marvels of nature, the natural precursors, perhaps, of that "sense of the holy" that is so distinctive of religious communities. Perhaps, too, the awareness of the beauty of nature and of the greatness of the privilege of being alive leads to some intimation of the goodness of God, so that He is conceived not only as Mind and Power, but also as Goodness.

Philosophical reflection on the awesome spectacle of order in nature cannot take us beyond the bare knowledge of God's existence and the faint intimation of some few of His attributes. But it *can* take us *that* far. We may or may not then turn to religion to further enrich our conception. That is another matter altogether. Philosophy is not theology, and philosophical understanding is not religious faith. But the understanding that philosophy can give us, limited though it is, may serve as a foundation for faith.

STUDY QUESTIONS

1. What relevance, if any, does the discussion of "the sense of wonder" have for the subsequent discussion of the teleological argument?
2. Look up St. Thomas Aquinas' fifth way (*Summa Theologica*, Part I, Question 2, Article 3), and compare it with the argument given in this chapter. What similarities do you find between the two arguments? what differences?
3. How does one go about identifying an instance in nature of "means ordered to ends"? What right have we to say, for example, that the "end" served by the ferocity of the tiger is the self-preservation of the tiger rather than the death of its prey? Is some criterion at work here that has not been made explicit?
4. Is the analogy between "order in nature" and "order in human contrivances" sufficiently close to support the second premise of the teleological argument? How important is this alleged analogy to the argument?
5. "Evolution, far from destroying the teleological argument, provides new evidence of adaptation of means to ends and thus supports the God hypothesis that it is the purpose of the teleological argument to establish." What is your opinion?

20

THE NONEXISTENCE OF GOD: A NATURALISTIC REJOINDER

It is a fundamental tenet of philosophical naturalism that the whole of reality consists of objects and events occurring in space and time and that the system of spatiotemporal events that we call the world is self-dependent and self-operating. It is an obvious negative corollary of this view that there is nothing real that transcends this world—no gods, no values, no anything. To say that something exists is to say that it is, or is reducible to, some spatiotemporal events that we can perceive or could perceive under such and such circumstances or that (at a minimum) are causally related to events of this kind. It makes sense to say that grasshoppers exist, because we can see them. It makes sense to say that mountains exist on Venus, because we know what mountains are and what it would be like to see them through a telescope. It makes sense to say that electrons exist, because the event that we call the existence of an electron is causally related to other events that we perceive. It does not make sense, in any of these ways, to say that God exists.

But no sooner do naturalists point out that the statement "God exists" is, at best, exceedingly odd (and at worst, meaningless), than theists turn this very observation against us. "Quite so," they say, "but the reason is that the existence of God is a unique instance. Grasshoppers, mountains, and electrons exist only *contingently*, but God's existence—the only one of its kind—is *necessary*. That is why the statement 'God exists' strikes us as being so odd." On this whole question of the existence of God I would like to make just one assertion and then be done with it: The statement "God exists" has no clear meaning; it is as senseless to deny it as it is to affirm it. But in view of the rejoinder ("This is a unique case"), we have no choice but to go over the worn-out old arguments to show why they do not establish the proposition "God exists" in any meaningful acceptation of those terms. What follows, then, is a *disproof of the proofs* for the existence of God.

The Ontological Argument

There is one very strong prima facie reason for doubting the soundness of the ontological argument and that is that practically everybody who has studied it carefully has in the end rejected it. St. Anselm, of course, who invented the argument, believed it to be sound; so also did René Descartes and Gottfried Wilhelm von Leibnitz. But Gaunilon in the eleventh century, Aquinas in the thirteenth, Hume and Kant in the eighteenth, and nearly every major philosopher since then have rejected it. If we can determine the soundness of an argument on the basis of the consensus of those who are most competent to judge, the ontological argument must be adjudged a failure.

The critics of the ontological argument have rejected it principally for three reasons, all of which I consider valid. First, if the reasoning contained in the ontological argument were sound, it should be applicable in other instances as well—namely, to the superlative instance of any positive quality. It should be possible to prove (by a parallel argument) the existence of an island than which none more beautiful can be conceived (this was Gaunilon's example), a mountain than which none taller can be conceived, and so on. But this is clearly absurd. It seems evident, therefore, that something is wrong with the argument.

We begin to understand just what is wrong with it when we consider, in the second place, that it really is not the case that when anyone either affirms or denies the existence of God, a being than which none greater can be conceived "exists in the understanding." Let it be granted that we can utter the *words* "a being than which none greater can be conceived"; I contend that we have no *concept* of a being so described.

The third reason for rejecting the argument is the most decisive. Existence, as Kant said, is not a predicate. To assert that something is *red,* for example, is to make an assertion that requires us to alter our concept of that thing; "red," therefore, is a predicate. But the assertion that something *exists* in no way modifies our concept of that thing. The ontological argument hinges on an alleged contrast (Proposition 3 of the summary) between (a) a being existing only in the understanding and (b) an otherwise identical being existing both in the understanding and in reality. But this is a contrast, a distinction in thought, that it is not possible for us to make. Our *concept* of a real Dalmatian differs in no way from our *concept* of an imaginary one. The difference between the two consists not in anything found in the concepts themselves but rather in the different ways in which they are related to our (actual or possible) perceptions. Hence, even if it were possible to form a concept of a being than which none greater can be conceived (and I have questioned this), it still would not be possible to conclude to the existence of God; the crucial distinction upon which the whole argument turns is one that it is impossible to make.

The Cosmological Argument

There are many forms of the cosmological argument, and it would be a tedious job to review and criticize each in detail. Chapter 18 presents the argument in a form that nearly all contemporary supporters regard as persuasive, and I shall restrict my remarks to this version. Anyone who understands what is wrong with the argument in this form will have no difficulty in detecting the weaknesses in any other form of the argument.

The cosmological argument as stated suffers from three serious defects. To begin with, the first premise ("Some contingent beings exist") is either unintelligible, or it is a truism. If it is unintelligible, it is not deserving of serious consideration. If it is a truism, nothing of importance follows.

I am at this moment looking at an ashtray. It presumably is one of the "contingent beings" that this premise says exists. Very well. What does it mean to say that this ashtray is "contingent"? I can think of three possibilities. It may mean that (a) there was a time when this ashtray did not exist and now it does—it has "come into being" and will, presumably, some day cease to exist. Or it may mean that (b) the nonexistence of this ashtray is conceivable. Or it may mean that (c) there are certain things without which the ashtray would cease to exist. If a, nothing of importance follows. You may, if you wish, argue to the existence at some time in the past of an ashtray-maker, but this is quite obviously beside the point. If b, again nothing of importance follows. We can conceive of the nonexistence of anything simply by thinking of it as occupying space and then imagining that space to be empty. If c is meant, the situation is a little more complicated, but the result is the same. It is apparent, for example, that the continued existence of this ashtray depends on the continued validity of certain laws of physics—the cohesion of its parts, its tolerance of the temperature levels to which it is subjected, and so on. But this does not take us any distance at all toward establishing the proposition "God exists."

If the proposition "Some contingent beings exist" does not mean one of these three things, I can only insist that I find it unintelligible. If there is something else that I am supposed to "see directly," I can only confess that I do not see it. Until the defenders of the cosmological argument tell us plainly and explicitly what they mean by the statement, I think we are justified in suspecting that they do not see it either. Either they mean one or more of the three things suggested above, or they mean nothing at all.

Let us, however, be as charitable as we can. Let us suppose that the supporters of this argument do mean something when they assert that "Some contingent beings exist." What might they mean? Option c would seem to be their most promising choice. They might insist that something of significance does follow from it because we cannot be satisfied with an infinite regress. If something Z (the ashtray, for example) is dependent on something else Y for its continued existence, they might say, then we can ask the same question about Y. Is it contingent or not? Eventually we must come to a *noncontingent* cause, and this is what we mean by God.

But there is something very wrong with this argument from ashtrays to physics to God. We know that by means of physical laws we can reason only to other physical laws or to some spatiotemporal event or events. Physical laws are passports that enable us to move from one range of phenomena to another *in the natural world.* They do not give us an exit visa to pass outside spatiotemporal reality. Moreover, what is wrong with a series of contingent causes, even an *infinite* series of contingent causes? In this case every member of the series is contingent in the sense defined above, and there is no first member. Is this any harder to conceive of than an infinite mathematical series, or infinite space?

Finally, the conclusion of the argument is so ambiguous that it seems quite impossible to either affirm it or deny it. How could anyone decide for or against the statement "A noncontingent ground of being exists"? What concrete difference would it make in your experience or mine whether this statement (if it is a statement) is true or false? None whatsoever. It is a meaningless combination of ponderous words, designed to intimidate rather than to elucidate. But one thing is clear: whatever these words are supposed to mean, the premises that precede them do not establish the existence of God. We may not like it, but it happens to be the case that this world and its laws are the only reality there is. Any attempt to reason from this or that feature of the world to some reality not of the world is sheer fantasy.

The Teleological Argument

Although it is popularly regarded as one of the most persuasive of the traditional arguments for the existence of God, the teleological argument is by far the weakest. Since the defects of the argument have only to be pointed out to be seen, I shall restrict myself to a very summary statement of them.

The assertion "Nature exhibits a number of instances of means ordered to ends" is subtly ambiguous. What nature exhibits is a high degree of *lawlike regularity.* If this is all that is meant by "means ordered to ends," all well and good; but it seems that more than this is intended. The language suggests "purposiveness," or "ordering," and thus subtly suggests *in an allegedly factual premise* that we ought to look for a "purposer," or "orderer." We seem to have here a case of syllogistic smuggling.

Furthermore, the alleged analogy between the lawlike regularity that we find in nature (to substitute for the offending terms) and that which we find in human contrivances is notably weak. We do indeed posit a human intelligence whenever we encounter an implement that (*a*) serves some conceivable purpose and (*b*) is evidently not altogether a product of nature. But neither of these characteristics applies to the regularities that we find in nature, not even to those offered by the author of Chapter 19 as examples of the sort of thing he has in mind. On what basis, then, are we supposed to see an analogy?

It is quite beside the point to argue that "the analogy between [order in nature] and the order found in contrivances known to be the product of intelligent purpose is infinitely stronger than any other analogy so far suggested." This may well be. I am no more impressed than was Hume, for example, by the suggestion that the universe could be likened to a giant plant or to a spiderweb rather than to a machine. But why should it be likened to anything at all? A human contrivance, after all, utilizes in some way or other certain laws of nature that man, by careful inquiry or by good luck, has discovered. May not these laws be themselves the ultimate facts to which appeal can be made, and may not the universe itself be the model of regularity in relation to which every other instance of regularity is only a pale analogy?

Moreover, even if the argument were sound, the being whose existence it establishes would be nothing more than a finitely wise, finitely powerful architect. The inventor of a machine does not create the materials with which he works; he only shapes them. Hence the "orderer" whose existence is supposedly established by this argument is merely a craftsman, not a creator. The argument, if it is sound, requires only that this cosmic "orderer" be very wise and very powerful. Hence, it does not establish the existence of an *infinitely* wise and powerful being. The argument requires nothing at all in the way of goodness. Since there is evil in the world that he is supposed to have designed, it may be assumed that he is something less than perfectly good; at best he must be considered amoral, at worst malevolent. This is hardly a description of God in any religiously meaningful sense of the term.

Finally, even if the argument did establish the existence of this strange being, it would establish only his past existence, not his present one. The existence of a watch implies only the existence of a watch-maker *at the time the watch was made;* it does not in any way assure me of his *present* existence. Similarly, if the existence of an ordered universe implied anything at all (which I doubt), it would be that once upon a time, long, long ago, there was a world-maker. He may since have died or changed his occupation.

The teleological argument is not a good one. It derives its prestige entirely, I suspect, from the fact that it unites the "natural wonder" of which we heard in the last chapter with the apparently kindred feeling of "reverence" in a way that is satisfying to religious people. It may even be that the feeling of reverence arose originally out of this feeling of natural wonder. Be that as it may, it is perfectly evident that the belief in the existence of God did not come about because of the cogency of the teleological argument.

A Final Word

None of the arguments for the existence of God is able to withstand careful scrutiny. Why, then, do so many people believe that God exists? The answer can only be that this belief is irrational—an illusion (Sigmund Freud), a personification of society (Émile Durkheim), or something else. The persistence of this belief in spite of the demonstrable fallaciousness of the arguments used to support it suggests that it must fulfill some very deep emotional need of many people. Therefore, it may be thought cruel to show, as I have done, how weak those arguments are. However, since people who believe in God obviously did not arrive at this belief by means of rational argument, it is unlikely that the removal of the arguments will by itself destroy that belief. People who need this particular illusion will probably keep it, with or without intellectual props. Moreover, we have addressed ourselves to this problem only in the interest of knowing the truth. Are there or are there not rational grounds for believing in the existence of God? As a convinced naturalist, I hold that there are not. I think that this is the truth. If the truth is painful, it is still the truth. Things are the way they are; the best we can do is to try to see them that way, not the way we might like them to be.

STUDY QUESTIONS

1. What objections does Naturalist bring against the ontological argument? Are they all sound objections, in your opinion? (Compare Naturalist's third objection with the defense of Proposition 3 in Chapter 17.)
2. What are Naturalist's objections to the cosmological argument? Do they apply with equal force to Aquinas' third way and to the shorter formulation offered in Chapter 18?
3. What are Naturalist's objections to the teleological argument? Do they apply with equal force to Paley's argument and to Aquinas' fifth way? Do you think Naturalist is right in calling this "by far the weakest" of the arguments for the existence of God?
4. Select whichever of the traditional arguments you consider to be the strongest and attempt to defend it against Naturalist's criticisms.

21

THE FAILURE OF
THE ARGUMENTS: A
SYMPATHETIC APPRAISAL

In the debate about the existence of God there would seem to be only two plausible positions: either (a) there is some sound argument for the existence of God, and everybody ought to believe that God exists; or (b) there is no sound argument for the existence of God, and everyone ought to hold that the existence of God is improbable or, at best, highly problematic. The absence of an argument proving that something exists does not, of course, prove that the thing in question does not exist. It must be admitted, however, that the burden of proof rests with those who make the affirmative claim. (For example, I cannot prove that there are little two-headed green animals living on the planet Venus; there may well be, but sanity seems to require that I assume that there are none unless, or until, some evidence is produced to indicate that there are.)

I find myself in disagreement with both positions and therefore, I fear, my own position must, at first, seem somewhat strange. I hold, with the author of the last chapter, that there is no sound argument for the existence of God; but I also hold, with the authors of the previous three chapters, that God exists and His existence can be known by us. This position represents, I think, the only possible way in which the impasse between theists and naturalists concerning the problem of the existence of God can be overcome.

Arguments and Rational Grounds

One way of stating the position that I should like to defend is this: There are no sound *arguments* for the existence of God, but there are, nonetheless, valid *rational grounds* for believing in His existence. Naturalists are right in rejecting the arguments for the existence of God but wrong in denying His reality; theists are right in affirming the reality of God but wrong in insisting that His reality is capable of proof.

Strictly speaking, it is not possible to *prove* the reality of anything. Reality manifests itself to us, or it does not; only in the former case is it possible for us to know it. One cannot even prove the reality of the physical world, as the futile discussions between realists and phenomenalists over this very question show. Solipsism is the only consistent alternative to a direct cognition of the reality of that which manifests itself to us as real.

Few philosophers who have addressed themselves to the realist-phenomenalist controversy have realized, I suspect, that their reflections concerning that problem are intimately related to the question of our knowledge of the reality of God. But they are. The root question, in both cases, is, How do we cognize *reality*? How do we get beyond perception and feeling to an awareness of the reality of that which seems to lie behind them? The solution to both the realist-phenomenalist controversy and the problem of the reality of God depends on the answer to this question.

The chief obstacle to satisfactorily resolving these and a number of other related problems is the very limited (and limiting) concept of *reason* that prevails in our culture at the present time. In the great classical tradition of Western philosophy—and I include all of the major figures from the Golden Age of Greek philosophy down to and including the German Idealists of the nineteenth century—reason was conceived as the structure of the conscious self by virtue of which man is able both to grasp and to shape reality. It is one and the same reason, according to this view, that seeks to know the true, to love the good, and to appreciate the beautiful. Man, it is evident, relates to his world in a variety of ways, each qualitatively different from the others: he knows (cognition), he feels (emotion), he appreciates (taste), he strives (conation), he acts (practice). Reason, in the classical view, is the ground and locus of all of these; it expresses the unity of the self even as it acknowledges the multiplicity of its relations to the world.

In our culture, however, this concept of reason has been lost. Reason is regarded by most people today simply as man's capacity for *reasoning*. Its function is conceived to be purely cognitive, and all the other functions formerly assigned to reason are therefore judged to be "irrational." Feelings, it is alleged, may be appropriate or inappropriate, but they cannot be rational; acts may be discreet or indiscreet, but they cannot be right or wrong (consistent with or contrary to right reason). Even in its cognitive function, the scope of reason has been radically narrowed. To espouse a moral or aesthetic value is no longer to cognize something but simply to express a private taste. The whole business of reason is, in short, to attain scientific knowledge, and what is not scientific knowledge is not considered knowledge at all. It is, in other words, irrational.

If any culture were absolutely consistent in maintaining this view, the consequences would be truly appalling. The outstanding characteristics of such a culture would be an impressive degree of technical competence, that is, an ability to do an enormous variety of things exceedingly well, and a complete lack of conviction as to whether any of these things are really worth doing. People in such a culture would be (as F. Scott Fitzgerald once described himself) like a little boy alone in a big house, who now that he was free to do anything, suddenly discovered that there was nothing he wanted to do. The whole life of man, on such a view, must be made up of technical knowledge and totally irrational feelings and inclinations. Such technical knowledge could not even include a knowledge of the reality of the world toward which it is supposedly directed.

Fortunately, no culture, not even ours, has been absolutely consistent in maintaining this view; but ours has gone far in this direction. We are more than a little embarrassed about espousing values that cannot be defended "scientifically." We are reluctant to engage in public discussion of issues that do not admit of clear-cut factual answers—issues such as the responsible use of atomic power or the obligations of industrialized nations toward underdeveloped countries.

No argument for the existence of God can be successful, for argument does not belong to the level of reason where the reality of God is manifest. Argument belongs to the level of "technical" or "scientific" reason; it can take us no further. On this point, naturalism is right. But then, without making some gratuitous assumptions, no argument for the existence of anything else can succeed either. If we are to know of the reality of anything, reality must disclose itself to us; there is no other way.

Our knowledge of the reality of God might be described as "nontechnical," "nondiscursive," "nonargumentative," or even "nonscientific"— but not as "nonrational." Too much of what is of value in human life belongs to the deeper levels of reason to allow scientific reason alone to determine what is rational and what is not. That scientific reason is and must be supreme in its own sphere is an important truth that was established only after a long and bitter struggle (witness the experience of Galileo). That the sphere of scientific reason is limited is also an important truth, however, one our culture is dangerously close to forgetting. The penalty for ignoring the former was the temporary retardation of the progress of modern science, and that was most unfortunate. But the penalty for forgetting the latter would be an overwhelming sense of the futility of life, and that, if it occurred, would be disastrous. Man can abide discomfort, but robbed of meaning he is reduced to nothing.

The Self-Disclosure of God

Material reality manifests itself to us in sense experience. The reality of the tree that I see through my office window is disclosed in the very process by which I see it. I do not first have sense data and then infer that there is something "real" corresponding to them. Investigation, experimentation, and reasoning may tell me much about *what* it is, but they cannot tell me *that* it is. Either its reality is immediately evident to me or I must remain ignorant of it. Scientific reason cannot persuade me of the reality of the tree; indeed, it is only as this reality is given that scientific reason can begin its work.

Human reality manifests itself in *interpersonal communication,* notably in conversation. Scientific reason cannot demonstrate the existence of other minds: this is the inescapable conclusion of the endless discussions of this topic carried on ever since Hume. In love, in friendship, even in our relations with the countless people whose lives barely touch ours, the reality of other rational selves is manifest to us. Here we are more aware, perhaps, of the limitations of scientific reason than in the case of material objects, for we know full well that the richness of a human personality defies exhaustive description; we know, but sometimes we forget.

God manifests Himself to us in the event called *revelation.* I do not mean by this anything odd or unusual—nothing in the way of an "ecstatic vision" or anything of that sort. I mean simply that our longing that life shall have some significance, our desire that the future shall have some hope, and our anxiety over the transitoriness and insecurity of everything that we perceive are somehow overcome. I do not think that any human being is without this experience. There is a need, a longing, an anxiety, a concern, an emptiness in human life. Somehow, from deep within ourselves, these are overcome. The void is filled, and we find courage. This "finding of courage," or "being grasped by meanings," or "being sustained in the conviction of the significance of life" is what I mean by revelation. The source or ground of this experience is what we are talking about when we use the term "God."

Please note that I am *not* setting forth here another argument for the existence of God. I reject all such arguments, including the argument from religious experience. What I am saying is that at a level of our selves far deeper than that at which reasoning and argumentation occur, God discloses Himself to us. We are, all of us, implicitly aware of the reality of God. We may choose to call this reality by some other name—that is a very trivial matter. Or we may turn away from this deeper dimension of our selves and try to live without meaning and without courage—and that is not a trivial matter.

I have no serious quarrel with the definition of God suggested in the introductory chapter and basically adhered to by the other writers. The reality that is disclosed to us in the way I have described does, indeed, reveal itself as the ground of being and value. There can be little doubt that if and when we are moved to an act of worship, it is this reality that is the intended object of our devotion. But precisely because we are dealing with a reality that is apprehended by reason in its depth rather than by scientific reason, this concept is bound to be obscure. Theology is an attempt, among other things, to make the concept "God" more precise; but the best theologians know that you cannot give this concept scientific precision without robbing it of its deepest meaning. "The heart has its reasons, which reason does not know." [1] The "reasons of the heart" are not blind, irrational emotions. They are a function of reason itself in a dimension vastly more profound than that with which we engage in scientific "reasoning."

This matter of the inevitable obscurity of the concept "God" deserves to be emphasized more than it has been thus far. H. D. Lewis is right when he says:

> the skeptic and agnostic do not so much find themselves unconvinced that in fact there is a God as fail to see what is meant by "God"; and we cannot first tell them what we mean and then proceed to show that God is also real. If they can be induced to see what we mean when we speak of God they will at one and the same time be convinced of His existence . . .[2]

The chief difficulty in acknowledging the reality of God, however, is not the inescapable ambiguity of the concept; it is rather the fact that in popular religion the concept *has* been made precise, but in an absurdly childish way. Often, people who do not believe in the existence of a Bearded Father somewhere off in space mistakenly think that this constitutes disbelief in the existence of God. But the God who is the ground of being and value, whose reality is manifest to every person in the deepest reaches of his self, bears little or no resemblance to this Celestial Despot of popular fantasy. To deny the reality of the latter is to topple an idol and so to be on the side of God; to seriously deny the reality of the former is impossible.

Another Look at the Arguments

If, now, we look at the traditional arguments from the perspective developed briefly in this chapter, it is not difficult to see why the debate concerning them has been so inconclusive. The critics of the arguments have, quite rightly, found fault with their argumentative form; the supporters of the arguments have defended their implicit meaning. For reasons already given, the arguments cannot succeed *as arguments;* on this point the critics are right. But the arguments do express, albeit inadequately, the awareness of the reality of God that is embedded deep in the consciousness of every human being.

---

[1] Blaise Pascal, "Fragment 277," *Pensées* (New York: Everyman's Library, 1932), p. 78.

[2] H. D. Lewis, *Our Experience of God* (London: Allen & Unwin; New York: Macmillan, 1959), p. 44.

The ontological argument attempts to put this fundamental awareness of the reality of God into a form acceptable to scientific reason. It affirms, accordingly, that *the proposition "God exists" is self-evident*. This, as the critics of the ontological argument have pointed out, is not the case; hence, the argument is no good as an argument. But the self-disclosure of God to reason in its depth is not the same thing as the alleged self-evidence of the proposition "God exists." As an argument the ontological argument is a failure; but the insight that it intends to express in this very inadequate way is both true and important.

The cosmological argument seeks to express this same insight in a slightly different way. The truth of the cosmological argument is that we are aware, in the depth of our selves, of the reality of the ground of our being and of all being. But the cosmological argument distorts this fundamental insight by attempting to exhibit it to scientific reason as a bit of propositional knowledge that can be gotten by correct syllogistic reasoning. This, as the critics of the cosmological argument have correctly pointed out, cannot be done: the cosmological argument is no good as an argument. However, the insight that it is attempting to express and that no argument can adequately express is both true and important.

This insight is most weakly reflected in the teleological argument, which, at least in the form made popular by Paley and other writers in the eighteenth century, almost inevitably conjures up the image of an Ultimate Artisan going about the business of making a world. This conception expresses little, if anything, of what is meant by the concept "God." Often when we look upward on a starry night, there is indeed a sense of mystery, which is probably best understood as a momentary heightening of our awareness of the reality of the ground of all being; but very little of this sense of mystery carries over into the teleological argument itself. People who find the teleological argument impressive are not usually convinced by the argument as such. They respond to it because it directs their consideration to certain features of the universe that tend to enhance the awareness of God that all human beings have. If the argument does this for some people, to that extent it is of value; but its value is that of poetry, not logic.

Former Harvard president Nathan M. Pusey once said, "It would seem to me that the finest fruit of serious learning should be the ability to speak the word God without reserve or embarrassment, certainly without adolescent resentment; rather with some sense of communion, with reverence and with joy." [3] To do this we must rid ourselves of concepts and images that make God into a thing among things, whose existence is accordingly open to question. Even our secular age knows, though it does not acknowledge, that there *is* a depth of reason and of

---

[3] Nathan M. Pusey, *The Age of the Scholar* (Cambridge, Mass.: Harvard University Press, 1963), p. 145.

reality. Without this awareness there would be no sense of worth, destiny, or hope. When we learn once again that it is at this level of our being that the reality of God is manifest, we shall learn "to speak the word God without reserve or embarrassment . . . ; rather with some sense of communion, with reverence and with joy."

STUDY QUESTIONS

1. How does the author of this chapter propose to overcome "the impasse between theists and naturalists concerning the problem of the existence of God"?
2. What exactly is the distinction drawn in this chapter between *arguments* and *rational grounds*?
3. What do you make of the discussion of the various dimensions of reason? Is it true that there is a tendency today to limit reason to what is here called "scientific reason"? Are you at all persuaded by the suggestion that there are dimensions of reason other than the "scientific"?
4. Is it correct to say that existence is not capable of demonstration—that either we must recognize it directly or else be ignorant of it? Is this true, for example, of our knowledge of the existence of physical objects? of other minds?
5. What does the author of this chapter mean by "revelation"? Is this, in fact, another argument for the existence of God?
6. Is there, as this writer affirms, an analogy between this problem and the realist-phenomenalist controversy?

Alston, William P. "The Ontological Argument Revisited," *The Philosophical Review*, 69 (1960), 454–474.

Anselm of Canterbury. *Proslogium*, in S. N. Deane, *Anselm*, 2nd ed. LaSalle, Ill.: Open Court, 1962.

Aquinas, St. Thomas. *Summa Theologica*. Many editions. See Part I, Question 2.

Bowker, John. *The Sense of God: Sociological, Anthropological, and Psychological Approaches to the Origin of the Sense of God.* Oxford: Clarendon Press, 1973.

Brown, Patterson. "St. Thomas' Doctrine of Necessary Being," *The Philosophical Review*, 73 (1964), 76–90.

Ducasse, C. J. *A Philosophical Scrutiny of Religion.* New York: Ronald Press, 1953.

Ebersole, Frank B. "Whether Existence Is a Predicate," *The Journal of Philosophy*, 60 (1963), 509–524.

Ewing, A. C. *The Fundamental Questions of Philosophy.* New York: Macmillan, 1951, chap. 11.

Flew, Antony. *God and Philosophy.* London: Hutchinson, 1966. Detailed critique of arguments for theism.

Harris, E. E. *Revelation Through Reason.* London: G. Allen & Unwin, 1959.

Hartshorne, Charles. *Anselm's Discovery: Re-examination of the Ontological Proof of God's Existence.* LaSalle, Ill.: Open Court, 1966.

————. *The Logic of Perfection and Other Essays in Neoclassical Metaphysics.* LaSalle, Ill.: Open Court, 1962.

————, and W. L. Reese. *Philosophers Speak of God.* Chicago: University of Chicago Press, 1963 (paperbound).

Hawkins, D. J. B. *The Essentials of Theism.* London: Sheed and Ward, 1949.

Hick, John. "God as Necessary Being," *The Journal of Philosophy*, 57 (1960), 725–734.

Hume, David. *Dialogues Concerning Natural Religion*, ed. by Norman Kemp Smith. Indianapolis, Ind.: Liberal Arts Press, 1962 (paperbound).

Hurlbutt, Robert H. *Hume, Newton and the Design Argument.* Lincoln, Nebr.: University of Nebraska Press, 1966.

Jack, Henry. "A Recent Attempt to Prove God's Existence," *Philosophy and Phenomenological Research*, 25 (1965), 575–579.

Kant, Immanuel. *Critique of Pure Reason*, tr. by Norman Kemp Smith. New York: St. Martin's Press, 1965 (paperbound). See section entitled, "The Ideal of Pure Reason."

Kenny, Anthony. *The Five Ways: St. Thomas Aquinas' Proofs of God's Existence.* London: Routledge and Kegan Paul, 1969. Detailed analysis by a competent and sympathetic critic.

Lewis, H. D. *Our Experience of God.* London: G. Allen & Unwin; New York: Macmillan, 1959.

McIntyre, John. *St. Anselm and His Critics.* Edinburgh, Scot.: Oliver and Boyd, 1954.

Malcolm, Norman. "Anselm's Ontological Arguments," *The Philosophical Review*, 69 (1960), 41–62.

Martin, C. B. *Religious Belief.* Ithaca, N.Y.: Cornell University Press, 1959.

Mascall, E. L. *Existence and Analogy.* London: Longmans, Green, 1949.

Mavrodes, George I. (ed.). *The Rationality of Belief in God.* Englewood Cliffs, N.J.: Prentice-Hall, 1970.

Mill, John Stuart. *Three Essays on Religion.* New York: Henry Holt, 1874.

Paley, William. *Evidences of the Existence and Attributes of the Deity.* Many editions. Originally published in 1802.

Plantinga, A. (ed.). *The Ontological Argument from St. Anselm to Contemporary Philosophers.* Garden City, N.Y.: Doubleday, 1965 (paperbound).

Reichenbach, B. R. *The Cosmological Argument: A Reassessment.* Springfield, Ill.: Charles C Thomas, 1972. Sympathetic to this type of argument.

Smart, Ninian. *Philosophers and Religious Truth.* New York: Macmillan, 1970 (paperbound).

————. *Reasons and Faiths.* New York: Humanities Press, 1958.

Smith, J. E. *The Analogy of Experience.* New York: Harper & Row, 1973. A point of view somewhat similar to the last chapter in this unit.

Taylor, R. *With Heart and Mind.* New York: St. Martin's Press, 1973. Again, somewhat similar to the last chapter in this unit.

Tillich, Paul. *Systematic Theology*, vol. 1. Chicago: University of Chicago Press, 1951, pp. 204–235.

Torrance, Thomas F. *God and Rationality.* New York: Oxford University Press, 1971.

PART V

THE PROBLEM
OF EVIL

22

GOD AND EVIL

Shortly before his death Robert F. Kennedy published a book bearing the title *To Seek a Better World*, in which he discussed various programs that he believed should be adopted in order to cure some of the major ills of society. Ironically, Senator Kennedy himself fell victim to the violence that has been one of the characteristic ills of recent years, and the search for a better world was left to others.

Can you and I not imagine a world better than the one we know? Surely we can. We can imagine a world, for example, in which there would be no illness, no suffering, no starvation, no violence, no death. In such a world parents would not have to stand helplessly by as the bodies of their children waste away under the onslaught of some dread disease, nor would children be left homeless and orphaned, innocent victims of the ravages of war. There would be no earthquakes, no hurricanes, no floods, in such a world, for nature would be congenial to human life. And the Kennedy brothers and Martin Luther King, Jr., would not have been cut down in the prime of life by the bullets of three assassins. Every time we support a "cause," every time we seek constructive change—whether we seek a cure for cancer, try to find a solution to poverty, work for improved government, long for peace—we are affirming our belief in the possibility of a better world.

No doubt, if a group of us were to discuss this matter thoroughly we would disagree in some respects about what would constitute an "ideal" world. You might insist, for example, that everyone in the world should subscribe to the principles of a certain political party, or the creed of a certain church—and I might very well contend with you on this. Or you might be willing to allow certain lifestyles which someone else feels should not be tolerated in an "ideal" world. We are, after all, amateurs in the art of world-making and some disagreement is to be expected. Certainly, however, we can agree that the things we have enumerated above—illness, suffering, starvation, violence, death—would not exist in an "ideal" world, and that he who works to eradicate these things from human life, who visits the sick or feeds the hungry or comforts the suffering or works for peace or restores life to those who are dying, is doing a good work. In this respect, surely, we would be in agreement about what would constitute a perfect world.

In whatever degree the world is less than perfect, to that degree the world is "evil." Evil is that which takes the place of a good that can be conceived to exist but that cannot come into being unless the evil is destroyed: it is to good as illness is to health, hunger to satiety, death to life. Let all evil be destroyed, and this would be a perfect world.

Evil as a Problem

The problem of evil arises for any world-view that affirms that the universe is constituted in such a way that we might reasonably expect that it would contain no evil. If the universe is the result of the mindless working of purely natural forces, as naturalism affirms, then it is not surprising that the world is the way it is. If, however, the universe as we know it is the creation of a God who is all-knowing, all-powerful, and all-good, then it *is* surprising that there is evil in the world; for one would expect that such a God, if He is going to create a world at all, would create a *good* one. Indeed, one would expect Him to create a perfect world, a world containing no evil of any kind.

The dilemma facing the theist may be stated as follows. According to traditional theism, all of the following statements are true:

1. God is perfectly good.
2. God's power is unlimited (i.e., He is omnipotent).
3. God is all-knowing (omniscient).
4. God is the sole creator of everything that exists.
5. There is evil in the world.

Note that if any one of these statements is held to be false, the problem disappears. If, for example, one denies that God is perfectly good, then the occurrence of evil can be understood as a consequence of God's willing it to exist. If one denies that God's power is unlimited, then God can be absolved of responsibility for evil on the ground that He did His best. If God's omniscience is denied, He can be excused on grounds of ignorance. If He is only a cocreator of the world, then perhaps evil can be attributed to the other creator(s) (though this apparently entails a denial of God's goodness, omniscience, or omnipotence as well). And finally, if one denies that there really is evil in the world, there is nothing left to be explained.

David Hume once put the theist's dilemma like this: "Is God willing to prevent evil, but not able? then is he impotent. Is he able but not willing? then is he malevolent. Is he both able and willing? whence then is evil?" [1] *How is the fact of evil in the world to be reconciled with belief in a creator who is perfect in goodness, knowledge, and power?* That is the problem with which we shall be concerned in the present section.

The technical name for an essay or treatise that attempts to achieve such a reconciliation is *theodicy.* A number of theodicies have been written by such writers as St. Augustine, Leibnitz, and F. R. Tennant. Chapter 23, "The Exoneration of God," summarizes the principal arguments usually put forward by theodocists. The following chapter, "A Skeptical Rejoinder," subjects these arguments to a critical analysis and concludes that they are unsuccessful.

Solutions Not Open to Theists

Before turning to a consideration of the principal attempts by theists to reconcile the apparent contradiction between their theological beliefs and the fact of evil, it may be useful to review two philosophically interesting "solutions" to this problem that are not available to the theist.

The first of these is the solution offered by Plato. In his great creation myth *Timaeus*,[2] Plato depicts the originator of the material world as a divine Craftsman who makes the ordered universe out of preexisting matter according to a plan, or "blueprint," of a perfect world. The Craftsman, says Plato, is perfectly good: His desire in making the world is to create an absolutely perfect world, one in which there would be no evil of any kind. If He could succeed in making the material world according to this plan, it would in fact be a perfect world. Why, then, is there evil in the world? Because, says Plato, the matter with which the Craftsman has to work contains a certain resistance to order which He cannot wholly overcome. God did the best He could, says Plato—no evil that exists is to be ascribed to Him—but His best was simply not sufficient to mold a recalcitrant matter into an altogether perfect world. Thus there is evil in the world.

Such an explanation of evil is, of course, not acceptable to a theist for at least two reasons. First, it denies the omnipotence of God, for according to traditional theism, God can do anything that does not imply a contradiction. Second, it assumes that matter is itself eternal (or at any rate, not a product of God's creative activity), and thus denies that God is "Creator of heaven and earth, and of all things visible and invisible" (Nicene Creed).[3] Indeed, from the point of view of traditional theism this

---

[1] David Hume, *Dialogues Concerning Natural Religion*, ed. Henry D. Aiden (New York: Hafner, 1957), p. 66.

[2] See B. Jowett (ed.), *The Dialogues of Plato* (New York: Random House, 1937), vol. II, pp. 13–14.

[3] The Nicene Creed is one of three ancient creeds of the Christian church (the other two

account is objectionable in yet another way, for the plan according to which Plato's Craftsman is said to have formed the world is also independent of the Craftsman; it is a preexisting plan that the Craftsman, like a builder who is not his own architect, must follow as best he can.

Another philosophically interesting explanation of evil is that offered by an ancient Persian religion called Zoroastrianism (also known as Zarathustrianism), according to which the world as we know it is the joint creation of a good deity (Ahura Mazda) and an evil deity (Angra Mainyu). All that is good in the world is due to the former, all that is evil, to the latter. Every human life is a battleground for the struggle between these two deities, which is to say, the struggle between good and evil. In the end, according to Zoroastrianism, the evil deity will be conquered, and evil will be destroyed forever; but in the meantime, life and history must be lived out in a world where good and evil are intermingled in countless ways.

Although to some people this account could be made quite acceptable by the simple expedient of substituting the more familiar names Jehovah and Satan for Ahura Mazda and Angra Mainyu, it requires but little reflection to see that it cannot be reconciled with traditional theism, for roughly the same reasons that Plato's account is unacceptable to theism. If God is conceived as the Creator of everything that exists, then it is no more acceptable to affirm the existence "from the beginning" of an evil deity (whatever be his name) than it is to affirm the eternal existence of a recalcitrant matter. Moreover, if God is indeed infinite in power, there does not seem to be any reason for Him to delay until some unknown (but presumably remote) future date the final overthrow of evil.

In the final analysis, then, Platonism and Zoroastrianism both explain the existence of evil by affirming an ultimate ethical dualism. God is thereby relieved of responsibility for evil in the world—and of the possibility of being proclaimed omnipotent and Creator of everything that is.

Whatever may be said in favor of ethical dualism as an explanation of the existence of evil, therefore, it is evident that such an explanation is not acceptable to theism. Hume's taunt remains: Is God both able and willing to prevent evil? *"Whence then is evil?"* Let us see how a theist might attempt to take up this challenge, and how a critic might respond to such an attempt.

STUDY QUESTIONS

1. What is the meaning of the term "evil"? What characteristic(s) must something have in order to be properly described as evil?
2. What, exactly, is the *problem* of evil? For whom does this problem arise? For whom does it not arise?

being the Apostles Creed and the Athanasian Creed). It dates from the Council of Constantinople, held in 381.

3. What is Plato's solution to the problem of evil? Why is it not acceptable to a theist?
4. What is the Zoroastrian solution to the problem? Why is it not acceptable to a theist?

23

THE EXONERATION
OF GOD

That there is evil in the world obviously constitutes a serious problem for theism, for it does indeed appear to be a contradiction to say that our imperfect world is the creation of a God who is perfect in knowledge and power and goodness. The contradiction might be stated thus:

> If God is perfect in knowledge, power, and goodness, then any work that He performs or has performed will be altogether good.
> This universe is a work that God has performed, but it is not altogether good.
> Nonetheless, God is perfect in knowledge, power, and goodness.

How shall we resolve the contradiction? Shall we deny the first premise? That does not seem very promising, since one would then be in the position of asserting that God directly and knowingly causes evil. Shall we deny the second premise? It appears that we cannot do that either, for it merely affirms that the universe is God's creation, and that there is evil in it. How then can we avoid drawing the conclusion that God must be lacking in knowledge, power, or goodness?

Apparent Evil and Real Evil

The first observation that I wish to make is that *some things that we call evil are merely things that are not to our liking*. In some respects we are all like the little child who cries bitterly because his mother will not allow him to have everything he wants. We desire something and count it an evil that other people possess it and we do not. Or we desire to do something—to play tennis, let us say—and we count it an evil that the weather does not cooperate. Much of our muttering about evil is nothing more than the tantrum behavior of God's spoiled children.

Some philosophers have gone so far as to say that *everything* that we call evil is, rightly considered, simply that which is contrary to our wishes. "The perfection of things," said Spinoza, "is to be reckoned only from their own nature and power; things are not more or less perfect, according as they delight or offend human senses, or according as they are serviceable or repugnant to mankind." [1] One suspects, however, that the victims of Auschwitz or Hiroshima or My Lai might find this view a bit difficult to swallow.

We who would "justify the ways of God to man," as John Milton put it, must be careful that in our great concern to exonerate God we do not become insensitive to the reality of pain and suffering in the world. There *is* evil in the world, and our clear duty as human beings is to help bear the burden of those who suffer evil, and to do all in our power to eliminate it. Yet we should recognize that some things perceived as evil are not really so, but are simply the consequence of our desiring more in the way of pleasure or possessions than it is reasonable for us to expect.

Evil as an Instrumental Good

Second, I would observe that *some things that are indeed evil in and of themselves are nonetheless productive of a good that could not have been produced in any other way.* We clearly recognize this principle in the case of surgery: the pain experienced by the patient, considered simply as an instance of suffering on the part of a sentient creature, is certainly evil; but it is an evil that is willingly endured because it is a means to a good end, that is, healing and health.

What I am suggesting, then, is that evil may play a role in the total economy of the universe analogous to the role of pain in the process of surgery. The patience that comes through enduring hardship over a long period of time, the joy that accompanies the achievement of a long-sought goal—these would not be possible in the absence of all difficulty and want. It is not unthinkable that God in His infinite wisdom should have allowed some evil in the world so that He might use it for man's moral training and thus for his ultimate good.

Evil as a Logical Corollary of Good

Third, I would point out that *some things that are indeed evil are logical corollaries of certain goods.* Consider, for example, the virtues of compassion, sympathy, and generosity. A world having these qualities is clearly better than one devoid of them. Yet, these virtues would be nonexistent in a world in which there was no pain, no suffering, no want of any kind.

---

[1] Benedict Spinoza, *The Ethics,* Appendix to Part I, in *The Rationalists* (Garden City: Doubleday, undated), p. 215.

The point, of course, must not be overdrawn. There is obviously much suffering, much want, much sorrow, that does not call forth any such corollary sentiment or act of love. Moreover, it is extremely difficult to say what measure of, say, compassion would morally compensate for a given quantity of want or pain. All I wish to suggest is that there are some undoubted goods that could not exist without the correlative evils, and it is quite possible that a world lacking those goods *and* evils would in fact be poorer than the world as it is.

Evil as a Consequence of Human Actions

A more profound understanding of the occurrence of evil in the world begins, however, when we recognize that *much of the evil in the world is man's doing, and could have been prevented by God only at the price of making us all automata.* Consider for a moment how very much of what we normally regard as evil in the world is accounted for by (*a*) individual human acts of cruelty, (*b*) war, and (*c*) man-made social structures and customs that enable the strong to oppress the weak. If we who are so quick to point an accusing finger at God could only eliminate from this world the evil that *we ourselves* do, the evil that would remain to be explained would be but a fraction of that which we now observe.

It is of course true that God could have prevented all the evil attributable to man had He simply made him incapable of doing evil. Such a creature, however, would hardly be worthy of being called a man, for he would be like the lower animals in that he would do everything by necessity rather than by free choice. And the universe, which would then be rid of all the evil that is now caused by man, would lack that remarkable being who is certainly the crowning glory of God's creation by virtue of the fact that he can *freely choose* to do the good.

Consider a simple analogy. As a parent, I desire that my child should be spared as much pain and sorrow as possible when he goes out into the world. Now it would be theoretically possible for me (though admittedly grotesque) to protect him from whatever dangers may await him out in the world by literally *imprisoning* him in my home, and perhaps "brainwashing" him from childhood to believe that life within the confines of one small house is quite enough for him. But though my child would in this way be spared some things that might indeed be painful and unpleasant, no one in his right mind would approve of my treating him in this way. Why? Because it is the universal judgment of mankind that to be deprived of one's freedom—even the freedom to be hurt—is an incomparable loss, and that freedom with its concomitant dangers is preferable to the kind of safety that can be purchased only at the price of giving up one's freedom. I demonstrate my love for my child, not by absolutely preventing him from being harmed, but by giving him his freedom in the hope that he will use it in ways that prove to be for his good.

If it is granted that the creation of beings capable of doing either good or evil is consistent with belief in a God who is perfect in knowledge, power, and goodness, then it is possible to extend the same reasoning to account for *all* evil in the world, not just that directly attributable to man. For according to a very ancient teaching, the whole creation as we know it is "fallen" from its original perfect state, and all the evil that we observe is a result of its fallenness. The precise nature of this fall from an original perfection is admittedly a mystery, and I shall not pretend to be able to trace every example of evil in the world to a specific aspect of the rebellion against the Creator that is the essence of the idea of the fall. To one who is sincerely seeking a solution to the agonizing problem of evil, however, the doctrine of the fall is a highly plausible and strangely comforting doctrine. Indeed, it is, in the last analysis, the only possible explanation of why there is evil in a creation that was once pronounced "very good" by its Creator.

The Best of All Possible Worlds

The proposition that we must finally defend if we would convincingly exonerate God of blame for the evil in the world is the proposition that this is the best of all *possible* worlds. God could have willed not to create any world at all, in which case He alone—He who is infinitely good—would exist. Or He could have created any one of an infinite number of possible worlds which He did not in fact create. Undoubtedly among those possible worlds that God chose not to create are some that would have been free of everything that we call evil. Why, then, did God choose to create this world, knowing (as He must have known) that it would contain much evil? The only possible answer is that of all the worlds He might have created, the one He did create—this one—contains more total good than any other world that He could have created. "The best plan," said Leibnitz, "is not always that which seeks to avoid evil, since it may happen that *the evil be accompanied by a greater good.*" [2]

It is of course easy for us to sit back smugly and say (in the spirit of Voltaire), "How can this be the best of all possible worlds when it contains such horrors as Auschwitz and My Lai? Even *I* can imagine a better world than that!" The problem is that we *cannot* really imagine a better world than that *because we do not know all the ways that God would have had to alter the design of the world in order to ensure that such things did not occur.* We are all Monday-morning quarterbacks when it comes to the game of world-making.

Consider, for example, the assassination of President Kennedy. I do not deny that this was an evil thing, for the violent death of a human being whenever it occurs is a tragedy that mars the perfection of the

---

[2] Gottfried W. Leibnitz, *The Philosophical Works of Leibnitz*, tr. George M. Duncan (New York: Tuttle, Morehouse and Taylor, 1890), p. 195.

world. Undoubtedly, in my view, God in His omniscience knew "from the beginning" that this tragedy was going to occur, and could in fact have created the world in such a way that it would not occur. But what would God have had to do in order to prevent it? It is impossible for us to say. Perhaps, as I suggested earlier, He would have had to deprive all men of their freedom in order to prevent a Lee Harvey Oswald from exercising his freedom with such tragic consequences. Or perhaps, like a celestial Superman who always manages to deflect the bullet before it reaches its intended target, He would have had to personally intervene whenever man's misused freedom was about to produce some evil result—with the further consequence, perhaps, that man would never learn to use his freedom responsibly, since God would always be seeing to it that no matter what he did, things turned out right.

Now, to say that we would prefer a world without freedom or a world with a "Divine Intervener" to the world as it actually is would be simply naïve, not because we positively know that such a world would be inferior to the world as it is, but precisely because we do *not* have a sufficient knowledge of what such a world would be like to say that it would be preferable to this one. It certainly appears that such a world would be inferior to the actual world at least in this, that it would lack some of the undoubted goods that this world clearly does contain; but that is not the point I am chiefly trying to make. The main point is that the concept of an alternative world is so complex that we can never know whether the difference we glibly say we would prefer, *together with all of the other differences that this would entail in the infinitely complex system of the world,* would yield a world that would in fact be preferable to the world as it is.

The Contradiction Revisited

Returning now to the apparent contradiction with which we began, it is evident that the thrust of our argument is to challenge the assertion that "if God is perfect in knowledge, power, and goodness, then any work that He performs or has performed will be altogether good." We have argued, rather, that any work that God performs will be productive of a greater *total* good than any alternative work that He might have performed. In order to show God blameworthy for the evil in the world, therefore, a critic would have to describe in complete detail an alternative world, a possible world, containing more total good than we find in the world as it actually is. It seems to me that this is in principle impossible, both because of the limitations of our knowledge of the world and because we cannot predict how much good will yet emerge in the infinite future that is revealed to us but one moment at a time; from which it follows that no one can ever be in a position to criticize God for making the world the way He did.

STUDY QUESTIONS

1. "Everything that we call evil is, rightly considered, simply that which is contrary to our wishes." Attack or defend this statement.
2. Is God "exonerated" to the extent that some evil can be shown to be a necessary condition of the existence of some good? Defend your answer.
3. Is it true that a world in which there are human beings who exhibit the virtues of compassion, sympathy, and generosity is better than one in which no such qualities would be present? What relevance does your answer have for the controversy concerning the problem of evil?
4. "The creation of beings capable of doing either good or evil is consistent with belief in a God who is perfect in knowledge, power, and goodness." Attack or defend this statement.
5. Theodicist argues that, contrary to what might appear to be the case, we cannot in fact imagine a better world than the one that actually exists. Summarize his argument in support of this proposition.

24

A SKEPTICAL REJOINDER

As I read Theodicist's "exoneration" I was reminded of a famous passage in David Hume's *Dialogues Concerning Natural Religion* in which Philo (a principal spokesman in the *Dialogues*) likens the world to a house or palace so ill-planned that "there [is] not one apartment convenient or agreeable." It simply would not do in such a case, says Philo, for the architect to point out that if this or that feature of the structure were altered, even greater ills would result. Philo continues:

> What [the architect] says may be strictly true: the alteration of one particular, while the other parts of the building remain, may only augment the inconveniences. But still you would assert in general that, if the architect had had skill and good intentions, he might have formed such a plan of the whole, and might have adjusted the parts in such a manner as would have remedied all or most of these inconveniences.[1]

Philo expresses precisely my own sentiments as I prepare to respond to the arguments of the preceding chapter. I concede that the problem is more complex than it might initially appear to be. Before one considers the matter carefully, one is indeed inclined to say that it is self-evident that the occurrence of evil in the world is inconsistent with belief in a God who is perfect in knowledge, power, and goodness. Theodicist's arguments at least succeed in destroying this illusion of self-evidence. But do they really succeed in "exonerating" God of blame for the evil that is in the world? I think they do not. Let me explain why.

Moral Evil and Natural Evil

Philosophers who are concerned with the problem of evil make a distinction—an important one for our purposes—between *moral* evil

---

[1] David Hume, *Dialogues Concerning Natural Religion*, ed. Henry D. Aiken (New York: Hafner, 1957), p. 72.

and *natural* evil. Any evil that occurs as a result of man's deliberate doing is termed moral evil. Any evil that occurs as a result of the ordinary working of natural laws is termed natural evil. An act of murder would be a typical example of the former, animal suffering (other than that inflicted by man) an example of the latter. There is nothing difficult about this distinction, and everyone can easily supply additional examples of both types from his own knowledge and experience.

There are, to be sure, instances of evil that appear to be "mixed" evils, that is, both natural and moral in certain respects. Suppose, for example, that a building contractor (perhaps with the collusion of the fire-safety inspector) constructs a building that he knows does not meet certain standards of fire safety, and suppose further that the building is struck by lightning with an ensuing fire that results in serious injury and loss of life. Are the suffering and death in this case instances of natural or of moral evil? The answer appears to be that they are both. The building contractor is culpable because he knowingly subjected the inhabitants of the building to a hazard that he could have and should have prevented, though he did not explicitly will that the building should catch on fire or that his negligence should lead to suffering and death. The occurrence of lightning, however, is a natural phenomenon that sometimes causes suffering and death even in the absence of any negligence such as we have just described, and the fact that human negligence was a contributing factor in this particular case does not prevent this from being an instance of natural evil as well. Again, it would not be difficult to invent (or perhaps recall) numerous additional examples of evils that appear to be the joint product of man's negligence or evildoing and natural occurrences.

For our present purposes, however, we need not be concerned about these instances of mixed (natural and moral) evils. There are plenty of examples of *un*mixed evils of both kinds to support the distinction, and once we have the distinction clearly in mind, we may begin to see what is wrong with Theodicist's account.

God and Moral Evil

Consider first Theodicist's account as it applies to moral evil, which is the kind that he appears to have principally in mind. All such evil, he says, may be understood as a consequence of man's misuse of his God-given freedom. But is not God then blameworthy for having made man capable of misusing his freedom in this way? No, says Theodicist, for a world in which there are creatures who have the freedom to choose good *or* evil is intrinsically better than one in which there are no such free creatures, even though the latter world would be free of all moral evil. Indeed, if we are to take Theodicist's second argument seriously, he seems to be suggesting that the occurrence of moral evil is only an episode in the moral training of man—that evil is really good in the way that surgery is, because it leads to a good result that could be gotten in no other way.

But I must ask, Is not Theodicist forgetting that the God whose innocence he is trying to establish is supposed to be omnipotent? How then can he say that the good things that God is allegedly trying to accomplish by subjecting the world to the "surgery" of evil "could not have been produced in any other way"? If God is omnipotent, then He can do anything that does not imply a contradiction. Why, then, could God not have created man *already morally trained,* thus by-passing the horrors of assault and murder and oppression and war and the whole long litany of woes that result from man's terrible inhumanity to man? Where is the contradiction in that? If a surgeon were capable of producing health without subjecting his patient to the pain of surgery, we would not think well of him if he put his patient through the operation anyway. How, then, is God, if He is omnipotent, not blame-worthy for subjecting His creatures to the consequences of man's cruelty when presumably He could have achieved His end without such terrible means?

Theodicist says that we can never "be in a position to criticize God for making the world the way He did" because we do not know all the ways that God would have had to alter the design of the world in order to ensure that evil did not occur. Note, however, that Theodicist's "moral training" argument posits a world at some future time that *is* better than this world at the present time by virtue of the "moral training" that is supposed to occur between now and then. I admit the ignorance with which Theodicist charges all of us. I confess that I do not know how to alter the system of the world to make it better—less evil—than it is. But God apparently does, for He is using evil (says Theodicist) "for man's moral training and thus for his ultimate good." But why, if He is omnipotent, does He not produce this good result immediately, without all that suffering in between? Why must an omnipotent God act like an irresponsible surgeon?

God and Natural Evil

If Theodicist's arguments fall short of exonerating God with respect to the occurrence of moral evil, they are even less adequate as an attempt to explain the occurrence of natural evil in the world.

Consider, for example, animal suffering. If we pay attention to the terror and the suffering, the history of the evolution of animals is one of the most depressing stories imaginable. Think of it! Millions upon millions of sentient creatures were cast forth into a world in which the prevailing law was simply "The fit shall survive for awhile, the unfit shall perish immediately." Countless millions of creatures were able to survive for but a moment in such a hostile world before becoming the prey of other animals whose own survival depended upon using them for food. And if one of them happened to survive, he in turn sought out other animals that were *his* natural prey, and terrorized and killed them even as he would eventually be terrorized and killed by his natural enemies. The present state of affairs in the animal world is just the same: the strong prey upon the weak, species is at war with species, terror and suffering and violent death are the rule rather than the exception.

How do Theodicist's arguments speak to this dimension of the problem? They hardly touch it, so far as I can see. Animal suffering certainly is not something that can be dismissed as a mere "apparent evil" (argument 1). It can hardly be said to make any contribution to man's moral training (argument 2). It is difficult to see what goods might be "corollaries" of such suffering (argument 3). Theodicist must be arguing, then, that animal suffering is somehow a characteristic of a world that is "fallen" from its original state of perfection, and that such suffering is somehow consistent with the idea that this world is nonetheless the best of all *possible* worlds.

I do not want to caricature Theodicist's view of the matter, but in all honesty I do not see how it can reasonably be argued that the "law of the jungle" with all the animal suffering that it entails, is a consequence of the "fallenness" of the world, or how that would absolve God of responsibility even if it were the case. It is a basic fact of every ecosystem that *life feeds upon life.* It is only in the poet's imagination that the lion and the lamb live at peace with one another: In the real world the lion who will not eat an innocent lamb dies of starvation, and the less peace-loving sort live on to propagate the species. In a world capable of sustaining only a finite number (albeit a very large number) of living beings, every living thing is potentially at war with every other living thing. A world "before the fall" in which all of God's creatures lived together in a presumed perfect harmony defies imagination.

Moreover, even if such a state of affairs could be imagined, there is nothing in Theodicist's account to explain why God is not responsible for the animal suffering that is said to be a feature of the "fallenness" of this world. What has the lamb done to deserve a cruel death in the clutches of a hungry lion? Nothing. What has the lion done to deserve the spear of the man whose lamb he has just killed? Nothing. If the "fall" occurred as a result of *man's* rebellion against God, then it is unjust that animals should suffer the consequences of that fall. And is not He who is reputed to have set the rules for this whole sorry game then guilty of a terrible injustice? Is it not implausible—really implausible—to argue that this world in which most animals (though innocent of any wrongdoing) live a pitifully short life characterized by terror, suffering, and violent death is *the best of all possible worlds?*

Nor is animal suffering by any means the only kind of natural evil that cries out for a better explanation than Theodicist has given us. Who is responsible for the famine that is ravaging the inhabitants of central

Africa at this very hour? How shall we explain the suffering and death that result from such natural occurrences as hurricanes and earthquakes in a world that is supposed to be the handiwork of a God who is perfect in knowledge, power, and goodness? What account can be given of the occurrence of disease in the best of all possible worlds? We search in vain through all the theodicies that have been written for an answer that will stand the test of careful scrutiny, but always we come away as empty-handed as we began. Evil simply *does not make sense* in a world whose creator is all that God is said to be.

God and Evil

We must conclude, therefore, that the fact that there is evil in the world cannot be reconciled with belief in a God who is perfect in knowledge, power, and goodness. If we believe in the existence of God—and in the absence of such a belief we ought to have no interest in this problem— then we must reexamine our *concept* of God to see if we cannot bring it into conformity with the facts. Can we accept the idea of a God whose knowledge, though great, is limited? Then God may be excused for the evil that is in the world on grounds of ignorance. Can we live with the idea of a God whose power, though great, is less than infinite? Then God may be excused for the evil that is in the world on the ground that He did the best He could—and we may dare to hope that in the very long run evil will be overcome. These, it would appear, are our only alternatives, for it would hardly be exculpatory to suggest that there is evil in the world because God's goodness is limited. He who would believe in God in a world such as ours must, therefore, choose between a God who is limited in knowledge and one who is limited in power. Or else he must live with the recognition that deep within his world-view there is a contradiction between his knowledge of the world and his beliefs about God, a contradiction that is and will forever remain unresolved.

STUDY QUESTIONS

1. How does Skeptic propose to distinguish between "moral evil" and "natural evil"? Is this a valid distinction? What relevance (if any) does it have for the discussion of the problem of evil?
2. Skeptic asks, "Why must an omnipotent God act like an irresponsible surgeon?" Translate this rhetorical question into an argument against Theodicist's position.
3. Does Theodicist's argument provide a way to account for animal suffering? disease? natural disasters? Are these unexplainable evils, as Skeptic implies?
4. "He who would believe in God in a world such as ours must . . . choose between a God who is limited in knowledge and one who is limited in power." Is this correct? If not, what are the remaining alternatives?

FOR FURTHER READING

Adams, Robert Merrihew. "Must God Create the Best?" *The Philosophical Review*, 81 (1972), 317–332.

Ahorn, M. B. *The Problem of Evil*. New York: Schocken Books, 1971. Argues that the problem of evil leaves the existence of God an undecided issue.

Augustine, St. *On Free Will*. Several editions.

————. *The Nature of the Good*. Several editions.

Bayle, Pierre. *Bayle's Historical and Critical Dictionary—Selections*, ed. by Richard Popkin. Indianapolis, Ind.: Bobbs-Merrill, 1965 (paperbound). Contains Bayle's objection to theism based on the problem of evil. Leibnitz seeks to answer Bayle in his theodicy.

Farrer, Austin. *Love Almighty and Ills Unlimited*. Garden City, N.Y.: Doubleday, 1961.

Ferre, Nels. *Evil and the Christian Faith*. New York: Harper & Row, 1947. A defense of theism.

Hick, John. *Evil and the God of Love*. New York: Harper & Row, 1966. From a theistic standpoint.

Hume, David. *Dialogues Concerning Natural Religion*, ed. by Norman Kemp Smith. Indianapolis, Ind.: Liberal Arts Press, 1962 (paperbound). See Parts 10 and 11.

Leibnitz, G. W. *Theodicy*, tr. by D. M. Huggard, ed. by Diogenes Allen. Indianapolis, Ind.: Bobbs-Merrill, 1966.

Lewis, C. S. *The Problem of Pain*. New York: Macmillan, 1962. A readable defence of theism.

Madden, E. H., and P. H. Hare. *Evil and the Concept of God*. Springfield, Ill.: Charles C Thomas, 1968. Critical of theism.

Mill, John Stuart. *Three Essays on Religion*. New York: Henry Holt, 1874.

Pike, Nelson (ed.). *God and Evil*. Englewood Cliffs, N.J.: Prentice-Hall, 1964 (paperbound). Contains Pike's reply to Hume.

PART VI

RELIGIOUS LANGUAGE

25

THE PROBLEM OF RELIGIOUS LANGUAGE

One of the most prominent characteristics of British and American philosophy recently has been its profound interest in language. Never before has language itself been made the object of so much painstaking study as it has in the past twenty or thirty years, and there can be little doubt that some of the resulting conclusions about the nature of language are of considerable philosophical interest.

Nor is it surprising that the careful scrutiny of language should have raised anew the problem of the meaningfulness of religious discourse, for the affinities of most contemporary philosophers are not with the humanities and theology but with the natural sciences, particularly physics. Philosophers today tend to be empiricists in their epistemology, conventionalists in their view of language, and skeptics with respect to the claim that the language of religion is in some way descriptive of transcendent reality. As a result of this preoccupation with language, and more especially as a result of certain negative implications drawn from a theory of language widely held by contemporary British and American philosophers, the problem of religious language has become a widely discussed issue in contemporary philosophy of religion.

Background of the Problem

Lest we become too myopic in our approach, however, it should be noted that the problem is by no means a new one. It is well over two thousand years since Plato wrote:

> The father and maker of all this universe is past finding out; and even if we found him, to tell of him to all men would be impossible. . . . If, then, Socrates, amid the many opinions about the gods . . . we are not able to

give notions which are altogether and in every respect exact and consistent with one another, do not be surprised. Enough, if we adduce probabilities as likely as any others.[1]

St. Augustine, who wrote a great deal about God, was also quite cognizant of the difficulty; on one occasion he even went so far as to suggest that we speak of God "not in order to say something, but in order not to remain silent." [2] Theologians of every age have often echoed St. Augustine's sentiments.

The problem achieved what might be termed its first definitive formulation in St. Thomas Aquinas' great *Summa Theologica*. The question as put by Aquinas is, "Whether what is said of God and of creatures is univocally predicated of them?" Translation: Do terms normally applied to finite objects have the *same meaning* when they are applied to God? Aquinas thought that the reply could not be affirmative, for when we apply a given term ("wise") to, say, a man, "we signify some perfection distinct from a man's essence, and distinct from his power and being," whereas when we apply the same term to God, "we do not mean to signify anything distinct from His essence or power or being." On the other hand, if we say that terms are predicated of finite objects and of God "equivocally," that is, in such a way that the same word has a totally different meaning in the two cases, then "the reasoning would always be exposed to the fallacy of equivocation." We would be concealing our complete ignorance about God under a camouflage of words that appear to be meaningful only because they are meaningful in their ordinary application. Aquinas' solution is to go between the horns of the dilemma. There is, he says, a third way, namely, the *way of analogy*: "Whatever is said of God and creatures is said according as there is some relation of the creature to God as to its principle and cause, wherein all the perfections of things pre-exist excellently." [3] Translation: Since this world is God's creation, it reflects —albeit imperfectly—the attributes of its creator. Therefore it is appropriate to ascribe the virtues that we observe here to God, recognizing however that when applied to God they no longer connote finitude and imperfection as they do when applied to creatures.

The contemporary version of the problem of religious language is, however, much more radical than the one that Aquinas attempted to solve, because two basic assumptions that Aquinas made are now generally rejected. Although remarkably cautious in his claims regarding our knowledge of God, Aquinas did assume, first, that we know a good many things about the nature of God. The question for him was how our language could *express* this knowledge. He also assumed that

---

[1] Plato, *Timaeus*, I, in *The Dialogues of Plato*, tr. B. Jowett (New York: Random House, 1937), vol. II, p. 13.

[2] St. Augustine, *To Simplician: On Various Questions*, II, 2, 1. Many editions.

[3] St. Thomas Aquinas, *Summa Theologica*, I, ques. 13, art. 5, in Anton C. Pegis (ed.), *Basic Writings of St. Thomas Aquinas* (New York: Random House, 1945), vol. I, p. 120.

somehow or other our language about God is meaningful. He wanted to know only *in what way* it is meaningful. The way of analogy is offered by Aquinas not as a solution to the problem of how language about God can have any meaning at all, but as an account of the particular *kind* of meaning "God talk" is supposed to have, it being assumed by everyone concerned in his day that talk about God has some kind of meaning.

The Problem Today

The problem of religious language was raised anew in the twentieth century by the formulation of *the empiricist criterion of meaning,* according to which a proposition is said to be factually meaningful if and only if some empirical facts are relevant to determining its truth or falsity. Philosophers who defend this criterion hold that there are only three kinds of linguistic expressions: empirical statements, analytic truths, and nonsense. Empirical statements are factually meaningful. Analytic truths simply express certain meaning relations among the terms of which they are composed; they say nothing about any matter of fact. All other linguistic expressions, regardless of their face value, are literally meaningless: they have no cognitive meaning whatsoever.

If we accept this criterion, however, we cannot avoid asking, Is it possible to speak meaningfully about God and, if so, how? Statements about God do not appear to be either confirmable or disconfirmable on the basis of any empirical observations; therefore, they do not appear to be factually significant. It is evident (to most observers, at least) that they are not analytic truths. Are they, then, altogether meaningless—a particularly prevalent form of linguistic nonsense? So it seems to some.

Philosophers who hold that all sentences purporting to say something about God are literally meaningless do not mean to suggest, of course, that they are obviously so. Indeed, their point is precisely that the nonsensical character of such utterances is extremely *unobvious*—so unobvious, in fact, that well-meaning people have talked about God for centuries as if what they were saying were literally significant. These philosophers point out, however, that once we understand the conditions that must exist for language to be meaningful, we can see that some of these conditions are lacking in the case of language about God; hence, they say, we are driven to a negative conclusion.

Nor do these philosophers deny that sentences purporting to say something about God may have for some people certain kinds of "meaning" other than descriptive significance. The linguistic expression "God loves His people and watches over them continually" may be emotionally comforting or aesthetically satisfying, or it may serve as a reinforcement of moral commitment. In these senses, it may be considered subjectively meaningful to the person who utters it. But the utterance cannot be literally significant even to a believer, say these philosophers; it does not assert anything that is capable of being either true or false.

Further, these philosophers maintain that in order for a linguistic expression to be factually significant, it is necessary that we be able to specify a state of affairs that, if it were the case, would render the statement in question false. I may or may not be able to actually determine whether the state of affairs to which I have reference obtains; that is purely a question of empirical possibility and does not affect the logic of my statement. But if I cannot specify a state of affairs that, if it were the case (whether or not I can ascertain if it is the case), would render my statement false, then, according to this view, I am not really saying anything.

Suppose, now, that someone were to ask a person who affirms the above utterance about God, "What would have to be the case in order for you to withdraw your statement that God loves His people and watches over them continually?" What could such a person say? We can imagine a conversation something like this:

Believer: I can't think of anything that would make me withdraw the statement. God just does love His people—we know that—and whatever happens, we have to go on believing that God loves us.

Critic: Let me see if I can help you. Surely the fact of human suffering—except, perhaps, for that inflicted by other men— counts against your statement?

Believer: No, not at all. Because, you see, God's love is not like human love. God's love is greater, more encompassing, more . . .

Critic: Wait a minute! How can you say that God's love is *greater* than human love? When men are suffering, other men usually try to do something about it. God, apparently, does not do anything at all. I should think we might be justified in concluding that God's love is inferior to human love, or even nonexistent.

Believer: You do not understand the infinite difference between God and man.

Critic: I see a difference, but the contrast, I must say, is not particularly flattering to God. And the "love of God" of which you speak seems to mean nothing whatsoever. With or without this love, there would be human suffering—no more and no less than there is now. With or without this love, the world would apparently be just the way it is now. Your alleged "assertion" about the love of God is no assertion at all.

This question of the *meaningfulness* of statements about God must not be confused with the quite different question of determining whether this or that theological statement is *true*. The first question belongs to the logic of religious discourse, the second to the epistemology of religious truth claims. The first question, moreover, is logically prior to the second. If the negative view on the significance of religious assertions should be sustained, religion could make no truth claims, in which case the epistemological question could be ignored.

It is no answer to the present question to say, "We know God loves His people because it says so in the Bible." The question is, What, if anything, do sentences about God *mean*, whether or not they are authorized by any religious authority? Are they factually significant at all? Are they, can they be, assertions? And if so, how do they get their meaning?

Some Alternatives

It is very difficult to classify the many ways in which various philosophers have attempted to deal with this problem, and it is impossible in principle to determine all of the possible ways of responding to it. Many philosophers have taken the position that the empiricist criterion of meaning makes it evident that talk about God is and always was nonsensical. People may keep on using this kind of language, but if they think that they are thereby asserting anything, they are just deceiving themselves. For someone who holds this view, the status of religious language is no longer a problem: religious discourse is clearly ruled out, and that is the end of the matter.

Others, however, have addressed themselves to the problem out of a desire to show that the empiricist assault on religious language need not be as fatal as the attackers seem to think it is. It is at this point that the picture becomes rather confused, because several different lines of defense have been attempted.

First, we may distinguish a group of writers who have accepted the empiricist criterion of meaning and the conclusion that religious language is devoid of literal significance, but who have argued (in a variety of ways) that this conclusion need not distress religious people, since the meaning and importance of religious language lie in an entirely different dimension. According to these philosophers, if we carefully examine the ways religious utterances are used, we will find that they serve an important function—though, to be sure, that function is not, as people may have once thought, factual description.

Chapters 26 and 27 represent two alternative ways of accounting for the nature of religious language along these general lines. The *ethical way*, developed in Chapter 26, goes back to Immanuel Kant, whose epistemological studies drove him to deal with this problem long before the empiricist criterion of meaning made its debut on the philosophical scene. The *existential way*, developed in Chapter 27, is of more recent vintage and has a number of contemporary proponents. In both of these cases, however, the claim is made that the referent of religious language is subjective rather than objective: talk about God, correctly understood, is just a very special kind of talk about ourselves.

Other writers have insisted on the more traditional view that religious language is descriptive of an objective reality, and they have attempted to show how this position can be maintained in the face of the empiricist attack. Some (few) writers have attempted to maintain that the empiricist criterion of meaning need not force the conclusion that talk about God is meaningless. This position is developed in Chapter 28. Others have argued that the empiricist criterion of meaning is itself inadequate, and they have attempted to affirm the factual significance of religious assertions in a way that, if accepted, would require the rejection of the empiricist criterion. This approach, as the writer of Chapter 29 points out, has much in common with the way of analogy of Aquinas.

One cannot wrestle for long with the problem of religious language without facing the question, What is religion? Is it basically a moral code? Then perhaps it can get along without talk about God. Or is it at root a set of beliefs about a being who transcends space and time, is the ground of being and value, and is worthy of man's worship? If so, religion clearly cannot tolerate the elimination of language about this being. To adopt a view—any view—about the nature of religious language is, therefore, to take an important step toward adopting a view about the essential nature of religion as well. For anyone who regards the truth claims of religion as important, therefore, the problem with which we shall be concerned in this section is anything but trivial.

STUDY QUESTIONS

1. What, specifically, are the kinds of religious utterances that some philosophers say are meaningless? Consider the following:
   a. Jesus was born in Bethlehem.
   b. The Holy Spirit proceeds from the Father and the Son.
   c. God answers prayer.
   d. Prayer changes things.
2. What is meant by the terms "univocal" and "equivocal"? What are St. Thomas Aquinas' objections to saying that certain things are predicated of God and of creatures "univocally"? What are his objections to saying that certain things are predicated of God and of creatures "equivocally"?
3. What is the empiricist criterion of meaning? How does this create a problem so far as religious language is concerned?
4. Is the question about the meaningfulness of religious language separable from, and logically prior to, the question about the truth of religious truth claims? Explain.
5. Formulate a concise statement of the problem of religious language as you now understand it. What do you understand to be the alternative ways of responding to this problem?

26

THE LANGUAGE
OF MORAL RESOLVE

It is more than a little misleading to call the criterion referred to in Chapter 25 a criterion of *meaning*. It is, more correctly, a criterion of *factual significance*. To say that a certain statement is "devoid of factual significance" is one thing; to say that it is "sheer nonsense" is quite a different matter. The prejudicial language in which the problem of religious discourse has been discussed in recent years has done much to further confuse an issue that is desperately in need of elucidation and, if possible, solution.

Although I consider the terminology in much of the recent discussion to be highly misleading, I do think that the empiricist criterion of factual significance (as I shall call it) is valid. No sentence can be significant—factually or otherwise—unless (*a*) its terms are understood and (*b*) it is in tolerable conformity with the syntactic rules of the language in which it occurs. ("Some drapples are snark pling" fails to meet the first requirement; "Pickle ostrich many seven" fails to meet the second.) If, however, a sentence is to be factually significant, in addition to fulfilling these two requirements it must also be the case that (*c*) it purports to describe some theoretically verifiable state of affairs. This, it would seem, is what we mean by calling it "factually" significant. If a person who claims to be uttering a factually significant statement can specify no state of affairs that, if it were the case, would render his statement false, it would seem fair to conclude that he is not really uttering a factually significant statement. The empiricist criterion is nothing more than a definition of what we mean by "factually significant." I do not see how we could reject it without blurring the rather obvious distinction between factually significant sentences and other kinds of sentences.

Nor can there be any doubt that according to this criterion religious language is not factually significant. Sentences of the type "God is three in one" and "God loves His people and watches over them continually" describe no states of affairs that are either confirmable or disconfirmable by any conceivable data. Such sentences are all right as far as their syntax is concerned. They may be all right as far as their terms are concerned. But they are not factually significant. They are descriptive of nothing. They are, therefore, neither true nor false.

This conclusion regarding the nonfactual character of religious language is regarded by many people, including some philosophers, as seriously objectionable. Most of the religions of the world claim to assert some matters of fact when they utter sentences about God, though Zen Buddhism appears to be an exception. But I think that the pseudodescriptions into which most religions seem to have fallen are a spurious element in those religions. The supposed assertions are not, *qua* assertions, essential to religion; their true (nondescriptive) significance lies in another dimension, as I intend to demonstrate.

Religion and Morality

Construed as assertions of fact, statements about God are entirely vacuous. Their true meaning, I suggest, consists in the fact that they express the *moral resolve*—that is, the intention to act in certain ways—of the person who sincerely utters them. I shall indicate some of the reasons for adopting this view and then give a few examples showing how some very common sentences having "God" as their subject ought to be construed.

We may begin with the observation that, whatever the view on the question of religious language, it is evident that morality constitutes an exceedingly important *part* of religion. What would Judaism be without the Ten Commandments, or Christianity without the Sermon on the Mount and the teachings of St. Paul, or Buddhism without the Noble Eightfold Path? Indeed, at the heart of every religion is a system of *moral precepts*, rules for behavior that the adherents of that religion are expected (and frequently exhorted) to observe.

Every religious group, as a matter of fact, constitutes an ethical community. Corporate worship is a solemn act in which the ethical community is reminded of its moral duty and given an opportunity to reaffirm and deepen its moral resolve. Religious practices and ceremonies are also easily explicable in this context. In the Christian religion, for example, baptism is a rite in which the young are formally inducted into the ethical community; communion is a rite in which the members of the local unit of the community affirm their identity with the larger community in the pursuit of a common ethical task. We would not, in fact, be far from the truth if we were to define religion as the *solemnizing of ethical commitment.*

Parables and Other Stories

Since, as I have argued, the chief function of religion is to encourage certain kinds of moral behavior, it is natural that every religion has a body of linguistic materials that tend to support this function. There are numerous stories, for example, some that are told as if they were historical (the crossing of the Red Sea or the conquest of Jericho), others that are frankly fictional (the parables of Jesus). Whether or not a given story is really historical, however, is of no great importance. The historicity, for instance, of the story of the "rich young ruler" who came to Jesus for advice or of the Good Samaritan who befriended the man who had been set upon by thieves is inconsequential. In both cases, the intent is to encourage a certain kind of behavior.

The genius of such stories lies in the fact that they make vivid, and thus lend powerful psychological support to, the ethical duty of the adherent. The injunction "Love your neighbor as yourself" is undoubtedly an excellent summary of the Christian ethic, but it is rather abstract. The story of the Good Samaritan reveals in a vividly concrete way what it means to love your neighbor as yourself. So also with the injunction to love your enemies and to return good for evil: it is not the general precept but the often retold story of Jesus forgiving those who crucified him, even as he hung upon the cross, that moves Christians to act in a like manner. Countless additional examples could be given from the literature of all religions.

Yet if people are to be persuaded to live in the prescribed ways, it is not enough that they be shown how to act: they must also be given some volitional support. Many stories in religious literature encourage adherents to act in the desired way by promoting, in varying degrees, two motives: gratitude and fear. In some religious communities the former motive seems to predominate, in others, the latter. But both are present in some degree in all religions. The people of Israel are to obey the law given at Sinai out of gratitude to the God who has delivered them from Egypt "with a strong hand and an outstretched arm"; at the same time, they are to recognize that their God is a "jealous" God, who will tolerate no worship of other gods and will severely punish those who disobey Him. St. Paul appeals to his readers "by the mercies of God" to act in certain ways; but the New Testament also warns of "the outer darkness" and the "weeping and gnashing of teeth" that await those who disobey. Sometimes the Buddha smiles and sometimes he frowns; but always he enjoins the extinction of desire as the key to a proper mode of life.

If we add to these stories the poems and hymns that reinforce the attitudes that the stories and the experience of the community have succeeded in creating, and that encourage the further development of such attitudes, it is apparent that a very considerable amount of the linguistic materials of religion can be satisfactorily accounted for. Even prayers, perhaps, might be explained as verbal expressions of the community's (or the individual's) sincere desire to achieve more fully the ethical ideal of the community, though the fact that they are customarily addressed to God calls for further explanation. A great many things that are otherwise extremely puzzling about religion fall nicely into place as soon as we recognize that a religious group is essentially an ethical community.

The Attributes of God

It is in this same context that language about God is to be understood. Sentences of the form "God is . . ." are not descriptions of an Absent Potentate; their truth does not depend on the veracity of certain esoteric sources of information. Like all the linguistic materials of religion, statements about God are to be understood in terms of their function in relation to the moral resolve that is the very raison d'être of the community. The question that we must ask is, How do statements about God function in relation to the life of such a community?

How, in fact, do religious people think of God? Chiefly, it would appear, as the giver and enforcer of the moral law. And because God is so conceived, He is also thought to embody all the virtues enjoined in the moral law. *God is the personification of the ethical ideal of the religious community.* Therefore, all moral virtues espoused by the community— love, mercy, wisdom, forbearance, compassion, and so on—are ascribed to God.

Every statement about God is in reality an assertion of some aspect of the ethical ideal of the community and an affirmation of the community's sincere intention to act according to that ideal. "God is love" means, in a Christian community, "We value self-denying love such as that enjoined and practiced by Jesus of Nazareth and do firmly resolve to act in this way ourselves." The mercy of God, the wisdom of God, the compassion of God, the forbearance of God, can easily be understood, *mutatis mutandis,* in the same way.

Let us return to the statement "God loves His people and watches over them continually." This expresses the community's corporate concern for each of its members—its ideal, if you will, that every member of the community shall act in such a way as to serve the needs and the welfare of every other member. The concern of one person for another who is ill (or otherwise in need) *is* the "love of God" of which the statement speaks. The meaning of the statement consists precisely in the fact that it honors such concern and enjoins each and every member of the community to incarnate this concern in his day-to-day dealings with his fellow-men. Behind every statement of this kind about God is the implied injunction "You shall be perfect as your Heavenly Father is perfect."

How Some Religious Language Can Be Meaningless

Although a great deal of discourse about God is, so to speak, "legiti-
mized" in this way, it does not necessarily follow that all of it is. Many
sentences having "God" as their subject can be regarded only as
absolutely meaningless. Examples of such sentences would be "God is
three persons in one," "God is able to do anything that He wants to do,"
and "God knows Himself perfectly and in knowing Himself knows the
world."

Sentences such as these, however, are not the kind that come
spontaneously to the lips of a devout member of a religious community.
They are not specimens of the language of living religion; they are the
products of academic theology. Many sincere laymen, in fact, instinctively feel that such statements are unrelated to the real life of the
religious community. They are impatient with "theological abstractions"
and prefer to hear their ministers talk about things that are "relevant to
life."

Since theologians are not a unique species of human beings, however,
it seems reasonable to suppose that their formulations must have some
basis in the conceptual framework within which the language of living
faith occurs. Such a basis is to be found in the personification of ethical
ideals that gives rise to the very idea of God. Once the notion of a
supremely perfect Person is established, it seems natural to ask, What is
He like? Much of what is said in answer to that question will faithfully
express the ethical ideal of the community, and so the community will
recognize in what is said a true description of "their God." Given the
supposition that talk about God is talk about a personal being, however,
certain other things will follow as logical consequences: God does not
change (for the ethical ideal is constant); God does not alter his plans or
feel either joy or sorrow (for to do so would involve change); and so on.
Immense efforts have been expended by theologians to achieve logical
coherence in their concept of God, with the result that innumerable
things have been said about God that, in my view, are quite meaningless.

What our proposal really comes down to is this: The proper criterion
for judging the meaningfulness of statements about God is not the
criterion of *factual* significance but the criterion of *ethical* significance.
No statements about God are factually significant; but many of them are
ethically significant nonetheless: they express the ethical ideal of the
religious community that asserts them and record the community's
resolve to act in ways consistent with this ideal. To construe statements
about God in this manner is to preserve everything that is of importance
to a religious community. It is, at the same time, to acknowledge the
indisputable validity of the empiricist criterion of factual significance. It
seems, therefore, a completely satisfactory solution to the problem of
religious language.

STUDY QUESTIONS

1. What position does Moralist take with respect to the empiricist criterion? Does he endorse it? modify it? reject it? reinterpret it?
2. Moralist represents religion as "the solemnizing of ethical commitment" and interprets various things—rites, religious literature, and so on—in terms of this definition. Is he right about this? Can you think of any elements that are constitutive of religion that cannot be interpreted in this way?
3. What concept of God does Moralist recommend as being closest to the view held by most religious people? Why? As far as you can judge, do you think he is right on this point?
4. How exactly does Moralist propose that we construe statements about God? Apply his proposal to several examples other than those that he himself offers.
5. According to Moralist, there are some things that religious people ought to stop saying, since, in his theory, they are meaningless. Make a list of statements that appear to fall in this category. Are they, as he suggests, superfluous to religion—"spurious elements"?

27

THE LANGUAGE
OF HUMAN EXISTENCE

Because I agree with Moralist about the validity of the empiricist criterion of factual significance, and because I share his concern that religious language not simply be cast aside as meaningless, it is not surprising that I should find his view extremely attractive. Like Kant, from whom he evidently has learned much, he presents a very plausible account of religion and of religious language, and in so doing he preserves meaning for at least certain kinds of talk about God.

We cannot hold it against this account that it dismisses much that religious people have always supposed they were saying when they uttered statements about God. Popular piety unquestionably *does* conceive of God as a kind of Great-Grandfather-in-the-Sky, who "has" His various attributes in the same way that Mr. Jones has red hair; and such literally ascriptive meaning clearly cannot be allowed by the empiricist criterion. Popular piety, and probably also academic theology, want our language about God to be objectively descriptive, and this it cannot be. Any dissatisfaction with Moralist's account that arises solely because he does not allow this kind of meaning to religious language is, therefore, quite illegitimate.

Although I share Moralist's view regarding the nonobjective character of religious language, I am not satisfied with his positive account of that language simply as an expression of moral resolve. Religion is more than a "solemnizing of ethical commitment," and the peculiar language of religion is more than an articulation of the intention of some group of people to act in certain ways. It is my purpose in what follows to indicate what that "more" is and to suggest an account of religious language that takes proper cognizance of it.

Religion and the Human Situation

Religion is a product of man's response to what we may call "the human situation"—the existential conditions within which his life as an existing individual is and must be lived. To say that these are *existential* conditions is to say that they are implicit in the very structures that determine human existence: they cannot be removed by any improvement in man's external environment, by any increase in his wisdom, or by any advance in his understanding of himself. They are there. They profoundly condition his existence at its very center. They can be acknowledged and accepted, but they cannot be removed. They are a part of what it means to be an existing human being.

That every human life stands under the terrible threat of total personal nonfulfillment is the first "existential fact" relevant for a proper understanding of religion. To be a human being is to know that there is a way that we ought to go, a life that we ought to live—and to know, at the same time, that we may miss it altogether. This is the threat of being "lost" of which all religions speak. It is because all humankind knows this threat and because religion addresses itself to it that the appeal of religion is so universal.

The threat of personal nonfulfillment—the fear, deep within everyone, of being utterly and irrevocably "lost"—expresses itself in a variety of ways. One form it takes, for example, is the horror of death. What a mockery death makes of human life! Here a young man full of promise, there a mother of several little children, and there a brilliant statesman in whom millions of people had placed their hope are taken by death. And each such event reminds us that we, too, must die. The single fact of death renders absurd the hopes, the plans, the words and works, that occupy us all. To reflect upon this, to see death as the final absurdity in a life that is nothing but "a tale told by an idiot, full of sound and fury, signifying nothing" [1] is to feel at least something of the threat of nonfulfillment.

This threat expresses itself also in a sense of guilt because of real or imagined wrongdoing. All men know this sense of guilt—whether or not it attaches itself to particular overt acts—for it is simply the recognition of having "missed the way," of not measuring up to what we might and ought to have been. The religious term for this is "sin," which connotes a profound *lack* in human life.

The threat of personal nonfulfillment is also manifest in the sense of meaninglessness that perpetually haunts human existence. If I have missed the way and if death has the last mocking word, then anything that I may set my hand to now must be utterly devoid of meaning. Nothing that I might do can have any meaning unless there are at least some proximate values for me to pursue; and there can be no proximate values unless they, in turn, are steps toward the realization of ultimate

---

[1] William Shakespeare, *Macbeth*, Act 5, Scene 5.

values. But death robs me of the latter. I am left with drabness and weariness, an unlovely Chekhovian world in which "all is vanity and a striving after wind." [2]

However, this is only one side of the dialectic within which we must try to understand religion. It accounts for the negative, or threatening, elements in religion: the wrath of God, the threat of Hell, the possibility of remaining bound to the cycle of rebirths (Buddhism), and so on. Every religion exhibits some elements of this type, but no religion consists exclusively of these elements. Indeed, it is precisely the claim of religion to point a way in which this ultimate threat to human existence is overcome, a way, to use the religious term, of *salvation*. "Salvation" means the complete fulfillment of self, the overcoming of the threat to self-fulfillment. There is, according to all religions, a grace in human existence by which this threat is accepted and conquered. Grace, too, is experienced in many forms, of which we may pause to mention just three.

It is experienced, first, as the conquest of the horror of death. There seems to be no distinctive word for this experience in our language, but religious literature abounds with references to such things as "deliverance from death unto life," "the conquest of man's last enemy," and so on. "O death," writes St. Paul, "where is thy sting? O grave, where is thy victory? Death is swallowed up in victory." [3] The doctrinal expression of this experience is the doctrine of personal immortality (and its many variants).

Grace is experienced also as forgiveness, an acceptance of oneself despite having "missed the way" and a confidence in that continued acceptance of self into an unknown future. (Note that there is no particular reason for preferring the religious term "forgiveness"; we could simply call this a sustaining sense of personal worth.)

Third, the experience of grace is manifest in human experience as a sense of meaning, a feeling that somehow the whole human enterprise is worthwhile and that each individual's part in that enterprise shares in that worth. Meaninglessness and despair, we realize, do not have the last word in human life after all: values thrust themselves upon us, tasks really worth doing lie before us, and life itself seems eminently worth living. We know the threat of meaninglessness, but we also know the overcoming of this threat.

All religions are shaped and formed by the dialectic that I have briefly described. The several religions use an infinite variety of pictures, symbols, and ideas, but their function is always the same: to assist their adherents in achieving the "way of salvation" by which the threat to self-fulfillment is overcome in all its varied forms.

---

[2] Ecclesiastes, 1:14.
[3] I Corinthians, 15:54, 55.

Our Language About God

It is correct, as far as it goes, to say that God is conceived by religious people as "the giver and enforcer of the moral law"; but it does not go far enough. More important, He is conceived as the giver of life and of salvation, the conqueror of death, the forgiver, the savior. *God is the supposed source of the grace that overcomes the "lostness" that threatens and oppresses human existence.* Of course, He is also conceived as giving and enforcing the moral law, but this is only because the moral law is thought to define in part the way that God would have us walk.

What each religion sets before its adherents is not simply a distinctive moral code but a concrete, all-inclusive *existence-possibility*. This includes, in addition to a moral code, a distinctive set of symbols, through which the adherents of a particular religion will be taught to conceptualize various dimensions of their experience; and certain rites, in which the peculiar religious needs developed in a group will find appropriate expression. A religious group is not only, or even primarily, an ethical culture society. It is a fellowship of human beings who are seeking the way of salvation together and who have learned to employ a common set of symbols to mark their progress on that way.

It is not at all difficult, against this background, to understand the ritual use of language that refers to God. He is addressed as a very exalted person not altogether unlike ourselves, and He is made the object of both prayer and praise. In prayer, the worshiper expresses both fear (which is never wholly overcome) and confidence that the Giver of salvation will supply his need. In praise, the worshiper expresses gratitude for blessings received and most especially for the incomparable gift of salvation.

But what, according to this view, can be the meaning of a theological assertion of the form "God is . . . (good, wise, holy, just, etc.)"? According to the empiricist criterion of meaning, such statements cannot signify what religious people typically think they do. What, then, is their meaning?

I think the answer is as follows. Theological statements of this kind have two elements: they express (a) the existential ideal of the community and (b) the gratitude of the community for blessings received. It is the intertwining of these two elements that gives such statements their peculiar character.

Let us consider first the existential ideal. St. Anselm's statement is particularly apt: "God is everything that it is better to be than not to be." [4] God is conceived by the faithful to realize in His own nature all of the goodness that He looks for in them, not only moral goodness but also such nonmoral qualities as wisdom and prudence. Much talk about God

---

[4] St. Anselm, *Proslogium and Other Writings*, tr. S. N. Deane (LaSalle, Ill.: Open Court, 1962), p. 11.

is, therefore, as Moralist says, a way of setting before the community the ideal to which the community is committed. But the ideal is not merely an ethical ideal: it is an ideal that encompasses the whole of life.

The picture is complicated by the fact that such talk about God also includes a great deal that is purely honorific. The feeling of gratitude that characterizes the religious life leads .the spokesmen of religion, the theologians, to ascribe to God, who is conceived as a. very exalted person, all kinds of qualities that no mere human being could ever have or hope to have in like degree—power, majesty, might, ubiquity, and so on. Such attributions have meaning, not as an expression of the community's existential ideal, but rather as an exaggerated expression of its gratitude. The gratitude is real and legitimate, but the expression of it by the ascription to God of qualities such as omnipotence and omnipresence is very misleading.

Talk about God is meaningful not as a description of an Unseen Being but as an expression of the existential ideals and the innermost feelings (of gratitude, etc.) of human beings. There may or may not be a Being who charts the way that we ought to go and grants forgiveness and salvation. But the way, forgiveness, and salvation are real components of our existence, and we live every moment in relation to them. The meaning of talk about God depends on the ways in which that talk reflects our experience of lostness, forgiveness, and salvation; we have these experiences firsthand and can discuss them as meaningfully as we can discuss anything else.

STUDY QUESTIONS

1. What does Existentialist mean by "existential conditions"? What existential conditions does he suggest are relevant for a proper understanding of religion? To what extent does Existentialist's account of religion involve a rejection of Moralist's account, and to what extent could it be construed as simply supplemental to that account?
2. Is there some connection between (a) a view of the nature of religion, (b) a concept of God, and (c) a view regarding the meaning (or lack of meaning) of religious language? Illustrate your answer by reference to the theories discussed in this and the preceding chapter.
3. What does Existentialist suggest is the "peculiar character" of religious language? Does this strike you as a plausible suggestion?

28

THE EMPIRICAL FOUNDATIONS OF RELIGIOUS LANGUAGE

A person who has gone through a substantial portion of his life complacently believing that his discourse about God is, at least in some respects, descriptive of a transcendent reality must be taken aback by the suggestion that this is not so. Surely, he thinks, there is some relatively easy solution to the problem. But there is none: the empiricist criterion of factual significance is a very restricting doctrine. And so, in desperation, he may tend toward desperate solutions.

I think that the two proposals just presented are examples of this "strategy of desperation." There is no doubt that a "way of life," or a "pattern of existence," is an important element within the whole fabric of a religion. It is not surprising, therefore, that elements of "moral resolve," or "existential orientation," are to be found in the language of religion. However, there is equally no doubt that religion is not simply a matter of moral resolve and/or existential orientation and that the language of religion cannot, as a consequence, be accounted for simply in those terms.

Suppose that I say, "My grandfather was one of the kindest men I ever knew: I want to be more like him." In speaking this way I am, of course, expressing a wish and an intention—recording my "moral resolve," if you wish—to act in a certain way. It may well be, further, that I have been taught from childhood to feel love and gratitude for Grandfather—through stories of things he did for me when I was small and of kindnesses he performed for other people whom I love, and so on. Under circumstances such as these my statements about Grandfather would take on a certain "moral" or "existential" flavor. They would, *among other things*, record my own feelings, intentions, and aspirations.

But surely my statements about Grandfather would also, and primarily, still be statements *about Grandfather.* Whatever it may say about my own intentions, the statement "Grandfather was a very kind man . . ." is a statement about Grandfather. It may be true, or it may be false. It may also, incidentally, be quite beyond verification. But whatever else it may express, it chiefly expresses my belief that Grandfather was a man of such and such a character.

Something of this nature must be said, I think, about religious language. No doubt it does express the kinds of things that Moralist and Existentialist say it expresses. But this is not all. Language about God is, first and foremost, language *about God*—about a reality whose existence or nonexistence is a matter of profound importance to us, and whose real possession or nonpossession of the attributes of love, mercy, compassion, and so on, determines whether or not our language about Him is true. Religion is not purely a matter of moral resolve and/or existential orientation; it is also a matter of belief. Without belief, neither moral resolve nor existential orientation would be called "religion."

It seems clear, therefore, that those who today are content to adopt one or another of the "subjectivist" solutions to the problem of religious language are living on the capital of their forefathers. They revere the way of life exemplified by their elders and they suppose that it can be preserved without the beliefs that created it. Should this way of life survive the rejection of the beliefs upon which it was based, however, it will be not a religion that has survived but merely an ethic. Religion implies belief; the language of religion attempts to express belief. And beliefs, all beliefs, are either true or false.

Religious Discourse and "Facts"

If we are persuaded of the validity of the empiricist criterion of factual significance, then there are only two alternatives: either we must show that statements about God are factually significant according to the criterion, or we must draw the unhappy conclusion that religious people are all mistaken in thinking that their language about God is expressive of beliefs. Since the latter alternative seems preposterous, I propose to defend the former. I think that statements about God are factually significant.

The empiricist criterion of factual significance, it will be recalled, requires that for a sentence to be accounted factually significant, some empirical data must be relevant to its truth or falsehood. That this is the case with respect to at least some statements about God is evident, I would argue, from the fact that religious people are concerned about the problem of evil. The occurrence of evil in the world (a fact of empirical observation) is a problem for religious people precisely because it appears to be inconsistent with belief in the perfect wisdom, power, and goodness of the Creator. If God were limited in wisdom, He could be excused because of ignorance. If He were limited in power (as Plato held), He could be excused on the ground that He did the best He could. If He were limited in goodness, then the occurrence of evil along with good is just what might be expected. But if God is said to be altogether wise (omniscient), powerful (omnipotent), and good, then the occurrence of evil counts against the statement. It is, in the sense demanded by the criterion, relevant to the truth or falsity of the statement. If it were not, there would be no point in the concern with the existence of evil that religious people have always had.

Nonetheless, the occurrence of evil does not conclusively falsify the statement "God is perfectly wise, powerful, and good," precisely because there is an important difference between religious truth claims (of the troublesome kind) and scientific truth claims. It is characteristic of scientific truth claims that (a) they yield precise predictions regarding what will occur under such and such prescribed conditions and (b) they are falsified by the nonoccurrence of what is predicted. In the case of religious truth claims, however, the situation is different. A theological belief leads not to precise predictions but to certain general expectations. Job believed that God, being just, rewards the righteous and punishes the wicked according to their deserts, and, being a righteous man, he consequently expected to experience health, long life, and prosperity. When expectations are disappointed, the result—as in Job's case—is not the *falsification of a theory* but the *calling in question of a belief*, what religious people call a temptation to unbelief. In such a situation a person may cease to believe; but when this does happen, it is not the refutation of a theory; it is the collapse of a faith.

The chief difference between religious beliefs and scientific hypotheses is not that the latter are alleged to be factually significant whereas the former are not. The difference consists, rather, in the radically different ways, or attitudes in which, the respective beliefs are maintained. Scientific hypotheses are, quite properly, held in the tentative, provisional way with which we are all familiar: they are always open to revision, and every fact not explicable in the context of the hypothesis becomes a challenge to create a better hypothesis. Beliefs about God obviously are not, and cannot be, held in this way. The belief that God is powerful, wise, and good is not a hypothesis to be discarded as soon as some untoward event occurs. It is an article of faith, and as such it can be given up only through and with great anguish. The belief is part of a total and (ideally) unconditional *commitment*—what Friedrich Schleiermacher called "absolute dependence" and Paul Tillich called "ultimate concern." To be "absolutely dependent" on or "ultimately concerned" about anything other than God is what is called "idolatry"; but whatever the object of ultimate concern, whether God or anything else, one's beliefs about that object cannot be held in the mood of detachment appropriate to a scientific hypothesis. They can be held only in the passion that is the appropriate mood for faith.

Empirical Grounds for Theological Assertions

Thus far I have been arguing only that acceptance of the empiricist criterion of factual significance does not necessarily force acceptance of the conclusion that statements about God are devoid of factual significance: empirical observations do in fact count against certain statements about God, but they do not conclusively falsify them because of the way in which theological beliefs are held.

It may be protested that this takes us only a very small part of the way toward solving the problem of religious language. It takes us beyond the empiricist criterion of factual significance, but leaves us with the problem that our language, though admirably suited to the description of ordinary objects, evidently cannot be properly descriptive of God. It also leaves entirely unanswered the question of what, if anything, may be adduced as counting *in favor of* theological assertions. If nothing were to be said about these two problems, there would be scant comfort in the knowledge that there are some empirical facts that appear to count *against* such utterances.

What makes the problem of theological language seem so difficult is the common supposition that what demands to be proved is that language can be meaningfully descriptive of a *wholly transcendent reality*. But surely it is evident that it cannot. A "wholly transcendent reality" is beyond the realm of all possible experience and, according to the empiricist criterion, what is beyond the realm of all possible experience is also beyond the realm of factual significance. We are altogether ignorant of that of which we have no experience, and we cannot speak of that of which we are ignorant.

There is, however, no good reason for such a one-sided emphasis on the transcendence of God. High religion, it is true, has always affirmed the transcendence of God—and has been healthily agnostic about our capacity to know anything about this aspect of God's nature. But it has also spoken of the *immanence* of God, and it is at this point that our language about God can be seen to have some intelligible meaning. To say that God is immanent is to say that He *is* present in human experience and that our language can be descriptive of Him in the same way that it can be descriptive of any other experienced reality.

The primary meaning of the term "God" is "a reality that saves man from the powers and processes that are destructive of his humanity and that is (as a consequence) eminently worthy of his unconditional commitment." Such a reality is experienced by us, I maintain, in the *creative intercommunion with other men* that characterizes interpersonal relations at their best. Here and here alone do we encounter a creative power that truly transforms us, that overcomes the guilt, the meaninglessness, and the triviality of our existence, and that enables us to fulfill our human potentialities. Here is salvation, in the only sense of that word that I can understand. Here, therefore, is God as He is experienced by us.

It is such creative intercommunion that originates and sustains the human mind and personality, that saves and transforms him who gives himself to it without reservation. It is in this reality that we find that deep acceptance of ourselves in spite of ourselves which is the essence of forgiveness. To him who thus commits himself, this reality gives peace, courage, comfort, and renewal of mind. If this is God, then God is in very truth that omnipresent reality in whom we live and move and have our being.

How perfectly natural, then, and how profoundly meaningful (because so thoroughly interwoven in the very fabric of our experience) to say, "God creates," "God sustains," "God forgives," "God saves," "God transforms," "God loves." In this power of creative intercommunion— this power that is among us, and in us, and is infinitely more than the sum of our individual powers—we experience a reality to which it seems natural and appropriate to ascribe the attributes of deity. It is not surprising that this is so: the true lovers of God have been those deeply involved in the common life of man, rarely metaphysicians. "God" means "creative intercommunion among men"; when we are moved to prayer or praise, it is to this reality that we make our offering.

What we experience is in very large part a function of what we have been trained to notice. A symphony is one thing to a novice and quite a different thing to a trained musician (and even among trained musicians a given symphony may be experienced quite differently). The novice hears "a lot of sound" and either likes it or does not. The musician hears themes, harmonies, progressions, varying timbres, tempos, and dynamics; he discerns structure and form and he compares a given interpretation of the piece with others that he has heard. Because he knows what to listen for, he perceives many things that the novice does not.

Most people today are not attuned to the kind of experience that I have been attempting to describe—the experience of God. God is a reality in our midst, but He is almost unknown. The reason He is unknown is that we do not pay sufficient heed to that dimension of our experience in which He is manifest to us. We are novices in religious experience. What chiefly occupies our attention is things: how to get them, how to manipulate them, how to derive pleasure from them. We notice objects, we notice regularities, we notice mathematical relations —but we do not notice God. Hence, it is no wonder that our experience is shallow and our talk of God empty. We do not need an alternative to the empiricist criterion; we need to redirect our attention and enrich our experience. Otherwise all our talk of God, with or without the criterion, is meaningless.

STUDY QUESTIONS

1. Is Empiricist right in his contention that "religion implies belief"? Support your answer with specific illustrations.
2. What exactly is Empiricist's position on the problem of religious language? On

what point or points is he in agreement with the previous two writers? On what points is he in disagreement with them?

3. What difference does Empiricist find between scientific truth claims and religious truth claims? Do you agree? Are there other differences as well?

4. What concept of God is suggested by Empiricist? Can one talk about God *thus conceived* in a way that is consistent with the empiricist criterion? Would this solution to the problem be apt to satisfy most religious people? Explain.

5. What, according to this account, is the meaning of each of the following: "God creates," "God sustains," "God forgives," "God saves," "God transforms," "God loves"?

29

RELIGIOUS LANGUAGE AS SYMBOLIC

It is regrettable that much of the philosophical discussion of religion in recent years has been directed toward the solution of the problem posed by the empiricist criterion of factual significance. The effect of this unfortunate narrowing of the discussion has been to trivialize the philosophical interest in religion. In the all-but-unanimous endorsement of this vaunted criterion, and the resulting consternation of some philosophers (as well as theologians) about the apparent consequences for religion and theology, ancient insights of great and permanent importance have been overlooked. I shall attempt to redress the balance.

A Critique of the Criterion

The status of our language about God aside, the empiricist criterion ought to be rejected as a general criterion of meaning (which is what its supporters usually claim it to be). Not only theological language is consigned by this criterion to the limbo of meaninglessness; so also are (a) statements about events alleged to have occurred in the past ("The Battle of Gettysburg occurred in 1863"), (b) statements about other minds ("Mr. Jones is worrying about how he is going to send his son to college"), and (c) statements postulating the annihilation of all perceivers ("Should a full-scale atomic war occur, all life will be destroyed"). We do know what statements of these three kinds mean; yet, according to the empiricist criterion, none of them is meaningful.

Moreover, the status of the empiricist criterion itself is a matter of considerable embarrassment to its supporters. The most plausible account of it is as an *empirical hypothesis*—an inductive generalization about the conditions of meaningfulness, derived from careful observation of statements adjudged on other grounds to be meaningful. If this is the case, however, it is evident that the "criterion" is not really a criterion at all. It cannot determine what is or is not meaningful, since the method by which the theory is erected presupposes that one already knows, *on some other basis,* which statements are meaningful and which are not. It is only fair to say that the supporters of the criterion have by and large recognized this problem and have tried to deal with it. It is also only fair to say that their attempts to do so have not been very convincing even to themselves.

As a general criterion of meaning, the empiricist criterion is, therefore, grossly inadequate. What it defines is not the conditions of meaningful discourse in general but the conditions of meaning commonly applied in the natural sciences. Therefore, if we assume that it is correct in what it does describe (a question for the philosophy of science), it follows that no statement which fails to satisfy this criterion will qualify as a *scientific* statement (in the narrow sense of "scientific" currently in vogue). It by no means follows that the statement in question is completely meaningless.

A Deeper Problem

Although preoccupation with the empiricist criterion (construed as a general criterion of meaning) has indeed trivialized the philosophical interest in religion, the discussion of this problem has produced some valuable results. It has demonstrated, for example, that there are ethical and existential dimensions to the meaning of religious language, as previous participants in the present discussion have made clear. Moreover, it has demonstrated that the question of the meaningfulness of our *language* about God cannot be separated from the question of the meaning of the *concept* "God"—as even Empiricist's account makes evident (Chapter 28).

In all the excitement over the apparent consequences of the empiricist criterion, however, an older and much more serious problem has been largely overlooked: Whatever the general conditions of meaningful discourse, how is it possible for a language whose form and structure are patterned after a world of finite objects to be descriptive of an infinite and transcendent reality? This was Aquinas' problem, referred to briefly in the introductory chapter. It is an inescapable problem for any philosophy that seriously affirms the possibility of meaningful discourse about God.

Aquinas' own proposal vis-à-vis this question, as has already been pointed out, is the classical answer to it. He said that God the Creator stands as "principle and cause" in relation to the things He has created and that "all the perfections of things pre-exist excellently" in Him. Thus, according to Aquinas, it is permissible to ascribe to God the perfections that we perceive in creatures, provided we bear in mind that in God they exist fully and perfectly, whereas in creatures they exist only fragmentarily and imperfectly. In the two sentences "God is wise" and "Socrates is wise" the meaning of the term "wise" is neither absolutely identical (univocal) nor absolutely diverse (equivocal): it is analogical. Socrates is wise in the way that wisdom is appropriate to a finite and imperfect being; God is wise in the way that wisdom is appropriate to an infinite and perfect being. "In analogies," said Aquinas, "the idea is not, as it is in univocals, one and the same; yet it is not totally diverse as in equivocals; but the name which is thus used in a multiple sense signifies various proportions to some one thing." [1]

The theory of analogical predication is both ingenious and profound, and it is worthy of great respect. It provides, as any adequate theory of theological language must, for both continuity and discontinuity between God and the world. It allows us to affirm both the transcendence of God (by virtue of which our language is not *properly* applicable to God) and the immanence of God (by virtue of which our language has *some* meaning when applied to God). It permits us to say the kinds of things that we want to say about God (as none of the theories presented in the previous three chapters do), yet it preserves a healthy agnosticism about the propriety of our language. In short, it reminds us that no description of God is really adequate to the reality of the divine mystery. It seems evident, therefore, that any theory that (*a*) presupposes that "God" means an immanent-transcendent reality as conceived in classical theism and (*b*) affirms the possibility of meaningful discourse about this reality must in the last analysis be something very similar to, or perhaps only a variant of, this theory.

Analogical predication consists, actually, in a very clever combination of positive and negative predication. It is evident that some statements about God are purely negative: they merely deny that God is thus and so. It seems appropriate, for example, to say that God is not composite, not corporeal, not finite, and not subject to change. These assertions are also commonly expressed by saying that God is simple, incorporeal, infinite, and immutable. There is evidently no mystery about how such talk about God can be meaningful, since the predicates employed are all being used in their proper everyday sense.

The analogical way of talking about God is in very large measure a further extension of this negative way. To be sure, in analogical predication we are attempting to make a positive statement about God—to say something about what God *is* rather than about what He is *not*. But the negative way continues to function by attempting to remove from the positive meaning of the predicate whatever it would not be appropriate to attribute to a being who is not composite, not corporeal, not finite, and so on.

Thus stated, however, the theory of analogical predication is open to

---

[1] St. Thomas Aquinas, *Summa Theologica*, I, ques. 13, art. 5, in Anton C. Pegis (ed.), *Basic Writings of St. Thomas Aquinas* (New York: Random House, 1945), vol. I, p. 120.

one very serious objection. If the analogical meaning of a given predicate as applied to God is its ordinary meaning minus those elements that render it incapable of describing the divine reality, it follows that the relation between a given term as applied to God and the same term as applied to creatures is in part equivocal and in part univocal. Insofar as "wise" connotes finitude, corporeality, and so forth, it refers only to creatures: to this extent "wise" as applied to God and "wise" as applied to creatures are *equivocal* terms. But what of the meaning that remains once the objectionable elements have been removed? To that extent, "wise" as applied to God and "wise" as applied to creatures are *univocal* terms. And so, it would seem, all of the objections to "univocity" apply with equal force to the analogical theory.

This is, in my opinion, a sound objection, though I would add that it touches only the letter and not the spirit of the theory of analogical predication. I think that the intention of the many philosophers who have supported the theory of analogical predication can be preserved through what I shall call the theory of *symbolic* predication. It is a kind of analogical theory, but with sufficient differences from the traditional theory to warrant a special name.

Symbolic Predication

The real purpose of the analogical way is to emphasize that (as well as to show how) our language about God is qualitatively different from our language about finite objects. The theory of analogical predication fails, not because it does not recognize this important insight, but because it tries to express it in an inadequate way—namely, at the level of discursive meaning. At that level, however, there are just three formal possibilities: (*a*) the meaning of a term in each of two instances is identical (univocal); (*b*) the meaning of a term in each of two instances is absolutely different (equivocal); (*c*) the meaning of a term in each of two instances is partly identical and partly different (analogical). To affirm that our talk about God is analogical, if this is what is meant by analogical, is not to escape the difficulties of univocal predication at all.

The kind of meaning that our language about God can have is, however, closely related to the kind of knowledge that we have of Him. If it were the case that we had some straightforwardly empirical knowledge of God, then there would be no problem at all in accounting for our language about God. This, however, is not the case. Our apprehension of God's reality and our knowledge of His nature do not occur at the discursive level. It is not "technical," or "scientific," reason that knows God but reason in its depth; hence, the language of scientific discourse (including the ordinary language of everyday experience) cannot adequately express this knowledge.

When we use language with reference to God, therefore, we are using it not in its ordinary literal meaning but *symbolically*. When we say that

God is good, wise, or merciful, we are not saying that in the same way that some persons are good, wise, and merciful He is too (only more so), nor are we saying that He is these things minus whatever elements of meaning connote finitude and imperfection. We are saying, rather, that God is *not* these things in the literal sense of "good," "wise," or "perfect," but that these terms point beyond themselves to realities in the ground of goodness, wisdom, and mercy—realities that cannot be grasped discursively, that can only be acknowledged as dimensions of the divine mystery.

To say that our language about God is symbolic is not to say that it is thereby inferior to literally descriptive language. On the contrary, it is to affirm that the mystery of the divine being so far surpasses our understanding that the descriptive language of everyday discourse is altogether inadequate to describe it. He knows God best who acknowledges that whatever he thinks and says about God must fall short of what God really is. Our language cannot describe God, even imperfectly; it can only point to Him. And this function of "pointing to" is precisely the function of a symbol.

What governs our choice of symbols? Why do we say (symbolically) that God is "good" and "wise" but not that He is "material" or "numerous"—for surely He is the ground of matter and number as well as of goodness and wisdom? The answer is that it is our apprehension of the divine reality itself that governs our choice. Just as discursive reason learns the art of choosing terms to describe the realities with which it is conversant, so reason in its depth learns the art of choosing symbols to indicate the divine reality. Talk about God is, in the last analysis, an attempt to *make language revelatory* of the divine nature. It is the language that is adjudged successful in this effort that is retained as the language of theology.

Whether or not it is possible to speak meaningfully about God, and, if so, what sort of meaning theological talk must have, cannot be decided on the basis of purely logical considerations. We must first take a stand on some very important ontological and epistemological problems: Does the term "God" denote a reality? Do we have any knowledge of this reality? The theory of theological language suggested here presupposes an affirmative answer to both these questions. The view that theological language is meaningless—though it may claim to be nothing but the plain implication of a neutral principle of logic—just as evidently presupposes a negative answer to one or both of these questions. A theory of theological language that pretends to be neutral with respect to these questions succeeds only in confusing the issue.

This being the case, the current uncertainty about the meaningfulness of theological language appears to be little more than a pale reflection of the frighteningly evident waning of our awareness of the divine reality. We human creatures have always known that God is not a thing among things; hence, we have always known that there is something peculiar, something unique, about our language with respect to Him. But only those for whom God has altogether ceased to be—only those for whom, as Friedrich Nietzsche said, God is dead—could seriously hold that our language about God is altogether devoid of meaning. Let the awareness of the divine reality be reborn among us and our doubts about the meaningfulness of theological language will quickly disappear. Pending that, our talk about God must be empty, and our talk about that talk an exercise in futility.

STUDY QUESTIONS

1. Symbolist rejects the empiricist criterion as a general criterion of meaning. On what grounds? What more limited role does he assign to it? Do you agree with him on this?
2. Why according to Symbolist is the status of the empiricist criterion "a matter of considerable embarrassment to its supporters"? Can you think of any way by which an advocate of the criterion might get around this difficulty?
3. What is the "older and much more serious problem" to which Symbolist invites our attention? Is it in fact a different problem from the one discussed in the three preceding chapters?
4. What exactly is "analogical" predication? What does Symbolist have to say in support of this proposal? What objection does he raise against it? Is the objection, in your opinion, a sound one?
5. What is Symbolist's own proposal regarding the meaning of statements about God? Does it overcome the objection that he raised against the analogical theory?

Aquinas, St. Thomas. *Summa Theologica*. Many editions. See Part I, Question 13.

Ayer, A. J. *Language, Truth and Logic*, 2nd ed. New York: Dover, 1946 (paperbound).

Braithwaite, R. B. *An Empiricist's View of the Nature of Religious Belief*. Cambridge, Eng.: Cambridge University Press, 1955.

Brown, Stuart C. *Do Religious Claims Make Sense?* New York: Macmillan, 1970.

Carnap, Rudolf. "The Elimination of Metaphysics Through Logical Analysis of Language," in A. J. Ayer (ed.). *Logical Positivism*. New York: Free Press, 1957.

Christian, William A. *Meaning and Truth in Religion*. Princeton, N.J.: Princeton University Press, 1964.

Coburn, Robert C. "The Hiddenness of God," *The Journal of Philosophy*, 57 (1960), 689–712.

Donnelly, J. (ed.). *Logical Analysis and Contemporary Theism*. New York: Fordham University Press, 1972. Analytic studies sympathetic to Theism.

Ewing, A. C. "Religious Assertions in the Light of Contemporary Philosophy," *Philosophy*, 32 (1957), 206–218.

Ferré, F. *Language, Logic and God*. New York: Harper & Row, 1969.

Flew, A., and A. Macintyre. *New Essays in Philosophical Theology*. New York: Macmillan, 1964 (paperbound).

Hempel, C. G. "Problems and Changes in the Empiricist Criterion of Meaning," in A. J. Ayer (ed.). *Logical Positivism*. New York: Free Press, 1957.

Hick, John. *Faith and Knowledge*. Ithaca, N.Y.: Cornell University Press, 1957.

High, D. M. (ed.). *New Essays on Religious Language*. London: Oxford University Press, 1969.

Lazerowitz, M. *The Structure of Metaphysics*. New York: Humanities Press, 1955.

Macintyre, A. (ed.). *Metaphysical Beliefs*. London: SCM Press, 1957.

Marhenke, P. "The Criterion of Significance," in L. Linsky (ed.). *Semantics and the Philosophy of Language*. Urbana, Ill.: University of Illinois Press, 1952.

Mascall, E. L. *Words and Images*. New York: Ronald Press, 1957.

Miles, T. R. *Religion and the Scientific Outlook*. New York: Humanities Press, 1959.

Mitchell, Basil (ed.). *Faith and Logic*. London: G. Allen & Unwin, 1957.

Munz, Peter. *Problems of Religious Knowledge*. London: SCM Press, 1959.

Ramsey, Ian T. *Christian Discourse*. London: Oxford University Press, 1965.

———. *Religious Language*. New York: Macmillan, 1963 (paperbound).

———. (ed.). *Words About God: The Philosophy of Religion*. New York: Harper & Row, 1971.

Tillich, Paul. *Systematic Theology*, vol. 1. Chicago: University of Chicago Press, 1951, pp. 235–289.

Wieman, H. N. *Man's Ultimate Commitment*. Carbondale, Ill.: Southern Illinois University Press, 1958, chaps. 1–7.

PART VII

MIND
AND BODY

30

THE MIND-BODY PROBLEM

Man, it has been said, is a mystery to himself. He knows that he is a part of nature, and yet he feels that he stands outside nature as does no other species. He knows that he shares a common evolutionary heritage with everything on this planet that is alive, yet he believes that human reality—Homo sapiens—is not merely another link in the evolutionary chain but a radically different and higher form of being that cannot be adequately comprehended in the categories appropriate to even the highest forms of nonhuman animal life. Socrates' ancient dictum "Know thyself" identifies a task that man apparently can neither avoid nor complete.

This is not of course to deny that the *scientific* study of man has achieved impressive results in modern times. We understand a great deal today about the workings of the human organism—about the mechanical and chemical and electrical processes involved in the various systems necessary to human life—that was not understood as recently as two or three decades ago. This new understanding has enabled medical science to achieve astonishing results in the prevention and cure of disease, in the implantation of "borrowed" organs (heart and kidney transplants, for example), and even in the creation of artificial organs. There is certainly every reason to believe that further medical research will continue to enlarge indefinitely our knowledge of the human organism, and will enable us to prolong and restore useful life where at present we are unable to do so.

One of the most puzzling questions that man has ever posed about himself, however, is one that falls outside the scope of biological and medical science. That is the question regarding the relation of *mind* and *body*.

Mental Events and Physical Events

We are all acquainted with a class of events that it seems natural and proper to describe as "mental" events. We know what it is like, for example, to have pleasurable and unpleasurable sensations: a cool shower after a hard day of work provides an example of the former; a dentist's drilling too close to a nerve, an example of the latter. We know, moreover, what it is like to experience *emotions:* love, hate, affection, concern, jealousy, and so on. Certain kinds of *activities* also appear to be mental, or at least partly mental, such as perceiving, remembering, imagining, deliberating, and inferring. Finally, *volition*—willing or deciding to do something in preference to something else—is a mental occurrence.

Events of the kinds just mentioned appear to be different in a number of ways from "physical" events. The most obvious apparent difference is that mental events, unlike physical events, are not publicly observable. If I am in pain, for example, nobody but me *feels* the pain. Other people may, of course, infer that I am in pain from the way I act (I may grimace, cry out, or perhaps clutch the part of my body that has been injured), but they cannot feel the pain that I feel. Indeed, I can fool other people into inferring that I am in pain by going through the motions of someone who is in pain; but I cannot fool myself on this score. Either I feel pain or I do not; it makes no sense to say, "I thought I felt a pain, but I was mistaken." (At this point we need not raise the question of how we are aware of such mental events. The question is worth consideration, but it will come up only incidentally in the discussion that follows. We may observe, however, that the name that some philosophers use for this process by which we appear to be directly aware of our own mental states is *introspection.* We know our own mental states by introspection and the mental states of others, if at all, by inference.)

A second feature of mental events that distinguishes them from physical events is that they cannot properly be said to be locatable in space. With respect to a physical event it is always meaningful to ask, Where, exactly, did it occur? But with respect to a mental event, such a question (unless it is construed to mean, Where were you when you felt, or decided, thus and so?) has no precise meaning. A volition, an emotion, or a recollection is not the sort of thing that can occur, say, on the sidewalk in front of the White House, about six feet in front of the main gate, whereas an explosion, a collision, a demonstration, or anything else that we would classify as a physical event is.

The differences, most people would say, result from the fact that the subjects of physical events are *bodies*, whereas the subjects of mental events are *minds*. Bodies occupy space and are locatable in space; hence, the events in which they participate are also locatable in space. Minds, however, do not occupy space (they are neither round, nor square, nor any other shape, nor do they come in various sizes) and are not, properly speaking, locatable in space; consequently, the events of which they are the subjects are not locatable in space.

What, precisely, is this notion of "mind" (or "consciousness") that is so deeply embedded in the commonsense view of man? It is difficult to say precisely. It involves, certainly, the idea of something that is the subject of what we call mental events—feeling, willing, desiring, thinking, and so forth—and it involves the denial that it can be described in terms of shape or size or other qualities applicable only to bodies. It is evidently closely associated with the brain, but because the brain is locatable in space (and for other reasons), mind is not usually considered identical with brain. It probably does no injustice to the commonsense view to say that each mind is thought to "inhabit" a particular body; in any case, it is clear that each mind is believed to be intimately related in some way or other to some particular body.

We do sometimes use spatial language in talking about certain mental phenomena. We say things like "I can't seem to get this idea *into my head*," and "Intentions are hard to detect because they occur *in a person's mind* where no one else can see them"; but when we speak in this way, we clearly are using spatial language metaphorically. We could, without altering the meaning of these statements, say instead, "I can't seem to comprehend this idea" and "Intentions are hard to detect because they are mental events and thus not publicly observable." It seems very doubtful, in any case, that the commonsense view of the nature of mind would allow that spatial categories are properly applicable to it.

There is something else about body and mind that is a part of the commonsense view, however, and that is that a given mind and the body with which it is associated mutually influence one another. The mental event that we call "seeing a flash of lightning," for example, seems to be related causally to a series of physical events involving an event in the sky, light waves, the optic nerves, and so on. The mental event that I call "feeling a pain" seems to be causally related to (a consequence of) certain physical events occurring in my body: the flame touching my finger, the bee stinging my ear, the dentist drilling my tooth, and so on. To be sure, I cannot always infer a physical event from the mental event of feeling a pain. Some pains are "psychosomatic"; they do not appear to be caused by the organic disturbances that normally cause such pains. In very many cases, however, the mental event that we call "feeling a pain" does seem to be caused by a physical event that we might call "receiving an injury"; and this supposition—that some mental events are caused by some physical events—seems clearly to be a part of the commonsense view.

It is also commonly supposed that some causal series run in the opposite direction—that some mental events cause, or at least partly cause, some physical events. At the present moment, for example, I am engaged in writing, which obviously consists of a series of physical (publicly observable) events. But at least part of the cause of my writing now is the fact that some time ago I decided to spend this particular day in this way. Our thoughts, our wishes, our decisions—mental events—seem to make a difference in the content and form of our speaking and acting, which are physical events.

These commonsense beliefs about body and mind may be stated in two simple propositions: (1) body and mind are two distinct entities, neither of which can be adequately explained as simply a special form of the other; (2) body and mind are capable, nonetheless, of causally acting on each other. The first proposition states the central thesis of what is called *mind-body dualism*. The second, which presupposes the first, states the central thesis of the view called *interactionism*. Interactionism, then, is simply the technical name for the "plain man's" view regarding the relation of body and mind.

Some Questions Regarding the Commonsense View

To most people the facts that we have just recounted seem commonplace enough, and for them the mind-body problem never arises. Many philosophers, however, find some features of the commonsense view extremely puzzling, chiefly because of (a) the alleged unclarity of our notion of "mind"; (b) certain difficulties in the way of knowing that such an entity exists; (c) the difficulty of understanding how there can be causal relations between physical and nonphysical entities; and, more recently, (d) the belief of some philosophers that the interactionist account presupposes metaphysical views that they regard as incorrect. The effect of these problems is to raise doubts about the correctness of the commonsense (interactionist) account and subsequently to initiate a search for a more adequate alternative.

The mind-body problem may be considered in terms of two related questions arising out of the commonsense view: Are body and mind two distinct entities, neither of which can be explained as a form or function of the other? and, How are the apparent two-way causal relations between them to be understood? The first part of the problem calls in question the dualism implicit in the commonsense view. The latter part asks for some explanation of the fact that body and mind appear to be involved in mutual causal relations.

Historically, it was the latter part of this problem that first caught the attention of philosophers; the dualism implicit in the commonsense view was simply taken for granted. During the sixteenth and seventeenth centuries the question that philosophers debated was, How are we to understand the apparent mutual causation between body and mind? A number of interesting (and sometimes far-fetched) answers were forthcoming.

René Descartes (1596–1650), whose reflections on the problem really launched the modern discussion, advocated the interactionist view. Body and mind, said Descartes, are radically distinct entities, two different kinds of substances, neither of which is reducible to the other: body is "extended, unthinking substance" and mind is "thinking, unextended substance." Nonetheless, Descartes thought it evident that body and mind interact and even conjectured that the precise point where this interaction occurs is in the pineal gland—for which, it may be said in his defense, no one had previously found any worthwhile function.

Descartes' successors by and large accepted his dualistic account of man, but some of them found his pineal-gland theory rather unconvincing. A number of alternatives to interactionism were therefore proposed. Gottfried Wilhelm von Leibnitz (1646–1716), for example, advocated a theory known as parallelism. Body and mind do not interact, said Leibnitz, but they appear to do so because God has created the world in such a way that there is a perfect "preestablished harmony" between any given series of mental events and a corresponding series of physical events. Mental events are always caused by prior mental events and physical events by prior physical events, but thanks to God's thoughtful provision for a perfect harmony between the two kinds of events, the appearance of interaction results. Nicolas de Malebranche (1638–1715), a contemporary of Leibnitz, advocated a special form of parallelism known as occasionalism, which might be described as harmony on the installment plan: God, said Malebranche, did not establish perfect harmony between physical and mental events "in the beginning," but as the occasion arises (presumably rather frequently), He does what needs to be done to keep the two series parallel. The result is the same, except that Malebranche's theory provided for the possibility of a certain kind of freedom for mind that Leibnitz's theory did not. Benedict de Spinoza (1632–1677) advocated what has been called a double-aspect theory, the details of which we shall not pause to recount. Suffice it to say that none of these proposals has commended itself to more than a few, and it seems safe to conclude that anyone who wishes to maintain the dualism that is inherent in the commonsense view must be prepared to maintain interactionism (mutual causation) as well. In the discussion that follows, in any case, we shall ignore all except the interactionist version of the dualistic account.

The Alternatives

Are body and mind two distinct entities, neither of which can be understood as a form or function of the other? There appear to be only three possible answers to this question.

First, it is possible to deny that they are radically distinct and to argue that mind is a determination of matter—that mind is, so to speak, a purely physical phenomenon that is governed by, and explicable according to, the same laws as any other physical phenomenon. Mind, in this view, is not ontologically unique: it is not a "spiritual substance," a nonphysical reality, that acts apart from and independent of the laws of nature. It is a part of nature, even a product of nature, and wholly subject to its laws. The collective name for views that attempt to account for the relationship between mind and body in this way is *identity materialism*.

Second, it is possible to take a position just opposite to that of identity materialism—to reject the dualism implicit in the commonsense view and to argue that body is explicable in terms of mind rather than the reverse. It would be tempting, for the sake of terminological consistency, to call this view "identity mentalism," or something of that sort, but common usage dictates otherwise. We shall, accordingly, refer to this view as *panpsychism*.[1]

Third, it is possible to hold that the commonsense view in this matter is the correct one—that is, to maintain the interactionist position, which we have already described. It then is necessary to show that the interactionist position, with whatever problems it may involve, has at least as much to commend it as either of the other two alternatives.

All three positions have one task in common, however, and that is to give some account of the apparent causal relations between mind and body. Whether we adopt the identity materialist, the panpsychist, or the interactionist position, the problem with which the philosophers of the sixteenth and seventeenth centuries wrestled so unsuccessfully remains a genuine problem that demands some kind of answer.

A Word About Metaphysics

To make any headway with this problem, we are going to have to venture into the rather forbidding area of metaphysics. None of the views we shall be considering really stands by itself: each is integral to a particular metaphysical position and can scarcely be made intelligible apart from the more inclusive view. Identity materialism, for example, is not just one view among many with respect to the mind-body problem; it is the view of man, and especially of mind, that is implicit in *monistic materialism*, that is, that the whole of reality consists of matter and its determinations. The panpsychist view of mind and body, on the other hand, is implicit in the broader metaphysical view of *panpsychism*. And interactionism, or at any rate the mind-body dualism that it presupposes, is the view of man that is implicit in *ontological dualism*, that is, that matter and mind are ontologically distinct and that reality includes both. It is possible to carry on the discussion for a greater or shorter period of time without explicitly bringing in these wider metaphysical views, but

[1] Strictly speaking, panpsychism is a general metaphysical theory, whereas identity materialism is a theory about the relation between mind and body. There is no parallel term for the panpsychist theory of mind and body, however, so we shall have to use the single term "panpsychism" for both the metaphysical theory and the theory of mind and body that it entails.

they are always hovering in the background when the problem of mind and body is being discussed.

It has been said that the mind-body problem has given rise to more "isms" than any other problem in the history of philosophy, and this is probably true. The mind-body problem is a complex one. We have attempted in this introductory chapter to narrow it down somewhat in order that we may concentrate on just three theories—identity materialism, panpsychism, and interactionism. Any theory on the nature of body and mind, it would seem, must be reducible to one of these three types, and a comprehension of them will enable an understanding of related matters with little difficulty.

STUDY QUESTIONS

1. Give some examples of what are here called "mental events" and "physical events." Do you in practice have any difficulty in distinguishing the two? By what criteria do you make the distinction?
2. Summarize what you understand to be the commonsense view regarding body and mind. Is this also your view? What "puzzles," if any, seem implicit in this view?
3. What exactly is identity materialism? panpsychism? interactionism? Do these three exhaust the logically possible alternatives with respect to the mind-body problem? Explain.
4. Is anything of importance at stake in the discussion of this problem? Do you see any possible implications for psychology? for sociology? for ethics? for religion? Be specific.

31

IDENTITY MATERIALISM

There are four main reasons why people generally have adopted—or perhaps have unconsciously presupposed—the dualist view regarding mind and body. First, the apparent irreducibility of "mental events" and "physical events" seems to imply that they occur, respectively, in "minds" and "bodies." Thinking, feeling, desiring, wishing, willing, and the like, appear to be different in kind from moving, being moved, accelerating, decomposing, and so on. The most plausible explanation of this difference, it is asserted, is that mind is the subject of the one set of events and body the subject of the other. Hence, it is concluded, mind and body must be regarded as two distinct entities.

Second, the fact of personal continuity seems to favor the dualist account. Not one single particle of the matter of which my body is now composed was in my body twenty years ago, yet it seems that there is some sense in which I am the same "person" that I was twenty years ago. The only acceptable explanation of this fact, it is held, is that there is something that remains unaltered by these physical changes, namely, my "mind" or "soul." So on this ground, too, it appears that "mind" or "soul" must be something different from body.

Third, certain facts alleged to be discoverable by introspection—for example, our awareness of acting "deliberately" or "purposively"—are sometimes said to demonstrate that conscious activity cannot be adequately described as a physical process. In the act of "weighing alternatives," for example, it seems that I am directly aware of the fact that I am not simply observing a process that is going on, say, in my brain: I am actively doing something, and this something that I am doing, it is held, is irreducibly "mental." The point of this argument is that we are directly aware of the uniquely "mental" character of such activities in the act of performing them; hence, they are not reducible to some other kind of process different from what we allegedly know them to be.

For many people the same conclusion is strongly reinforced by a fourth and very different sort of consideration. In Western culture a widespread belief in, and hope for, life after death prevails. This evidently presupposes a "soul" capable of existing apart from the body, for it is evident that after the event that we call "death," the body decomposes and is eventually reduced to its basic elements. If, then, we are to give any meaning to the phrase "personal immortality," something must be presupposed in the constitution of man that is not subject to the process of decomposition; and this something is called the "soul," "mind," or "consciousness." The emotional fervor with which the dualistic account is sometimes maintained is, in my opinion, largely a result of this consideration.

These, then, are what I take to be the chief grounds upon which the dualist theory of body and mind has been erected. Some of these reasons are very persuasive, since they exhibit the dualist theory as an explanation of certain undeniable facts—facts that must obviously be accounted for in some way or other by any theory that may be proposed. Nonetheless, a number of other considerations provide strong grounds for doubting the correctness of this account, and I propose now to indicate in some detail what they are.

Reasons for Doubting the Correctness of the Dualist View

The dualist theory is suspect, in the first place, because it is impossible to form a clear concept of an entity called a "mind," "soul," or "consciousness." We have here a case parallel to that of the now thoroughly discredited idea of a "material substratum," which John Locke defined as "something I know not what that supports qualities." [1] Mind, apparently, is a something we know not what that thinks, feels, decides, and so on. It is the name for our ignorance of the true nature of mental events. To infer mind as the cause of mental events is equivalent to inferring wind gods as the cause of the blowing of the wind: the inference, in both cases, is vacuous.

In addition, whatever it is that is supposed to be meant by "mind" or "soul," there seem to be insuperable difficulties in the way of our knowing that any such entity exists. That some organisms are capable of perception and feeling seems evident: more or less definite criteria can be established to determine when such an event is or is not occurring. But there appear to be no criteria on the basis of which we could say in any given instance, "There is a mind." There is nothing that we can see, hear, taste, touch, or smell—no observational evidence, in other words

---

[1] John Locke, *An Essay Concerning Human Understanding*, II, xxiii (New York: Dover, 1959).

—that is in any way relevant to confirming or disconfirming the statement "A mind exists." To the purely conceptual difficulty of trying to understand just what it is that is being affirmed to exist when mind is being affirmed to exist, we must, therefore, add the epistemological difficulty that there seems to be no conceivable way by which the existence of these elusive entities could ever be known.

Even if it were possible to give conceptual clarity to the notion of mind, and even if some evidence could be adduced to render the existence of mind probable, it would still be quite impossible to conceive how mind could be involved in causal relations with body. Let me illustrate. Given a minimal knowledge of the laws of physiology, I can understand without too much difficulty how the movement of an arm, say, can be caused by the contraction of certain muscles, how the contraction of those muscles can be caused by certain nerve impulses, and how the nerve impulses can be caused by certain neural events— events occurring, that is, in the brain. All of these, it will be noted, are physical processes that are theoretically observable by anyone who approaches them with the proper instruments and the requisite knowledge. But how are we to understand these neural events as being "caused" by an allegedly nonphysical event called a "volition"? Is volition a sort of causation—perhaps an instance of pushing or pulling, or the passage of an electrical current, or what? No answer given to this question would be intelligible; that is what I mean when I say that it is impossible to conceive how body and mind can be involved in causal relations. The same difficulty arises, of course, whether it is mind that is alleged to act causally upon body (as in volition) or body upon mind (as in sensation).

Moreover, what we know about the structure of the nervous system makes it extremely unlikely that the process of deliberation, for example, and the purposive behavior that commonly follows it are different in kind from processes universally taken to be nonmental. Indeed, it seems very likely that the only difference between purposive activity and the reflex action of higher animals is degree of complexity. It is only because of the lapse of time between the stimulus and the response that we regard purposive behavior as something different in kind from reflex action.

Another very serious objection against the interactionist view is that if it were true, it would violate the principle of the conservation of energy, for which there is a vast amount of supporting evidence, including experimental evidence with regard to human activity. Briefly, the principle of the conservation of energy may be stated thus: In all physical processes, the total amount of energy in the universe remains constant; its form may be altered, but never its quantity. Moreover, every instance of causation known to us involves the transference of energy from the cause to the effect. If, then, it is said that some events in the body have effects in the mind, there must be some transfer of energy from the body to the mind. Since mind is allegedly unperceived, this energy should supposedly "disappear" for a time: the measurable energy in the body should decrease. And if the mind causes effects in the body, the amount of energy in the body should then increase. This does not appear to be the case. Thus, either body-mind interaction does not occur or body-mind interaction is a remarkable exception to the principle of the conservation of energy.

Finally, it seems implausible to me that there should be one large class of events—those associated with "mind" or "consciousness"—that cannot be understood in terms of the same principles that explain all other phenomena. Scientific research is steadily revealing to us a world that is best understood as an immense mechanism whose parts are interrelated and interdependent. That this system is incredibly complex is obvious. Indeed, some subsystems (that is, identifiable parts of the total system) are so complex that it takes many years of painstaking research to understand their workings (the genetic code, for example). Nonetheless, area after area of inquiry is yielding its secrets to the patient efforts of scientific researchers. It is simply unbelievable that "mental" phenomena should be the lone exception to a world that otherwise can be understood in terms of the laws of physics.

I think it must be conceded that the objections to which I have called attention constitute very substantial grounds for doubting the correctness of the dualist theory and thus justify the search for a more adequate alternative. Such an alternative is to be found, in my opinion, in the materialist view of mind.

A Materialist Theory of Mind

One difficulty of a purely semantic nature stands in the way of the general acceptance of a materialist view of mind: the term "materialism" frequently has strong negative connotations, due chiefly to its association with some rather crude theories advocated about a century ago. Let me make it clear, then, that I do not propose to account for mind in terms of tiny nuggets of matter that act and react upon one another according to Newton's Laws of Motion: nothing except a few fairly simple macroscopic phenomena can be accounted for in this way. Nor is it my intention, in this account of mind, to "dehumanize" man in any way. Man is clearly a noble and fortunate creature, and his capacity for intelligent behavior remains his most noble endowment, however it is to be understood.

Suppose that we try to understand man without positing a nonmaterial "mind" or "consciousness." How, then, must he be conceived? Clearly, he must be seen as a complex psychophysical organism capable of correspondingly complex behaviors. Some of these behaviors may sometimes be described (and appropriately so) in mentalistic terms, but there will be no activities of this organism that are purely "mental" activities, no activities that could only be understood as activities of a "mind" or "consciousness."

What I am asserting is that the universe as I understand it contains *no minds:* it contains organisms that behave in ways that have led some philosophers (and most nonphilosophers) to draw the erroneous conclusion that there are some entities called "minds." There is no such thing as a mind activity that might be called "thinking"—but there is a kind of human behavior that can rightly be described as "thoughtful." Similarly, there are no mind activities that can properly be called willing, remembering, wishing, and so on—but human beings do sometimes behave purposively, reflectively, or with desire. Mentalistic terms, in short, denote some of the ways in which human beings behave; they do not denote the activities of an unperceived nonspatial entity that is somehow "within" man. The dualist account of body and mind has been aptly called "the dogma of the ghost in the machine." [2] Identity materialism is sometimes thought to consist simply in exorcising the ghost, leaving only the machine. I am arguing, on the contrary, that man is neither a ghost nor a machine: he is a complex psychophysical organism capable of a peculiarly complex type of behavior that we sometimes describe in mentalistic terms.

"But surely," it will be objected, "people do not only behave thoughtfully; they also *think.* They not only act purposively; they *will,* they *decide.* Thinking, willing, choosing, sensing, deciding—surely these are activities in which human beings engage, not merely adverbial dimensions of other kinds of behavior. How can identity materialism account for such activities?"

It is evident that a complete answer to this objection would require an extensive analysis of each of the types of events commonly called "mental." Limitations of space make this impossible, and we must accordingly be selective. Let us take, then, the alleged mental process that we call "thinking." If we can show that thinking is capable of being understood without recourse to a substantival theory of mind, we may justly claim to have defended our view in what must be regarded as a crucial test case; for thinking is without doubt the activity *par excellence* of which minds are supposed to be the subjects.

A typical example of what we call "thinking" would be a student's attempting to solve a problem, say, trying to find the square root of 196. What does the student do? If he does not know the procedure for finding square roots, he will have to tackle the logically prior problem of finding out how to do them. If he does know the procedure, he will simply apply it, presumably with the help of pencil and paper. And if he is a bright student with a lot of practice solving problems of this sort, he may even be able to dispense with paper and pencil and do it, as we say, "in his head."

---

[2] Gilbert Ryle, *The Concept of Mind* (New York: Barnes & Noble, 1949), p. 15 and elsewhere.

But what is going on "in his head" when he is attempting to solve this problem? The answer seems to be that certain processes are occurring in his brain. He may, as an aid to these processes, put some numbers down on paper, but this is not essential to the process itself. (It is not even essential to such a process that the person engaged in it be directly aware of what he is doing: mathematicians frequently are able to give the answer to a problem without consciously going through the steps by which the answer is deduced. The same conclusion can be drawn from the fact that we sometimes wake up knowing the answer to a problem that we tried unsuccessfully to solve the night before: the relevant "thinking" occurred, apparently, during sleep.) What is essential is only that the answer he comes up with should in fact be the square root of 196—that he should end up by "knowing" what is the square root of 196.

A number of further considerations may be adduced in support of the view that thinking consists in a physical process that presumably occurs in the brain. For one thing, we are able to do it better at some times than at others. When we are fatigued, for example, we do not do it nearly so well as when we are rested. Also, our ability to think can be enhanced or decreased by administering certain drugs. Drugs and fatigue do have certain effects on the body, including the brain; hence, it seems likely that the process itself is a process occurring in the brain.

It may be objected that *awareness* of thinking is not itself a process going on in the brain. Perhaps. But this awareness, as we have already noted, does not always accompany the process that we call "thinking," though sometimes, admittedly, it does. Moreover, to explain this awareness we should have to analyze introspection; and this, too, is a physiological process, as are all of the phenomena we call "mental events."

Replies to Objections

The most serious objections that could be raised against the materialist view of mental occurrences are precisely those considerations that led to the adoption of the dualist theory in the first place. The apparent irreducibility of "mental events" and "physical events" amounts, in my opinion, to little more than the irreducibility of the *language* of personal experience to the *language* of objective occurrences. We recognize that the sentence "I am seeing a blue object" is not translatable into a sentence of the form "Such and such processes are occurring in my brain," and we conclude from this that the two sentences are not about the same thing. That we have these two kinds of language to describe mental events is undeniable, but no conclusion about the status of such events follows from this fact.

The notion of personal continuity is something of a puzzle. That it is not to be accounted for by positing a "soul" or "self" that persists throughout all bodily changes is evident, however, when we consider that institutions and other complex existences are also said to exhibit continuity. Take, for example, a university that has been in existence for a century or more. None of the original faculty, students, administration, or regents are now associated with the university. It is very possible that none of the original books are any longer to be found in the library and that no building now on the campus was there in the beginning. Yet in *some* sense it is said to be the "same" university, for over relatively short spans of time a number of the elements that constitute the university— physical plant, faculty, and over shorter spans, the student body—for the most part remain unchanged. Perhaps continuity in the case of persons ought to be understood in much the same way. My continuity with the self of yesterday consists in the fact that in looks, habits, faults, abilities, physical structure, and so forth, I am for the most part identical with that person—but only "for the most part." Continuity, then, consists in the fact not that some one element remains constant throughout but that change occurs in the context of a relatively stable structure.

No conclusion about the status of mind can be drawn, it seems to me, from the fact that we are allegedly directly aware on occasion of acting "deliberately" or "purposively." We are apparently in a position to know our own mental states in a way that others are not (although it is to be noted that fairly precise criteria can be established for judging some-one's behavior to be "deliberate" and/or "purposive"), but it can scarcely be argued that it therefore follows that a mental state consists in some determination of a nonphysical entity that we call our "mind." It is just as plausible to hold that this awareness is simply one of the by-products of the occurrence of such and such a neural process.

On the question of life after death, certainly the hope for such a thing does not constitute a valid reason for holding that the conditions for it do, in fact, obtain. In the materialist view of mind, when death occurs, mind perishes no less than body; it is as meaningless to talk of the continuation of mind after the deterioration of the brain as it is to talk of the continuation of running after the deterioration of someone's legs. "Mind" is the collective, and misleading, name for those dimensions of human behavior that we call "intelligent." When the human organism dies, it ceases to behave at all; thus intelligent behavior also ceases. When running stops, "swiftly" cannot continue by itself; when behavior ceases, "mind" no longer has any meaning.

The old puzzle about how mind and body could interact, or how the appearance of interaction was to be accounted for, is evidently a consequence of the mistake of separating body and mind in the first place and regarding the latter as a substantial entity that has then to be rerelated to body in some odd way. Mind is minding; it is adjectivally, adverbially, related to the body and its behavior. But body is explicable in terms of the laws governing matter, particularly matter as organized in complex living organisms; hence, mind, too, is explicable in terms of those self-same laws.

STUDY QUESTIONS

1. What are suggested in this chapter as the main reasons why people generally have tended to favor the interactionist view of body and mind? Can you think of any additional reasons for this? How would you rank these reasons, from "strongest" to "weakest"?
2. Summarize Materialist's reasons for doubting the correctness of the dualist view. Which list of reasons—this list or the one written in answer to the previous question—strikes you as being the most convincing?
3. What exactly is the view of mind that Materialist is proposing? What arguments does he use to support this view?
4. What are Materialist's answers to what he regards as the chief arguments in favor of the interactionist view? Which do you personally find more convincing, the arguments in support of the interactionist view or Materialist's replies to them?

32

PANPSYCHISM

If we are to arrive at an acceptable view on the question of mind and body, it is important to distinguish carefully between (a) the considerations against the dualist account and (b) those supporting a materialist theory. It is sometimes assumed that if the dualist theory can be shown to be inadequate, the materialist account of mind will readily be seen as correct. This idea, I am convinced, is erroneous. I hope to show that the correct view is, instead, that body, or "matter," is to be understood mentalistically.

I should like to begin by reinforcing an observation made incidentally in the introductory chapter of this section. Although the problem of the relation between body and mind appears to be straightforwardly about how we are to understand *man*, at root it is a metaphysical problem. To argue that mind is nothing but a particular determination of matter is simply not plausible. No one, I think, who confined his attention to the known facts about the relevant physical and psychological phenomena would ever be tempted to subscribe to such an account. The philosophers who nonetheless do take this approach do so, I think, out of a prior conviction that *all* phenomena are ultimately to be understood in terms of matter and its laws. They are, in other words, committed from the start to the metaphysics of monistic materialism. The existence of mental phenomena, therefore, constitutes an embarrassing problem for them, and they are accordingly compelled to try to "reduce" mind to matter on pain of having their metaphysical theory discredited. This is true whether the metaphysics that inspires the attempt is overt, as in the case of the nineteenth-century materialists, or covert, as it is with many philosophers at the present time.

The materialist account of mind, to me, is so unconvincing that I would prefer to simply ignore it and proceed directly to a far more plausible alternative. However, many people today do find monistic materialism very attractive, so I must take time to point out some of the most serious inadequacies of Materialist's account. And since identity materialism is needed to maintain the metaphysics of monistic materialism, my critique of the materialist theory of mind may also be construed as a *reductio ad absurdum* of that metaphysical theory.

Critique of the Materialist Theory of Mind

The materialist theory of mind is inadequate in at least four respects. First, this theory does not provide a believable account of what is happening when we are thinking, feeling, perceiving, remembering, desiring, willing, and the like. Let us consider "thinking," since this is the example that Materialist has briefly discussed. It seems evident that (*a*) whether or not a neural process of some unique sort is occurring whenever a person is thinking of some particular thing, this certainly has never been shown to be the case; and (*b*) even if thinking of a determinate sort is always accompanied by some corresponding neural process, it does not follow that thinking simply *consists in* this neural process. The question of what neural processes are correlated with what mental states is, surely, an empirical question, and the investigation of this matter has not yet proceeded to the point where anyone can claim a one-to-one correspondence between the two. Even if this were to be established, however, it is extremely implausible to hold that thinking is the *same thing* as the neural process that accompanies it. A well-designed and properly programmed computer, for example, is capable of solving certain kinds of problems far more quickly than even the brightest of mathematicians; yet we should not (except metaphorically) describe the process by which it does so as "thinking." What is the difference? The difference is that to say that something is an instance of thinking is to posit a mind, a consciousness, as the subject of the thinking; nothing other than metaphysical prejudice could ever induce someone to give a different answer.

Materialist has, in a way, attempted to answer this objection. He says the apparent irreducibility of mental events and physical events amounts to little more than the irreducibility of the language of personal experience to the language of objective occurrences. But this way out of the difficulty is not open to the materialist. If the materialist account of mind is correct, then a sentence like "I am seeing a blue object" *ought to be* logically equivalent to the sentence "Such and such processes are occurring in my brain." The statement "Rutabagas do not taste good," for example, can be translated "So and so does not like rutabagas," since these statements are *about* the same thing—the likes and dislikes of some particular person or persons. Alternative descriptions of the same state of affairs are always interchangeable. If, then, it is conceded that in the present case the two descriptions are not interchangeable, then they obviously are not describing the same state of affairs: mental states are not *equivalent to* neural processes.

Materialist's account of personal continuity is also quite obviously inconsistent with what we know about this phenomenon from the one case each of us actually experiences—*his own* continuity. My knowledge that I stand in a relation of continuity with that certain person born on such and such a date at such and such a place who is I rests, surely, on the fact that I have recollections of experiences that are so related that I necessarily see them as members of a single series. I know that I am the "same person" who last evening watched a baseball game, last year took a trip to Chicago, some years ago attended a certain university, and before that lived in a certain city, because I *remember* having the experiences that constitute these several events. It may well be that the "stuff" of which my body is composed has been completely changed during this long span of time; but certain patterns, a certain more or less constant organization of this "stuff," and certain serially related memories have endured. It is to these that I have reference when I say that throughout this time I have been the "same person."

It seems grossly misleading, therefore, to explain personal continuity on the analogy of the continuity of a nonorganic complex like a university. The analogy, if there is one, must surely be applied in the other direction. An institution has, admittedly, a kind of fictional unity that bears some analogy to the unity of a person (as does a nation, a club, a political party, etc.); and the recorded history of an institution might be compared in some ways to the remembered experience of a human being. We can even personify a university and sing "her" praises in song and verse, but we know well enough that the "person" we thus posit does not really exist except in a metaphorical sense. It is not nearly so evident that Materialist is aware of the fact that he is using a metaphor, and a misleading one at that, when he attempts to "thingify" our experience of personal continuity.

One final objection. The materialist theory of mind implies that people never act in terms of conscious purposes freely chosen but only as a result of external causes. In our own experience, at least, we know that this is not true. Despite Materialist's disavowal of the older mechanism, his position involves a mechanistic view of human behavior; and mechanism, old or new, is a bitter pill to swallow. We surely believe ourselves to act freely and purposively a good deal of the time. Indeed, I should say that we know ourselves to do so. Unless we are to regard this knowledge as no knowledge, as illusory, we must reject the materialist account of mind. If we do adopt that account, we must accept its mechanistic consequences.

Another Alternative

So far we have agreed with Materialist that the dualist account of body and mind—the view that body and mind are two distinct entities involved in mutual causal relations—is untenable, and we have rejected the materialist alternative of attempting to account for mind as a peculiar determination, or set of determinations, of matter. There now appears to be only one possibility remaining, and that is to regard *mind* as fundamental and body as explicable in terms of mind. What case can be made for this alternative? Since we have acknowledged that any resolution of this problem presupposes some metaphysical theory, let us begin by noting some of the more important features of such theories.

Metaphysics consists in the attempt to elaborate a system of concepts in terms of which every phenomenon that we encounter can be interpreted and understood. The requirements that a metaphysical system must meet are that (a) some phenomena shall be explicable in terms of it, (b) no phenomena shall be inexplicable in terms of it, (c) it shall be internally consistent, and (d) it shall not have implications that are absurd or contrary to fact. The method by which such systems are elaborated consists in (a) generalizing some concepts that are known to have application in some limited sphere and (b) attempting to apply the concepts thus developed to all phenomena—attempting, in other words, to give them a universal application. Monistic materialism, for example, is a metaphysical system whose central concepts were originally adapted from the science of mechanics. My criticism of it is that it does not provide a plausible explanation of mental, or psychological, phenomena.

Suppose, then, that we relinquish the idea that everything that occurs is explicable in terms of tiny units of lifeless matter that act and react upon one another according to certain laws. Let us see if we can give a better account of things by saying instead that the ultimate constituents of which the universe is composed are to be conceived on the analogy of *mind*. Everything is to be conceived as being composed of a greater or lesser number of "droplets of experience," or "atoms of consciousness," each of which is in some degree aware of the environment that constitutes its world, and each of which accordingly takes account of its environment in a way that is appropriate to its particular level of awareness. Following Alfred North Whitehead (1861–1947), we shall call such a center of experience an "actual occasion." [1]

Since the idea of an actual occasion is derived from our direct awareness of our own selfhood, it is natural that we should develop the idea in terms of other concepts derived from there as well. We know, for example, that our own lives are describable as careers in which we are constantly obliged to make choices. Our past and the constitution of the rest of the world severely limit the possibilities open to us, but there are some possibilities for each of us, a variety of alternatives from which we must choose. Let us say, then, that the life of every actual occasion is a

---

[1] See Alfred North Whitehead, *Process and Reality* (New York: Harper & Row, 1960), p. 113.

career in which it must choose, from among the possibilities available to it, what it is to become. Its possibilities, like ours, are determined by (a) its past, (b) the constitution of the rest of the world that it has to take into account, and (c) its own level of awareness. Every actual occasion, then, will experience something—something appropriate to its own level of awareness—analogous to what in man is called perception, feeling, remembering, willing, and so on.

According to this account, what is a "material object," for example, a stone? Let us call it a "society of actual occasions," an aggregate of actual occasions united together in a quasi unity analogous to that of a society of persons. No doubt the level of awareness of the actual occasions that compose a stone is of a very low order—lower, for example, than that of the lowest organism—and the alternatives open to them are so severely limited that so far as we can see they do little more than perpetuate themselves virtually unchanged from moment to moment. So unvarying are their choices, in fact, that we can observe statistical uniformities in the behavior of the society, can formulate, in other words, certain laws descriptive of the behavior of the aggregate. We can do the same thing, it is to be noted, with respect to a colony of ants or bees.

Our way of taking account of such aggregates is through what we call "perception"—in the case of our perceiving a stone, by means of sight and touch. Its way of taking account of us is to resist our efforts to penetrate it, to allow itself to be moved on occasion, and so on.

The level of awareness of actual occasions appears to vary greatly, and the options available to an actual occasion seem to widen as the level increases. In inorganic substances, the level appears to be at its lowest: we cannot even begin to imagine what it would be like to *be* a grain of sand or a particle of calcium. With the simplest organisms, the level is higher: the very simplest plants are able to exercise a degree of freedom that is unknown to any particle of inorganic matter. The level increases when we come to insects, still more when we come to the higher animals, and reaches its fullest realization in man. So great is it in even the case of the higher animals such as dogs, horses, monkeys, and the like that we can almost imagine what it would be like to be such a creature; in any case, we cannot seriously doubt that they have a consciousness in many ways similar to our own.

How, then, ought we to conceive of man? As a society of actual occasions of varying levels of awareness. Some one of these dominates and gives unity to the society; this we call the "mind" or "soul." In the experience that we call perception—feeling a pain, for example—the pain is experienced by the finger, say, as a pressure or a piercing, by the nerves as an electrical current, by the brain as certain brain waves that occur in it, and by the mind as the feeling of pain. The experience that we call willing is experienced by the mind as deliberation and decision, by the brain as a directive to enact such and such an alternative, by the nerves as electrical impulses of a certain kind, and by the appropriate muscles as a directive to contract in such and such a way. The society, when it is healthy, is a cooperative society, each member doing its part to ensure the welfare of the whole under the guidance of its dominant member. When a hostile "foreigner" enters (as in infection), or when some members of the society become uncooperative (as in cancer), the whole society suffers; and if it cannot repel the invaders, or get rid of the uncooperative members, the whole society may be destroyed.

Limitations of space have permitted only the very briefest sketch of the metaphysical scheme in terms of which, I believe, the relation of body and mind can be correctly understood. Much more detail and countless additional examples of its explanatory power would have to be provided before I could hope to persuade many of my readers that what I am suggesting is at least in the direction of the truth. Here, I must be content to let the plausibility of my proposal rest on its ability to solve the familiar puzzles of the relation between body and mind: (*a*) the alleged impossibility of forming a clear concept of "mind," (*b*) the alleged difficulty of knowing that any such entity exists, (*c*) the difficulty of trying to understand how unthinking body and unextended mind can interact, (*d*) the problem of how we are to conceive of personal continuity in the case of conscious organisms, and (*e*) the problem of how certain "mental events" are related to the so-called physical events with which they are associated.

My answer to each of these puzzles is as follows. First, there is no difficulty whatsoever in forming a perfectly clear concept of mind unless we demand that the concept be formed in spatial terms. The question, What kind of body is a mind? is not a proper question and deserves no answer. I cannot form an "image" of a mind because a mind is not the sort of thing that occupies space, and only things that occupy space can be "imaged." But I know as clearly as I know anything what a mind is: a conscious center of feelings, perceptions, thoughts, and volitions.

There is also no difficulty in knowing that mind exists. In the very act of thinking, feeling, doubting, and so forth, I know that I exist. In the intelligent behavior of other organisms, especially in the intelligible communication that I have with other minds, I know that other minds also exist.

There are no unthinking bodies; hence there is no "gap" between body and mind that has to be bridged by some half-mind–half-body "connecting link." There are only minds of varying levels of awareness; and every mind is able to take account of those that constitute its world in ways appropriate to its level of awareness. (Minds at a relatively low level of awareness, for example, take account of one another by means of what we call "mechanical causation.")

Personal continuity in the case of any organism—whether or not it is "conscious" in the strict, unextended, sense of that word—consists in the persistence of its structural unity and its unique relation to its past history, which past history it must take into account in choosing the next stage in its career. Something analogous to memory, therefore, must characterize the experience of every actual occasion.

There are no such things as purely physical events properly so-called. Everything that occurs is an event in the career of some actual occasion or society of actual occasions. It is only when we abstract from this and view it, so to speak, "from the outside" that we get the derivative notion of a "physical event." A given event may be perceived as a feeling of pain by the actual occasion (mind) that is dominant in the society constituting a human brain; the same event may be perceived by a neurosurgeon as the occurrence of certain neural processes. It all depends on how one actual occasion takes account of the experiences of other actual occasions, which in turn depends in large part on the particular ways in which that actual occasion happens to be related to them.

STUDY QUESTIONS

1. What inadequacies does Panpsychist claim to find in the materialist theory of mind? Do these seem to be serious objections to the materialist theory? How might Materialist attempt to answer them?
2. What precisely is panpsychism? How well, in your opinion, does it measure up to the "requirements that a metaphysical system must meet" as itemized by Panpsychist?
3. What theory of man does Panpsychist propose? How is this theory supposed to provide a solution to the mind-body problem?
4. What at this point seem to be the strongest arguments in favor of the panpsychist theory of body and mind? What seem to be the strongest arguments against it?
5. Write a critique of panpsychism from the point of view of a materialist, answering the objections raised by Panpsychist against the materialist theory and raising appropriate objections to the panpsychist theory.

33

DUALISM RECONSIDERED

Let me begin this defense of dualism by saying that on at least two points I am in very close agreement with Panpsychist. First, I think he is quite right when he says that there is no special difficulty in forming a clear concept of "mind"—except for those who are really looking for an *image* rather than a *concept.* No nonspatial entity can be "imaged," since "image-ing" is modeled after visual perception, and visual perception is always spatially determined. Any attempt to form an "image" of mind or soul—such as Plato's famous word picture (in the dialogue *Phaedrus*) of the two horses and the charioteer—clearly must be metaphorical in character, at best, a pale reflection of reality itself. I find nothing obscure, however, in the concept of mind as a conscious center of feeling, perception, thought, and volition.

Second, I agree with Panpsychist that there is no special difficulty to knowing that mind exists. Descartes was essentially right, I think, in saying that our own existence as a thinking being (*res cogitans*) is the most indubitable fact we can know. Even if we doubt that anything else exists, we must exist in order to do the doubting. As for the existence of other minds, we obviously have to infer from the outward behavior of the other person that he or she is in a mental state such as we know ourselves to be in when we behave in such and such a way (tears when we are sad, grimaces when we are in pain, laughter when we are happy, etc.). But our inferences in such cases are as warranted, surely, as any inference can be.

I am not at all persuaded, however, by Panpsychist's suggestion that the problem of how mind and body can interact, or appear to interact, is to be solved by simply disallowing that there is any such thing as body, any more than I am by Materialist's mechanistic explanation. Communication between minds by means of intelligible discourse, and communication between bodies by means of mechanical causation, are two processes I can understand well enough not to feel puzzled about them. Now whatever it is that goes on between mind and body—in perception and in volition—does not seem to be reducible to either of these. We must look further for our explanation of body-mind intercausality.

Is it, indeed, even meaningful to say that the ultimate constituents of which a stone, for example, is composed are "minds with a very low level of awareness"? It makes sense, I think, to talk about animals and insects having something like a human consciousness, because something like the behavior that we know to be associated with consciousness in man is to be observed in the behavior of animals. We have, in this case, three points of reference in relation to which we can fill in the fourth: human consciousness is to certain kinds of human behavior as x is to somewhat similar animal behavior. But in the case of stones, and in the case of individual parts of the human body, we lack the "similar behavior" that would permit us to work the sum. What, then, does it mean to posit "low-level consciousness" in such things? Nothing at all.

With respect to the nature of personal continuity, I am not sure that I understand what Panpsychist is suggesting; consequently, I am not sure whether I agree or disagree with his view. It seems clear to me, in any case, that our awareness of our own personal continuity is tied up with our awareness of having a mind that is one and the same mind from the beginning to the end of our life. In the strict sense of the word, therefore, I do not think that we should attribute personal continuity to any beings except those who have minds like ours. In an analogous sense, however, we can attribute continuity to animals on the ground that they possess a consciousness somewhat similar to our own, and we can attribute organic continuity to any organism so long as it maintains its organic structure and unity. Aggregates of inorganic matter—stones, for example—can be said to have continuity only in the sense that they have a relatively stable structure, but this is a very loose application of the notion of continuity: a piece of a stone is itself a stone and has as much structure as the larger one from which it came.

Finally, it appears wholly gratuitous to say, as Panpsychist does, that there are no such things as physical events "properly so-called." In one sense of this statement, it is obviously false: there *are* lightning flashes, thunderclaps, planetary motions, and things of that sort. These are surely more properly described as "physical events" than as anything else we might be inclined to call them. But this, obviously, is not what Panpsychist means to deny. What he is contending is, rather, that we should not think of such events as the consequences of the actions and reactions of bits of lifeless, unconscious matter operating according to certain invariable laws. What is really the case, he wants to say, is that everything that exists—including electrons, protons, and so on—is composed of tiny "droplets of consciousness" and everything that occurs—including what we call "physical events"—is, properly understood, an experience in the career of some such droplet or droplets. This whole account seems to me, for reasons already given, altogether gratuitous, fantastic, and meaningless; it is, as someone has said, so incredible that no one but a very learned man could ever have thought of it.

Therefore, the attempt to reduce body to mind must be regarded as a failure, just as the attempt to reduce mind to body has been shown to be a failure. Since, then, there appears to be no viable alternative to the dualist view of body and mind that is alleged to involve insuperable difficulties, we should look once again at these difficulties to see if they cannot be removed without doing violence to our sense of what is credible. Certainly the prima facie evidence must be conceded to be on the side of dualism: it is only the so-called difficulties of this view that have led to the fruitless search for a monistic alternative. Let us see whether on this matter common sense cannot, for once, be vindicated.

The Alleged Difficulties of the Dualist View

The difficulties alleged to be inherent in the dualist view of body and mind have been nicely summarized by Materialist as follows: (a) the conceptual difficulty of trying to understand what the term "mind" is supposed to denote; (b) the epistemological difficulty of knowing anything about such an entity, if there is one; (c) the alleged impossibility of conceiving how body and mind could interact; (d) the alleged impossibility of distinguishing between purposive behavior and "reflex action" behavior in view of the fact that the same nervous system is apparently involved in both; and (e) the suggestion that interaction, if it occurred, would violate the principle of the conservation of energy. We shall consider each of these difficulties in turn.

To what I have already said regarding the first two points I should like to add that it is materialistic dogmatism alone that creates the first-mentioned difficulty and empiricist dogmatism alone that creates the second. Otherwise, enough has already been said on the first point; anyone who is able to distinguish between a concept and an image should have no difficulty forming a precise concept of mind. On the second point, I can only say, "*Of course* we cannot see, feel, taste, touch or smell minds: they are not the sort of thing that can be perceived in that way." But we have already discussed this point sufficiently in our earlier remarks.

Let us leave the interactionist puzzle for a moment and consider the two quasi-scientific arguments. With respect to what I shall call the "nervous system argument," there surely must be *some* difference between deliberate actions and reflex actions that leads us to make the distinction in the first place. What is it, then, that leads us to call some instances of behavior—blinking, sneezing, flinching, and so on—reflex actions? The answer, surely, is that these actions occur without deliberation or decision on our part: there is a stimulus (a thrown object, a tickle in the nose, a loud noise) and the response follows immediately—"automatically," as we say. We do not have to decide to do something in such cases; we just do it. Reflex actions are, as it were, natural habits of the human organism. With deliberate actions, the situation is different: we must decide both what we shall do and when we shall do it; and the process of deliberation may be as brief or as protracted as we choose to make it.

It is not at all plausible to argue that the difference between these two kinds of behavior is due only to the relatively greater complexity of the neural processes involved in deliberate behavior, for even if these processes are more complex than those involved in reflex action (whatever "complexity" means in this context), it does not follow that this is the only difference. Certainly the same nervous system must be employed in the two cases: it is the only nervous system we have. But our own experience tells us that there is, nonetheless, a qualitative difference between the two. The most plausible explanation of this difference is that in the one case mind is active and in the other case it is not; in the one case mind is agent and in the other it is only a spectator. The "nervous system argument," therefore, has no force whatsoever as an objection to the dualist view.

Nor, I think, is the "conservation of energy" argument any more convincing. There are, actually, two different forms of this argument. One would have it that the dualist theory implies that in man the principle of the conservation of energy is violated, and that because we know this principle to be universally valid, the dualist theory is therefore false. The other reasons that the dualist theory implies that in man the principle of the conservation of energy is violated, and that because we have experimental evidence to show that this is not the case, the dualist theory must be false. The argument, in either form, is usually put forward with a great show of scientific learning, leaving the impression that either the dualist or the late Professor Albert Einstein must be mistaken—and there is little doubt, in such a contest, who will be the winner.

Whether or not the principle of the conservation of energy is universally valid is a question for physicists to decide, and neither Materialist nor I have any basis for an opinion. Be that as it may, however, the argument cannot succeed unless it can also be shown that the interaction of body and mind, if it does occur, involves the transference of energy from one to the other. This has never been demonstrated: it has only been presupposed. It may well be that every instance of purely physical causation involves such a transference of energy; this, again, is a question for the physicist, not the philosopher, to decide. But it is surely begging the issue to simply presuppose that body-mind interaction, if it occurs, must be an instance of physical causation and must therefore conform to the laws governing such events.

Both the "nervous system argument" and the "conservation of energy" argument are thinly veiled attempts to bring not scientific facts but scientific *prestige* to bear against the interactionist view. Neither argument arises because of any puzzles inherent in the dualist view: they are arguments invented for the purpose of discrediting the dualist view after that view has already been rejected on other grounds. These grounds, as I think Panpsychist has amply shown, are metaphysical ones: the dualist view of body and mind is distinctly uncongenial to the metaphysics of materialism. We are left, then, with only one difficulty in the way of adopting the dualist view of body and mind, that of understanding how body and mind can interact. What is it about this phenomenon that strikes us as being so odd?

Why Interaction Is Puzzling

Perhaps the reason that mind-body interaction appears so puzzling is that mind and body seem to be so dissimilar to one another. How can a nonspatial and nonphysical entity like a *mind* be involved in mutual causal relations with an unthinking physical entity like a *body*? But a moment's reflection makes it evident that this question does not locate precisely the source of our bewilderment, for there are innumerable examples of causation between dissimilar entities that pose no such puzzlement. We believe without difficulty that there is a causal relation between a mosquito bite and malaria, between the throwing of a switch and the blowing of a siren, between the pressure on an accelerator and the increasing speed of an automobile; yet the two terms in each of these examples are highly dissimilar. We must look further for the source of our bewilderment.

Perhaps the reason that we are mystified about apparent instances of mind-body interaction in a way that we are not mystified by instances of intraphysical causality is that in cases of the latter kind we conceive of the cause and the effect (however dissimilar they may be) as being parts of a *single system*, governed by the *same laws*. We assume that there is some coherent set of laws—chemical, physical, biological—in terms of which the several series of events from the mosquito bite to the malaria, the throwing of the switch to the blowing of the siren, and the pressing of the accelerator to the increase in speed of the automobile are all explicable. If we are mystified at this level, it is because we do not know which laws are relevant to the phenomena in question. (Compare: How do mosquitoes cause malaria? How do burns cause feelings of pain?) In the case of mind-body interaction it seems that we have to deal with two "systems," and the laws governing the interaction of body and mind do not seem to be assimilable to either.

Let me illustrate. We can explain a burn—up to a point. We can, with the help of the relevant physical laws, relate the occurrence of the flame to the increase of temperature on the surface of the skin; this increase in temperature to the occurrence of tiny electrical impulses in certain nerves; and the occurrence of these impulses to the occurrence of a certain pattern of brain waves. But then we reach a gap in our explanation: we have no laws—none that are coherent with, or a part of, the system of laws we have been using thus far—that will enable us to relate the occurrence of the brain waves to the feeling of pain in the consciousness of the injured person.

Once we posit the feeling of pain in that consciousness, however, we have no difficulty understanding subsequent mental events. The injured man "deliberates" between going to the doctor and treating himself; he "remembers" that his wife warned him to be careful about lighting camp stoves; he "decides" to treat the burn himself; and so on. Once we get to *mind*, we can "lock in" on the other system, and everything is all right. But then there is volition and the ensuing behavior (brain waves, nerves, muscles, etc.), and once again we encounter the gap.

Our puzzlement about the interaction of body and mind is, therefore, an expression of our desire to reduce all phenomena to some single unitary system, with one set of laws applicable to all events. But the only possible ways of fulfilling this desire would be to explain mental phenomena in terms of physical laws (identity materialism), or physical phenomena in terms of mental laws (panpsychism), and neither of these explanations is adequate to the facts. We are left, therefore, with an ultimate and irreducible dualism, a dualism that may leave us puzzled and dissatisfied but which we must, nonetheless, accept.

Although we cannot understand mind-body interaction either in terms of the laws governing physical phenomena or in terms of the laws governing mental phenomena—cannot construe it, that is, either as a physical phenomenon or as a mental phenomenon—we have the best possible evidence that such interaction does occur, namely, our own experience. Physical events *do* cause mental events: we know this from countless instances of what we call perception. Mental events *do* cause physical events: we know this from countless instances of willed, deliberate behavior. These are the facts, and they cannot be denied, however puzzled we may be about the *modus operandi* of that unique mode of causality that occurs in the mutual relations of body and mind.

To realize why we find it difficult to comprehend mind-body interaction, however, is in some degree to rid ourselves of the puzzle. We then understand why this particular sort of causality seems so odd, and we are free to look at it without being tempted to deny the obvious in order to assimilate it to some other mode of explanation; we are no longer "bothered" by its oddness. It is only in this sense that an informed dualism constitutes a "solution" to the mind-body problem. The odyssey that begins with common sense and that seeks a solution to its puzzles in either materialistic or mentalistic monism reaches its culmination in a view that might be best described as common sense made sure of itself. To accept such a view is to accept the puzzle of how mind and body interact in preference to the even more bewildering puzzles that result if the reality of either is denied.

STUDY QUESTIONS

1. On what points does Dualist agree with Panpsychist? What objections does he raise against Panpsychist's position? Could Materialist, without abandoning his own position, join Dualist in urging these same objections?
2. Write a defense of panpsychism against the objections raised by Dualist. Which of Dualist's arguments do you find most difficult to refute?
3. What is the "nervous system" argument against dualism, and how does Dualist attempt to answer it? Who do you think has the strongest case on this particular point?
4. What is the "conservation of energy" argument against dualism? What is Dualist's answer to this argument?
5. What is it, according to Dualist, that makes apparent mind-body interaction so puzzling? Do you think he is right about this? Are you satisfied with his final answer to the puzzle?

Armstrong, D. M. *A Materialist Theory of the Mind.* London: Routledge and Kegan Paul, 1967.

Aune, Bruce. "Feelings, Moods, and Introspection," *Mind,* 72 (1963), 187–207.

————."The Problem of Other Minds," *The Philosophical Review,* 70 (1961), 320–339.

Borst, C. V. *The Mind-Brain Identity Theory.* London: Macmillan, 1970 (paperbound). A collection of papers pro and con.

Broad, C. D. *The Mind and Its Place in Nature.* Paterson, N.J.: Littlefield, Adams, 1960 (paperbound), chaps. 3 and 14.

Campbell, Keith. *Body and Mind.* Garden City, N.Y.: Doubleday, 1970 (paperbound). Contains a good bibliography.

Cornman, James W. *Materialism and Sensations.* New Haven, Conn.: Yale University Press, 1971. Defends an adverbial theory.

Dewey, John. *Experience and Nature.* LaSalle, Ill.: Open Court, 1958 (paperbound).

Ducasse, C. J. *Nature, Mind and Death.* LaSalle, Ill.: Open Court, 1951.

Evans, C. O. *The Subject of Consciousness.* London: G. Allen & Unwin, 1970.

Ewing, A. C. *The Fundamental Questions of Philosophy.* New York: Macmillan, 1951, chap. 6.

Feigl, Herbert. *The "Mental" and the "Physical."* London: Oxford University Press, 1968 (paperbound).

————. "The Mind-Body Problem in the Development of Logical Empiricism," in M. Brodbeck and H. Feigl (eds.). *Readings in the Philosophy of Science.* New York: Appleton-Century-Crofts, 1953, pp. 612–626.

Grossman, Reinhardt. *The Structure of Mind.* Madison, Wis.: University of Wisconsin Press, 1965. Detailed critique of arguments for phenomenalism from a realist perspective.

Hume, David. *A Treatise of Human Nature.* Many editions. See Book I, Section VI.

Joske, W. D. "Behaviorism as a Scientific Theory," *Philosophy and Phenomenological Research,* 22 (1961), 61–68.

Krikorian, Y. "A Naturalistic View of Mind," in Y. Krikorian (ed.). *Naturalism and the Human Spirit.* New York: Columbia University Press, 1944, pp. 242–269.

————. "The Publicity of Mind," *Philosophy and Phenomenological Research,* 22 (1962), 317–325.

Lachs, John. "Epiphenomenalism and the Notion of Cause," *The Journal of Philosophy,* 60 (1963), 141–146.

Laird, John. *Our Minds and Their Bodies.* London: Oxford University Press, 1925.

Laslett, Peter (ed.). *The Physical Basis of Mind.* Oxford: Basil Blackwell, 1951.

Lewis, H. D. *The Elusive Mind.* London: G. Allen & Unwin, 1970. Defends mind-body dualism against its major contemporary critics.

Locke, Don. *Myself and Others: A Study in Our Knowledge of Minds.* London: Oxford University Press, 1968. Current and lucid.

Malcom, Norman. "Knowledge of Other Minds," *The Journal of Philosophy,* 55 (1958), 969–978.

O'Connor, John (ed.). *Modern Materialism: Readings on Mind-Body Identity.* New York: Harcourt, Brace & World, 1969. Useful bibliography.

Rosenthal, D. M. (ed.). *Materialism and the Mind-Body Problem.* Englewood Cliffs, N.J.: Prentice-Hall, 1971.

Russell, Bertrand. *The Analysis of Mind.* New York: Humanities Press, 1958.

Ryle, Gilbert. *The Concept of Mind.* New York: Barnes & Noble, 1965 (paperbound).

Shaffer, Jerome. "Could Mental States Be Brain Processes?" *The Journal of Philosophy,* 58 (1961), 813–822.

Skinner, B. F. *Science and Human Behavior.* New York: Macmillan, 1953. See "The Self," pp. 283–294.

Smythies, J. R. (ed.). *Brain and Mind.* London: Routledge and Kegan Paul, 1965. A valuable collection of essays by various writers.

Spicker, Stuart F. (ed.). *The Philosophy of the Body.* New York: Quadrangle Books, 1970 (paperbound). Classical and contemporary selections.

Strawson, P. F. *Individuals.* Garden City, N.Y.: Doubleday, 1959, pp. 87–116.

Vesey, G. N. A. *The Embodied Mind.* London: G. Allen & Unwin, 1965. A Cartesian view in modern dress.

Wiggins, D. *Identity and Spatio-Temporal Continuity.* Oxford: Basil Blackwell, 1967.

Wisdom, John. *Other Minds.* New York: Philosophical Library, 1952.

———. *Philosophy and Psychoanalysis.* New York: Philosophical Library, 1953.

———. *Problems of Mind and Matter.* New York: Cambridge University Press, 1963 (paperbound).

PART VIII

FREEDOM
AND
DETERMINISM

34

THE PROBLEM OF
FREEDOM AND DETERMINISM

We turn now to one of the most frequently discussed and most vexing problems in philosophy: determinism and free will. It is a problem in which almost everyone is interested—the scientist, the theologian, and the ethicist, as well as the philosopher and the man in the street. More than likely, you yourself have encountered it in some form or other many times before.

The Problem

Like many philosophical problems, the free-will problem arises because of an apparent conflict between beliefs based on two different groups of facts. On the one hand, certain facts of moral experience convince most of us that we are accountable for our actions. For example, we praise and blame one another on the basis of observed behavior, and we accept praise and blame from others (and occasionally from ourselves) for our own acts. We say things like, "I ought not to have done that," "What he did was shameful," and so on. In other words, we believe ourselves to be morally responsible, and we treat others as if they were too. It would naturally seem to follow that if we are morally responsible, then we must be free: moral responsibility seems to presuppose moral freedom. This is one side of the picture.

But there are other facts that seem to support the view called universal determinism, the theory that every event in the universe is an inevitable consequence of antecedent causes. It seems self-evident to many people, for example, that "every event has a cause." Every scientific inquiry seems to presuppose that the phenomena under investigation are governed by some laws and that these laws are capable of being discovered and stated with mathematical precision. We all act, as a matter of fact, as if the universe is orderly: we expect pure water always to freeze at 32° Fahrenheit at sea-level barometric pressure; we expect the laws of aerodynamics to remain constant when we take a plane trip; and so on. Moreover, an immense and steadily growing quantity of scientific evidence appears to bear out the hypothesis that this is an orderly universe, that every event has a cause, that everything that occurs is an inevitable consequence of antecedent causes. Thus, we are also readily persuaded that the determinist hypothesis is correct.

However, if we try to affirm both these views, we encounter a serious problem. How can we be free in the way required to render us morally responsible if every event in the universe (including our decisions and our actions) is an inevitable consequence of antecedent causes? Does this not imply that we are not the real agents of our acts, and that our belief that we are morally responsible is mistaken? Or, if we are indeed free in the sense required to render us morally responsible, how can every event be an inevitable consequence of antecedent causes? Do moral responsibility and the freedom it requires contradict the mass of evidence supporting our belief in the orderliness and regularity of the universe?

It is apparent that a correct understanding of "moral freedom" is imperative. So far we have spoken of moral freedom simply as that freedom (whatever its nature) that is a condition of moral responsibility. But what is the nature of this freedom? Is such freedom consistent with universal determinism or is it not? If not, which is the case?

Three Alternatives

This question about freedom and determinism can be answered in three different ways. One answer is, (a) The freedom that is a condition of moral responsibility is not compatible with universal determinism and (b) universal determinism is the case; therefore (c) man is not free in the sense required to render him morally responsible. This position is commonly called *hard determinism*. It has been maintained by a large number of eminent thinkers and is more plausible than it appears when stated in summary form as it is here.

A second answer is, (a) The freedom that is a condition of moral responsibility is not compatible with universal determinism and (b) man has this freedom; therefore (c) universal determinism is not the case. This position is commonly called *libertarianism*. It also can claim a large number of eminent defenders and is probably the view of most people prior to systematic reflection on the problem.

The third possibility is, (a) The freedom that is a condition of moral responsibility is compatible with universal determinism, and so (b) man may be morally responsible even if determinism is the case. This view is commonly called *soft determinism*. It has been supported by such well-known philosophers as David Hume and John Stuart Mill and is probably the dominant view among British and American philosophers at the present time.

It should be noted that a soft determinist is no less a determinist than a hard determinist: both hold that every event in the universe is an inevitable consequence of antecedent causes. The difference between them is only in the consequences that they draw from this view. A hard determinist, because he believes that the freedom that is a condition of moral responsibility is not compatible with universal determinism, draws the "hard" conclusion that man is not morally responsible. A soft determinist, because he sees no incompatibility between universal determinism and moral freedom, draws the "soft" conclusion that man may be morally responsible even though universal determinism is the case. This is a point that people who are only casually acquainted with the freedom-determinism problem often fail to understand.

Terminology

Before considering the grounds upon which any one of these positions is maintained, it is advisable to clarify some of the technical terminology that enters frequently into discussions of this problem.

Let us consider first the terms "determinism" and "indeterminism." Determinism (or universal determinism, as we have called it above) is a theory about the universe—the theory that every event in the universe is an inevitable consequence of antecedent causes. According to this theory, the state of the universe at any given moment determines *in every detail* what it will be like at any future moment. An omniscient scientist, if he existed, could (according to this theory) predict with perfect accuracy each and every detail of the future—precisely when each organism would come into being, every detail of its life, the exact moment of its death, and so on. That we cannot in fact make such predictions now, say determinists, is due only to our ignorance of the relevant laws. If we did know the relevant laws—as we do in the case of the motions of the planets—such prediction would be relatively easy.

Indeterminism is simply the denial of determinism. Like determinism, therefore, it is a theory about the universe. It asserts that the universe is so constituted that some events occur that are not the inevitable (and therefore theoretically predictable) consequences of antecedent causes but are, rather, uncaused, spontaneous, original. This does not mean, of course, that the universe as conceived by the indeterminist is utterly chaotic. An indeterminist readily admits that there are vast areas of the universe in which events are not only theoretically predictable but actually predictable. His position is simply that however wide the domain of causal law may be, it is not universal. Some events are not subject to it; they are not inevitable, and our hypothetical omniscient scientist could not have predicted them despite his exhaustive knowledge of the universe.

We may also observe at this point that since determinism either is or is not true, and since indeterminism is identical with the view that determinism is not true, it is evident that either determinism or indeterminism must be the case. A great deal of confusion in the literature relating to this problem might have been avoided if this simple point had been clear to everyone who has written on it.

Two other theories that must be clearly understood are *behaviorism* and the *free-will theory*. Unlike determinism and indeterminism, these theories are about man rather than the universe.

Behaviorism may be defined as the view that man is so constituted that the whole of his behavior—his every wish, thought, decision, and act—is the inevitable consequence of antecedent causes. Behaviorism, then, is determinism as it applies to man. Man, according to this view, is not in any degree the original cause of his own actions; his decisions and his choices are merely links in a complex chain of causes whose ultimate origin lies outside himself.

The free-will theory, stated negatively, is simply the denial of behaviorism (just as indeterminism is simply the denial of determinism). Positively stated, the free-will theory may be defined as the view that man is so constituted that he is in some degree the original cause of his own actions—that it is impossible in principle to predict every detail of a man's behavior, since some of the causes of his future behavior are not now present. Similarly, it is impossible in principle to reduce a given act to a set of antecedent conditions lying outside the agent. However strong the influence of antecedent conditions may be, they are not, according to this view, sufficient to produce the act.

We shall have occasion in a later chapter to note in some detail the difficulties surrounding this notion of free will. For the present, however, the student should concentrate on what the theory denies rather than what it affirms. We may justly expect of Libertarian (who is committed to affirming the free-will theory) that he will give a positive account of this theory in the course of stating and supporting his position.

Assuming the definitions that have just been given, the logical relations that obtain among these four theories may be summarized as follows:

1. If determinism is true, then
   a. indeterminism is false
   b. the free-will theory is false
   c. behaviorism is true
2. If determinism is false, then
   a. indeterminism is true
   b. the truth or falsity of behaviorism is unknown
   c. the truth or falsity of the free-will theory is unknown
3. If indeterminism is true, then
   a. determinism is false

    b. the truth or falsity of behaviorism is unknown
    c. the truth or falsity of the free-will theory is unknown
4. If indeterminism is false, then
    a. determinism is true
    b. behaviorism is true
    c. the free-will theory is false
5. If behaviorism is true, then
    a. the free-will theory is false
    b. the truth or falsity of determinism is unknown
    c. the truth or falsity of indeterminism is unknown
6. If behaviorism is false, then
    a. the free-will theory is true
    b. indeterminism is true
    c. determinism is false
7. If the free-will theory is true, then
    a. behaviorism is false
    b. indeterminism is true
    c. determinism is false
8. If the free-will theory is false, then
    a. behaviorism is true
    b. the truth or falsity of determinism is unknown
    c. the truth or falsity of indeterminism is unknown

Two other more or less technical terms sometimes encountered in discussions of this problem are *fatalism* and *predestination*. We shall not use them in the debate that follows, but it seems advisable to clarify them briefly in order to avoid future confusion.

Fatalism may be defined as the view that (*a*) determinism is true, therefore (*b*) whatever is going to happen is going to happen, no matter what anyone does. Fatalism implies what might be called a what-the-hell attitude toward life, since it would make no sense to try to bring about some result when its occurrence depends in the first place solely on whether or not the desired result is "fated" (determined) to occur. For the same reason, obviously, it would make no sense to take any steps to prevent some event from occurring. A fatalist would say, "I'll go when my time comes—and until then, no matter what I do, I'm safe; when that time comes, nothing can save me." Fatalism, then, is not so much a theory as an attitude toward life. Insofar as it is a theory, however, it is clearly mistaken in asserting that on the premise that determinism is true it follows that whatever will be will be *no matter what you or I or anyone else may do*. What determinism implies is that what you or I or someone else may do can be very influential (as intermediate causes) in determining events, but that our behavior, whatever it may be, is of course itself determined by antecedent causes. Much more could be said on this topic, but perhaps these few remarks are sufficient to show that fatalism is not a particularly useful concept in attempting to understand the free-will–determinism problem.

An equally unhelpful concept for our purposes is predestination. This is a theological concept, and in Christian theology at least it has a very precise meaning. It is the view that God determines absolutely, without regard to any quality or condition in man, who shall be saved and who damned; it has to do only with this alleged decision, nothing else. Its only relevance to the free-will–determinism controversy is that it denies that man is free to decide what his eternal destiny will be. Since we have no need for this concept in the following discussion, there is no need to say any more about it.

It is crucially important for the discussion that follows, however, that the four concepts discussed earlier—determinism, indeterminism, behaviorism, and the free-will theory—be clearly and thoroughly understood. They will bear occasional review as we proceed with the debate.

STUDY QUESTIONS

1. State in two or three different ways what you understand to be the freedom-determinism problem.
2. How might this problem arise for each of the following: a physicist? a psychologist? a sociologist? a theologian? a juror?
3. Is it true that this problem is capable of being answered in just three ways? If so, explain why; if not, describe the additional alternatives.
4. Define carefully each of the following: hard determinism, soft determinism, universal determinism, indeterminism, libertarianism, behaviorism, free-will theory.
5. X says, "I do not believe in either determinism or indeterminism: I believe in *self*-determinism." Criticize this statement.

35

THE CASE FOR
HARD DETERMINISM

It is my purpose to show that of the three possible alternative answers to the question posed in the preceding chapter, hard determinism is the most plausible. I shall begin by pointing out exactly what, as a hard determinist, I am obliged to defend. I shall then go on to support this position with what seem to be the strongest arguments available.

What Hard Determinism Is

Hard determinism is the view that (a) the freedom that is a condition of moral responsibility is not compatible with universal determinism and (b) universal determinism is the case; therefore, (c) man is not free in the sense required to render him morally responsible. I hold, that is to say, a certain view of what would have to be the case if man were to be morally responsible; I hold that this condition of moral responsibility is not compatible with universal determinism; and I hold that universal determinism is true. I conclude, therefore, that man is not in fact morally responsible. This conclusion—the assertion that man is not in fact morally responsible—cannot be avoided if my two premises are true.

What Constitutes Moral Freedom?

It is first advisable to distinguish two different meanings that are often conveyed by the single word "freedom." One is "the opportunity to do what you want to do." In this sense, we have the freedom to do whatever we are not hindered from doing by external constraints or natural limitations. Thus I am "free" at this moment to write or not to write, to remain sitting at my desk or to get up and leave it, to open my office door or to keep it closed. I am not "free" to help myself to all the money in the vault of the nearest bank (because of external constraints) or to jump thirty feet into the air (because of natural limitations). Let us call this kind of freedom the "circumstantial freedom of self-realization." [1]

It is apparent that freedom in this sense varies greatly, depending on abilities and circumstances. The strong are "free" to do some things that the weak are not; the rich are "free" to do some things that the poor are not; the average citizen is "free" to do some things that the prison inmate is not; and so on. Circumstantial freedom of self-realization, the opportunity to do what we want to do, is a matter of degree.

In another sense, freedom is seen as a power of the self to enact any one of a number of genuinely open alternatives. This is what libertarians ascribe to man when they credit him with having a "free will." The essential idea here is that of being an *original cause* of some action. We shall call this kind of freedom the "natural freedom of self-determination."

I want to urge my readers to think very carefully about the distinction that I have just made between these two conceptions of freedom, for the distinction is absolutely essential to a proper understanding of this whole problem. The first conceives of freedom as an *opportunity*; the second, as a *power*. To assert that man is free in the first sense is to assert something about his external circumstances; to assert that man is free in the second sense is to assert something about his internal make-up. Opportunity/power; external/internal; freedom A/freedom B: these are the contrasts that we must hold firmly in mind as we try to decide what position to take with respect to this very important problem.

I assume that everyone will allow that freedom in the first sense—the circumstantial freedom of self-realization—is a necessary condition of moral responsibility. We do not hold people responsible for not doing something if we are satisfied that they wanted to do it but were simply unable to. This much is agreed to by everyone who is a party to the freedom-determinism dispute.

It is my view, however, that although the circumstantial freedom of self-realization is indeed a *necessary* condition of moral responsibility, it is not a *sufficient* condition. The libertarians are right in affirming that if man is to be regarded as morally responsible, it is also necessary to ascribe to him the natural freedom of self-determination, or "free will" as they like to call it. They are wrong, however, in affirming that man has it.

The question of what constitutes moral freedom is a very difficult one, and we must be careful not to get lost in a forest of abstractions and arbitrary definitions. It would be easy indeed to arbitrarily define moral

---

[1] The terminology is borrowed from Mortimer J. Adler, et al., *The Idea of Freedom* (New York: Doubleday, 1958). This study constitutes the definitive analysis of the concept of freedom, and it is highly desirable that its terminological recommendations be adopted by all participants in the dispute over determinism and free will.

responsibility in such a way that the circumstantial freedom of self-realization would be a sufficient condition of its possibility. But we are not at liberty to define moral responsibility according to our fancy. What we really mean by moral responsibility is implicit in the ways in which we ascribe praise and blame and consider ourselves and others as deserving of reward or punishment.

In order to decide, therefore, whether or not the natural freedom of self-determination is a condition of moral responsibility, we have only to scrutinize the kinds of moral judgments we make. Then we may ask ourselves, Would we or would we not alter our judgment if we were persuaded that the agent of the act was not "free" in the sense of possessing the natural freedom of self-determination? I am confident that anyone who reflects carefully on a few hypothetical cases of this kind will find that we would alter our judgment, thereby demonstrating that our moral judgments do presuppose that man is free in the sense of possessing the natural freedom of self-determination.

Consider this hypothetical example. Two boys, Tom and George, are apprehended attempting the armed robbery of a supermarket. Subsequent questioning reveals that the holdup was first suggested by Tom, but that the detailed planning of the robbery was done in cooperation and that the two participated equally in the actual attempt. Therefore, both are guilty of committing a felony, and they are presumably deserving of equal punishment before the law.

If we were given no more information than this, our moral judgment on the matter would probably be nearly parallel to the legal judgment. Tom and George, we would say, are equally blameworthy for planning and attempting to execute this act. Indeed, if there is any difference at all in the blame attaching to the two boys, the greater blame must be Tom's, since it was he who first suggested the idea. Nonetheless, we would say, both are highly blameworthy and deserve the punishment that they will now presumably receive at the hands of the law.

But suppose we then learn that Tom was raised in a family of habitual criminals and from earliest childhood had been taught that armed robbery was a feat of heroism rather than a blameworthy act. Suppose we also learn that George was the product of a very different kind of home: his father was governor, his mother a leader in civic affairs, and his elder brother a congressman. Would we now alter our previous moral evaluation? I am certain that we would, and in some readily predictable ways. We would say that George, having had the advantages of his upbringing, is more deserving of blame than Tom. We would say that Tom, owing to the untoward circumstances in which he was raised, is almost more to be pitied than to be blamed. Whatever the status of these two before the law, we would maintain that so far as their moral guilt is concerned, they are not deserving of equal blame.

But what is the principle according to which we alter our judgment of moral guilt? Why do we judge Tom less harshly than George? Clearly it is because we partly attribute Tom's act to causes lying outside himself—to the environment in which he was raised—whereas we attribute George's act to his own perverse choice. In other words, *we do not hold a man responsible for any act insofar as we believe that act to be the consequence of causes lying outside himself.* Anyone who objectively considers a number of hypothetical cases of moral judgment will readily agree that this is an important principle on which our everyday moral judgments are formulated.

A person is morally responsible for his or her actions, then, only if, and insofar as, he or she is the original cause of them. Moral freedom— the freedom that is a condition of moral responsibility—includes the natural freedom of self-determination. Without this—without "free will," as the libertarians say—there is no moral responsibility.

The Case for Determinism

Unfortunately, it is impossible for man to have the natural freedom of self-determination, because this is a deterministic universe. To complete my case, I shall set forth a number of arguments that make it necessary to adopt the determinist hypothesis.

First, every instance of regularity in nature supports the hypothesis that all macroscopic phenomena are reducible to the regular operations of natural laws. The quantity of evidence now available from the many special sciences is so great as to make the contrary hypothesis exceedingly improbable.

The era of modern science began when men ceased asking for the *purposes* of natural phenomena and asked instead for their *causes.* To the question, What is the purpose of the revolution of the heavenly bodies? all sorts of fanciful answers are possible, and no answer can ever be demonstrated to be the right one. But to the question, What *uniformities* are exhibited in the motions of the heavenly bodies? or, What are the *causes* of celestial phenomena? clear and mathematically precise answers can be given.

For a long time it was assumed that "lawlike regularity" applied only to the realm of inanimate matter and that human behavior, at least, was exempt from the reign of such laws. Severe doubt was cast on this view by the work of Charles Darwin, however. A short time later, research was undertaken by Sigmund Freud and others on the supposition that human behavior, like any other phenomenon, is governed by laws that may be discovered by painstaking inquiry. This supposition has been progressively verified by Freud's successors. As B. F. Skinner says, "We cannot apply the methods of science to a subject matter that moves about capriciously." [2] Every advance in descriptive psychology, every discovery that is made with respect to the laws governing human

---

[2] B. F. Skinner, *Science and Human Behavior* (New York: Macmillan, 1953), p. 6.

behavior, adds to the rapidly growing evidence that human behavior, too, is thoroughly subject to the vast network of causes that govern all phenomena.

Should anyone be disposed to quarrel with what has just been said, let him reflect for a moment on what it would be like for a scientist to abandon the determinist hypothesis. Given the determinist hypothesis, a scientist can ask about any phenomenon he has chosen to investigate, What are its causes? What are the uniformities, the laws, exemplified in this phenomenon? Without the determinist hypothesis, he could not ask such questions. He would have to ask instead, Does this phenomenon have any causes—or is this perhaps one of those things that occur haphazardly, one of those things that do not have any regular causes? And this, I submit, would be absurd. It would cut the nerve of the whole scientific enterprise, which has made its advances on precisely the opposite supposition.

In a less rigorous but perhaps equally important way, we all make a similar supposition whenever we predict the behavior of other human beings. We know, for example, that if we want to avoid an argument, we had better stay off the subject of politics whenever Uncle George is around; and we know this because, in a rough and ready way, we know some of the "laws," the "regularities," that govern Uncle George's behavior. Consider any person with whom you are reasonably well acquainted. Is it not true that you could, with a high degree of accuracy, predict how he or she would act in a wide variety of situations? To acknowledge this is to acknowledge that his or her behavior exhibits certain uniformities, uniformities that differ from the uniformities exhibited in the motion of planets, the interactions of chemicals, and the migration of birds only by virtue of being less well understood.

That human behavior is not exempt from causal laws also becomes evident when we reflect on the experience of "choosing among alternatives." Here, if anywhere, we would expect the "natural freedom of self-determination," which libertarians defend, to be evident. But it is not. Consider: We never choose without a motive. Just as motives are determined by desires, so choice is determined by motive: we always choose that alternative for which we have the strongest motive. But what constitutes the strongest motive for any given individual depends on his personal likes and dislikes, which are, in turn, the consequences of his heredity and environment. Thus, the "chain of causes" leading to an act stretches back indefinitely; "decision" is not an original cause but merely one link in the chain.

I have dwelt at length on this matter of human behavior because it is, so to speak, the last outpost of indeterminism. If it is conceded that human behavior is as completely subject in principle to causal explanation as are other phenomena, then so far as I can see there will remain no further objection to adopting the determinist hypothesis. Thanks to the efforts of psychologists and sociologists, we have already come a long

way toward adopting a behaviorist view. We now speak without
hesitation of "the causes of crime," "the conditions that create antisocial
attitudes," and the like. We still have, admittedly, much to learn about
the laws that govern human behavior. But it is not unreasonable to hope,
with Skinner, that

> eventually a science of the nervous system based upon direct observation
> rather than inference will describe the neural states and events which
> immediately precede instances of behavior. We shall know the precise
> neurological conditions which immediately precede, say, the response, "No,
> thank you." These events in turn will be found to be preceded by other
> neurological events, and these in turn by others. This series will lead us
> back to events outside the nervous system and, eventually, outside the
> organism.[3]

The foregoing considerations do not, of course, conclusively demonstrate the truth of the determinist hypothesis. However, they do suggest
quite clearly that it is more reasonable to affirm the determinist
hypothesis than it is to affirm its only alternative—indeterminism. And
this is the conclusion that I have been attempting to establish.

I want to deal briefly with one objection that is frequently raised
against the determinist position. It is sometimes stated that the principle
of indeterminacy, which was first formulated by the German physicist
W. K. Heisenberg and which is now an accepted part of modern physical
theory, demonstrates that determinism is not the case and lends
empirical support to the libertarian position. Now I will concede that it is
possible that there is a real indeterminacy in the behavior of subatomic
particles, as Heisenberg's theory affirms, although it seems to me most
improbable that this is the case. The principle of indeterminacy is best
understood, I think, as a limitation in *our knowledge* of subatomic events
rather than a real hiatus in the network of mutually interacting events of
which the universe is composed. Suppose, however, that I should turn
out to be mistaken on this point. Suppose there is a real indeterminacy at
the subatomic level. What are the consequences? I would, of course, be
compelled to concede that in this one class of cases there does indeed
seem to be some real indeterminacy in the universe, and that to that
extent determinism is incorrect. But this admission would in no way
bolster the libertarian view that *man's* decisions or actions are undetermined. To be sure, hard determinism is in considerable part an inference
drawn from the belief that determinism is true, and to this extent hard
determinists would (if Heisenberg's principle does in fact point to a real
indeterminacy) have to modify their position. But the consequences for
ethics are the same whether one is a determinist or merely a behaviorist,
and the Heisenberg principle does nothing to undermine the behaviorist
view. Thus the objection, while it is not exactly irrelevant to the issue we
are discussing, suggests nothing that could be of any help to the
defenders of moral responsibility.

---

[3] *Ibid.*, p. 28.

Consequences for Ethics

The conclusions to which the foregoing considerations force me are, I confess, somewhat disturbing. Since moral responsibility presupposes the natural freedom of self-determination (free will), since this freedom is not compatible with universal determinism, and since universal determinism appears to be the case, it seems evident that—contrary to what most people certainly believe—man is not morally responsible. And this inference, in turn, carries with it consequences such as the following:

1. No human act, however "noble" or "base," is ever worthy of either praise or blame. John F. Kennedy's heroism and dedication were as much a product of his heredity and environment as Lee Harvey Oswald's hatred and perversion were a product of his.
2. Punishment (or "retributive justice" as it is sometimes called) cannot be defended on the ground that a person who acts in a certain way is "guilty" and therefore "deserving of punishment." It makes no sense to talk about a criminal "paying his debt to society." Like everybody else, the criminal has acted in the only way possible for him (given his heredity and environment) and therefore has incurred no such debt.
3. If we are to continue to praise and blame or reward and punish people on the basis of their behavior, it can only be on the ground that such things will tend to influence their behavior in certain desirable ways.

These are "hard" conclusions. I will even admit that personally I do not like them and that I in fact continue to make judgments of praise and blame just as everyone else does. But as a philosopher I know that such judgments have no rational justification. Our beliefs about moral responsibility and what we now know about the structure of the universe (and about man in particular) are in hopeless and irremediable contradiction. As a philosopher I have felt obliged to point out this contradiction notwithstanding the unpalatable consequences for ethical theory.

STUDY QUESTIONS

1. What precisely is the difference between "the circumstantial freedom of self-realization" and "the natural freedom of self-determination"? In what sense, according to Hard Determinist, must man be free if he is to be morally responsible? Do you think he is right about this?
2. What is the point of Hard Determinist's insistence that in the discussion of this question one must constantly refer to the "facts concerning the actual ways in which we handle the categories of moral responsibility"? Does this seem to be at all important?
3. Does Hard Determinist's example bear out his claim that we do not hold a person responsible for an act insofar as we believe that act to be the consequence of causes lying outside himself? Suggest three or four additional examples that either confirm or disconfirm this principle.

4. What arguments does Hard Determinist offer in support of the truth of the determinist hypothesis? Does this evidence seem to be conclusive? Can you think of any additional arguments in support of this hypothesis that Hard Determinist has failed to mention?

5. Do the "disturbing consequences" that Hard Determinist itemizes at the end of his essay really follow from his view, as he says? Are there other similar consequences that Hard Determinist has neglected to mention?

36

THE CASE FOR
SOFT DETERMINISM

It must certainly be acknowledged that Hard Determinist has made a strong case for determinism and the impossibility of the freedom without which man cannot be morally responsible. His arguments in support of the determinist hypothesis are particularly cogent, and I am delighted to accept everything he has to say on that score as a part of the case that I propose to build in defense of *soft determinism*.

Before I do this, however, I should like to note that I do not care for the name "soft determinism" that is commonly used to describe my position. There are two reasons for my dislike of this title. The first is that it was invented by William James, a noted libertarian, who coined it precisely for the purpose of disparagement. Just listen to James:

> Nowadays, we have a *soft* determinism which abhors harsh words, and, repudiating fatality, necessity, and even predetermination, says that its real name is freedom; for freedom is only necessity understood, and bondage to the highest is identical with true freedom.[1]

Now, if to avoid confusion, I allow my position to be called "soft determinism," I insist that James's pejorative connotations be laid aside and that my position be considered simply on its merits. If I reject Hard Determinist's conclusions with respect to ethics, it is not because I am "soft" but because I think his conclusions are unwarranted.

The second reason for my displeasure with the name "soft determinism" is that it has led to a great deal of confusion concerning what my position really is. I am no less firm in my adherence to determinism than is Hard Determinist. I, too, maintain that the universe is so constituted that absolutely everything that occurs, including actions by human

[1] William James, "The Dilemma of Determinism," in *The Will to Believe and Other Essays in Popular Philosophy and Human Immortality* (New York: Dover, 1956), p. 149.

beings, is an inevitable consequence of antecedent causes. Both Hard Determinist and I are what may be called "strict determinists." The difference between us is not that he is more consistent in his determinism than I, but that he draws certain consequences from his determinism (with respect to ethics) that are in my view unjustified. I propose now to show where Hard Determinist makes his mistake and how it is possible to maintain a consistent determinism without drawing the dire conclusions that he insists must be drawn.

Moral Freedom

The crucial question that must be asked about the vexing problem of moral freedom is, *In what sense* must man be "free" if he is to be morally responsible? Hard Determinist has argued that he must be free in a contracausal sense, that is, that he must possess a natural freedom of self-determination. My view, on the contrary, is that the circumstantial freedom of self-realization—the opportunity to do what you please—is a necessary *and sufficient* condition of moral responsibility. I think that a careful consideration of the ways in which we actually ascribe praise and blame will demonstrate that this view is the correct one.

Let us suppose that Hard Determinist were right in his contention that man could be morally free only if this were not a deterministic universe, that is, that man could be held morally responsible for an act only if that act were not the inevitable consequence of antecedent causes. We would then be in the position of saying that a person is responsible for an act if and only if that act is uncaused. But to say that something is uncaused is to say that it is a "chance" event, a mere random occurrence. Apart from the difficulty of even conceiving of such a thing, it is absurd to maintain that a person could be morally responsible only if his actions, or some of his actions (those for which he would be held responsible), occurred "by chance." This is not what we have in mind when we say "So and so is morally responsible for doing *r*."

What, then, do we have in mind? Simply, I submit, that the agent had the opportunity—the circumstantial freedom—to do a number of things, and that he did what he did *because he wanted to*. When appraising praiseworthiness or blameworthiness, we do not ask whether the agent could have desired to do otherwise than he did, because that is not relevant to our judgment of his actions. What we do ask is whether the agent could have done otherwise had he so desired.

Let us consider a hypothetical example. Johnny has been instructed always to come directly home from school, and his mother has learned (through repeated observation of Johnny's arrival time) that when he does, he normally arrives home no later than 3:15 P.M. A few times, however, Johnny has arrived home at a slightly later time, but on each of these occasions his mother has determined that "he could not have done otherwise": he had to stay after school, the extreme cold made it necessary for him to stop briefly at a store to warm himself, and so forth. But one spring day Johnny arrives home at nearly five o'clock, and Mother naturally asks, "Johnny, where have you been?" Johnny replies, "I've been playing in the puddles." "But Johnny," Mother objects, "don't you know that you are supposed to come directly home from school?" "Yes." "Well, why didn't you?" "Well, I just didn't want to. I wanted to play in the puddles." "Well, son, you will have to be punished for this." "But Mother," Johnny cries, "you can't punish me for that. I couldn't *want* to do anything else."

We obviously do not, and would not, consider Johnny's objection relevant. Why? Because in holding someone responsible for something, we do not ask why he wants to do such and such but only whether his doing such and such was a result of his wanting to do it. So long as Johnny's late arrival was unavoidable—so long as his wanting to be home on time was thwarted by circumstances—Johnny was not held responsible for his late arrival; but when his late arrival was the consequence of his wanting to do something that caused him to be late, he was immediately held responsible *no matter what may have been the causes of his wanting to play rather than obey.*

Let us consider a second hypothetical case. The manager of a supermarket is apprehended in the act of removing the contents of the store safe at 2 A.M. and, of course, is suspected of attempted theft. Investigation discloses, however, that (a) a gunman is holding the manager's wife and children hostage and has threatened to harm them if the manager does not comply with orders; (b) a second gunman has forced the manager to drive to the supermarket and open the safe; and (c) the manager tried unsuccessfully to attract the attention of the police (at risk of his life) by exceeding the speed limit and running through a red light en route to the market.

Knowing these facts, we would not hold the manager responsible for the attempted theft, because we would then be satisfied that he was not doing what he wanted to do. And the reason that he was not doing what he wanted to do was that he did not have the circumstantial freedom, the opportunity, to do it.

Who was responsible, then, for the attempted robbery? Obviously, the gunmen, for *to be morally responsible is to be the person whose motives, whose desires, need to be changed if a given kind of behavior is to be encouraged or prevented.* We do not blame people for doing what, under the circumstances, was the only thing they could reasonably have been expected to do. We do blame them if a different desire on their part would have been sufficient to produce a more desirable kind of behavior.

Reasons for Confusion

The problem of freedom and determinism has been debated vociferously and inconclusively for many hundreds of years. Why should this be so if the solution is really as simple as I have suggested? Since this question may itself hinder acceptance of my position, I should like to deal briefly with it.

There are two reasons why the true solution to this much discussed problem has proved consistently elusive. The first, and in my judgment the most important, is that the nature of moral judgments has been misunderstood. To be morally responsible, as we said above, is to be the person whose motives need to be changed if a given kind of behavior is to be encouraged or prevented. Moreover, the function of moral judgments is precisely *to alter the motives of the person being judged and thus to influence his future behavior.* Praise and blame are simply mild forms of reward and punishment. The reason for employing either is always to discourage or prevent certain kinds of undesirable behavior (blame or punishment) or to encourage certain kinds of desirable behavior (praise or other rewards).

Let us now suppose that someone makes a moral judgment without understanding the true nature of moral responsibility. In all likelihood he would construe such judgments on the analogy of statements of fact. Accordingly, he would interpret blameworthiness and praiseworthiness as "intrinsic qualities" of the persons or acts being judged. From this mistaken starting point it is a very short step to the view that some obscure power ("freedom") *within the agent* is a condition of moral responsibility.

The second reason involves a series of semantic confusions over the terms "law" and "freedom." One understanding of "law" derives largely from its use in connection with statutes and ordinances—the kinds of things enacted by city councils, legislatures, and parliaments. It is the very nature of this type of "law" to prescribe behavior—indeed (by virtue of the threat of punishment) to coerce behavior. Implicit in every such law is the "or else" embodied in the system of fines or punishments that await the offender. If we disobey, we become subject to the prescribed punishment; because we fear the punishment, we usually obey, whether or not the prescribed behavior is what we ourselves really want to do.

But in science the term "law" is used to designate something very different, namely, an observed uniformity. Scientific law is merely a report about what has actually been observed to be the case in such and such a class of phenomena. Here there is no coercion, no "or else." Pure water (at sea level) is not compelled or constrained to freeze whenever the temperature reaches 32° Fahrenheit. It just does. And the "law" that states this is simply a description of what in fact has been observed to occur.

Had this distinction between prescriptive and descriptive law been clearly recognized, it probably would never have occurred to anyone to insist that moral responsibility requires exemption from the laws of nature. Moral responsibility does indeed require exemption from coercion, but the laws of nature do not coerce. The opposite of causality is acausality, or indeterminism, whereas the opposite of compulsion is freedom. Hence, the failure to distinguish the two different kinds of law led to the absurd view that moral responsibility requires a contracausal, or indeterministic, freedom.

Moral Responsibility Requires Determinism

Thus far I have argued only that moral freedom is consistent with the determinist hypothesis and that we do not need to conclude with Hard Determinist that man cannot be morally responsible in a deterministic world. It may appear that I am being purely defensive—that I am trying to "salvage" whatever I can of human moral responsibility in a deterministic universe. By way of countering this impression, which is implicit in James's unfortunate labeling of my position as "soft" determinism, I should like to conclude by taking the offensive in this argument. The thesis I propose to support is this: Not only is moral responsibility consistent with the determinist hypothesis, but *moral responsibility would not be possible in anything other than a deterministic universe.*

That moral responsibility requires determinism is evident, in the first place, from my earlier argument concerning the absurdity of maintaining that a person can be responsible for only those of his acts that occur "by chance." For any event whatsoever, we can conceive of only two possibilities: either it has a cause or it does not have a cause. If it has a cause, then it is explicable within the context of the determinist hypothesis. If it does not have a cause, then it is a "chance event." To reject determinism, therefore, on the ground that it is incompatible with moral responsibility—or, alternatively, to reject moral responsibility on the ground that it is not possible in a deterministic universe—is to adopt the absurd position referred to above.

My thesis can also be supported in another way. Let us suppose that this were not a deterministic universe—that some things that occur were not the inevitable consequences of antecedent causes—and that a given set of circumstances would not, therefore, always produce a predictable effect. In such a universe it would be impossible to hold a man responsible for *anything,* because he could never know what would be the result of any act he might perform. In such a universe the glass of water that yesterday quenched the thirst of a dying man might today poison him, or turn him into a giraffe, or do any one of countless other thoroughly unpredictable things. It is only insofar as we can predict what the effects of a given course of action will be that we can act responsibly; hence it follows that we can act responsibly only in a universe where certain predictable effects follow inevitably from certain causes. An indeterministic universe, in which the orderly sequence of events is interrupted by more or less frequent "chance events," would be a moral chaos. It is doubtful if life would even be possible in such a universe. Certainly responsible behavior would not.

It seems, therefore, that the time has come to lay this old problem to rest. What is really of concern to Hard Determinist is the truth of the determinist hypothesis. It is this that he feels obliged to insist on, and in this he is right. What is really of concern to Libertarian is the truth of the conviction that man is morally responsible. This is what he feels obliged to insist on, and in this he is right. Where both Hard Determinist and Libertarian err—and this is the unargued assumption that has kept the debate alive for many years—is in assuming that moral responsibility requires a contracausal freedom in man. Once the absurdity of this assumption is perceived, the problem is solved.

STUDY QUESTIONS

1. Where precisely does Soft Determinist agree with Hard Determinist, and where does he disagree with him? Is there any difference between them regarding the *method* by which each thinks this question must be decided?
2. Does it follow from Hard Determinist's position, as Soft Determinist says, that "a man is responsible for an act if and only if that act is uncaused"? How might Hard Determinist defend himself against this objection?
3. Do the two hypothetical examples offered by Soft Determinist support his claim that the only relevant question in deciding moral responsibility is whether the person involved did what he did because he wanted to? Could Hard Determinist explain these examples in a way consistent with his position?
4. What does Soft Determinist say is the meaning of "moral responsibility"? Do you think he is right? If not, what alternative would you suggest?
5. What considerations does Soft Determinist offer in support of his claim that moral responsibility actually *requires* determinism? Do you agree or disagree with this thesis? Why?

37

THE CASE FOR LIBERTARIANISM

In spite of the formidable array of arguments that Hard Determinist and Soft Determinist have presented in support of their respective positions and against libertarianism, I am convinced that libertarianism can be shown to be true, and I welcome the opportunity to demonstrate how the various objections raised against it can be rather easily overcome. Let me begin by indicating where I agree and disagree with each of my opponents.

Hard Determinist has argued that determinism is true and that the freedom that is a condition of moral responsibility is not compatible with determinism. From these two premises he has drawn the unhappy conclusion that man is not morally responsible. My position vis-à-vis Hard Determinist is clear: I reject his first premise, affirm his second, and, of course, do not accept his conclusion. I believe it can be established on independent grounds that man is morally responsible and that therefore determinism is not the case. I shall attempt to show in due time that the consequences of accepting this conclusion are not nearly so dire as some determinists would lead us to believe.

Soft Determinist offers a more elusive argument, so naturally it is more difficult to state precisely where we agree and disagree. Our prime disagreement, of course, centers on determinism. He holds that it is the case, I hold that it is not. We disagree, moreover, about the kind of freedom required to render a man morally responsible. He holds that the circumstantial freedom of self-realization is a sufficient condition of moral responsibility; I hold (in agreement with Hard Determinist) that man is not morally responsible unless he possesses also the natural freedom of self-determination.

It may seem as if Soft Determinist and I agree on one point, namely, that man is morally responsible. But anyone who is acquainted with both his position and mine will immediately recognize that our agreement is only verbal. When he says that A is morally responsible, he means that A is the person whose motives need to be changed if a certain kind of behavior is to be encouraged or avoided. When I say that A is morally responsible, I mean that he is fittingly, or deservingly, subject to praise or blame, reward or punishment.

Despite the fact that it is very widely held, soft determinism, I am convinced, is not a tenable position. Hard determinism, on the other hand, is a position worthy of respect, though I consider it mistaken nonetheless. At any rate, I believe that for any clear-thinking person the final choice must be between libertarianism and hard determinism, and I shall do my best to show that the strongest considerations are on my side.

Refutation of Soft Determinism

I have the greatest sympathy for the considerations that led Soft Determinist to adopt his position. The conclusions that Hard Determinist draws with respect to man's moral responsibility are "hard" indeed, and it is not surprising that some determinists have sought a way to avoid them within the context of their deterministic beliefs.

Nonetheless, the mistake that Soft Determinist makes—the mistake that vitiates his whole position—is incredibly obvious. Starting from the assumption that determinism is true, Soft Determinist (a) arbitrarily redefines "moral freedom" in such a way as to render it compatible with determinism, and (b) arbitrarily redefines "moral responsibility" in such a way as to make "moral freedom" as he has defined it a sufficient condition thereof. He then proudly announces that he has "reconciled" determinism and moral responsibility, and that the traditional problem that has long divided libertarians and determinists has at last been solved. But all that has been accomplished by this little verbal sleight of hand is a blurring of the relevant concepts and a further confusion of the issue. That moral responsibility *as this concept is employed in our everyday judgments of praise and blame* is compatible with determinism is not shown to be true in the slightest by Soft Determinist's argument.

Consider an analogy. Suppose that we are interested in the question, Are all the citizens of Flamenco absolutely loyal to their government, or do some of them occasionally commit acts of treason? Two straightforward answers are possible: Either (a) all citizens are absolutely loyal ("hard loyalism") or (b) treasonous acts are sometimes committed ("occasionarianism"). But it would be distinctly unhelpful to have someone say, "Look, I can define treason in such a way that occasional acts of what is now called treason do not contradict the view that all the people of Flamenco are absolutely loyal to their government." We do not want to know whether treason *as thus redefined* can be made to square with "universal loyalism." What we want to know is whether treason in its ordinary unaltered meaning is compatible with "universal loyalism"; and it is evident that it is not.

Hard Determinist has already cautioned us to remember that we are not at liberty to define moral responsibility to suit our fancy. What we really mean by moral responsibility is implicit in the ways in which we ascribe praise and blame and deem ourselves and others deserving of reward and punishment. If one attends carefully to the actual employment of judgments of praise and blame, he will shortly discover, I am confident, that "being morally responsible" means more than simply "being capable of having behavior altered through an alteration of motives."

Consider for a moment some of the absurd implications of the view that moral responsibility means what Soft Determinist says it means. In the first place, it would follow that we ought to hold animals morally responsible no less than we do men, for there is every reason to suppose that reward and punishment will influence the behavior of dogs and horses just as much as they will influence the behavior of men. But, of course, although we do indeed reward and punish animals, we do not apply moral judgments to them.

Further, if moral responsibility means what Soft Determinist says it means, it would make no sense whatsoever to speak of a deceased person as "responsible" for something, since on this hypothesis there is no one whose motives could be influenced in such a way as to bring about a different sort of behavior. Yet, we do blame deceased persons for acts committed by them: Hitler and Stalin are examples.

And again, in judgments of praise and blame we commonly "make allowances" for such things as a poor childhood environment. The child who grew up in the slums, whose father was a petty thief, and so on, "did not have the chance" (as we say) that his more fortunate fellows did, so we judge him less harshly. On Soft Determinist's ground we would have no reason to judge him less harshly, since we have no reason to suppose that his behavior is either more or less subject to influence than anyone else's. Indeed, if Soft Determinist is right, we ought, if anything, to judge such a person more harshly, since there is reason to suppose that more counteracting influences are needed if his behavior is to be brought into tolerable conformity with society's norms.

Thus, at a number of crucial points Soft Determinist's account of moral responsibility is at variance with our actual judgments of praise and blame. Since it is in reference to such judgments that we must decide this matter, Soft Determinist's inability to account for the cases just mentioned must be regarded as decisive against his position.

Soft Determinist has argued that moral freedom consists simply in having the circumstantial freedom of self-realization and that this view is supported by the fact that in concrete cases we never inquire about anything else. "It is significant," he writes, "that the only question relevant to determining moral responsibility . . . is, Was the agent able to do what he wanted to do? That is, did he have the *circumstantial freedom* to actualize his own wishes?" But surely the reason for this is that we assume that every normal and healthy person has the natural freedom of self-determination—free will—at all times, and so we do not feel the need to inquire about it in each particular case. The reason Johnny's mother (in Soft Determinist's example) does not accept his objection that he "could not want to do anything else" is not that his objection, if true, is not relevant, but rather that she does not believe him. If she were to become convinced that he had suddenly been afflicted with a puddle-playing syndrome that literally *compelled* him to want to play in puddles, her attitude would be very different.

We may safely conclude, therefore, that the recent attempts of some determinists to affirm the moral responsibility of man without relinquishing their belief in determinism do not succeed. If man is to be regarded as morally responsible, it is necessary, as Hard Determinist has argued, that he have both the circumstantial freedom of self-realization (the opportunity to do what he wants to do) and the natural freedom of self-determination (free will). And since, as Hard Determinist has shown, the latter is not compatible with determinism, the choice must rest between Hard Determinist's position and my own.

Replies to Objections

Hard Determinist has admirably stated the arguments that he thinks effectively support the determinist hypothesis. Nevertheless, his arguments are not convincing. Let us review them once more.

First of all, he asserts that "every instance of regularity in nature supports the hypothesis that all macroscopic phenomena are reducible to the regular operations of natural laws" and that "the quantity of evidence now available from the many special sciences is so great as to make the contrary hypothesis exceedingly improbable." However, the determinist hypothesis is not a "superhypothesis," progressively being established by mounting evidence; it is rather a heuristic principle[1] that is presupposed in each particular scientific inquiry. It is important to scientific research that there be no preestablished limits to the scope of natural laws, since such limits would arbitrarily prevent inquiry beyond a certain point. But it is not important to the scientific enterprise to maintain, either as a dogma or as a hypothesis, that there are no such limits.

Suppose, for example, that my view that man is free in a contracausal sense were correct. This would not, so far as I can see, in any way hinder the scientific study of man. My view does not deny that there are some laws governing human behavior: it denies only that human behavior is *completely* explicable in terms of such laws. Let the scientific study of

[1] See Glossary.

man proceed as rapidly and as far as it can; let the independent variables affecting man's behavior be discovered and stated with as great precision as possible; there will still remain the "freedom factor," as a consequence of which man's behavior will not become perfectly predictable and as a consequence of which man is and will remain morally responsible. This factor may be more or less influential in determining a person's behavior than we now commonly suppose; outside influences may, as psychologists and sociologists are inclined to believe, play a much greater role in determining behavior than was once assumed. But unless and until laws have been discovered in terms of which *every detail* of man's behavior is explicable, there is no reason whatsoever to deny the presence of this "freedom factor." Indeed, as we shall see presently, there is excellent reason to affirm it.

Hard Determinist's admission that the principle of indeterminacy might turn out to be a case of real indeterminacy in the universe illustrates my point exactly. Physicists have lived with this concept for many years now, and it has not appeared to hinder their research in the least. They have simply been forced to accept the fact that when they are dealing with subatomic particles, they have reached one of the limits of universal law, a realm where lawlike regularity apparently does not obtain. That the human will should constitute another such limit would not appear to raise any new problems. Certainly I do not mean to suggest that the discovery of the principle of indeterminacy constitutes evidence in support of the freedom of the will: Hard Determinist is quite right in denying that this principle has any such direct relevance for the free-will problem. I do emphatically assert, however, that the fact that scientists have been able to accept with equanimity the principle of indeterminacy, astonishing as that principle was in the context of classical theory, completely destroys Hard Determinist's claim that the possibility of indeterminacy such as would be required by a belief in free will would "cut the nerve of the whole scientific enterprise."

Hard Determinist's second argument in support of determinism (actually it is in support of behaviorism) is that we can, in a rough-and-ready way, predict the behavior of people whom we know well. This, he contends, supports the hypothesis that their behavior is governed by certain "laws" or "uniformities," which we vaguely discern in making our prediction.

I grant that we can, within certain limits, make some informed guesses about how people that we know well will act in certain situations, but I fail to see how this in any way supports the behaviorist thesis. Such consistency of behavior as we actually observe in people of our acquaintance may be due to either (a) external causes such as a behaviorist believes completely dominate human behavior or (b) habits of character acquired through many years of training and experience— or both. Even if we grant that to some extent a is the case, we can still reasonably hold the libertarian view in the absence of evidence that a is the case totally. And to the extent that *b* is the case, we can plausibly hold that a man's character is in part a product of his past choices freely made, and that it may be further modified by future choices. Thus it seems clear that such regularity as we do observe in the behavior of individuals in no way supports the hypothesis that *all* human behavior is the product of causes lying ultimately outside the agent.

Hard Determinist's third argument is that reflection on the experience of "choosing among alternatives" makes it evident (*a*) that we always do that for which we find the strongest motive and (*b*) that what constitutes the strongest motive for any individual depends on causes lying outside himself. In one form or another, this is one of the oldest and most persuasive arguments used against the libertarian position. The refutation of it must, unfortunately, be somewhat complex.

The apparent force of this argument lies in the tacit adoption of a mechanical model to describe and explain human volition and action. According to this model, the self is conceived as a "thing" that is pulled (or pushed) in various directions by "motives" and is inevitably moved in the direction of the strongest pull (or push). But the model is not adequate. Selfhood cannot be conceived "from the outside"; it must be conceived from within, in terms of what it means to *be* a self. The reality of responsible selfhood cannot be adequately described in the paramechanical language of motives-determining-acts; it can be expressed only in the personal-life categories of decision and choice.

Space does not permit the detailed development of an alternative to the mechanical model employed by Hard Determinist. However, we may observe that it is the moral freedom of man, not the indeterminacy of some "faculty" of man, that is here in question. As moral agents we know (*a*) that there are some situations in which we are "morally obliged" to act in a certain way—there is something that we "ought" to do—and (*b*) that very often in such situations there is something that we "desire" to do that differs from what we "ought" to do. I am willing to allow that a person is not free to choose what shall be his strongest desire in any given situation: that, it seems to me, is determined by his character in relation to all the other details of that situation. I would insist, however, that in any given situation a person need not act in accord with his strongest desire; he may, instead, act contrary to his desire because he believes it is his *duty* to do so. He alone decides whether his action shall correspond to duty or to desire; hence he alone is answerable for his behavior.

This is admittedly a gross oversimplification of the matter, since in actual experience the conflict between duty and desire is seldom so sharp and explicit as this account suggests. It is, nonetheless, truer to our actual experience as moral agents than the mechanistic model we are attempting to refute. Anyone wishing a fuller explanation of this matter can (and should) at some later time inquire further into the notion of the self. For the present we have only to acknowledge that a self is not a "thing" and that its operations cannot be understood in terms of a mechanical model appropriate only to "things."

The Basis for Libertarianism

Even if my arguments succeed in removing the chief objections to libertarianism, the libertarian position is yet to be established. What is still required is some positive ground for its affirmation.

There is one, and only one, ground upon which libertarianism rests: that we know ourselves to be morally responsible, and that therefore we also know that whatever is necessary to render us morally responsible must be the case. There are, indeed, times when we have only one avenue of action open to us, and in such situations we accept neither praise nor blame for doing what, under the circumstances, was the only thing we could do. But more commonly we are faced with a variety of alternatives, some of which are in varying degrees attractive to us (instances of desire) and some of which may appear to make some moral claim on us (instances of duty). Here we must choose among the alternatives; and in the experience of choosing, of saying Yes to one of the alternatives and No to all the rest, we know directly that it is *our choice* that determines what shall be done. Our choice is not arbitrary: we can always give a reason for it ("I wanted to," "I felt it was my duty," etc.). But neither is it predictable, because we alone decide whether and to what extent to follow duty or desire.

Since we are, and know ourselves to be, morally responsible, the universe must contain the possibility of moral responsibility. Therefore it cannot be strictly deterministic, for in such a universe, moral freedom and responsibility could not exist. But neither, obviously, can it be a chaos, since in such a universe we could never accurately predict the result of any of our acts. (This last condition is the answer to Soft Determinist's claim that moral responsibility *requires* determinism. What moral responsibility does require is that the universe exhibit sufficient uniformity to enable us to know the probable consequences of this or that act.) The universe must, therefore, be sufficiently uniform in its operations to enable us to "count on" certain actions producing certain effects, and it must be sufficiently "loose" in its structure to permit human beings to make genuinely free and responsible decisions.

Fortunately, from my point of view, that is just how the universe appears to be. There certainly is a very large area in which perfect uniformity appears to prevail: hence, I can depend, say, on food to nourish, and I can feed the hungry confident that my action will not produce unintended results. Whether I actually do feed the hungry is up to me; consequently, I am fittingly held responsible for what I do or fail to do. Because there is a considerable degree of uniformity, science is possible; and I would not want to set any a priori limits to the extent of that uniformity. But because there is also a certain amount of "looseness" in the universe, moral freedom and responsible behavior have found a place as well; and I would be equally reluctant to set any a priori limits to the extent of man's moral responsibility. In a strictly deterministic universe science would presumably be possible, but moral freedom and responsibility would not. In a chaotic universe neither science nor morality would be possible. In the universe as it is, however, highly uniform but not strictly determined, there is ample room both for scientific knowledge and for moral freedom and responsibility. To abandon either would be to err in our understanding of man and his world.

STUDY QUESTIONS

1. Where exactly does Libertarian agree, and where does he disagree, with each of the two previous writers? Where on each of these points do your own sympathies lie at the present time?
2. How, according to Libertarian, has Soft Determinist accomplished the apparent reconciliation of determinism and moral freedom? Is this an accurate description of what Soft Determinist has done? If not, where does it go wrong?
3. Libertarian offers a *reductio ad absurdum* of Soft Determinist's account of moral responsibility. Summarize the argument. Does it succeed in your opinion?
4. What is a "heuristic principle"? How does the suggestion that the determinist hypothesis is a heuristic principle tend (if it does) to weaken Hard Determinist's case?
5. Summarize Libertarian's replies to Hard Determinist's arguments in support of determinism. Which of them, if any, do you find most convincing? Which least convincing?
6. What does Libertarian say is the "one, and only one, ground upon which libertarianism rests"? Do you find his argument at this point convincing? Why or why not?

Adler, Mortimer, et al. *The Idea of Freedom.* Garden City, N.Y.: Doubleday, 1958.

Ayers, M. R. *The Refutation of Determinism.* London: Methuen, 1968.

Beardsley, Elizabeth L. "Determinism and Moral Perspectives," *Philosophy and Phenomenological Research,* 21 (1960), 1–20.

Bergson, Henri. *Time and Free Will.* New York: Harper & Row, 1962 (paperbound).

Berofsky, Bernard. *Determinism.* Princeton, N.J.: Princeton University Press, 1971.

———— (ed.). *Free Will and Determinism.* New York: Harper & Row, 1966. A valuable collection of writings from many sources.

Brand, Myles (ed.). *The Nature of Human Action.* Glenview, Ill.: Scott, Foresman, 1970 (paperbound). An anthology. A basic issue: can sufficient explanations of human actions be given by references to causes?

Campbell, C. A. *In Defense of Free Will.* London: G. Allen & Unwin, 1967. A collection of essays by a prominent proponent of libertarianism.

————. "Is 'Free Will' a Pseudo-Problem?" *Mind,* 60 (1951), 441–465.

————. *On Selfhood and Godhood.* New York: Humanities Press, 1957.

Cranston, M. *Freedom—A New Analysis.* London: Longmans, Green, 1953.

Dworkin, Gerald (ed.). *Determinism, Free Will and Moral Responsibility.* Englewood Cliffs, N.J.: Prentice-Hall, 1970 (paperbound).

Eddington, A. S. *The Nature of the Physical World.* Ann Arbor, Mich.: University of Michigan Press, 1958 (paperbound), chap. 14.

Edwards, Jonathan. *Inquiry Concerning the Freedom of the Will,* ed. by Paul Ramsey. New Haven, Conn.: Yale University Press, 1957.

Ezorsky, G. (ed.). *Philosophical Perspectives on Punishment.* Albany, N.Y.: State University of New York Press, 1972. Classical and contemporary selections.

Farrer, Austin. *The Freedom of the Will.* New York: Scribner, 1960.

Fingarette, Herbert. *The Meaning of Criminal Insanity.* Berkeley, Calif.: University of California Press, 1974 (paperbound).

Flew, Antony. *Crime or Disease?* New York: Harper & Row, 1973. An examination of the concept of mental illness as it relates to the legal and moral issues raised.

Franklin, R. L. *Freewill and Determinism.* London: Routledge and Kegan Paul, 1968.

Halverson, W. H. "The Bogy of Chance," *Mind,* 73 (1964), 567–570.

Hampshire, Stuart. *Freedom of Mind and Other Essays.* Princeton, N.J.: Princeton University Press, 1971. Favors "free will."

Honderich, T. (ed.). *Essays in the Freedom of Action.* London: Routledge and Kegan Paul, 1973. Contemporary sources.

Hook, Sidney (ed.). *Determinism and Freedom in the Age of Modern Science.* New York: New York University Press, 1958.

Hospers, John. "Free-Will and Psychoanalysis," in W. Sellars and J. Hospers (eds.). *Readings in Ethical Theory.* New York: Appleton-Century-Crofts, 1952.

Hume, David. *A Treatise of Human Nature.* Many editions. See Book II, Part III.

James, William. "The Dilemma of Determinism," in *The Will to Believe and Other Essays in Popular Philosophy and Human Immortality.* New York: Dover, 1956 (paperbound), pp. 145–183.

Laird, John. *On Human Freedom.* New York: Hillary House, 1947.

Lehrer, Keith. "Can We Know that We Have Free Will by Introspection?" *The Journal of Philosophy,* 57 (1960), 145–157.

MacMurray, John. *The Self as Agent.* New York: Humanities Press, 1957.

Matson, W. I. "On the Irrelevance of Free-Will to Moral Responsibility," *Mind*, 65 (1956), 489–497.

O'Conner, D. J. *Free Will*. Garden City, N.Y.: Doubleday, 1971 (paperbound).

Pears, D. F. (ed.). *Freedom and the Will*. New York: St. Martin's Press, 1963.

Rankin, K. W. *Choice and Chance: A Libertarian Analysis*. Oxford: Basil Blackwell, 1961.

Rashdall, Hastings. *The Theory of Good and Evil*. Oxford: Oxford University Press, 1924, bk. III, chap. III.

Schlick, Moritz. *Problems of Ethics*, tr. by David Rynin. Englewood Cliffs, N.J.: Prentice-Hall, 1939 (Originally published in German in 1931), chap. 7.

Sidgwick, Henry. *The Methods of Ethics*, 7th ed., rev. by Constance Jones. Chicago: University of Chicago Press, 1962.

Skinner, B. F. *Beyond Freedom and Dignity*. New York: Knopf, 1971. A famous psychologist argues that the concept of free-will has adverse social consequences and offers an alternative approach to various social problems.

——. *Science and Human Behavior*. New York: Macmillan, 1953, chap. 1.

Smart, J. J. C. "Free Will, Praise and Blame," *Mind*, 70 (1961), 291–306.

Stebbing, L. S. *Philosophy and the Physicists*. New York: Dover, 1958 (paperbound).

Stevenson, C. L. *Ethics and Language*. New Haven, Conn.: Yale University Press, 1960 (paperbound), chap. 14.

Wilson, John. "Freedom and Compulsion," *Mind*, 67 (1958), 60–69.

PART IX

MAN'S
HIGHEST
GOOD

38

THE STRUCTURE
OF ETHICAL THINKING

It is an interesting and perhaps important fact about us that we regularly appraise our own behavior and that of our fellows in moral terms. Some behavior is appraised positively: an act is said to be good, or noble, or generous, or right; its enactor, benevolent, kind, humane, virtuous. And some behavior is appraised negatively: an act is said to be evil, or vile, or selfish, or wrong; its enactor, malevolent, bestial, inhumane, corrupt. Man cannot escape involvement in a moral community. His life is enveloped by what we may call "the moral sphere."

The Moral Sphere

What distinguishes that kind of behavior which we consider subject to moral appraisal? What are the defining characteristics of the moral sphere?

First, it is apparent that we appraise only *human* behavior morally. Until men landed on it, we did not subject anything that ever happened on the moon to moral appraisal. Again, we do not apply terms of moral appraisal to the behavior of animals or insects. We do not criticize the mating practices of antelopes, or the predatory habits of leopards, or the "slave" systems of ants or bees. Only human beings and their behavior are called good or bad, right or wrong, virtuous or vicious.

Second, it is only human behavior involving *choice* that we regard as appropriately subject to moral judgments. We assume, when we ascribe praise or blame to some particular human behavior, that other alternatives were available to the person whose behavior is being judged. We neither praise nor blame a person for doing something if we believe that, under the circumstances, it was the only thing he or she could have done.

277

Third, even when choice is involved, not all instances of human behavior belong to the moral sphere. Under ordinary circumstances, for example, my decision to have juice and cereal for breakfast rather than eggs and toast has no moral significance. (Of course, we can imagine a set of unusual circumstances in which this choice would have moral significance—if, say, I and another person were both on the verge of starvation, a single serving of each kind of breakfast was available, and he was seriously allergic to eggs, whereas I was not.) The third defining characteristic of the moral sphere is, then, that some *moral rule or principle* is relevant to the behavior in question: there is something that a human being in a given situation ought or ought not to do, some choice that he ought or ought not to make, simply by virtue of the fact that he is a human being in those particular circumstances. It would be morally wrong for me to contribute knowingly to the demise of my allergic friend by eating the cereal that could sustain his life when another alternative is available to me. Why? Because I have a moral obligation to preserve human life when I can. The generalized verson of this idea—that one ought to preserve human life when one has the opportunity—is an example of a moral rule or principle.

Normative Ethics

All of us, then, act in ways that are or may be subject to moral appraisal, and all of us make moral judgments about the behavior of others. In clear-cut cases we make these judgments without difficulty: we praise a man who risks his life to prevent a homicide or a mother who rushes into the flames to rescue a child. In such cases we judge almost instinctively, as if there were no reasoning involved.

In other cases, however, our moral judgments are more problematic. Is mercy killing ever morally defensible, and if so, under what circumstances? Is conscientious objection morally superior to being a soldier? Are some wars morally defensible and others not? Was it or was it not morally right for the United States to drop atomic bombs on Hiroshima and Nagasaki? In such cases we tend to be less certain about our answers, and we often disagree with one another in the answers we give. When we do disagree, we appeal to relevant general principles of right and wrong and try to show that the position we hold is consistent with those principles.

Normative ethics is an attempt to answer the question, What kinds of things really are right and wrong, and why? The aim of the ethical theorist is to introduce order and consistency into our ethical beliefs and to relate them, if possible, to some universal principle or principles from which they supposedly derive their validity as rules for the guidance of our behavior. If I ought to help old Mrs. Jones cross a busy intersection when I see her standing there apprehensively, it must be because there is some rule or principle that prescribes what I ought to do and in terms of which I will be appropriately praised or blamed for what I do or fail to do. And if I also ought to attempt to rescue a child who is drowning, the same reasoning applies. The ethical theorist asks, What is it that these two cases, and hundreds of others that might be mentioned, have in common? Is there not some general principle that governs these and all other cases of moral obligation? To ask and attempt to answer such questions is to engage in the peculiar sort of inquiry called normative ethics; to exhibit a set of ethical beliefs as a coherent system deducible from one or more general principles is to construct an ethical system.

Two Types of Ethical Thought

The efforts of philosophers to introduce order and consistency into our thinking about the moral sphere have resulted in two general types of ethical systems.

The first type may be termed *teleological*. The moral value of any act, according to this type of theory, consists in the tendency it has (or is intended to have) to produce a good or bad result. Some things are intrinsically good, and other things are good or bad depending on their tendency to promote or to hinder that which is intrinsically good. If health is considered intrinsically good, for example, then the praiseworthy character of certain acts (giving food to the hungry, medical care to the ill, etc.) and the blameworthy character of other acts (knowingly selling or serving contaminated food) can be understood in terms of their relation to this good. Everything that is morally praiseworthy, according to this type of theory, is so because of its tendency to realize that which is intrinsically good: the intrinsically good is the end (*télos*), or goal, at which all behavior having moral value is aimed. We shall return to a further consideration of this type of ethical system shortly.

Not all ethical theorists are convinced, however, that the whole moral sphere can be understood in terms of the relation of various acts to whatever may be said to be intrinsically good. Some acts, say these theorists, are obligatory in themselves, quite apart from any tendency they may have to produce an intrinsically good result. It may be argued, for example, that a person has the moral obligation under virtually any set of conceivable circumstances to tell the truth or to keep a promise, whether or not he believes that by so doing he will promote the realization of the intrinsically good. Some acts are "morally right" in and of themselves; they are not right merely by virtue of their tendency to realize some other good. Ethical systems that attempt to understand the moral sphere along these lines are variously termed *formalist* or *deontological* theories.

The Summum Bonum

Among many philosophers who have attempted to understand the moral sphere in teleological terms, a much discussed question has been, What is man's *summum bonum*—man's highest good? Some of man's "goods" are obviously good solely because of their instrumental value. Medicine, for example, is good only because of its value in producing health. Very well, let us then consider health. Why is it good? If we say that health is good because it is a precondition of being able to engage in enjoyable activity, then it too is an instrumental good (though it may also be an intrinsic good). Well then, why is enjoyable activity good? Is it instrumentally good in that it contributes to the realization of some higher good? If so, where does this process come to an end? What is man's "highest" good? What is the one good that (*a*) is worthy of being desired in and of itself, (*b*) is not instrumentally good, and (*c*) is the cause of the goodness of other things insofar as they contribute to its realization?

Note that our question is open-ended. It can logically be answered in an infinite number of ways, though few of the answers would be likely to appear plausible. Let us look briefly at a few of the answers that have seemed sufficiently credible to win the support of at least some philosophers.

Some Possible Answers

It can be plausibly argued that *pleasure* is man's highest good, indeed, that it is the only thing that is good in and of itself. This view is called *hedonism* (from the Greek *hedone*, meaning "pleasure"). One of its earliest and best-known advocates was the Greek philosopher Epicurus (341–270 B.C.), who wrote:

> We recognize pleasure as the first good innate in us, and from pleasure we begin every act of choice and avoidance, and to pleasure we return again, using the feeling as the standard by which we judge the good.[1]

Some critics of hedonism contend that such a view treats man as if he were a lower animal, a merely sensuous being. The truth is, they say, that man's uniqueness consists in the fact that he is a rational being. Man's highest good, therefore, is not pleasure—which may indeed be the highest good of a pig or a dog—but *activity according to reason*. This view we shall call *rational eudemonism* (from the Greek *eudaimonia*, meaning "happiness"). It was first advocated by Aristotle (384–322 B.C.), the great Greek philosopher and tutor of Alexander the Great.

Some ethical theorists have concluded that there is no one thing that is man's highest good, but that several things are worthy of being desired for their own sakes and that man's highest good consists in realizing as many of these intrinsic goods as he can. This view, also advocated by a number of philosophers, we shall call *ethical pluralism*.

It seems evident, finally, that religious claims have some bearing on the question concerning man's highest good. We shall, therefore,

---

[1] Epicurus, "Letter to Menoeceus," in Whitney J. Oates (ed.), *The Stoic and Epicurean Philosophers* (New York: Random House, 1940), pp. 31–32.

consider the view that man's highest good consists in a state of affairs that is incapable of being fully realized in this life, that the ultimate fulfillment of man's deepest needs and longings lies beyond the temporal sphere. This view, which we shall call *theological eudemonism*, has been advocated (with numerous differences in detail) by many philosopher-theologians including St. Augustine (A.D. 354–430) and St. Thomas Aquinas (A.D. 1225–1274).

Although these four are the answers that have been given most frequently to the question we are now considering, it is obvious that they by no means exhaust the possibilities. We shall, however, limit our consideration to these four, beginning with some of the arguments that may be adduced in support of hedonism.

STUDY QUESTIONS

1. What are suggested in this chapter as the defining characteristics of the moral sphere? Do you agree with this definition? Can you think of an example of human behavior that you would regard as being appropriately subject to praise or blame that does not fall within the moral sphere as so defined? Can you think of any example of behavior that fits this definition, but which you would exclude from the moral sphere?
2. What is normative ethics?
3. What precisely is the difference between teleological ethics and deontological (or formalist) ethics?
4. Precisely what are you asking when you ask, What is man's highest good? Rephrase the question in a way that you think exhibits more clearly the point of the question.
5. In addition to those suggested in this chapter, can you think of any plausible answers to the question, What is man's highest good?

39

THE CASE
FOR HEDONISM

Critics of hedonism seem to have rather consistently exhibited a perverse determination to misunderstand and misrepresent what its advocates are trying to say. The reason for this, I suppose, is that there is a simple-minded line of reasoning that appears to lead from the assertion "Pleasure is man's highest good" to the assertion "The highest rule of morality is, Enjoy yourself!" Since it seems obvious to everyone (including hedonists) that the injunction to enjoy oneself is not a very promising starting point for ethics, it is lightly concluded that the fundamental axiom of hedonism—that pleasure is man's highest good—is mistaken.

In order to rid our consideration of hedonism of this spurious reasoning, I propose that we begin our deliberation at a somewhat different point. Let us suppose that you and I are engaged by a very wealthy man to look after the raising of his children. His instructions to us are as follows: "The care of my children is entirely in your hands. You are to spare no effort and no expense to assist them in every possible way to achieve the very best life of which they are capable. Everything that would be for their good you are to provide; everything that would be for their evil you are, so far as possible, to omit from their experience. I leave it to you to judge what would truly be for their good and what would not."

If we are to carry out these instructions, we now have some very important decisions to make. We must decide what really is good—indeed, what really is best—for our charges. On what principle shall we decide? I say on the pleasure principle and would like to persuade you to agree with me.

The Pleasure Principle

When I assert that pleasure is man's highest good, I am *not* asserting that sensuous gratification is man's highest good. Man is not a pig. Man's highest good consists in the optimum realization of the pleasures of which *man* is capable. Man is capable, to be sure, of pleasures of sensation, and such pleasure is most certainly to be preferred to pain. But man is capable also of what may be termed the "higher" pleasures. He is capable, for example, of experiencing intellectual pleasure, by virtue of which knowledge is a great human good. He is capable of experiencing pleasures of feeling and imagination, by virtue of which he perceives poetry, music, painting, and the other products of the visual and performing arts as goods. He is capable of experiencing pleasure in the very act of serving a human need, by virtue of which the moral sentiments acquire for him an intrinsic value all their own. Man's highest good is *human* pleasure. What is pleasurable for man, and therefore good for man, is different from what would be pleasurable for a creature with more limited capacities.

Pleasure is an experience, a state of being, that occurs whenever an awakened desire is satisfied. There is pleasure in eating food when you are hungry and in drinking a glass of cold water when you are thirsty. There is pleasure also in beholding a beautiful sunset when inspired by a love of beauty, and in mastering a theorem when stimulated by a hunger for knowledge. Any good thing that you or I can do for any other human being will be, must be, a contribution to his pleasurable experience. To say that an act of such and such a kind is morally good or right is to say that it is the sort of act that on the whole tends to enhance human pleasure. You see, then, how very far we hedonists are from asserting that the first principle of ethics is "Enjoy yourself!" Such a principle cannot be derived from anything I have said and is in fact as repugnant to me (as a moral principle) as to any other ethical theorist.

Two questions now need to be clearly distinguished. The first is, What is man's highest good? I have replied that pleasure (as defined above) is man's highest good. A second and very different question is, About whose good ought I, as a moral agent, to be concerned? To this question I would reply that I ought to be concerned about the good (the pleasure) of all men, myself included. To be concerned exclusively about my own good (my own pleasure) would be sheer selfishness and would therefore be deserving of moral disapproval. To be as concerned about the good (the pleasure) of others as about my own is the essence of morality and is summed up in the admonitions "Do unto others as you would that others do unto you" and "Love your neighbor as yourself."

Supporting Arguments

The assertion that pleasure is man's highest good is not capable of strict and conclusive proof. Its probability can, however, be established by two persuasive arguments.

To say that something is man's highest good implies that it is worthy of being desired for its own sake. The intrinsic desirability of pleasure is rendered highly probable, it seems to me, by the fact that it is universally desired. That something is visible is indicated by people's actually seeing it. That something is audible is shown by people's actually hearing it. In like manner, I would suggest, the desirability of pleasure is evident from the fact that people actually desire it.

This argument is weakened not at all by examples of individuals who have freely subjected themselves to experiences that they fully expected to be more or less painful. Consider a father who permits one of his kidneys to be transplanted into the body of his daughter, whose kidneys had been removed because of disease. Is this man demonstrating that he prefers pain to pleasure? Surely not. He demonstrates only that he is willing to suffer pain in order that his child may have an opportunity to experience the pleasures of a normal life. His pain is chosen not for its own sake but for the sake of the pleasure he might give to someone he loves. Every instance of pain freely accepted that I can think of can be understood in the same way: as a means to the enhancement of some human pleasure that is valued for its own sake.

Second, the assertion that pleasure is man's highest good is broadly supported by the fact that it renders intelligible the moral rules and principles by which most people agree we ought to try to live. Why is it morally wrong to steal? Because human pleasure is enhanced when people respect each other's property rights. Why is it morally wrong to lie? Because life proceeds more serenely, more happily, when people can be counted on to tell the truth. Why is it virtuous to feed the hungry, to visit the sick, to comfort the bereaved, to aid the destitute? Because in doing these things we are assuaging human pain and enhancing human pleasure. Hedonism, then, merely makes explicit the principle that has unconsciously guided the conscience of mankind through the thousands of years in which the moral code by which most civilized societies live has been developing. The explicit assertion of this principle makes possible the further development of the moral code as society moves rapidly into a new era in which the rules of the past may be insufficient to guide us in resolving the problems that we are likely to encounter.

Qualities of Pleasure

Let us now return to the point where we began: the task of providing for the children of our wealthy employer "everything that would be for their good" and shielding them from "everything that would be for their evil." How shall we proceed? What pleasures shall we teach them to enjoy? What pains shall we seek to eliminate from their experience?

We shall, of course, provide adequately for their physical needs: food, shelter, clothing, and the like. We shall let them feel the warmth of the sun on a summer day and the refreshing coolness of a stream when they are old enough to swim. We shall employ the best medical knowledge available to protect them from disease and to heal them when they are ill.

But clearly, if we are to provide "everything that would be for their good," we must do much more than this. We must awaken in them the higher faculties, the uniquely human desires, in order that they may experience the sublimer pleasures that man alone, so far as we know, is capable of enjoying. We shall attempt to awaken their thirst for knowledge, to make them curious about themselves, their world, and their fellows. Then we can guide them toward the discovery of answers in order that they may experience the incomparable pleasure of learning.

We shall also attempt to awaken in our young charges a love for beauty, so that they may experience the sublime pleasures of art, music, sculpture, and nature itself. We shall expose them to mountains and oceans and sunsets, to the paintings of the masters, to the mighty symphonies of Beethoven and the exquisite music of Mozart, to architectural creations of exceptional beauty, to theater, cinema, and dance. We shall cultivate in them a taste for beauty in form and movement, an aesthetic sense that will provide them with immeasurable pleasure throughout life.

We shall, finally, attempt to awaken in them a moral sense, a natural preference for good and an abhorrence of evil. We shall teach them to desire the pleasure of all men, indeed of all sentient creatures, and shall attempt to inculcate in them that natural kindness and generosity of spirit that is the essence of virtue. We shall not, certainly, seek to make of them either ascetics or grim moralists, but we shall teach them to value the pleasurable experience of every creature, and especially of every human being; and we shall teach them when the occasion demands it to forgo some pleasure themselves in order that some greater or rarer pleasure may be experienced by others.

"That all sounds very lovely," someone may say, "but let me ask a very practical question. If pleasure is man's highest good, why do you not simply maximize the *quantity* of pleasure for your young charges and stop worrying about the *quality*? If money were man's highest good, it would make no difference whether he got it in fives, tens, or hundreds; only the total quantity would be relevant. Why not with pleasure?"

To this question I would reply as follows: No man would be willing to exchange his higher faculties—his capacity to experience intellectual and aesthetic and moral pleasure—for any quantity whatsoever of merely sensual pleasure. Promise a man every variety of sensual pleasure, in any quantity imaginable, on the condition that he cease to be a man and become a lower animal, and he will refuse it. Why? Because, in fact, men do value some pleasures above others and are on occasion willing to endure a fair amount of physical discomfort for the sake of securing some of the higher pleasures. All pleasure, *qua* pleasure, is good and worthy of being desired; but in the judgment of those who have experienced a wide spectrum of pleasures (and they alone are competent to judge), some forms of pleasure are more valuable, more worthy of being desired, than others.

Our problem as tutors, then, is not merely to maximize the quantity of pleasure for our charges but to orchestrate the variety of pleasures in such a way as to guide them toward a truly satisfying life. This, admittedly, is no easy task, for there is danger of imbalance in many directions. We do not want them to become sensualists, or esthetes, or arid intellectuals, or rigid moralists: we want them to become well-rounded human beings, sensitively balancing the various forms of pleasure in their own experience and seeking to further a similar balance in the lives of others.

Let me conclude by underscoring the point with which I began. The greatest problem that we hedonists have to face is that our position is often misrepresented in such a way as to make it into something that no man with any sense of human dignity would espouse. This is usually done by defining pleasure in purely sensual terms and then suggesting that according to hedonism each individual should be concerned only about *his own* pleasure (so defined). But this, I repeat, is a gross parody of hedonism. Hedonism is indeed the view that pleasure is the greatest human good. But hedonists affirm that what is pleasurable for man is different from that which is pleasurable for a lower animal, because man is capable of enjoying a rich variety of pleasures. If moral virtue consists in desiring what is good for all men and doing what will tend to achieve it, then from a hedonist's point of view a moral agent must desire and work for human pleasure in all its various forms.

STUDY QUESTIONS

1. What exactly is pleasure? Write your own definition, then compare this with the definition in a dictionary.
2. "Any good thing that you or I can do for any other human being will be, must be, a contribution to his pleasurable experience." Do you agree? If you do agree, does that settle the issue for you—that is, does it follow that pleasure is man's highest good?
3. "The assertion that pleasure is man's highest good is not capable of strict and conclusive proof." Do you agree? In general, how would you go about trying to support the claim that *x* (pleasure, or what-have-you) is man's highest good?
4. Objection: If pleasure is man's highest good, then the more pleasure there is, the more good there is, regardless of the *quality* of pleasure involved. Do you agree?
5. Suppose that someone experiences pleasure in torturing animals. Is the pleasure good? Is the activity of torturing animals right? How might Hedonist respond to these questions?

40

A LIFE
OF REASON

I want to begin my contribution to this discussion by reintroducing the beautiful word "eudemonia" from Chapter 38. It is usually translated "happiness," but it means much more: literally, "having a good spirit"; connotatively, "good fortune," "fulfillment," "a rich destiny." Eudemonia is that for which a man would exchange all that he has. It is the pearl of great price, the goal and desire of every human being.

It is a mere tautology to say that man's highest good is to achieve eudemonia. The question is, In what does man's eudemonia consist? Hedonist tells us, in the experience of pleasure. I think he is mistaken in this assertion, and I shall attempt to show why.

Critique of Hedonism

Let us look first at Hedonist's reasoning. The intrinsic desirability of pleasure is evident, he says, from the fact that it is universally desired. For just as something is visible by virtue of the fact that people actually see it, and audible by virtue of the fact that people actually hear it, so a thing is desirable by virtue of the fact that people desire it. Ergo, he concludes, pleasure is desirable.

This reasoning is altogether specious; indeed, it is nothing more than a play on words. To say that something is visible or audible is to say that it is *capable* of being seen or heard. To say that something is desirable, on the other hand, is to say that it is *worthy* of being desired. "Desirable" is like "despicable" and "lovable," not like "visible" and "audible." That people desire something does not at all tend to show that it is truly desirable, that is, that it is *worthy* of being desired. It only shows that it is desired.

I must also take issue with Hedonist's attempt to square his assertion that pleasure is man's highest good with the idea that some forms of pleasure are more desirable than others by virtue of their higher quality. On the premise that pleasure is man's highest good, what can "higher quality" possibly mean? It can only mean, it seems to me, "more pleasurable": it can be of a higher quality only in the way that a ten-dollar bill is of a higher quality (if you want to put it that way) than a one-dollar bill. And if a man is criticized for neglecting his intellectual and aesthetic and moral development for the sake of being a pure sensualist, he could, on Hedonist's premise, convincingly defend himself by arguing that he finds sensual pleasure more pleasurable than other kinds. I know that Hedonist does not want to say this; indeed, his theory about "qualities of pleasure" is intended precisely to avoid this conclusion. My point is that he cannot have it both ways. If pleasure is man's highest good, then one pleasure can be "higher" than another only by virtue of being more pleasurable. If various forms of pleasure differ in quality, then they must differ by virtue of some component other than pleasure itself, and in that case pleasure is not man's highest good.

That Hedonist's argument contains some specious reasoning does not, of course, prove that he is mistaken in his assertion that pleasure is man's highest good. Good theories are sometimes supported with bad reasons, and in such cases we must be wise enough to look beyond those bad reasons and consider the theory on its own merits. Let us now do this with Hedonist's theory. Let us forget his faulty reasoning and consider directly whether or not pleasure is man's highest good. I shall, of course, argue that it is not.

First, imagine a person enjoying in a very high degree throughout a long life all the pleasures that Hedonist has described—sensual pleasures, intellectual pleasures, aesthetic pleasures, pleasures of every conceivable kind. According to Hedonist's theory, this person would have achieved man's highest good and should wish for nothing more. But let us suppose something more about this person. Though he possesses an abundance of pleasure at every moment, he does not possess memory, so he cannot remember that he has experienced pleasure in the past. Moreover, though he is experiencing immense pleasure moment by moment, he is not *conscious* of experiencing pleasure, nor is he able to anticipate that he will experience pleasure in the future. This person, in short, though by our hypothesis he experiences an abundance of pleasure, lacks those faculties by which he could be *conscious* that he was experiencing pleasure. Would we really say that he was realizing man's highest good? We would not. But if pleasure is man's highest good, we clearly should.

"Well," Hedonist may say to us, "you are just nit-picking. Any reasonable person must know that when I say that pleasure is man's highest good, I mean that the *consciousness* of pleasure is man's highest good. Certainly I don't mean to assert that pleasure, apart from the consciousness of pleasure, is good." Very well, let us accept this revision of Hedonist's theory. It still does not stand up under close scrutiny.

Imagine now that a person has been put to sleep with an anesthetic and that all necessary arrangements have been made to take care of normal bodily processes—supplying food and water, getting rid of bodily wastes, and so forth. In addition, medical science being at a very advanced stage, his brain is artificially stimulated in such a way that he has the *consciousness* of experiencing in a very high degree all the pleasures that Hedonist describes as constituting man's highest good. He experiences every imaginable form of sensual pleasure, every form of aesthetic pleasure, and the highest reaches of intellectual ecstasy. And let this experience of sheer ecstasy, unadulterated by any consciousness of pain, go on and on and on. Let it continue forever. Would we say that this man is an example of someone who was realizing man's highest good? We would not. Yet, if the consciousness of pleasure were man's highest good, we should assent to this.

Or consider this: If pleasure, or the consciousness of pleasure, were man's highest good, then the best of all possible worlds for man would be one in which half the people on earth were sadists and the other half masochists. There would, certainly, be a great deal of pleasure in such a world—much more, presumably, than there is now—but I for one would not call it a better world. Yet, if I were to accept the thesis that pleasure is man's highest good, I would be obliged to applaud such a world.

Hedonism, then, is not an acceptable theory about what constitutes man's highest good, man's eudemonia. Let me present an alternative view.

Rational Eudemonism

Suppose that we ask what constitutes the highest good of a fish. It is apparent that the eudemonia of a fish would be that state of affairs that would enable the fish to do those things that nature has equipped it to do, most prominently, swimming, an activity in which the fish expresses its uniqueness as a fish. In order to identify the highest good of any species of living thing you have first to identify what it is about that species that is unique; for the highest good of any creature is that activity or state of affairs in which it is, so to speak, fulfilling its unique destiny, realizing its unique purpose for being.

What, then, is unique about man? His capacity for growth and reproduction he shares with all other living things, plants as well as animals. His capacity to experience sensation (sight, hearing, touch, taste, smell) and to move about (locomotion) he shares with all the animals. That which is unique in man is not to be found in these areas. Man differs from every other species of living thing by virtue of his reason. Man alone is able to seek and to know truth, though admittedly he often falls into error in his quest for truth. This capacity to exercise reason, then, to seek understanding, knowledge, science, wisdom, is man's unique endowment.

Man's *highest* good, then, must consist in the exercise of his highest faculty. He has, to be sure, many lesser goods—food, companionship, pleasurable sensations, and the like. But man's highest good, that in which his eudemonia essentially consists, is the right exercise of his rational faculty.

In addition to seeking knowledge, however, it is the function of man's reason to instruct him regarding what is good and right. Thus man is exercising his rational faculty not only when he is searching for or contemplating truth but also when he is acting according to what reason tells him is good and right. Consequently we arrive at the view that man's highest good consists in *activity according to reason,* either in the quest for truth or in practical activity according to the moral dictates of reason.

I freely admit that this high goal of always acting according to reason is rarely achieved by man. For there is in man, as every serious student of the human psyche from Plato to Sigmund Freud has told us, a powerful irrational element that seeks expression in those very actions that we have said are supposed to be controlled by reason. Indeed, the sharp difference between Hedonist's position and my own is vividly illustrated at this point; for Hedonist is bound to say that insofar as the expression of libido is pleasurable it is good, whereas I affirm that insofar as it leads to behavior that is not in accordance with reason it is bad. Man progresses toward his highest good not by following the path of least resistance (which hedonism would appear to counsel him to do) but by striving—sometimes heroically—to bring his various drives and appetites under the control of a disciplined reason. This may not always be maximally pleasurable, for there is undoubtedly pleasure in the fulfillment of an awakened desire and disappointment in its denial, but it is the way to eudemonia.

We have noted that the view that there are various qualities of pleasure, and that the "higher" pleasures are to be preferred to the "lower" pleasures, is not consistent with the basic thesis of hedonism that pleasure constitutes man's highest good. I would now suggest that the concept of "qualities of pleasure," which does appear to be valid, can best be understood in conjunction with the theory I am here defending. For to say that one sort of pleasure is higher than another means, I suggest, that there is more reason in it. A child's delight in playing in the snow is surely as innocent as any pleasure imaginable, but it is of a lower order of pleasure because there is little reason in it. The pleasure of a student of physics in finally mastering relativity theory is of a higher order of pleasure because there is much reason in it. The scale according to which we rank pleasures as being higher or lower is the scale of reason.

In affirming that activity according to reason is man's highest good I am not denying that pleasure is a good. On the contrary, I hold that pleasure may be a very high-level good, and that it is worthy of being desired insofar as it does not detract from the pursuit of this highest good. We should aim, it seems to me, at being rational beings, at realizing in practice the goal of activity according to reason; it will then follow, as a natural concomitant of such a life, that we will experience such pleasures as are good for us.

STUDY QUESTIONS

1. What is Rational Eudemonist's objection to Hedonist's claim that pleasure is desirable because it is universally desired? Who is right on this point?
2. "If various forms of pleasure differ in quality, then they must differ by virtue of some component other than pleasure itself, and in that case pleasure is not man's highest good." Do you agree?
3. Rational Eudemonist presents two *reductio ad absurdum* arguments to show that pleasure is not man's highest good. Do they succeed? How might Hedonist defend himself?
4. How does Rational Eudemonist support his claim that man's highest good consists in activity according to reason? Do you find his argument at all convincing?

41

ETHICAL PLURALISM

Discussions about the *summum bonum* often seem to me to confuse several questions. Consequently, I want to preface what I have to say on the subject of man's highest good by distinguishing those questions that are sometimes discussed almost interchangeably and by indicating which of these questions I shall be answering in the remainder of this essay.

Four Questions

In asking, What is man's highest good? it is possible, first, to be asking for a description of the best conceivable state of affairs for man. In answer to this question we might posit, for example, a world in which the temperature at ground level is always 72° Fahrenheit, where no illness or suffering of any kind ever occurs, where people remain youthful forever, and so on. Such a description might even be of some practical value in defining a remote ideal toward which our efforts in the real world might fruitfully be directed, but it would not be a description of "man's highest good" in the sense in which I shall be discussing it.

Second, this question could be construed to mean, What is the best possible state of affairs for man, the laws of nature being what they are? In this case we would have to describe a kind of ideal society, in which all the remediable ills of society as we know it are somehow cured. Plato in the *Republic* and Thomas More in *Utopia* tried to do this; but this is not the question I shall be discussing.

A third possible meaning of the question concerning man's highest good is this: Of the various good things that man may for various reasons desire, which are most worthy of being desired for their own sakes? What are the principal intrinsic goods for man? I shall be addressing myself to this question shortly.

The fourth way in which the question may be construed is as follows: Of the various things that are worthy of being desired for their own sakes, which *one thing* is most worthy of being desired? This question assumes that there is a multiplicity of things that are intrinsically good but that some one of them is so much better than the others that it should be desired even at the cost of losing the other, and lesser, intrinsic goods. I shall have something to say on this point also in what follows.

Of these four questions, it seems to me that Hedonist has addressed himself to the third and Rational Eudemonist to the fourth. Hedonist has argued that pleasure alone is intrinsically good and worthy of being desired for its own sake, and that whatever else is good for man is good only insofar as it is productive of human pleasure. Rational Eudemonist, on the other hand, has conceded that pleasure is *a* good, perhaps even an intrinsic good, but has argued that another intrinsic good—activity according to reason—is the *highest* intrinsic good for man, that is, the intrinsic good most worthy of being desired.

In order to defend my position against both Hedonist and Rational Eudemonist, therefore, I am obliged to reply to these two questions. Against Hedonist I shall argue that pleasure is only one of several intrinsic goods for man; and against Rational Eudemonist I shall argue that man's highest good consists, not in the maximum realization of some one intrinsic good to the possible exclusion of all others, but rather in the maximization of all.

A Word About Method

It is notoriously difficult to argue for or against any theory about what things are intrinsically good and worthy of being desired as ends in themselves. Hedonist frankly admits that he cannot provide a "strict and conclusive proof" of his position; Rational Eudemonist does not even try. The method that seems to me most appropriate is what I shall call the method of *imaginative isolation*. Let us suppose that we are trying to decide whether x is intrinsically good. We then imagine a universe in which x is absent, and then another that is identical in all respects except that x is present. We then ask, Does the presence of x in the second case provide any reason for preferring the second universe over the first? If the answer is affirmative, x may be presumed to be intrinsically good; if the answer is negative, we conclude that x is not intrinsically good.

Pleasure

If we now apply this method to the case of pleasure, we shall not be surprised to discover that pleasure is indeed an intrinsic good. If we were to imagine, let us say, one universe in which sentient beings are always in pain and another identical in all respects except that sentient beings consistently experience pleasure, we would say without hesitation that the second universe is preferable to the first. In saying this we would be acknowledging that pleasure is intrinsically good.

However, not all pleasure is intrinsically good. For let us suppose that some great tragedy occurs—a hurricane, for example, that results in great loss of human life—and that someone contemplates this awful tragedy *with pleasure.* Surely, we would say, a universe in which tragedy produces sorrow is better than one in which it would produce pleasure, because pleasure of this kind is *not* good. Or suppose that someone experiences pleasure in doing some reprehensible act: a universe that lacked *such* pleasure, we want to say, is to be preferred over one that contains it.

These exceptional cases raise a very difficult question: if we assent to the proposition that, on the whole, pleasure is good and worthy of being desired, precisely why do we object to its occurrence in these cases? The answer would appear to be that it is not to the pleasure as such that we object but to pleasure caused by something intrinsically bad. All other things being equal, we prefer a universe where sentient beings experience pleasure to one in which they experience neither pleasure nor pain; but we should prefer the latter universe to one in which some sentient beings experience pleasure in contemplating the suffering or death of others.

The result of our analysis appears to be, then, that pleasure is good except in those cases in which it is caused by something that is intrinsically bad.

Knowledge

By using the same method we shall find that *knowledge* also is intrinsically good. Imagine a universe in which there is a definite quota of pleasure but no knowledge, and another in which there is an exactly equal quantity of pleasure but, in addition, widespread knowledge of the laws of nature and of human society. We would unhesitatingly choose the latter. And note that we do not (as Hedonist might argue) value the knowledge because of the pleasure it gives, for according to our hypothesis, the amount of pleasure in the two cases is exactly equal. It is clear, therefore, that we value the knowledge for its own sake.

Are there exceptions in the case of knowledge, as we discovered there were in the case of pleasure? It would seem so. Certainly most of us would feel obliged to conceal from a young child information that might be hurtful or acutely embarrassing to him—that his mother had abandoned him, for example, or that his father was a criminal. Eventually, we realize, the child should know even these painful truths, but while he is young and possibly capable of severe emotional damage, we would probably feel obliged to "protect" him from this knowledge. Again, in the case of a person of any age who is very ill, we can easily imagine information that we might conceal from him on the ground that knowledge of it would (we think) only aggravate his condition or add mental torture to the pain he is already suffering.

The generalization to which these considerations bring us is that knowledge is good except when it would lead to consequences sufficiently bad to outweigh the good. Perhaps we could even say that knowledge is always good; but there are cases in which this good cannot be realized without simultaneously realizing an evil of such magnitude that the good comes as a poor bargain.

Moral Virtue

At this point I do not wish to split hairs about the exact definition of moral virtue, but I cannot avoid mentioning it if my list of intrinsic goods is to be at all complete. By moral virtue, then, I mean what I think is just the common and accepted meaning of this phrase, namely, those qualities of character that predispose someone to act kindly toward his fellow-men and in general to behave in ways that he considers good and right.

Now it seems clear to me that such qualities of character and the actions in which they are expressed are intrinsically good. Again we apply our method of imaginative isolation. Consider a world that contains a definite quantity of pleasure and knowledge but no moral virtue, and consider another universe containing exactly the same amount of pleasure and knowledge but moral virtue as well. We would, I think, unhesitatingly choose the latter. If so, it is clear that we regard moral virtue as something that is good in itself apart from its consequences—though it is probably true that in actuality we prize it also for its consequences. Moreover, it seems to me that in this case the conclusion holds without exception: I can think of no case in which we would be inclined to say that it would be better for virtue not to exist because of its allegedly bad consequences.

Other Intrinsic Goods

Are there other things that, by a further application of the method of imaginative isolation, might be identified as intrinsic goods? I find it difficult to answer this question with any degree of confidence. Other candidates suggest themselves: justice, creativity, optimism, freedom, even life itself. But certain of these, I think, are reducible to some combination of the intrinsic goods we have already identified, and others appear to be merely instrumental goods. In any case, I am not willing to say flat out that pleasure, knowledge, and virtue are the only intrinsic goods for man, but I am unable at this time to extend the list any further myself. If imaginative isolation can identify other intrinsic goods, then so be it: it does not affect my argument in the least.

Man's Highest Good

Is some one of these intrinsic goods more worthy of being desired than others? Many philosophers would answer this question in the affirmative. Hedonist, for example, elevates pleasure to the highest level and treats all other goods merely as means to the production of pleasure. Rational Eudemonist, by elevating activity according to reason to the highest rank, ends up with a definite order of preference: knowledge, then virtue, then pleasure. So far we have not heard in this debate from anyone who holds that virtue is man's highest good, but we are reminded of the words of Socrates at the end of the *Apology*: "When my sons are grown up, I would ask you, O my friends, to punish them; and I would have you trouble them, as I have troubled you, if they seem to care about riches, or anything, more than about virtue . . ." [1]

If pleasure, knowledge, and virtue are indeed all intrinsic goods, it seems plainly foolish to elevate any one of them to the position of the *summum bonum* to the possible exclusion of the others. These three are related not as superordinates and subordinates but as coequal goods worthy of being desired by all men. Man's eudemonia consists not in being a mere pleasure seeker, nor in being an arid intellectual, nor in being a grim moralist: his eudemonia consists in being man. Insofar as he is intellect, his eudemonia consists in the acquisition of knowledge; insofar as he is will, in the cultivation of virtue; insofar as he is feeling, in the experience of pleasure. Man's *summum bonum* is to realize so far as possible every intrinsic good, in such balance and proportion as his natural endowments and his circumstances may permit.

STUDY QUESTIONS

1. What are the "four questions" that Pluralist attempts to distinguish on pp. 292–293? Is he right in saying that "Hedonist has addressed himself to the third, and Rational Eudemonist to the fourth"?
2. What is "the method of imaginative isolation"? How is it supposed to be useful in the discussion of the present issue?
3. List the things that Pluralist identifies as intrinsic goods. Do you agree that these are intrinsic goods? Would you add anything else to this list?
4. What is Pluralist's final answer to the question, What is man's highest good? Do you agree with him?
5. Suppose that Pluralist had an opportunity to obtain either one (but not both) of two intrinsic goods. On what basis, if any, could the choice of one over the other be made?

---

[1] Plato, *Apology*, in *The Dialogues of Plato*, tr. B. Jowett (New York: Random House, 1937), vol. I, p. 423.

42

THEOLOGICAL EUDEMONISM

I enter this debate as a modern advocate of a view that has a long and distinguished history. In the Greco-Roman world it vied successfully with several of the theories set forth in preceding chapters, and it was for centuries the universally accepted opinion regarding man's highest good. In recent years, however, this view has been abandoned by many people in favor of one or another of the alternative theories. I remain convinced, however, that it is the correct view and propose to present it as convincingly as I am able.

Some Generalizations

Let me begin by making some generalizations that seem to me to be warranted on the basis of the foregoing discussion. First, all parties to the debate appear to be agreed that man's highest good consists in the fulfillment of man's deepest longings and desires. Man is, so to speak, an "unfinished" creature. He longs for completeness, for fulfillment, for the satisfaction of his desires. The assertion that pleasure, or knowledge, or virtue, or all of these together, constitutes man's highest good really means that the realization of whichever of these is proposed will satisfy man's deepest needs and cause him to experience completeness. If it does not, then what is being proposed is not in truth man's *highest* good but merely, at best, some lesser good.

It follows, therefore, that any view about the *summum bonum* presupposes some judgment about man's deepest needs, some judgment about what it would take to render man truly complete. If you really believe that all that man lacks in order to be truly complete is a goodly quantity of pleasurable experiences of various sorts, then (and only then) are you justified in adopting hedonism; and so on for any other proposal that may be put forward.

Let us, then, ask the crucial question about each of the theories advanced thus far. Would an immense quantity of pleasurable experiences satisfy the deepest longing of the human heart? Clearly not. Would an immense amount of knowledge satisfy this longing? No. Would any amount of pleasure, knowledge, and virtue give man the completeness that he craves? It would not. These are goods, to be sure, but none is man's *highest* good. Our search must continue.

An Alternative View

Suppose that we press our search by asking the question, *Why* does man experience this incompleteness, this longing that cannot be satisfied by any imaginable quantity of pleasure, knowledge, or virtue? The answer, I would suggest, is that *man is separated from that to which he essentially belongs, and so long as that condition remains, man is restless and unfulfilled.* To understand what it is that constitutes man's highest good, we need first to understand the depths of his predicament.

To say that man is separated from that to which he essentially belongs is to say that man is "out of harmony" with himself, with his world, and with God. He experiences conflicts *within himself*—conflicts between the call of duty and the lure of desire, between the drive toward individuality and the desire to conform, between the longing for solitude and the need for companionship. He experiences conflict with *other human beings*—with people who seem "strange" to him because they are of a different race, a different nationality, a different economic or social class, a different faith, a different culture. And he experiences conflict with God, whose very existence seems doubtful to him, whose authority he resents, whose laws he hates, and whose nature he cannot comprehend. Let us call this situation *estrangement.* It is the universal human condition, the tragic predicament of fallen man.

If estrangement is the ultimate reason for the restless hunger of the human heart, then clearly man's highest good is that state of affairs in which estrangement is overcome and man is restored to a harmonious relationship with himself, with his world, and with God. Such a state of affairs is called "salvation." *Man's highest good consists in the reconciliation of that which is estranged, in the healing of broken relationships, in salvation.* Nothing short of this will ultimately satisfy the deepest longings of the human spirit.

Please note that in affirming that man's highest good consists in salvation I am at present talking about a this-worldly process, a good that is attainable in some degree here and now. The reconciliation of that which is estranged, the healing of that which is broken, is a process that is going on in the world here and now, a process that we enter into whenever we participate in the overcoming of enmity, conflict, and strife.

Indeed, if some of my readers find the term "salvation" too loaded with other connotations to convey the meaning I am trying to express, I suggest that they simply substitute the term "peace." Augustine once wrote (and note how he speaks to each of the elements of estrangement enumerated above):

> The peace of body and soul is the well-ordered and harmonious life and health of the living creature. Peace between man and God is the well-ordered obedience of faith to eternal law. Peace between man and man is well-ordered concord . . . The peace of all things is the tranquility of order.[1]

"The peace of all things"—that, I submit, is the state of affairs that all men desire above every other good. To the extent that such peace is achieved, man reaches his highest good. To the extent that it is not, he remains restless and dissatisfied.

Can this state of affairs be achieved by man in this earthly life? The answer would appear to be, Yes, in some degree. The faith by which Western man lived for many hundreds of years speaks of a God who with infinite love and patience seeks to reconcile to Himself a creation that has turned its back on Him. Insofar as God's creatures learn to love Him above all things, the "tranquility of order" of which St. Augustine speaks is restored. For the *disorder* that plagues our world is a consequence of our misdirected love—a consequence of loving the creature more than the Creator. In response to God's love, however, our love can be redirected, and we can begin to experience the wholeness, the peace, the tranquility, that we and all creatures would experience in its fullness if "the peace of all things" were fully achieved.

The Eternal Dimension

Every human life, then, is a quest for salvation, though salvation is sometimes wrongly sought in ways that only deepen estrangement. But every human life, however much it may experience reconciliation, falls short of a complete realization of the *summum bonum*, inasmuch as no one life can experience the perfection of salvation apart from "the peace of all things."

The full realization of man's highest good—the final reconciliation and peace of all things—lies, therefore, beyond this present life in a life of eternal blessedness. Indeed, every fundamental desire of the human spirit cries out for a fulfillment that cannot be completely achieved in this life.

As an intellectual being, man has an insatiable desire to know the truth. This is evident not only from our own experience of taking great

---

[1] St. Augustine, *The City of God*, XIX, xiii, in Whitney J. Oates (ed.), *Basic Writings of St. Augustine* (New York: Random House, 1948), vol. 2, p. 488.

delight in achieving some new understanding but also from observing that many persons spend their entire adult lives in pure research, with little or no thought to any possible practical consequences of their hard-won knowledge. As Aristotle remarked, "All men by nature desire to know";[2] this desire to know is not satisfied by any quantity of learning that may be achieved in this life.

As a moral being, there is also in man a desire to live rightly, to do what is good and just and to refrain from doing wrong—in short, to achieve the perfection of virtue. But this desire, however great its achievement by the noble few, is never fully satisfied in this life. Selfish desires, the lusts of the body, ignorance and frailty, conspire to prevent us from achieving moral perfection. That perfection, if it is ever to be achieved, must await another life.

There are, further, certain goods that we all desire as members of human society: among other things, honor and appreciation for the good that we have done; reputation among our fellows; and such riches as may enable us to be comfortable and secure as we face an uncertain future. Regardless of the magnitude of its realization, our desire for these goods is never fully satisfied in this life.

There is also in us, as Hedonist has emphasized, a desire to experience pleasure; indeed, so intense is this desire in some of us that we race from pleasure to pleasure as if believing that if only we could experience a sufficient quantity and variety of pleasures, our restless hearts really could be quieted. But from every such venture, however great the momentary ecstasy, we return to the world of reality to find that the void still remains and the spirit is still unsatisfied.

There is in us, finally, as Spinoza has beautifully put it, a desire to "persevere in our being . . . (through) indefinite time."[3] We do not want our life to come to an end, and we demonstrate this by taking all sorts of measures to protect ourselves from danger and to guard our health. Yet we know that this earthly life will eventually come to an end.

There is, to be sure, a kind of earthly happiness in such satisfaction of these several longings as we are able to secure in this life. But over all our futile searching for a paradise on earth stand those haunting words of St. Augustine in the opening chapter of *The Confessions*: "Thou has formed us for Thyself, and our hearts are restless till they find rest in Thee."[4] Man's highest good, man's true eudemonia, can be achieved only in a preliminary and fragmentary way in this life. Its perfection must await that life of eternal blessedness that God desires to give to all His children.

What do we mean by a life of eternal blessedness? First and foremost,

---

[2] Aristotle, *Metaphysics*, I, i, in Richard McKeon (ed.), *The Basic Works of Aristotle* (New York: Random House, 1941), p. 689.

[3] Benedict de Spinoza, *Ethics*, part III, prop. VI and VIII, in John Wild (ed.), *Spinoza Selections* (New York: Scribner, 1930), pp. 215, 216.

[4] St. Augustine, *The Confessions*, I, i, in Oates (ed.), *op. cit.*, vol. I, p. 3.

we mean a life in which man's estrangement is *totally* overcome and man is restored to a harmonious relationship with himself, his world, and God. In such a life, every good that man desires is achieved in its fullness. Our desire for knowledge is fully satisfied, for all that we are capable of knowing is known completely and without error. Our quest for virtue reaches its goal, for our characters at last reach the perfection that forever eludes us in our present life. Our desire for honor, fame, and wealth is fulfilled insofar as it is good for us and extinguished insofar as it is not. In this life of which I speak we shall experience pleasure of such purity and such permanence as we never dreamed of in this life. Finally, we shall no longer have to labor under the depressing knowledge that sooner or later our life will come to an end, for we shall have the blessed certainty that it will continue forever. Such a life, and nothing less than this, would constitute the true happiness, the eudemonia, the ultimate fulfillment, of a being whose needs and longings are what we know our own to be.

A Choice

If we grant that man really does have the needs and longings that I have enumerated, and that his highest good does not consist in anything attainable in this life, then there are three alternatives among which we must choose. We may assert, first, that eternal happiness is a real possibility for man, in which case we should spare no effort to attain such a life. Or, second, we may conclude (as many evidently have) that eternal life is not possible for man and that there is no chance of ever being truly and completely happy. If we accept this position, the practical alternatives are (*a*) to attempt to stifle our desires, since they cannot be satisfied (this is Stoicism), or (*b*) to sullenly accept some limited set of attainable goods as the best we can hope for. It is no accident, I think, that the prevailing ethic of our time is a strange mixture of Stoicism and a very superficial hedonism.

Given these three alternatives, in any case, I do not hesitate to adopt the first and to assert that eternal happiness is a real possibility for man. In the remainder of this essay I want to offer some persuasive reasons in support of this view.

Supporting Arguments

I am impressed, first, by the fact that for every natural appetite there is a corresponding way by which that appetite is naturally satisfied. For the appetite of hunger there is food, for thirst there is drink, for sexual desire there is sexual intercourse, for loneliness there is human companionship, and so on. Consequently, it is inconceivable to me that nature should have endowed man with a set of appetites if there were no way for them to be satisfied. If man's hunger for eternity—his deepest hunger of all—should turn out to be the one hunger for which there is no satisfaction, it would be a cruel trick indeed. Thus it seems probable that a state of eternal blessedness, in which this longing would be fully satisfied, is a real possibility for man.

I call your attention next to the fact that man is "overendowed" if this life is the only life for which he was intended. The evolutionary process has in general equipped each organism with just those qualities that it needs to survive in the struggle for life. Man, however, is a remarkable exception. His capacity for abstract knowledge, his moral aspirations, his love of beauty, his spiritual ideals, go far beyond what is needed to secure his mere earthly survival. These endowments mark him off as a creature destined for higher things—destined, indeed, for a life of eternal blessedness.

I appeal also to what I shall call the "presentiment of immortality" in the souls of virtually all men, ourselves included. The great spiritual leaders of mankind—Socrates and Plato and Kant, Buddha and Jesus and Mohammed, St. Augustine and St. Thomas Aquinas and countless others—have spoken unashamedly of this sense of immortality; their words express the hopes and feelings of the great majority of the human race. It is not unreasonable to hold that the sentiments expressed with such unanimity by those whom we revere as the greatest and holiest of men express a genuine insight into the true destiny of the human spirit.

There is even some straightforward empirical evidence in favor of human immortality as the result of research that has been done in the area of parapsychology. Numerous cases are on record of persons who have apparently conversed with deceased loved ones or acquaintances and in the course of these conversations have secured information they could have received from no other sources. The number of qualified researchers working in this area is, unfortunately, very small, because parapsychology does indeed regard as possible some things that are very unpalatable to the typical contemporary scientific mind. The evidence in support of the theory that the soul survives the death of the body is growing, however, and this theory is of course an essential part of the view that eternal life is a real possibility for man.

One further argument in support of human immortality may be suggested. If God exists, and if (as theism asserts) He loves His creation, then it is not unreasonable to assume that He desires and will provide for the preservation and happiness of man, the crown of His creation. If we are in doubt about the existence of God, then we have to resolve that question before we can decide on the merit of the present argument. If we believe in the existence of God, then a belief in human immortality seems more plausible than disbelief.

I acknowledge, however, that the evidence of these arguments is inconclusive: we cannot know with certainty that we shall or shall not survive death. We must, therefore, as Blaise Pascal said, wager one way or the other. It makes supremely good sense, I think, to wager on the possibility of an eternal life in which our every need and longing shall be fully satisfied; to do so gives to this present life a quality, a meaning, and a perspective that make it a much richer adventure than it otherwise would be. We may never succeed in making this world a paradise, but we need the concept of paradise in order that the ideal of the perfect life may ever be before us and in order that we may endure with tranquility the sorrows and disappointments that beset us as we make our way through life. If in wagering on a future life we should turn out to be mistaken, we shall still be the gainers by virtue of the richness lent to this life by the hope of another; and if we are right, we shall in due time experience in reality that eternal happiness in which our deepest longings and desires are at last fully satisfied.

STUDY QUESTIONS

1. "All parties to the debate appear to be agreed that man's highest good consists in the fulfillment of man's deepest longings and desires." How would Hedonist be likely to respond to this statement? Pluralist?
2. "Man is separated from that to which he essentially belongs." What, exactly, does this mean?
3. What exactly is the proposal of this chapter concerning man's highest good? To which of Pluralist's four questions does this theory appear to be addressed?
4. "If we grant that man really does have the needs and longings that I have enumerated, . . . then there are three alternatives among which we must choose." Do you agree? Do you agree with the "if" clause? What are the "three alternatives"? Are there others?
5. What arguments are offered in support of the view that "eternal happiness is a real possibility for man"? Do you find these arguments at all persuasive?
6. "It makes supremely good sense . . . to wager on the possibility of an eternal life in which our every need and longing shall be fully satisfied." Does it?

Aquinas, St. Thomas. *Summa Contra Gentiles*. Many editions. See Book III, Chapters 25–37, 48, and 60–63.

Aristotle. *Nicomachean Ethics*. Many editions. See Book I.

Augustine, St. *The City of God*. Many editions. Book XIX deals with the question of the *summum bonum*.

————. *The Morals of the Catholic Church*. Many editions. See Chapters 1–14.

Bennett, Jonathan. *Rationality: An Essay Towards an Analysis*. New York: Humanities Press, 1964.

Bentham, Jeremy. *An Introduction to the Principles of Morals and Legislation*. Several editions. See especially Chapters 1, 2, 4, and 10. Of interest especially because of its description of the "hedonistic calculus."

Broad, C. D. *Five Types of Ethical Theory*. New York: Humanities Press, 1956.

DeWitt, N. W. *Epicurus and His Philosophy*. Minneapolis, Minn.: University of Minnesota Press, 1954.

Epicurus. *Extant Writings* (Letter to Herodotus, Letter to Pythocles, Letter to Menoeceus, Principal Doctrines, Fragments, Diogenes Laertius' "Life of Epicurus"), in Whitney J. Oates, *The Stoic and Epicurean Philosophers*. New York: Random House, 1940, pp. 3–64.

Ewing, Alfred C. *The Definition of Good*. New York: Macmillan, 1947.

Gosling, J. C. B. *Pleasure and Desire: The Case for Hedonism Reviewed*. Oxford: Clarendon Press, 1969.

Lucretius. *On the Nature of Things*. Many editions. See Books III and IV. A well-known statement of the hedonistic view by an ancient admirer of Epicurus.

MacKinnon, D. M. *A Study of Ethical Theory*. London: A. and C. Black, 1957.

Mill, John Stuart. *Utilitarianism*. Many editions. A classic statement of the hedonistic theory.

Moore, G. E. *Principia Ethica*. Cambridge, Eng.: Cambridge University Press, 1903. Chapter 3 is a detailed critique of hedonism; Chapter 6 is a statement of the pluralistic view.

Murdoch, Iris. *The Sovereignty of Good*. New York: Schocken Books, 1971.

Passmore, John. *The Perfectibility of Man*. New York: Scribner, 1971.

Plato. *Philebus*. Many editions. Difficult reading, but of great interest for its critique of hedonism and its advocacy of a pluralistic view.

Ross, W. D. *Foundations of Ethics*. London: Oxford University Press, 1939.

————. *The Right and the Good*. Oxford: Clarendon Press, 1930. See Chapter 5 for a carefully reasoned statement of the pluralistic view.

Stocks, J. L. *Aristotle's Definition of the Human Good*. Oxford: Basil Blackwell, 1919.

Tsanoff, Radoslav A. *The Moral Ideals of Our Civilization*. New York: Dutton, 1942.

PART X

THE LANGUAGE OF MORALS

43

THE CENTRAL PROBLEM
OF METAETHICS

Anyone who is old enough to be reading a book on philosophy has certainly learned to use "the language of morals" with some facility, and probably uses it more or less unconsciously almost every day. We read of an act of cruelty and say, "How terrible!" Or we learn of an act of unusual kindness and say, "How nice!" We say that slavery and racial discrimination are "wrong," and that helping human beings to realize their potential is "right." We say that some things are "good" and other things are "evil," some acts are "right" and some are "wrong."

Not only do we use this kind of language; we also sometimes *disagree* with one another about what things really are good or bad, right or wrong. Indeed, we sometimes try to persuade those who disagree with us on an ethical matter that their opinion is mistaken. The current debate that is raging over the abortion issue, for example, is basically a case of ethical disagreement: the parties to the debate are disagreeing not about the empirical facts but rather about what *moral* appraisal (good, bad, right, wrong) is appropriate in light of those facts.

In using the language of moral appraisal, and in disagreeing with one another about moral issues, we assume, obviously, that we are using language *meaningfully*. Ethical discourse, then, has *some* kind of meaning. But exactly how is such discourse meaningful? *How are we using language when we say of something in a moral sense that it is good or bad, right or wrong?* This is the problem with which we shall be concerned in the present section.

Normative Ethics and Metaethics

Note that the question that we have just formulated is not the sort of question that concerns normative ethics. Normative ethics, we have said (see Chapter 38), deals with substantive ethical issues—for example, with what things really are intrinsically good, or what things are morally right or wrong, and why. Our question here is concerned, rather, with *the language in which we express* our opinions on such issues. We are asking not about what *is* intrinsically good but about what it means to *say* that something is intrinsically good; not about what *is* good or bad, right or wrong, but about what it means to *call* something good or bad, right or wrong.

The generic name for inquiries that have as their object the language of moral appraisal is *metaethics*. The raw material with which the metaethicist is concerned is the actual language that people use when they make moral judgments. The objective of metaethics is to produce a correct description of that language—to elucidate what is really being said when people say things like "Albert Schweitzer was a good man," or "The infliction of needless pain is morally wrong."

Suppose that after studying this matter for some time one finds that one is in genuine doubt about the meaning of such language. Ought one then to stop using "moral predicates" altogether? Certainly not, unless one is prepared to abdicate concern for many of the major problems that we as individuals and as a society must face in the years immediately ahead. Just as one can speak a language without knowing all the grammatical rules that govern that language, so one can use the language of moral appraisal without having a correct metaethical theory about that language. If all ethical discourse were to be prohibited until metaethics had completed its work, metaethics would have no subject matter upon which to begin. The business of metaethics is to describe how people do use the language of moral appraisal, not to prescribe how they may use it.

The Options

All language appears to serve four principal functions: to request information (the interrogative function), to convey information (the informative function), to direct behavior (the directive function), and to express feeling (the expressive, or emotive, function). If this analysis is correct, then it is evident that ethical discourse must also be reducible to one or more of these functions, or types of discourse.

It seems obvious that ethical discourse does not serve an interrogative function. However, it may be a species of informative language. Many metaethicists are agreed that it is. But what information does it give? Here opinions vary, with at least four different answers having been proposed.

Some philosophers hold that to apply a moral predicate to the appraisal of something is to assert the presence or the absence of a certain empirical quality or qualities in the thing being appraised. It may be said, for example, that to call an act "praiseworthy" or "good" is to say that it is productive of pleasure, and the question of whether or not an act is productive of pleasure is obviously an empirical question. Or it may be said that to call a certain form of conduct "good" is to say that it is characteristic of those beings who have proceeded the farthest or the highest along the evolutionary path, and this assertion, if spelled out in some detail, is also capable of being determined empirically. We shall call this view (which is developed in Chapter 44) *ethical naturalism*. It is also sometimes called *naturalistic objectivism*.

Other philosophers hold, however, that ethical discourse is informative in the sense that it asserts the presence or absence of some *nonnatural* quality in the thing being appraised. This was the view of G. E. Moore, who said:

> If I am asked, What is good? my answer is that good is good, and that is the end of the matter. Or if I am asked, How is good to be defined? my answer is that it cannot be defined, and that is all I have to say about it . . .
> My point is that "good" is a simple notion, just as "yellow" is a simple notion; that, just as you cannot, by any manner of means, explain to anyone who does not already know it, what yellow is, so you cannot explain what good is.[1]

This position, which is developed in Chapter 45, is variously called *nonnaturalistic objectivism* or, more commonly, *intuitionism*. The reasons for calling it the former are evident when one compares it with its "naturalistic" counterpart. The reason for calling it "intuitionism" is that since the quality in question is, according to the theory, nonnatural, it is not subject to empirical investigation and must, accordingly, be intuited, that is, rationally discerned. (The term "intuition," as used by philosophers, does not mean what it means in the everyday expression "a woman's intuition." It means, rather, direct apprehension, or rational discernment: it denotes the act by which, according to rationalists, the intellect directly grasps some truths. See Chapter 7 for a fuller exposition of the rationalist thesis.)

It may be, however, that ethical discourse is informative in a quite different way. It may be that "moral judgments," as they are called by some philosophers, convey information not about the object or the act being judged but about the likes or dislikes of (*a*) the person making the judgment or (*b*) some group of people for whom he speaks or to whom he has reference in making the judgment. Such views are called *subjectivist*, and depending on whether it is (*a*) the speaker's likes or dislikes or (*b*) the likes or dislikes of some group for which he speaks or to which he has reference, you have, respectively, *private subjectivism* (Chapter 46) and *cultural relativism* (Chapter 47).

Note that these four theories have one very important feature in common, namely, the belief that a moral appraisal is a truth claim: it

---

[1] G. E. Moore, *Principia Ethica* (Cambridge, Eng.: Cambridge University Press, 1959. Originally published, 1903), pp. 6–7.

asserts that something is the case. According to all these theories, therefore, moral appraisals are capable of being true or false. To know that a given moral appraisal is true or false is, according to these theories, to know that something is or is not the case; thus it is proper to speak of these as *cognitivist* theories.

It is possible, however, that ethical discourse is not informative of anything at all—that it is to be understood instead as a species of *directive* or *expressive* discourse. Theories affirming such a position are termed *noncognitivist,* with *emotivism* viewing ethical discourse as expressive and *imperativism* viewing it as directive. Both theories are discussed in Chapter 48.

To summarize, on the assumptions (*a*) that all language serves either an interrogative, an informative, a directive, or an expressive function, and (*b*) that ethical discourse obviously does not serve an interrogative function, we arrive at the following list of metaethical theories, each of which constitutes an answer to the question posed at the beginning of this chapter:

I. Cognitivist Theories
   A. Objectivist Theories
      1. Ethical Naturalism (Naturalistic Objectivism)
      2. Intuitionism (Nonnaturalistic Objectivism)
   B. Subjectivist Theories
      1. Private Subjectivism
      2. Cultural Relativism (Societal Subjectivism)
II. Noncognitivist Theories
   A. Emotivism
   B. Imperativism

We cannot state with certainty, however, that the theories we have just enumerated constitute all the possible ways of answering the question about the meaning of ethical discourse. This is true for at least two reasons. First, we cannot be sure that the four "functions of language" from which our analysis began are the only functions that an exhaustive study of language might reveal; and should some other function be identified, it is possible that a case could be made for the view that ethical discourse is a species of that function of language. Second, the specification of subtypes within each of the functions listed above is by no means exhaustive: language is capable of being informative, directive, and expressive in an immense variety of ways, and the theories listed identify only the particular ways that have commended themselves to philosophers as being the most plausible ways of construing ethical discourse.

All that can be claimed for the above classification, then, is that it is a reliable road map for one who is just beginning to learn his way around in the province of metaethics. It identifies six neighborhoods (to continue the metaphor) where all writers on metaethics currently reside, but, like any map, it omits a great deal of interesting detail. After one has become familiar with the province, the road map can perhaps be discarded, and one can then begin to explore more carefully the neighborhood or neighborhoods that seem most suitable for human habitation.

STUDY QUESTIONS

1. State whether you agree or disagree with the following assertions, and defend your opinion.
   a. Moral appraisal language occurs more or less frequently in the everyday conversation of most adult human beings.
   b. People sometimes disagree on ethical matters.
   c. People sometimes present rational arguments to persuade other people to change their ethical views.
   d. Moral appraisals have some kind of meaning.
   e. Some ethical issues are issues that most people regard as important.
   f. It is possible to have an opinion on an ethical matter.
   g. It is possible to be mistaken in one's opinion on an ethical matter.
2. What do you understand to be "the central problem of metaethics"? Does this seem to you an important problem? What bearing, if any, does it have on such matters as the controversy over the morality of abortion, or the legitimacy of the feminist demand for "equal rights"?
3. What do subjectivist theories regarding the meaning of moral appraisals have in common with objectivist theories? What is it that distinguishes them? What is the difference between ethical naturalism and intuitionism? between private subjectivism and cultural relativism? between private subjectivism and emotivism?
4. Why is it impossible to conclude with certainty that one has surveyed all of the possible answers to the question posed in this chapter?

44

ETHICAL NATURALISM

Ethical naturalism, or naturalistic objectivism, is the view that moral sentences—both those employed in everyday moral judgments and those employed by writers on normative ethics—are reports about the presence or absence of certain natural qualities in persons, acts, or state of affairs. They are, accordingly, translatable without loss of meaning into sentences that do not employ any of the so-called moral predicates (good, bad, right, wrong, etc.).

Since different definitions of the key moral predicates are compatible with the central features of ethical naturalism, I shall begin my defense of this position by indicating what all of its adherents hold in common and on what point they differ. I shall then go on to elaborate the particular version of ethical naturalism that I hold to be correct.

First, I want to make it clear that we who hold this theory, or any metaethical theory, are not offering an arbitrary verbal definition of key ethical terms, nor are we making a recommendation about how people generally *ought* to use these terms. Our claim is that the structure of language allows only certain ways in which a sentence can have meaning. Ethical naturalism is a theory about which of these ways correctly describes the particular kind of meaning that moral sentences have.

In holding that (a) to say that something is good or bad, right or wrong, is to say that it has, or does not have, certain empirically ascertainable qualities, ethical naturalism implies at least two other things about moral sentences that all its adherents hold in common: namely, (b) moral sentences are, like all informative sentences, true or false; and (c) questions about the truth or falsity of such sentences are resolvable by straightforward empirical means. These three points constitute the defining characteristic of ethical naturalism; anyone who holds this position must show that moral sentences do in fact exhibit these features.

There should not be any disagreement over the method by which this matter must be resolved. Since a metaethical theory deals with the meaning of moral sentences, we must always look to the actual judgments that people make: the theory must conform to real usage. To ask for the meaning of "good" in its moral sense is to ask for a definition of that term as used by ordinary folk and ethical theorists when they frame what we call "moral judgments." If we lose sight of this—if we depart from actual usage—we are bound to get lost in a never-never world of arbitrary definitions.

Having covered the areas of unanimity among ethical naturalists, we now come to the single point on which they disagree: just *which* qualities it is whose presence or absence is being asserted when something is judged to be good or bad, right or wrong. If, for example, someone says that "good" means "conducive to the development of socialism," or "conducive to the further evolution of man," he is expressing a naturalistic view, but in my opinion a mistaken naturalistic view. I shall not take time, however, to survey the various proposals that have been made by ethical naturalists on this point, but shall proceed directly to an exposition and defense of my own view. If I succeed in presenting a convincing case, then it will follow that ethical naturalists who disagree with me on this point, as well as metaethicists who hold fundamentally different views about the logic of ethical discourse, are mistaken.

The Meanings of "Good"

If any one term may be said to be of central importance among the moral predicates, that term is "good." Unfortunately, this term has so many meanings in both ethical and everyday usage that we shall have to analyze it very carefully in order to see its significance in ethical thinking.

The most important moral sense of "good" is as the antithesis of "evil." All of the other moral predicates are definable in relation to "good" and "evil," as I shall shortly attempt to show. But first, we must distinguish some other senses of "good" to avoid later confusion.

There is a completely *nonmoral* sense of "good" meaning the opposite of "poor." We speak, for example, about good knives and poor knives, about good novels and poor novels, about good runners and poor runners. In such cases we mean, apparently, "conforming to (good) or failing to conform to (poor) the criteria appropriate to the assessment of such items." A good knife is, among other things, one that cuts well, a good novel, one that makes for enjoyable reading, and a good runner, one who runs swiftly. A poor knife, or novel, or runner is one that does not meet these criteria. "Good" in this sense is not a moral predicate at all and must not be confused with "good" in its centrally important moral sense as the opposite of "evil."

There is still another sense of "good," however, in which it is the opposite of neither "poor" nor "evil" but of "bad"; and in this sense it usually is a moral predicate. (Not always, however: we talk about good and bad pitches in baseball, good and bad shots in basketball, and we clearly do not in such cases intend to make a moral judgment.) I shall speak of "good" in this sense as the *secondary* sense of "good" and of "good" when it stands opposed to "evil" as the *primary* sense of "good."

In this secondary sense there are four classes of things that we call good (or bad): people, certain of their mental acts (thoughts, intentions, desires, purposes), their overt acts, and the products of their overt acts (governments and other man-made institutions). I am unable to think of anything else that we would call good or bad in this clearly moral sense except in a metaphorical way. To say that something is good in the secondary sense is to say that it promotes, or tends to promote, what is good in the primary sense. "Good" as opposed to "evil" means *"intrinsically* good"; "good" as opposed to "bad" means *"instrumentally* good." This is the reason for calling the latter a secondary, or derivative, sense of "good."

All other moral predicates can be defined in relation to "good" in the primary sense. My "duty," for example, is to do what, all things considered, I ought to do. "Duty" and "what I ought to do" are synonymous expressions; and what I ought to do is the act that, among all the things I might do, will have the greatest tendency to promote what is good in the primary sense. Any act that tends to promote what is intrinsically good is to that extent *right;* any act that tends to hinder the achievement of what is intrinsically good, or to promote what is intrinsically evil, is to that extent *wrong.* An act that has no tendency to promote either good or evil is *morally indifferent.* It is evident, therefore, that "good" in the primary sense of "intrinsically good" is the key concept in our ethical thinking.

The Primary Meaning of "Good"

The crucial question that we must ask in metaethics, therefore, is, What is the meaning of "good" in the primary sense? To this question the correct answer, as I conceive it, is "pleasurable for human beings." This is what we *mean* by calling something "good" in the primary sense; everything else that depends on the disposition and choices of men is good or bad, right or wrong, praiseworthy or blameworthy, insofar as it tends to promote or to hinder the achievement of human pleasure.

Perhaps the best way to demonstrate the truth of what I am stating is to consider a hypothetical case in which two people are disagreeing about whether or not a certain proposed course of action is "right," say, the using of tear gas to quell a riot. A thinks it would be wrong to use it; B thinks it would be wrong *not* to do so.

How might either party attempt to support his view? The best way would be to indicate the probable results of the proposed action. A might argue, "If tear gas is used, the rioters will retaliate by using firearms, and the situation will be even worse than it is now. So far, all we have to worry about is a small riot; the course you are proposing could turn it into a civil war." B might argue, "I think you are mistaken. Tear gas has been thoroughly proven as an effective means of controlling riots, and it should be used immediately. The longer this situation is allowed to remain out of control, the greater is the danger of its turning into a civil war—the very thing you fear. I say tear gas should be used without delay."

It should be noted that both A and B are agreed that the "right" course of action is the one that will have the greatest tendency to promote human well-being, or what comes to the same thing, to prevent human suffering. If A were to become convinced that the result of using tear gas would be as B says, he would on his own premises have to concede that the proposed action is indeed right; and if B were to become convinced that the result would be as A describes it, he would have to concede to A. The argument of both assumes that what is right or wrong in the case in question can be decided only by attempting to calculate the human consequences.

The same point can be reinforced in another way. Suppose that a third party, C, enters the dispute. "I agree with B," says C. "I think tear gas should be used—although I agree with A that it will probably lead to civil war. Nonetheless, even though it will cause suffering for many people, I think it is the right thing to do." A and B, surely, would be equally astonished by such a statement. They could only ask, "What on earth does C *mean* by 'good'?" Obviously, C does not mean by "good" what most people mean by it, which is "that state of affairs, among the options available to us, in which the maximum of human pleasure and the minimum of human suffering are achieved." If this meaning is not assumed, the whole context in which the dispute was carried on is destroyed, and the dispute itself becomes unintelligible.

Let us consider a second example. Most people would agree, I think, that the excessive drinking of alcoholic beverages is morally wrong (if there are some who disagree, it makes no difference to the argument). Those who do take this position do so because of certain well-known consequences: exessive drinking is injurious to one's health; it is the most frequent cause of auto accidents; it can deprive a family of many of the conveniences and even the necessities of life (because of its cost per se, and also by often causing the loss of one's job); it poisons human relationships by making people who are normally pleasant and kind become belligerent and cantankerous; and so on. These consequences, it is evident, are all descriptions of some adverse effect that the act or habit in question has, or tends to have, on human beings. (If the excessive drinking of alcoholic beverages did not have these consequences, as the drinking of water in any quantity apparently does not, we would not regard it as wrong, and "drunkenness" would not be a term of moral disapprobation.) Thus it seems clear that it is human pleasure that is regarded as intrinsically good, and that everything else is regarded as being good or bad insofar as it tends to promote or to hinder that end.

One could continue to give examples indefinitely, but it hardly seems necessary. Consider any example you wish and you will discover that anything that people commonly assess in moral categories—people, their thoughts, dispositions, intentions, or acts—lends itself to such appraisal solely by virtue of its assumed tendency to promote or to hinder human pleasure. If we could know (a) what state of affairs would achieve the absolute maximum of human happiness together with a minimum of human suffering, and (b) what acts would have the maximum tendency to promote that state of affairs, we should have no difficulty in deciding in any particular case what is the right thing to do. The moral dilemmas that we face are due to our ignorance not of what "good" means but of what to do in order to achieve that ideal state of affairs in which the maximum of human pleasure and the minimum of human suffering are realized.

When I say that a moral judgment consists in the assertion that some empirically ascertainable qualities are or are not present in the thing being judged, I do not mean that these qualities are precisely ascertainable in the way that, say, the presence or absence of sodium chloride in a solution would be. I do mean, however, that there is nothing over and above the empirical facts to which we must attend in order to decide whether the judgment in question is true or false. The problematic character of many moral judgments is due, not to the supposed fact that "goodness" consists in some odd nonempirical quality, but to the fact that such judgments often involve suppositions—even conjectures and guesses—about the probable results of this or that action. Such uncertainty will persist until we are able to calculate much more precisely the human consequences of alternative courses of action.

The chief reason that this account is not as obvious to most people as might be expected (in view of the fact that they handle the language of moral appraisal without difficulty almost every day of their adult lives) is that most of us are taught moral principles in a way that does not clearly exhibit their relation to human pleasure. We are taught as children that certain kinds of things (like slapping or biting other children, or taking things that belong to them, or telling lies) are "naughty," and that certain other kinds of things (like paying compliments, helping people in need, or visiting the sick) are "nice." If we reflect on the many rules that we have learned in this way, we may be puzzled, and tempted to look for some odd quality that gives these rules their "obligatory" character.

What we fail to understand if we think in this way, however, is that the rules have been formulated precisely because they specify some of the most common ways in which human pleasure can be enhanced and human suffering minimized. To see moral principles in this light is to rid them of the purely arbitrary character they sometimes seem to have and to exhibit them as legitimate rules of behavior for anyone who desires to know and to do what is morally right.

I said earlier that anyone who holds the naturalist view must be prepared to show that moral sentences are true or false and that their truth or falsity is ascertainable by empirical means. Let us now consider these features as they apply to what might be thought to be a difficult case for an ethical naturalist to account for: one in which a particular person—Joe Doakes, say—is said to be (in the moral sense) "a good person" or "a good man."

Is there any evidence that would count against the statement "Joe Doakes is a good man"? Yes. If we were to learn that Joe is a heavy drinker, or that he commonly mistreats his wife and children, or that he is habitually careless in his work, or that he does not get along well with most people, we would be inclined to regard the statement as false. To say that Joe Doakes is a good man is to say that, for the most part, he acts in ways that are not compatible with those just described. The difference between these two kinds of behavior—what makes one type of behavior "good" and the other "bad"—is precisely the tendency of each to promote or to hinder human pleasure.

But the means by which it can be determined which of these ways is descriptive of Joe's behavior are clearly empirical. We must watch him to see how he behaves and listen to what other people say about his behavior. It is on that basis that we make up our minds. If Joe is like most of us, it is quite certain that he is neither unambiguously good nor unambiguously bad: sometimes he acts in ways that promote human pleasure and sometimes in ways that decrease it. It is the facts about Joe's actual behavior that determine whether and to what extent he is truly described as "good" or "bad," and these facts are ascertainable only by the empirical method of first- and second-hand observation of his behavior. Ergo, moral sentences are true or false and confirmable or disconfirmable by empirical means.

STUDY QUESTIONS

1. True or false: A number of mutually incompatible theories belonging to *normative ethics* could be correctly described as "naturalistic" theories. Why or why not?
2. True or false: Ethical naturalism is just another name for hedonism. Explain.
3. What does Ethical Naturalist (EN) say is "the method by which this matter must be resolved"? Is he right? How do you determine what method is appropriate? Is it implicit in the question that is being asked, or is it determined in some other way? Can you think of any reason why any of the other parties to the dispute might object to this method?

4. Do you think EN is on the right track in distinguishing three meanings of "good"? Suppose that he is right: does this in any way substantiate his main thesis? Does he claim that it does?
5. Is EN right in saying that the statement "Joe Doakes is a good man" can be refuted by empirical facts? How does this argument affect EN's case?
6. Summarize EN's arguments in support of his position. Can you think of any arguments against it?

45

INTUITIONISM

There are two kinds of hedonists: those who affirm that "good" just *means* "pleasurable" or "conducive to happiness" and those who maintain that whatever "good" means, pleasure (or happiness) is the only thing to which it applies. We might call these positions, respectively, *analytic hedonism* and *synthetic hedonism*, since according to the former the statement "Pleasure is good" is an analytic statement and according to the latter it is a synthetic one.[1] Both forms of hedonism, I am convinced, are mistaken; but hedonism in its analytic form is by far the more seriously in error of the two. And Ethical Naturalist, unfortunately, is an analytic hedonist.

Nevertheless, much of what Ethical Naturalist has said appears to me to be both true and valuable. He is quite right, for example, in distinguishing three meanings of "good" (the nonmoral sense and the instrumental and intrinsic senses of moral goodness). He is right also in his contention that most (though not all, in my view) other moral predicates can be defined in relation to the very important concept of intrinsic goodness. But the crucial question for metaethics, as he himself says, is, What is the meaning of "intrinsically good"? And on this question I think he is profoundly mistaken.

The Open-Question Test

There is a simple test, which I shall call the open-question test, by which we can easily assess the accuracy of any proposed definition. Let us call a word for which a definition is being proposed the *definiendum* and the

---

[1] See the Glossary for further clarification of the terms "analytic" and "synthetic." See also the discussion on p. 44.

definition that is proposed the *definiens*. If we ask a question of the form, Are all [definiens] really [definiendum]? it is evident that if our definition is accurate, we shall not be putting a significant (or open) question; and if our definition is not accurate, we shall. Suppose, for example, that I define "bachelor" as (*a*) an unmarried male and as (*b*) an unmarried adult male human being. If I apply the test, it is clear that in the one case I do have an open question, and that in the other case I do not. If I ask, Are all unmarried males bachelors? I have an open (significant) question to which the correct answer is No, because preadult human males and nonhuman males of any age are unmarried males who are not bachelors. But if I ask, Are all unmarried adult male human beings really bachelors? it is equally evident that I am not asking an open, or significant, question; for the briefest reflection makes it clear that the definiens is what I mean when I use the term "bachelor."

If, now, we apply the test to Ethical Naturalist's proposed definition of "intrinsically good," it is clear at once that this definition will not do. For the question, Are all instances of human pleasure really good? is an open question, to which it is highly unlikely that an affirmative answer would be correct. Consider a few examples. Is it plausible to maintain that the enjoyment that a young boy might get out of torturing a frog (or some other sentient creature), or the pleasure that a sadist might get out of tormenting another human being (even if his happiness should exceed his victim's suffering), or the perverted pleasure of a masochist who allegedly enjoys being punished are good? Clearly not. If we judge human pleasure to be good, the reason is not that goodness simply *means* human pleasure but that we discern that the quality denoted by the term "good" is present in most (but not all) instances of human pleasure. It is this insight that we express in our synthetic judgment "Human pleasure, by and large, is good."

There are, as Ethical Naturalist has pointed out, a number of rival theories of the naturalist type, and space obviously does not permit us to list them and apply our test to each of them in turn. It may fairly be said, however, that the hedonist version of this theory is by far the most plausible. Since it fails to pass the open-question test, we may be reasonably confident that any other theory of this type would also fail.

Refutation of Hedonism[2]

The inadequacy of hedonism can be demonstrated apart from the open-question test, which, it is to be noted, shows the incorrectness only of analytic hedonism. The arguments that I shall now put forward demonstrate the inadequacy of hedonism in both its analytic and synthetic forms. Our discussion will require a brief venture into the domain of normative ethics in order to present more clearly what I consider to be the correct metaethical theory.

---

[2] See also chapter 40, pp. 287–289.

The incorrectness of hedonism is evident, first, from the fact that there are a number of things other than pleasurable states of mind that we regard as being intrinsically good. W. D. Ross has shown, for example, that (a) virtuous disposition and action, (b) the apportionment of pleasure and pain to the virtuous and vicious respectively, and (c) knowledge and right opinion are *intrinsic goods* and that they cannot be reduced to pleasurable states of mind or to acts tending to increase the sum of human pleasure.[3] A universe in which these things obtain—quite apart from any consideration of the balance of human pleasure that they may or may not produce—is intrinsically better than a universe in which these things do not obtain. We have only to contemplate the two states of affairs, assuming the quantity of human pleasure to be equal in the two cases, to see that this is so.

The same conclusion may, however, be established in another way. There are some instances of human pleasure that, if we suppose them to occur, reduce the total quantity of goodness in the universe. Suppose, for example, that A suffers great misfortune; and suppose that B, who has long been jealous of A's earlier good fortune, contemplates A's misfortune *with pleasure.* Certainly in this case the quantity of pleasure in the universe is greater than it would be if B did not react in this way to A's misfortune; but it is equally clear that B's responding in this way is not a good but an evil. Indeed, it would be better under these circumstances if there were less pleasure in the universe, for there would be more good in the universe if B were sorrowful instead of happy. It seems obvious, therefore, that goodness is not simply identical with pleasure and that not all instances of human pleasure are good.

The inadequacy of hedonism can also be exhibited by the following *reductio ad absurdum* argument.[4] If human pleasure were the only thing that is intrinsically good, and if the amount of good in the universe depended entirely on the amount of human pleasure, then a universe in which there was but one individual who experienced a moderate quantity of pleasure *forever* would be intrinsically better than one in which a finite number of individuals experienced pleasure in whatever degree for any finite length of time. But we obviously do not think this to be the case. Even if we were persuaded that some one person could be made to experience moderate pleasure forever (thus producing an infinite quantity of pleasure and, *ex hypothesi*, goodness in the universe), we would not, if it were necessary, approve of the annihilation of all other human beings in order to achieve this, although, according to the hedonist hypothesis, their pleasure would be of a merely finite quantity and therefore inferior to that of our hypothetical eternal individual. Since we cannot draw the conclusion that would follow from the hedonist theory, it is evident that the hedonist theory is false.

---

[3] W. D. Ross, *The Right and the Good* (Oxford: Clarendon, 1930), Chap. 5.

[4] See Chapter 5 for an explanation of the *reductio ad absurdum* form of argument.

The Indefinability of "Good"

We have been speaking—without any misgivings about the meaningful-ness of what we have been saying—about a variety of things (states of mind, acts, states of affairs in the universe, etc.) that we would or would not call good. We have said that, contrary to the claim of ethical hedonists, we do not mean simply "pleasurable" when we call some-thing good (analytic hedonism), nor is it only pleasure that we regard as being good (synthetic hedonism). What, then, do we mean when we call something good? The correct answer to this question, I think, is the one given by G. E. Moore: we mean good, and nothing else. "Everything is what it is, and not another thing." [5] We can, indeed, find other words to denote the quality that we commonly denote by the word "good"; we can use the German word *gut*, or the French *bon*, or even the English phrase "worthy of being valued in and of itself"; but that which we denote in these various ways is a simple, indefinable, nonnatural quality whose presence in a person, act, or state of affairs is what makes us call it good.

"Good" is indefinable because it is a simple concept. In order to define a concept, it is necessary that that concept be complex, that it be composed of simpler concepts. One can define "daffodil," for example, as "a yellow flower of the genus *Narcissus*" because its various elements—being yellow, being a flower, and being of the genus *Narcis-sus*—are all constituent parts of the complex concept of a daffodil. Of these constituent elements, "flower" and "genus *Narcissus*" can also be defined. But, as Moore pointed out, "yellow" cannot be defined (except, of course, in the sense that one can point to examples of yellow objects) because it is a simple concept. All definitions must ultimately be built up out of such concepts, for the process of defining concepts by pointing to the elements of which they are composed cannot go on indefinitely: at length we must come to those elements that, like "good" and "yellow," are simple, and therefore indefinable.

"Good," like "yellow," is a simple and indefinable concept. But the quality it denotes, unlike the quality denoted by the term "yellow," *is not a natural quality*. By this I mean, simply, that the goodness of a person, act, or state of affairs is not something that can be perceived by the senses; it must be *rationally discerned*, or *intuited*, if it is to be apprehended at all.[6]

Let us consider again the illustration of the person who contemplates with pleasure the misfortune of another human being. There is no question here of the probable effects of B's malice: we can very well imagine that A is already dead, or that B expired shortly after enter-taining unkind thoughts about A's misfortune, and still we would judge

---

[5] Bishop Butler, quoted by G. E. Moore on the title page of *Principia Ethica* (Cambridge, Eng.: Cambridge University Press, 1959. Originally published 1903).

[6] See Chapter 7, pp. 49–56, for a discussion of this concept.

that B's malice was evil. But how do we know this? Certainly it is in virtue of the supposed facts that we render our judgment; but our judgment that "B's pleasure in A's misfortune is evil" is not simply a confused way of reporting that B did in fact entertain feelings of pleasure in contemplating A's misfortune. It is a judgment about the *moral significance* of those facts. And this judgment rests, not on the perception of some additional natural qualities or some supposed tendency of B's act (of contemplation), but on our direct intuition of the evilness of the act itself.

Consider a second example. X has borrowed a sum of money from his wealthy friend Y and has promised to repay him on a certain date. The date arrives and X, being a man who keeps his word, repays the loan. Although hardly an instance of moral heroism, this is, I presume, an act on which we would without hesitation pronounce a favorable judgment. Since it is an instance of promise-keeping, and promise-keeping is something that we regard as a moral duty under normal circumstances, the act in question is judged to be good. But note that no calculation of the probable consequences of alternative possible courses of action is involved in this judgment. Indeed, it is highly likely that the same sum of money given to a poor family would produce more human pleasure than it would if returned to the bank account of Y. But the calculation of consequences is not relevant in this case: X has contracted a duty in making a promise to Y, and that duty takes precedence over all but the most unusual of circumstances. We judge, therefore, that X's act of returning the money on the date promised is good.

What are we saying, then, when we say, "This act is good," and on what basis? Clearly we are not saying that X's act is the one that, of all the alternatives available to him, has the greatest tendency to increase the sum of human pleasure. Indeed, we can be quite sure this is not the case. We are saying that X's act, as an instance of promise-keeping, is good, and that is all we are saying. Our basis for saying this is, not that we perceive some empirical facts in addition to those that make us call this act an instance of promise-keeping, but simply that we apprehend such an act as being good.

There is, I realize, a widespread tendency among philosophers today to reject intuition, or direct rational insight, as a mode of acquiring knowledge and to insist that the only knowledge available to us must come by empirical means. This bias against rational insight explains, I think, the recent flurry of activity in the empiricist camp to find some way to account for our knowledge of ethical truths and our ability to make valid moral judgments, without admitting these as instances of rational, or nonempirical, insight. But the effort is doomed to failure. Even our judgment that human pleasure is, on the whole, good, is a synthetic judgment that we could not make apart from our direct apprehension that the quality of goodness is in fact present in most (but not all) instances of human pleasure. It is this apprehension, and this alone, that allows us to distinguish between those instances of human pleasure that are good and those that are not. What is apprehended, in such cases, is not "another thing" but *goodness itself*.

If this view is correct, any attempt to define "good" in terms of some natural quality or combination of natural qualities is mistaken: it confuses the nonnatural quality designated by the term "good" with something else that it is not. I propose, following Moore, to call this particular kind of mistake the *naturalistic fallacy*. It is a fallacy because it is an error in logic, and it is naturalistic because it is the specific error of confusing a natural quality with a nonnatural quality. It is this fallacy, which exists regardless of the set of natural qualities proposed as a definition of "good," that is effectively exposed by the open-question test. Many writers on ethics, as Moore has shown, have been guilty of it.

A Word About Moral Duty

Earlier I stated that I am not in complete agreement with Ethical Naturalist's suggestion that all other moral predicates can be defined in relation to the centrally important concept "good." My chief misgivings on this score concern the concept "moral duty." I do not think it is correct to say, as Ethical Naturalist does, that someone's moral duty is always to do the act that, of all the alternatives available, will produce the greatest total increase of good in the world. I think some acts have an obligatory character quite apart from their supposed consequences. But I want first to make a preliminary observation about moral duty that may be of some help in clearing up this rather elusive concept.

In order to make intelligible the very commonplace fact that a person can be mistaken about what his moral duty is in a given situation, it is important to distinguish between (*a*) objective duty and (*b*) apparent duty. "I believe it is my duty to do thus and so" is an intelligible statement, and its intelligibility rests on the assumption that what I *believe* to be my duty may be different from what really *is* my duty.

It is certainly evident that we cannot possibly know which of the many things that we might do at any moment will in fact produce the greatest increase of good in the world; so if this is what Ethical Naturalist means, his view would entail that we never know what our duty is. And this, I think, is absurd. We must, then, interpret him to mean that we ought always do that act which *we believe* will produce the greatest increase of good in the world. In other words, we must construe his remark as applying not to our objective duty but to our apparent duty. But even then, his view does not stand up; for what I believe to be my duty on many occasions is not at all the act that I believe is likely to produce the greatest increase of good in the world, all things considered. Neither objective duty nor apparent duty, therefore, seems to be definable in relation to "good."

The "obligatory" or "dutiful" character of certain kinds of acts is a quality of those acts that must be rationally discerned in the same way that the goodness of certain states of affairs must be rationally discerned. There are, as Ross has pointed out,[7] various kinds of duties—duties of fidelity (telling the truth, keeping promises), duties of reparation (making amends for wrongful acts), duties of gratitude (expressing thanks for favors done by others), duties of justice (assisting the needy), duties of beneficence (relieving suffering), and so on. No doubt we sometimes err in thinking a particular act to be our duty when it is not, just as we sometimes err in judging a given state of affairs to be good when it is not; for our knowledge of moral truths is not infallible. But our knowledge of moral truths, insofar as we have such knowledge, is nonempirical; the qualities that we judge when we make a moral judgment—both the goodness of good things and the obligatoriness of acts that are our duty—are nonempirical, or nonnatural, qualities.

STUDY QUESTIONS

1. What is the open-question test? Can you think of any examples in which the test fails to prove what Intuitionist says it proves?
2. What distinction does Intuitionist make between "analytic hedonism" and "synthetic hedonism"? What is the relationship between hedonism of these two types and ethical naturalism? How does Intuitionist attempt to refute hedonism of both types?
3. Would it be logically consistent for a person to be both (a) an intuitionist and (b) a synthetic hedonist? Explain.
4. Consider very carefully Intuitionist's examples of moral judgments. Does he convince you that they *cannot* be construed in the way that Ethical Naturalist would have us construe them? Does he convince you that they should be construed in the way he proposes? Try his proposal with a few examples of your own.
5. How does Intuitionist analyze moral duty? Would it be logically possible for Intuitionist to agree with Ethical Naturalist's analysis of moral duty?

---

[7] Ross, *op. cit.*, Chap. 2.

46

PRIVATE SUBJECTIVISM

Neither of the two preceding theories constitutes a truly adequate account of the logic of moral discourse. Each of them, it seems to me, explains some of the facts about the language of morals and each leaves certain facts unexplained. Let us try to separate truth from error in the foregoing accounts and proceed from there to develop a theory about the logic of moral discourse that is adequate to all the relevant facts.

Ethical Naturalist has affirmed the following propositions:

a. The term "good" has three distinguishable meanings: a primary moral meaning (good as opposed to evil), a secondary moral meaning (good as opposed to bad), and a nonmoral meaning (good as opposed to poor).
b. The most important concept for understanding the logic of moral discourse is "good" in its primary moral sense.
c. All other moral predicates are definable in terms of this concept.
d. The meaning of "good" in this primary sense is "pleasurable for human beings."
e. Moral judgments are, therefore, true or false.
f. The truth or falsity of moral judgments is ascertainable by straightforward empirical means.

Of these six propositions, Intuitionist has agreed, explicitly or by implication, with propositions a, b, and e, and has disagreed with the other three. In place of the propositions that he rejects, Intuitionist has offered the following:

g. The term "duty," at least, is not definable in terms of "good" in the primary sense.

h. The term "good" in the primary sense denotes a simple nonnatural quality, and by virtue of its simplicity is in principle undefinable.
i. The truth or falsity of moral sentences is ascertainable by nonempirical means (intuition).

Of these nine propositions I think we can, without further ado, simply accept propositions *a*, *b*, *e*, and *f*. My reasons for holding propositions *e* and *f* to be true are, however, quite different from those given by Ethical Naturalist, as will shortly be apparent. (I do think that moral sentences consist in the assertion—rather misleading—of some very commonplace facts. I am, therefore, bound to hold that the two propositions in question are true.) I have no wish to enter into the side argument between Ethical Naturalist and Intuitionist about whether or not "duty" is definable in terms of "good" in the primary sense; so I shall refrain from expressing myself on propositions *c* and *g*. I am inclined to doubt whether our moral concepts are as neatly organized into a coherent system as Ethical Naturalist has suggested; but I am even more certain that what we know when we know that something is our duty is not what Intuitionist says we know, nor do we know it in the way he says we do (proposition *f*). But this is, in any case, a trifling side issue, and I do not wish to commit myself to a definite position on it.

There are, then, three propositions among the nine that have been enunciated by my two predecessors—propositions *d*, *h*, and *i*—with which I definitely disagree. I propose to indicate briefly my reasons for rejecting each of them.

Let us consider first Intuitionist's claim that the truth or falsity of moral sentences is ascertainable by nonempirical means (proposition *i*). I disagree with this claim for two reasons. First, I hold that all our knowledge of synthetic truths arises out of experience: I am, in short, an empiricist. If there were some other convincing examples of synthetic truths that are known a priori—"intuited," as Intuitionist says—then we might, of course, entertain the possibility that the truth of moral sentences is also known in this way. But it has been amply demonstrated by many philosophers that the most plausible examples of such truths can be easily accounted for in a way that is consistent with empiricism.[1] Since this is the case, it seems unlikely that moral truths are an exception to the rule. Second, even if the correctness of the general thesis of empiricism be disallowed, it cannot be plausibly argued that moral truths are examples of synthetic truths that are known a priori. These truths do not exhibit the qualities of necessity and universality— or of self-evidence—that are alleged to be the hallmarks of a priori knowledge. There is, admittedly, a certain oddness about moral sentences; but this oddness, as we shall see, is due to something quite different from the alleged fact that they are truths that are directly "intuited" as Intuitionist claims.

---

[1] See Chapter 8 for a fuller explanation of empiricism.

As for proposition *h*, it is sufficient to point out that if proposition *i* is rejected, proposition *h* must be rejected as well—or else we must draw the conclusion that we are in complete ignorance with respect to moral truths. I think that usually when we say something is "good" or "right," we do know that what we are asserting is the case, though we are seldom explicitly aware of exactly what we are asserting. I, therefore, conclude that the theory that "good" denotes a simple nonnatural quality is incorrect.

Ethical Naturalist's thesis that "good" means "pleasurable for human beings" is inadequate in a number of ways. Intuitionist has pointed out, for example, that our judgment that a state of affairs is good, or that an act is right, does not vary exactly with the quantity of human pleasure supposed to be present; and I think that in this he is right. But the inadequacy of the theory can also be shown in another way. There is no valid argument by which we can, from premises containing no moral predicates, deduce a sentence that does contain a moral predicate. If Ethical Naturalist's thesis were correct, we ought to be able to argue as follows:

State X is a state of the universe in which there would be substantially more human pleasure than there is at present.
Act W is, of all the things I might do, the act that would be maximally conducive to the achievement of state X.

I *ought* to do act W.

Now it is apparent, I am saying, that we cannot validly argue in this way. The "ought" that appears in the conclusion is not deducible from the merely descriptive statements that constitute the premises of the argument, whereas according to Ethical Naturalist's thesis it should be. Moreover, insofar as we do feel that the conclusion is somehow appropriate to (even though not deducible from) those premises, it is because of another unexpressed premise—that one ought, on the whole, to do things that are conducive to human pleasure.

It seems to me, therefore, that the attempts of both Ethical Naturalist and Intuitionist to describe the peculiar logical structure of moral discourse must be regarded as failures. Moral predicates do not refer to either observable or unobservable qualities in the objects of which they seem to be descriptive. Hence, moral sentences are not informative in the sense of conveying some information about the object that is said to be good or bad, right or wrong. It remains to be seen, however, whether such sentences are not informative in another sense.

The Case for Subjectivism

An important fact about moral utterances, for which objectivist theories give no account whatsoever, is that they are always expressive of some attitude, either positive or negative, on the part of the person making the judgment. Some moral predicates, like "good," "right," "praiseworthy," and "virtuous," report what we may call a "pro- attitude"; others, like "evil," "bad," "wrong," "blameworthy," and "vicious," report an "anti-attitude." This fact about moral predicates and the sentences in which they are employed is a valuable clue to the logical structure of the language of morals, for it suggests that *what we are saying when we call something good or bad, right or wrong, is that we have, or tend to have, a favorable or unfavorable attitude toward it.* The real meaning of the statement "The infliction of needless pain is evil" is "I disapprove of the infliction of needless pain." Moral sentences, in short, are informative of the attitude of the person rendering the judgment, not of the qualities of the object being judged.

My point may be illustrated by considering the somewhat parallel case of food preferences. A says, "Rutabagas are good." B says, "I disagree: rutabagas are not good at all." On the surface of it, it looks as if A and B are engaged in a disagreement about whether rutabagas do or do not possess the quality of "tasting good." However, A and B are not really disagreeing about any empirical or nonempirical qualities of rutabagas at all. What A means by "Rutabagas are good" is "I, A, like rutabagas," and what B means by "Rutabagas are not good" is "I, B, do not like rutabagas." A and B have, then, different *attitudes* toward the taste of rutabagas, and their respective statements about the goodness or nongoodness of rutabagas are simply misleading ways of reporting their private tastes.

Moral sentences, I am suggesting, are misleading in exactly this way. Like statements about tastes, they look as if they are informative about the object that is said to be good or bad, right or wrong, but they are in fact informative only of the feelings, or attitudes, of the person making the statement. "Helping someone in need is praiseworthy" is like "Rutabagas are good," not like "Daffodils are yellow"; but the misleading character of moral sentences is less obvious than is that of sentences about food preferences.

There is one common, and at first sight quite plausible, objection to this view, namely, that on the theory proposed here it would seem that there is nothing to argue about in matters of ethical "disagreement," just as there is nothing to argue about if you like rutabagas and I do not: the most we can do is recognize that our tastes differ at this point, and that is the end of it. But, of course, people do argue about ethical matters, and they even cite empirical evidence in support of their views. How, then, can this be accounted for in the subjectivist theory?

The answer is that (a) by and large people do tend to approve and disapprove of the same "ends" and (b) when they disagree, their disagreement is usually about the most effective means of achieving those ends. Ethical Naturalist's example of the two people who disagreed about whether it would be right to use tear gas in a certain situation is a case in point. The two did not disagree in what we may call their basic moral attitude: they both favored a restoration of order and regarded with disfavor the occurrence of a civil war. Their disagreement was only about the likely results of using the tear gas; because they held different opinions on this point, they held different attitudes toward the proposed action. Since empirical evidence is relevant to assessing the probable consequences of this or that course of action, the citing of evidence is appropriate in such circumstances.

As a general rule, significant disagreement on ethical matters is possible only if, and insofar as, the disputants tend to hold the same basic attitudes toward the same actual or imagined states of affairs. If they reach agreement about the facts but still persist in holding conflicting attitudes, there remains nothing that can be settled by rational argument.

"But surely," it may be objected, "people do disagree in their basic moral attitudes and even try to persuade others to agree with them." Granted. People seem to feel more strongly about their moral attitudes than they do about their food preferences (we do not talk, for example, about our "culinary convictions") and are generally unwilling to accept questioning of them. But the only methods by which anyone can persuade another to change his basic moral attitudes are those not of rational argument but of nonrational persuasion: name-calling, intimidation, threats, and so on. This is probably why our language has words like "prude," "moral ignoramus," and the like.

Does this view lead to pessimistic conclusions about the possibility of achieving enough ethical agreement among men to make harmonious life possible? Not at all. To so conclude would be equivalent to a restaurateur's concluding that, since people's tastes differ, he might as well give up trying to develop a menu that will win the general approval of his customers. Fortunately, people by and large tend to approve and disapprove of the same kinds of things: that is why there is little disagreement with statements like "The infliction of needless pain is evil" or "It is good to help others who are in need." It is not the alleged objectivity of moral judgments but the substantial similarity of our basic moral attitudes that renders possible a reasonably harmonious society.

The Truth and Falsity of Ethical Statements

I have already stated that I agree with Ethical Naturalist's assertions that ethical statements are true or false and that their truth or falsity is ascertainable by empirical means. I want now to indicate why and in what sense I hold these assertions to be true.

Since according to my view ethical statements are reports about the speaker's attitudes, such statements are always either true or false: they are true if the speaker really has the attitude that he claims to have and false if he does not. Moreover, the means by which we determine whether a person has the attitude he claims to have are straightforwardly empirical: introspection in the case of ourselves and observation in the case of others. The evidence that Johnny does not like spinach is his behavior—the fact that he never voluntarily eats spinach, objects violently if told that he must eat some spinach, makes a face when a spoonful of spinach is put in his mouth, and so on. The evidence that a person who says that honesty is good really does approve of honesty is that he pays his bills, does not take things that do not belong to him, and in general behaves in ways that are consistent with what is normally meant by the term "honesty."

It seems to be possible, incidentally, for a person to be mistaken about his own attitudes and thus to make false ethical statements without any intent to deceive. At times a person can affirm general principles learned earlier in life, which may have been truly descriptive of his attitudes at that time, without realizing that his present attitude (as judged by his behavior) is no longer what it formerly was. A person who has been taught that all drinking of alcoholic beverages is wrong, for example, may continue to say this on occasion even if he engages in moderate drinking himself and has no objection to others doing the same. There is, so far as I can see, no logical inconsistency in this; it is just that the general principle learned earlier in life is no longer truly descriptive of this person's present attitude.

Moral Attitudes and Objectively Descriptive Inferences

There is a sense, however, in which moral utterances are implicitly descriptive of the objects that are asserted to be good or bad, right or wrong. It is true, as Ethical Naturalist says, that if someone is said to be "a good man," we should be very surprised to learn that he is a poor husband and father, difficult to get along with, careless in his work, and so on; and this gives some credence to the view that the statement "Joe Doakes is a good man" is an assertion to the effect that Joe Doakes has certain qualities and does not have others.

That the assertion "Joe Doakes is a good man" is not as straightforwardly descriptive as this example makes it appear to be, however, is apparent from the fact that what we would regard as its "objective descriptive content" would vary considerably depending on whether we understood the statement to have been uttered by (a) the president of the local temperance union, (b) a fundamentalist minister, (c) oneself, or (d) the head of the Mafia. There are some "objective descriptive implications" in each case, but their precise character varies depending on the speaker. How can this be?

The correct solution to the puzzle, I would suggest, is as follows. What is sometimes called the descriptive content of a moral utterance is a result of an inference that we make from (a) what we know or suppose about the basic moral attitudes of the speaker in conjunction with (b) the particular statement that he makes to the effect that so and so is good. We know, for example, that Mr. X, the head of the Mafia, generally approves of men who can rob a bank without getting caught, who always share their loot with the rest of the mob, and so on. If, then, Mr. X says "Joe Doakes is a good man," we infer that Joe Doakes is not a psalm-singing philanthropist but a man who exhibits the qualities that Mr. X is in the habit of commending. If we knew nothing about the attitudes of the speaker, we should be very much in doubt about what kind of a man Joe Doakes is even though he is said to be a "good" man.

If when we hear someone described as a "good" or "virtuous" person, we are not usually in doubt about what sort of person he is, it is not because "good" or "virtuous" directly mean such and such a combination of qualities, but because people by and large tend to favor certain kinds of qualities and behavior in their fellow-men. It is this fact that lends ethical naturalism whatever plausibility it has, and it leads us, mistakenly, to conclude that the primary meaning of moral utterances is their objective descriptive meaning. The variability of this descriptive meaning (depending on the basic moral attitudes of the speaker) makes it evident that this descriptive content is inferential rather than direct, and it is precisely the subjective theory of the primary meaning of moral utterances that enables us to account for this undeniable variability. I take this, therefore, as a most powerful confirmation of the correctness of the view here proposed.

STUDY QUESTIONS

1. What are the "three propositions" enunciated by one or the other of the two preceding writers with which Private Subjectivist (PS) feels obliged to take issue? With whom are you inclined to agree on each of these points? Why?
2. Is PS right in saying: "There is no valid argument by which one can, from premises containing no moral predicates, deduce a conclusion that does contain a moral predicate"? If he is right, is this fact damaging to ethical naturalism? Explain.
3. What exactly is PS's own view about the meaning of moral sentences? Do the examples he gives especially lend themselves to this kind of interpretation? Can you think of any examples that he might find it difficult to interpret in this way?
4. In what sense does private subjectivism maintain that ethical statements are capable of being true or false? How according to this view can the statement "The infliction of needless pain is evil" be contradicted?
5. What does PS mean by the statement that the "descriptive content" of ethical statements is inferential rather than direct? Do you think he is right?

47

CULTURAL
RELATIVISM

The view of moral judgments presented in the preceding chapter represents a decided advance over the two objectivist theories introduced earlier. It seems clear that pro- attitudes and anti- attitudes are involved in an important way in the meaning of moral judgments. Any theory that fails to take account of this fact must be regarded as inadequate.

Some things about Private Subjectivist's proposal, however, strike me as being very strange. I shall point out what I consider to be certain oddities in his theory, features that demonstrate beyond a reasonable doubt that it is not the whole and correct answer to our problem. I shall then suggest a slight emendation by means of which the difficulties inherent in the private subjectivist view can be overcome.

Some Oddities of Private Subjectivism

If we were to adopt the private subjectivist theory, we should have to conclude that moral judgments are never false except in the very unusual instance in which the person making the judgment has made some mistake in assessing his own attitude; and this seems very strange. Let us suppose that A and B are discussing the rightness or wrongness of r. A says, "r is right"; B says, "r is wrong." It would hardly be appropriate for A to say in this situation, "But B, you don't really disapprove of r, you do it all the time!" Even if A confronted B with evidence that he regularly had a pro- attitude toward r, this still would not make B withdraw his statement. We could imagine him replying, "I didn't say I *disapproved* of r, I said that r is *wrong*—notwithstanding the fact that I, reprobate that I am, approve of it." And B would not be talking nonsense.

This brings me to my second point. According to private subjectivism, it would be nonsensical (because self-contradictory) to say, "I approve of some things that are wrong," or "I disapprove of some things that are right." The self-contradiction is plain: "I approve of some things that are wrong" means, according to this theory, "I approve of some things that I do not approve of." But certainly it is not self-contradictory to speak of approving of some things that are wrong. A theory that requires us to banish such statements to the realm of nonsense is somehow mistaken.

There is another type of statement that has a perfectly legitimate use in ordinary discourse that becomes nonsensical according to the private subjectivist view. Consider the statement "We ought never to do anything that we believe to be wrong, even if we want to." Surely this is a statement that would be very natural in certain contexts—in a treatise on normative ethics, for example—and we should have no difficulty in understanding it or, probably, assenting to it. But according to the private subjectivist view this becomes a nonsensical statement because it means "I disapprove of people doing things that they disapprove of, even when they approve of them." Now the purpose of a metaethical theory is not to reform moral discourse but to explain it. Since we do have a use for statements such as this, and since private subjectivism does not allow that use, the theory surely needs some improvement.

Further, if the private subjectivist theory is correct, then it follows that treatises on normative ethics tell us nothing except the private likes and dislikes of their authors. This idea, to say the least, is a very strange one. No doubt the great ethical theorists of our cultural heritage—Aristotle, St. Thomas Aquinas, Immanuel Kant, and many more—did have their private likes and dislikes on moral questions, just as they presumably had their own peculiar tastes in food; but surely it is not because of a purely biographical interest that we read Aristotle's *Nicomachean Ethics*, St. Thomas Aquinas' *Summa Theologica*, or Kant's *Critique of Practical Reason*. We read them because we expect these men to help us understand, among other things, what we ought to approve of, what really is right or wrong, good or evil; and we should not be interested in such questions, or even be able to ask them, if moral appraisals expressed nothing but the speaker's private likes and dislikes.

Finally, it seems that part of the persuasiveness of Private Subjectivist's account results from a confusion of which he and many of his readers are probably aware. I suspect that the most convincing feature of private subjectivism for many people is its apparent capacity to account for shifts in the "objective descriptive content" of ethical statements depending on who makes the statement. We infer certain things about the object judged, says Private Subjectivist, on the basis of what we know about the general likes and dislikes of the person making the judgment. What Private Subjectivist fails to note, however, is that when the statement "Joe Doakes is a good man" is made by, say, the head of the Mafia, it is no longer a *moral* judgment: it is a judgment employing "good" in a *non*moral sense such as we find in the sentence "A Buick is a good automobile." When the head of the Mafia says that Joe Doakes is a "good man," he certainly does not mean that Joe is a paragon of virtue: he means that Joe is a good (effective) gangster, that he does well those things the speaker expects a gangster to do. How, then, do we distinguish between the moral and the nonmoral uses of "good"? Actually, we distinguish without difficulty: we recognize immediately, once our attention is called to it, that the statement about Joe Doakes by the number-one man in the Mafia is not a moral judgment, whereas the same statement made by you or me normally would be. Private subjectivism fails to recognize this difference and is unable to account for it. Hence, we must look further for a metaethical theory that is adequate to all the relevant facts.

An Alternative to Private Subjectivism

The theory I should like to offer is known as *cultural relativism.* Moral judgments, according to this view, are indeed reports about pro-attitudes and anti- attitudes (as they are according to the private subjectivist theory); but the attitudes that they purport to describe are not necessarily or exclusively those of the person making the judgment but rather those of some group with which he identifies or to which he has reference in making his judgment. Basic moral attitudes, in short, are never simply the private attitudes of this or that individual. They are always the common attitudes of some community of which the individual is a part. Indeed, it is precisely the generality of such attitudes—their nonprivate character, in other words—that gives them the force of moral principles. Let us see how the features of moral discourse that have proved to be perplexing for the private subjectivist theory can be understood if we construe moral sentences in the way I am proposing.

What meaning can be allowed for the statements "I approve of some things that are wrong" and "I disapprove of some things that are right"? Both of these, as we have seen, are meaningless if we interpret them according to the private subjectivist theory. According to my view, however, they are perfectly intelligible statements. "I approve of some things that are wrong" means "I approve of some things that are not generally approved of by people whose opinions I ordinarily respect"; and "I disapprove of some things that are right" means "I disapprove of some things that are generally approved of by people whose opinions I ordinarily respect." As soon as we recognize that the approval or disapproval expressed in a moral judgment is not necessarily or exclusively that of the speaker but represents some "community" with which he identifies, the apparent self-contradiction of such statements disappears.

There is a certain deliberate vagueness in the expression "generally approved of by people whose opinions I ordinarily respect," and it is in order to discuss it at this point. Considerable variation exists from one individual to another with respect to the "community" with which he identifies, and consequently with respect to the opinions he takes into account when making his moral judgments. In every culture—especially in a self-consciously pluralistic culture such as our own—there are various subcultures that in many cases are the "communities" of which their members feel themselves to be a part. No one is just an American, or a Russian, or a Swede. A given American, for example, may be at one and the same time (*a*) an American, (*b*) a Catholic, (*c*) a Democrat, (*d*) a college professor, and (*e*) a member of the Society for the Prevention of Cruelty to Animals. Each of these "communities" may, on different occasions, be the one to which he has reference when he calls something right or wrong, good or evil. Which community is relevant in a given case depends on the basic attitudes typical of each. For our hypothetical American it might vary depending on whether the topic under discussion is (*a*) the freedom of the press, (*b*) birth control, (*c*) the proper role of the federal government, (*d*) plagiarism, or (*e*) slaughterhouse procedures. It is to allow for this varying reference of moral judgments that I have used the phrase "generally approved of by people whose opinions I ordinarily respect," it being understood that *whose* opinions one respects varies greatly from one individual to another and even from one occasion to another (depending on what is being considered). "Morally neutral" would then mean "an object of neither pro- attitudes nor anti- attitudes in any of the communities whose opinions I tend to respect."

All the moral predicates are, I think, correctly construed as purported descriptions of the basic attitudes, positive or negative, of whatever community or communities the speaker has reference to in making his judgments. "Ought," however, is not a predicate, and it is not definable in terms of community attitudes. "Ought" is descriptive, rather, of the *expectations* of the community with respect to its members. To say "I ought to do such and such" is to say "It is expected of me by those whose good will I cherish that I do such and such." The meaning of the statement "We ought never to do what we believe to be wrong, even if we want to" is, therefore, rather complex: it means "It is expected of a person, by those whose good will he cherishes, that he refrain from doing the things they generally disapprove of, even if his personal inclination is to do them." This interpretation expresses exactly what we would understand a person to mean if he were to make the statement in question.

Cultural relativism also enables us to understand how a person can make a false moral judgment apart from the rather unusual circumstance in which he might be mistaken about his own attitude. According to cultural relativism, a moral judgment is true if the people in the community to which the speaker has reference have the attitude that he is attributing to them; it is false if they do not. It is quite natural that a person should occasionally be mistaken about the pro- and anti-attitudes of the members of his community with respect to some matter that he may never have had an opportunity to discuss with them—especially since most people are simultaneously members of several communities. Thus, at this point too, cultural relativism appears to solve a puzzle that the private subjectivist theory leaves unsolved.

What, finally, is the content of treatises on normative ethics? Why are these works not the mere expression of the private likes and dislikes of their authors, as private subjectivism would have them be? The answer is that an ethical treatise is an attempt by one member of a community to assist the other members to clarify their moral attitudes, to eliminate any inconsistencies that may be present (to render them "coherent"), and to adopt certain additional attitudes consistent with those already held. Indeed, a very daring and original ethical thinker may do even more: he may recommend adopting attitudes different from those currently held—in which case he will be regarded by the community either as a great teacher or as an eccentric, depending on whether or not his recommendations are accepted.

This brings us to the final difficulty that we noted in connection with the private subjectivist theory: the fact that no basis could be given for the difference we instinctively sense between moral and nonmoral meanings of "good." The question is, why do we assume that the statement "Joe Doakes is a good man," when spoken by the head of the Mafia, is not a moral judgment, when we assume that the same statement when spoken by someone else may be? I think the answer is as follows. The subculture to which the head of the Mafia has reference in calling Joe Doakes "a good man" is not a "community" in any meaningful sense of that word. It is only a group of men whose common bond is a parasitic relation to a community. If the head of the Mafia were to call Joe a good man in the *moral* sense of "good," he would have to have reference to the basic attitudes of the community, that is, to law-abiding society. And this, of course, would be tantamount to saying that Joe is quite unfit for service in the Mafia. Were he to call Joe a good man in the moral sense of "good," therefore, we could only construe it as an expression of his disapproval of Joe. ("Buy off Joe Doakes? Forget it. He's a *good* man, unfortunately.") However, if he says, "Joe Doakes is a good man," in an approving way ("You need somebody to help you on that Jones job? Take Joe. He's a good man."), we know immediately that what he is expressing is not a moral judgment at all but simply what we may call "goodness of function." (Compare: "You need another car for the Jones job? Take mine. It's a good car.")

Concluding Unphilosophical Postscript

It should be apparent that the view presented here not only solves the difficulties noted in the private subjectivist view but also retains everything that is most persuasive in that view. For example, the variability of the objective descriptive content of a moral judgment depending on who happens to utter it—a fact that is absolutely fatal to any objectivist theory—is easily explicable in terms of the different communities to which a given speaker may have reference (or, as we said before, in terms of the same speaker on different occasions or with respect to different topics). No doubt people's habits of approval and disapproval tend on the whole to coincide with those of the communities with which they identify. Therefore, from our knowledge of a person's general attitudes we can often infer directly the descriptive statements implied in his judgment that something is good or bad (in the moral sense). The fact remains that we can distinguish between a person's private attitudes and his moral convictions, and our theory provides a basis for this distinction, whereas the private subjectivist theory does not.

There is one further feature of moral judgments, which none of the previous writers has mentioned, that is rather important. The discussion of it will require us to venture briefly into the realm of social psychology, however, and here I can only offer my comments as a layman's surmise, a "concluding unphilosophical postscript" to what I have already said.

The feature of moral judgments to which I refer is what might be called their "constraining" or "obligatory" character. Moral principles sincerely held seem to make a claim, to demand (but not force) obedience. Discussion of moral issues, accordingly, always seems to be a matter of unique importance: we are concerned about them "in the center of our being," so to speak.

The explanation of this fact, I suggest, is as follows. As social beings, our acceptance by the communities with which we identify is deeply important to us. Consequently, our conformity to the expectations of the community and our identity with the community by way of sharing its basic moral attitudes are also very important to us. We exist not as isolated individuals but as human beings in community with other human beings. The attitudes and expectations of the community thus impinge upon us, constrain us, make demands on us: it is this that gives us our sense of duty and obligation and our attitudes concerning right and wrong, good and evil, virtue and vice. Morality is a social phenomenon and we are social beings; therefore, moral questions, problems, and principles strike us as being among the most important matters with which we can be concerned.

STUDY QUESTIONS

1. List the objections that Cultural Relativist (CR) raises with respect to private subjectivism. Are these serious difficulties for the private subjectivist view? Can you think of any way to defend private subjectivism against these objections?
2. What does CR offer as an alternative to private subjectivism? To what extent does this involve disagreement with Private Subjectivist's position?

3. What analysis does CR offer of the sentences that he earlier cited as being "nonsensical" if interpreted according to the private subjectivist theory? Are you satisfied with this analysis? Can you think of any moral sentences that CR might have difficulty in construing in a way consistent with his theory?

4. Do we know that the statement "Joe Doakes is a good man," spoken (in an approving way) by the head of the Mafia, is not a moral judgment? How? (If you are not satisfied with CR's account, devise one of your own.)

5. Would there be any inconsistency in being both a cultural relativist and a moral critic of one's own community or society? To what moral standard would such a person (qua critic) be appealing?

48

NONCOGNITIVISM

All the metaethical theories presented thus far assume that moral sentences are assertions. Ethical Naturalism construes moral sentences as assertions about the presence or absence of some natural quality (for example, pleasure-producing potential) in the act or state of affairs about which the alleged assertion is made. Intuitionism construes such sentences as assertions about the presence or absence of an alleged nonnatural quality (i.e., goodness) in the judged object. Private subjectivism construes them as assertions about the attitudes of the asserter. And most recently we have heard from Cultural Relativist, who advises us to construe such sentences as assertions about the feelings of approval and disapproval on the part not of the speaker but of some group with which the speaker identifies or to which he has reference in making his assertion.

The inadequacies of the first three of these theories have already been discussed. Cultural relativism is also inadequate in its own way, however, and I want to point out some of the most serious problems inherent in this view before going on to propose what I believe to be a more adequate alternative.

Critique of Cultural Relativism

First, when we "unpack" a moral sentence in the way that cultural relativism says we should, what we end up with is not a plausible account of the sentence with which we began. Consider, for example, the sentence (which one could readily imagine being uttered by a stern-voiced father) "Son, you ought not drive so fast." According to cultural relativism, the meaning of this sentence is roughly as follows: "You commonly drive at speeds that are excessive and if you continue to do so you are apt to become involved in an accident; moreover, your mother and I, and many others whose opinions you normally respect, have feelings of disapproval toward your so doing." Now this, I am saying, is not a plausible account of what we mean by the moral sentence "You ought not drive so fast." And this conclusion can be reinforced by applying the relativist theory to additional examples.

Second, cultural relativism obliterates the distinction between the manners and the morals of a given culture. We are in fact able to distinguish between the moral standards of a group of people and their standards of etiquette; indeed, we are able to make that distinction even with respect to our own culture. We consider it bad manners to make uncouth noises while eating, for example, but we do not consider it immoral to do so. Yet in both cases we have what might be described as "feelings of disapproval." If the sentence "X is wrong" means merely "The group of people whose opinions I normally respect disapprove of X," then we should not be able to make this distinction and, in fact, it should be correct to say (in our culture), "Eating noisily is morally wrong." Hence it is clear that moral sentences cannot be satisfactorily construed in the way that cultural relativism urges us to construe them.

Finally, if moral sentences mean what cultural relativism says they mean, we should not be able to meaningfully ask the question, Are all the things that my cultural reference group approves really right, and are all things that they disapprove really wrong? But we *can* meaningfully ask this question—indeed, as we noted a moment ago, we can readily think of examples of things that are the object of general approval or disapproval that nobody would think of calling right or wrong. Thus it is evident that "right" and "wrong" do not mean simply approval or disapproval by the appropriate cultural reference group.

Since all the theories that attempt to construe moral sentences as *assertions* of one kind or another have now been shown to be inadequate, it seems clear that our only alternative is to construe them as sentences of a very different kind—that is, as sentences that do not *assert* anything at all. Two such theories have been put forward in recent years, namely *emotivism* and *imperativism*. I shall cover emotivism only briefly, because I think it can be readily shown that it is not a promising alternative to the theories that have already been discussed. I shall then attempt to state the case for imperativism, which I believe to be the most plausible account of the meaning of moral sentences.

Emotivism

According to emotivism, the specifically moral character of moral sentences consists, not in the assertion that the speaker, or some group to which he has reference, has certain feelings, but in a nondescriptive *expression of* those feelings. Moral words, insofar as they have a distinctively moral flavor, are not descriptive either of the object being "judged" or of anybody's feelings: they are not descriptive at all. Grammatically, they have the status of an interjection. "You ought not drive so fast" means, roughly, "You commonly drive at excessive speeds: for shame!"

Emotivism acknowledges, however, that some moral sentences cannot be reduced to (a) a factual assertion ("You commonly drive at excessive speeds") plus (b) an expression of approval or disapproval ("for shame!"). A sentence like "Driving at excessive speeds is wrong," for example, has no factual meaning; its only meaning is therefore emotive, according to this view. It is as if someone said "driving at excessive speeds!" in a "raised-eyebrows" tone of voice, thus indicating his disapproval of the behavior in question. General moral sentences are neither true nor false according to the emotivist view. Someone who says, "Driving at excessive speeds is wrong," cannot be contradicted because he is not making an assertion; anyone who appeared to be disagreeing with him would only be expressing a contrary attitude.

Many people have great difficulty understanding the difference between emotivism and the private subjectivist view. The difference can be stated as follows: According to the private subjectivist theory, moral sentences are informative sentences; according to emotivism, they are not. Or the difference can be expressed in this way: According to the private subjectivist view, moral sentences are always either true or false; according to emotivism, they are not. According to the private subjectivist view, the statement "Driving at excessive speeds is wrong" can be contradicted by the statement "You do not really disapprove of fast driving." According to emotivism the utterance cannot be contradicted because it makes no assertion.

The difference between private subjectivism and emotivism is not over whether or not a person who utters a moral sentence has the feelings in question: both views assume that he normally does. The question is, Does the meaning of a moral sentence consist in an assertion by the speaker that he has such and such feelings, or is a moral sentence a nonreportive expression of those feelings? Private Subjectivist says the former, emotivism says the latter. The difference is subtle, but important.

I do not wish to dwell at great length on the defects of the emotivist theory. It has been widely and soundly criticized since it was first put forward some years ago, and many of its early supporters have abandoned it in recent years. I do want, however, to mention just three or four of the most serious objections that have been raised against the theory.

The emotivist theory does not do justice to the seriousness with which moral sentences are commonly uttered. Questions calling for moral appraisal and decision are frequently matters of great moment: the fates of men and nations are sometimes at stake. To say that the sentence "War is evil" means "Boo for war" or that the sentence

"Bravery is good" means "Hurray for bravery" is absurd. No doubt we frequently take ourselves too seriously, but we surely are not guilty of this when we say that our moral appraisals of war, of bravery, or of thousands of other things that we appraise in this way are important. The "boo-hurray" theory offends us because it makes light of serious matters. For this reason alone it deserves to be rejected.

Moreover, a number of odd and distressing consequences follow if we assume this theory to be true. For example, we can never be in error in making a moral "judgment," and from this it follows, in turn, that neither blame nor remorse is ever appropriate. Moreover, according to this theory, there can never be a rational basis for an ethical appraisal or decision. And most distressing of all, it would follow that ethical disputes cannot be resolved by rational means: if individuals or nations cannot agree on some matter of importance, there is nothing to do but to fight it out until the strongest wins.

The issue resolves itself, really, to this: Are moral utterances rational or are they not? The unanimous answer of our whole Western ethical tradition, from Plato and Aristotle to Kant, John Stuart Mill, Moore, and Ross, is that they are. The reply of the emotivists is that they are not. This is no trifling matter. If ethics can be rational, then moral progress— the gradual improvement of our moral principles by reflection and criticism—is possible; if not, such progress is not possible. Indeed, the very notion of "progress" becomes, in this theory, incomprehensible. Anyone concerned about the future of civilization would do well to ponder these consequences.

Let us look, then, at one last alternative, the noncognitivist metaethical theory known as imperativism.

Some Features of Directive Language

Rational beings employ language for a variety of purposes, only one of which is to convey information. Because so much of our use of language does consist in this informative function, however, conventional logic has dwelt almost entirely on the logical behavior of language so employed. But the directive function of language—the use of language to guide behavior—is an equally rational function.

The difference between these two kinds of language might be understood in terms of the types of questions each might be appropriate to in framing an answer. We use language informatively only in instances where we presuppose a question of the form, What are the facts? or What is the case? We use language in its directive function only in instances where we presuppose a question of the form, What shall I do? To a question of the latter type, any statement of fact would be inappropriate; to a question of the former type, a moral appraisal would be equally inappropriate.

There are many different instances in which the function of the language used is quite evidently directive. Consider the following list: a typical verbal communication from a sergeant to his platoon; a recipe; assembly instructions for a child's toy; instructions from ground control to a team of astronauts; a teacher's remarks in preparation for an examination; a parent's word to a small child who is dallying after bedtime. All these are instances of language being used directively—to guide behavior.

Language used directively, like language used informatively, envisages a fairly specific state of affairs. "Johnny, go to bed" (directive), like "Johnny is going to bed" (informative), anticipates Johnny's going to bed in the very near future. Both utterances are about Johnny's going to bed, but what is said about Johnny's going to bed is different in the two cases. The directive sentence is addressed to Johnny, and it might be translated "Johnny's going to bed: do it!" The informative sentence is addressed to anybody who cares to listen, and it might be translated "Johnny's going to bed: it is occurring."

Language intended to serve a directive function is typically addressed to the person or persons whose behavior is to be guided. Some directives are intended for some one specific individual ("Johnny, go to bed!"). Others are intended for whomever may be in a position to benefit from them ("Tear on dotted line"). Some appear to be addressed to everyone; that is, they are intended to be universally applicable ("Do not take for yourself what belongs to another"). We shall return to this shortly.

The directive function, like the informative, is *sui generis:* neither can be reduced to, or derived from, the other. A given sentence may, of course, serve both functions ("Bring me the book that is lying on the dresser"), but the functions themselves may, nonetheless, be distinguished.

We cannot determine the intended function of a sentence simply by identifying its mood. Function depends on the intentions of the speaker, whereas mood does not. The sentence in parentheses in the preceding paragraph, for example, is in the imperative mood, but it is bifunctional. "Johnny, go to bed" and "Johnny, it is past your bedtime" may both serve a directive function, but the two sentences differ in mood.

Ethical Discourse as a Species of Directive Language

Let us return to ethical discourse and see how the foregoing reflections on the nature of directive language may help us to understand this very common type of talk.

The vast majority of moral sentences are in the indicative mood. This may be one of the reasons why most of the earlier efforts to ascertain the status of moral sentences proceeded on the assumption that they must be understood as some subvariety of informative language. It is not at all inconsistent with this fact, however, to suggest that the function of moral sentences is to guide behavior—is, in short, directive.

Consider, first, the way in which children learn to use moral concepts. A typical instance is the following: Johnny accompanies his mother to the grocery store, and seeing some tasty-looking candy within reach, decides to help himself. Mother says, "No, Johnny, you must put that back. It is *wrong* to take something that belongs to someone else without paying for it." Three elements of this situation should be noted: (*a*) the moral sentence is uttered in a situation involving choice among alternative ways of behaving—a situation like many Johnny may be expected to encounter in the future; (*b*) the evident function of the moral utterance is to serve as a principle for the guidance of conduct—a rule that may help Johnny decide how to act in future situations of this type; and (*c*) the moral principle thus enunciated is universal in scope—it applies not only to Johnny but to everyone. It is chiefly this third characteristic that identifies it as a moral principle rather than a merely conventional rule.

Note also the situations in which we commonly employ moral talk: the same three features, it will be found, are always present. Moral principles, we might say, play a role among human beings analogous to the role of instinct in the behavior of animals. They serve as rules of conduct, guiding us in the multifarious choices that we are constantly called upon to make. Because moral principles are universal in scope, it is always appropriate to state them, even when we are alone. The fact that moral judgments are sometimes spoken in solitude (for example, "How noble!" or "How reprehensible!" uttered while reading something) in no way invalidates the claim that the primary and normal function of such utterances is to guide behavior.

We may observe, finally, that for several reasons it is absolutely impossible for human beings to live without principles of this kind. First, our knowledge of the probable consequences of acting in this or that way is severely limited. We need general rules of conduct, embodying the accumulated wisdom of preceding generations, to guide our behavior in those situations in which we do not know how to calculate the likely consequences of various alternatives. Second, however extensive our knowledge of probable consequences may be, we require principles that will provide reasons for preferring one set of consequences over another. This would be true even if we were omniscient, knowing in precise detail what would be the short- and long-range consequences of each alternative before us. Finally, without such principles we would not be able to accumulate practical wisdom and pass it on to our children. All learning, it must be remembered, involves generalization; it is only through generalizations that we escape the irrationality of sheer individuality. Moral principles are to the practical life what general truths are to the intellectual life; they are the generalizations that relate the particulars of experience, thus casting them into an intelligible pattern.

There is no danger that people will cease to have ethical principles as a consequence of this or that inadequate metaethical theory, however widely such a theory may come to be held. There is danger, however, that widespread bewilderment about the meaning of moral utterances may lead to a weakening of their directive power, and thus to a chaotic situation in which the groping for new principles goes on without the benefit of the foundation of the old. It is necessary and important that these principles change, else men would not be able to adjust to the constantly changing conditions in which they live. But if change is to be healthy, it must be orderly—a creation of the new by way of a modification of, and addition to, the old. This cannot occur if old principles are simply ignored or if they altogether lose their directive power. Hence, it is a matter of more than casual importance that their status be understood and their role duly respected.

STUDY QUESTIONS

1. Imperativist offers three arguments in opposition to cultural relativism. Summarize these arguments.
2. What, exactly, is emotivism? How does it differ from private subjectivism?
3. Summarize Imperativist's criticisms of the emotivist theory. Do these seem to you to be sound criticisms?
4. Summarize the "features of directive language" discussed by Imperativist. Do these features in fact distinguish directive language from informative language, as Imperativist apparently believes?
5. What arguments does Imperativist offer in support of his central thesis regarding the meaning of moral sentences? Do you find his arguments persuasive?
6. For what reasons, according to Imperativist, do we need moral principles? Is it possible to agree with him on this without accepting his main thesis?

Aiken, J. D. *Reason and Conduct: New Bearings in Moral Philosophy.* New York: Knopf, 1962.

Ayer, A. J. *Language, Truth and Logic,* 2nd ed. New York: Dover, 1946 (paperbound), chap. 6. States the case for emotivism.

Baier, Kurt. *The Moral Point of View,* abr. ed. New York: Random House, 1965 (paperbound).

Blanshard, Brand. *Reason and Goodness.* New York: Macmillan, 1961.

Brandt, R. B. "The Emotive Theory of Ethics," *The Philosophical Review,* 59 (1950), 305–318.

——. *Ethical Theory.* Englewood Cliffs, N.J.: Prentice-Hall, 1959, chaps. 7–11.

——. "The Status of Empirical Assertion Theories in Ethics," *Mind,* 61 (1952), 458–479.

Carter, C. L. (ed.). *Skepticism and Moral Principles.* Evanston, Ill.: New University Press, 1973. Contains Marcus Singer's criticisms of private subjectivism, cultural relativism, and emotivism.

Edel, Abraham. *Science and the Structure of Ethics.* Chicago: University of Chicago Press, 1961 (paperbound).

Edwards, Paul. *The Logic of Moral Discourse.* New York: Free Press, 1955 (paperbound), chaps. 7–9.

Ewing, A. C. *Second Thoughts in Moral Philosophy.* New York: Macmillan, 1959, chaps. 1 and 2.

Falk, W. D. "Goading and Guiding," *Mind,* 62 (1953), 145–171.

Feinberg, Joel (ed.). *Moral Concepts.* New York: Oxford University Press, 1970.

Frankena, W. K. "Moral Philosophy at Mid-century," *The Philosophical Review,* 60 (1951), 44–55.

Gewirth, Alan. "Meanings and Criteria in Ethics," *Philosophy,* 38 (1963), 329–345.

Hancock, Roger. "The Refutation of Naturalism in Moore and Hare," *The Journal of Philosophy,* 57 (1960), 326–334.

Hare, R. M. *Applications of Moral Philosophy.* Berkeley, Calif.: University of California Press, 1972.

——. *Essays on the Moral Concepts.* Berkeley, Calif.: University of California Press, 1972.

——. *Freedom and Reason.* New York: Oxford University Press 1963 (paperbound).

——. *Practical Inferences.* Berkeley, Calif.: University of California Press, 1972.

——. *The Language of Morals.* New York: Oxford University Press, 1964 (paperbound).

Harsanyi, J. C. "Ethics in Terms of Hypothetical Imperatives," *Mind,* 67 (1958), 305–316.

Hudson, W. *Ethical Intuitionism.* New York: Macmillan, 1967. A short historical study of the intuitionist theory.

Kerner, George C. "Approvals, Reasons and Moral Argument," *Mind,* 71 (1962), 474–486.

——. *The Revolution in Ethical Theory.* Oxford: Clarendon Press, 1966.

Ladd, John (ed.). *Ethical Relativism.* Belmont, Calif.: Wadsworth, 1973.

Mill, John Stuart. *Utilitarianism.* Indianapolis, Ind.: Liberal Arts Press, 1960 (paperbound).

Moore, G. E. *Principia Ethica.* New York: Cambridge University Press, 1959 (paperbound), chaps. 1–3.

Nowell-Smith, P. H. *Ethics.* Baltimore, Md.: Penguin Books, 1954.

Perry, R. B. *General Theory of Value.* Cambridge, Mass.: Harvard University Press, 1926.

Prichard, H. A. *Moral Obligation.* New York: Oxford University Press, 1949, chaps. 1, 2, and 5.

Prior, A. N. *Logic and the Basis of Ethics.* New York: Oxford University Press, 1949.

Raphael, D. Daiches. *Moral Judgment.* New York: Hillary House, 1955, chaps. 4, 7, and 8.

————. *The Moral Sense.* New York: Oxford University Press, 1947.

Ross, W. D. *Foundations of Ethics.* New York: Oxford University Press, 1939, chaps. 2, 3, and 11.

————. *The Right and the Good.* New York: Oxford University Press, 1930, chap. 2.

Sedgwick, Henry. *The Methods of Ethics,* 7th ed., rev. by Constance Jones. Chicago: University of Chicago Press, 1962, chaps. 3, 8, and 9.

Singer, M. G. *Generalization in Ethics.* New York: Knopf, 1961.

Smart, J. J. C., and Bernard Williams. *Utilitarianism: For and Against.* New York: Cambridge University Press, 1973. A debate between the two authors.

Stevenson, C. L. *Ethics and Language.* New Haven, Conn.: Yale University Press, 1960 (paperbound), chaps. 1, 2, and 4–6.

Stroll, A. *The Emotive Theory of Ethics.* Berkeley and Los Angeles: University of California Press, 1954.

Taylor, Paul W. *Normative Discourse.* Englewood Cliffs, N.J.: Prentice-Hall, 1961.

Toulmin, S. E. *The Place of Reason in Ethics.* Cambridge, Eng.: Cambridge University Press, 1960 (paperbound).

Urmson, J. O. *The Emotive Theory of Ethics.* London: Hutchinson's University Library, 1968.

Veatch, Henry B. *For an Ontology of Morals: A Critique of Contemporary Ethical Theory.* Evanston, Ill.: Northwestern University Press, 1971. From a Thomist background.

Warnock, G. J. *Contemporary Moral Philosophy.* New York: St. Martin's Press, 1967. See also a critical review of Warnock's book by R. M. Hare in *Mind* lxxvii, 307 (July 1968), 436–440.

Wellman, Carl. *Challenge and Response: Justification in Ethics.* Carbondale, Ill.: Southern Illinois University Press, 1971.

————. *The Language of Ethics.* Cambridge, Mass.: Harvard University Press, 1961.

PART XI

FREEDOM
AND AUTHORITY

49

SOCIETY AND
THE INDIVIDUAL

As John Donne once said, no man is an island. We are born into a world
that has been shaped and molded by those who lived before us, and we
live our entire lives surrounded by other human beings whose individual
and collective wishes impinge upon us in innumerable ways. During our
formative years we are surrounded by parents, teachers, and other
adults who make every effort to mold us, to fit us into the society into
which we have been born. We are taught to speak its language, adopt its
customs, espouse its values—so that they become our language, our
customs, our values. We are all members of human society; we cannot,
even by the most bizarre efforts imaginable, totally depart from its
influence. As in childhood, so in adulthood, society presents us with a
variety of *authorities* whose commands we are expected to obey.

The Concept of Authority

What does it mean to say of someone that he is an "authority"?
Evidently it can mean either of two things: (a) it might mean that he
possesses specialized knowledge in some particular area, that he is an
"expert" on some subject; or (b) it might mean that he has the right to
control (to some extent) the behavior of others.

There is no mystery about the former concept of authority. One
becomes an authority in this sense by learning more about a given
subject than is known by most other people. Such an authority does,
indeed, claim that others ought in general to believe what he says when
he speaks on his field of specialization, but only because he happens to
have investigated the field more thoroughly than most others and hence
is in a position to speak about the relevant facts on the basis of
knowledge that they do not possess. Theoretically, anyone can become

an authority on any subject he chooses, provided only that he pursues his inquiries to the point where his knowledge of that subject greatly surpasses that of most of his contemporaries.

But what does it mean to be an authority in the sense of having "the right to control (to some extent) the behavior of others"? This definition does not take us very far because it defines one puzzling word, "authority," in terms of another equally puzzling word, "right." It is no better than if we had said, " 'Authority' (in the second sense) means the *authority* to control (to some extent) the behavior of others." Clearly, that is not very helpful.

Let us consider a hypothetical case in which we would be inclined to say that someone is an authority in the second sense. Consider, for example, a judge in a court of law. When he is exercising his office rather than acting as a private citizen, he can do certain things that the generality of citizens cannot do: he can issue commands with the expectation that they will be obeyed ("Silence in the court!" "Proceed with the examination!" etc.); he can invoke force to compel obedience to his commands; he can make decisions (or, in some cases, participate in making decisions) about the guilt or innocence of persons charged with unlawful conduct; and he can impose penalties upon those who are judged to be guilty. He exercises his authority as a judge precisely insofar as he does these things that a private citizen could not do. In saying that he has the authority to do these things, what are we saying? That he has the right (that word again) and the power to control the behavior of others.

Suppose that in place of a judge on the bench we imagine these same prerogatives being exercised by the acknowledged leader of a small gang of thieves. An acquaintance of one of the gang members is suspected of tipping off the police about the gang's latest job, in which two members of the gang got caught. He is "brought to trial" before the gang, and the leader does the very things the judge was said to do when he was exercising his authority. He issues commands with the expectation that they will be obeyed ("Lefty, stand up!"); he invokes force to compel obedience to his commands ("Shorty, give Lefty's arm a twist and see if you can't make him a little more cooperative"); he decides that Lefty is "guilty"; and he imposes a penalty that will be enforced ("Be permanently out of town in one hour or you'll end up in the river"). We would not, in such a case, say that the gang leader was exercising "authority." Why not? Because, although he has the power, he does not have the right to act as he did.

We are in a dilemma. It appears that we can distinguish between a judge in a court of law (who is an authority in the required sense) and a gang leader who behaves in a judgelike way (but is not an authority) only by saying that the judge has the power *and the right* to act as he does, whereas the gang leader has only the power. What, then, is a "right"?

Let us try this: A right is an opportunity to act (or to refrain from acting) in some specified way, which opportunity is guaranteed by law or by the general consent of the community. What distinguishes the situation of the judge from that of the gang leader is that only the judge's exercise of power is sanctioned by the will of the community as expressed in the laws defining those powers. The judge is an authority by virtue of the fact that he exercises *legitimate* (according to law) power, whereas the gang leader's power has no such sanction.

If we accept this definition of "right," our definition of "authority" begins to make some sense. An "authority" is one who has the right (as defined above) to control (to some extent) the behavior of others and the power to enforce that control. Right + Power = Authority *whenever the right in question is the right to control the behavior of others.*

The exercise of authority involves, therefore, a limitation upon the freedom of the individual who is subject to that authority. If a police officer on traffic duty exercises his authority to tell me when I may and may not proceed through an intersection, or how fast I may drive, then my freedom to proceed through the intersection when I want to, or to drive at whatever speed I wish, is being curtailed accordingly.

The Authority of Society

Every society exercises some degree of authority over its citizens. It does this by passing laws that all citizens are expected to obey and by imposing penalties upon those who do not obey these laws. The paradigm examples of "authorities" are, indeed, those who are charged with the responsibility of enforcing the law, trying those accused of breaking the law, and punishing those subsequently adjudged guilty.

The philosophical question to which we shall be addressing ourselves in this section is this: On what grounds, if any, does society have the authority to restrict the freedom of the individual to do as he pleases? Society, we have said, exercises authority over its citizens. What is the source of this authority? What, if any, is the justification for society's exercise of authority over its citizens?

It will be readily acknowledged, I suppose, that this question has considerable relevance for the contemporary political situation in the United States and, indeed, throughout the world. Self-proclaimed "revolutionary" groups have arisen in various places, claiming that they are subject to no law except revolutionary law, no authority except revolutionary authority. Planes are hijacked, property is destroyed, men are executed, all in the name of this or that revolutionary cause; and those who perform these acts contemptuously dismiss existing law, the police, the courts, and the will of society as an oppressive rule that has no legitimate authority over them.

The question has, however, been discussed by philosophers for many centuries. Plato deals with it in *The Republic*, and Aristotle in *Politics*. It is, in some ways, the central question in political philosophy. Let us look briefly at the principal ways in which it has been answered.

Four Alternatives

It is possible to argue, first, that the laws of society have the force of law because (or insofar as) they are sanctioned by natural law. This view, called the *natural-law theory*, holds that there are certain fundamental principles of right and justice that human reason can discern by attending carefully to the propositions asserting those principles. Such a principle is expressed, for example, in the proposition "The needless destruction of human life is evil." This proposition, according to the theory, cannot be proved, nor does it need to be: any right-thinking person will, upon reflection, acknowledge its truth. Laws prohibiting murder, then, are derived from this principle. Society's right to restrict the freedom of its citizens (for example, to prohibit the taking of another human life) is based on its perception of what is right, that is, on its perception of what is prescribed or prohibited by eternal and immutable natural laws.

A second alternative is what is called the *social-contract theory*, according to which each citizen of the state, by virtue of accepting the benefits of an ordered society, gives his tacit consent to the government that maintains that order. Each citizen is, so to speak, agreeing with every other citizen to accept certain limitations on his own freedom in order to secure the greater security that is thereby made possible. This view was initially advocated by such theorists as Thomas Hobbes (1588–1679), John Locke (1632–1704), and Jean Jacques Rousseau (1712–1778), and was strongly influential in the thinking of the framers of the American Constitution.

One can also defend the legitimacy of certain restrictions on the freedom of individuals in society according to the theory of *social utilitarianism*. According to this theory, the natural function of government is to promote the general well-being of its citizenry, to secure the greatest happiness for the greatest number. The justification for restricting by law the freedom of each individual to do as he pleases is that such restriction will tend to promote the general welfare. It is a corollary of this view that any restriction of freedom that cannot be shown to actually promote the general welfare is unjustified.

A fourth alternative is to assert that there is no justification for society's restriction of the freedom of its individual members. This view, known as *theoretical anarchism,* asserts additionally that although society has no authority to impose itself on its members, it does so nonetheless because it has the *power* to do so and because it perceives a practical necessity to do so. What society calls "authority" is, therefore, merely superior power—whether it be wielded in the name of monarchy, or oligarchy, or even majoritarian democracy. Civil authority is always merely *de facto*, never *de jure*.

These, then, are the principal ways in which the question of the justification of society's restriction of individual freedom may be answered. Let us now consider in some detail the arguments that may be urged in support of each.

STUDY QUESTIONS

1. What are the two senses of "authority" distinguished in this chapter? Are you satisfied with the definition of "authority" offered on p. 353? If not, how would you improve on it?
2. Is a philosophy instructor an authority, and if so, in what sense?
3. What exactly is the question about authority that is posed in this chapter? List all the ways of answering this question that seem to you to have at least some measure of plausibility.
4. Do you think it is the case that any right-thinking person will, upon reflection, agree that "the needless destruction of human life is evil"? What apparent relevance does your answer have for the question at issue?
5. What is your present opinion regarding the question posed in this chapter?

50

THE NATURAL-LAW
THEORY

The question before us is, What is the justification for society's exercise of authority over its citizens? I shall argue that this authority is justified insofar as the laws through which society exercises its authority are derived from natural law. I shall, in short, defend the natural-law theory.

The Theory

The natural-law theory involves the following claims: (*a*) there are some basic and unchanging principles of right and justice that ought to govern the affairs of men; (*b*) these principles can be known by man; and (*c*) laws have the force and authority of law insofar as they are derivable from these principles.

No one has, to my knowledge, ever attempted to codify all of the basic principles of right and justice which together make up the natural law, but it is not at all difficult to produce numerous examples. The preceding chapter gave one example: The needless destruction of human life is evil. Many such principles are stated in the Universal Declaration of Human Rights adopted by the General Assembly of the United Nations, such as "All human beings are born free and equal in dignity and rights" (Article 1); "Everyone has the right to life, liberty and security of person" (Article 3); and "Everyone has the right to own property alone as well as in association with others" (Article 17 [1]). Additional examples could easily be given, but let these suffice.

Two things should be noted about these principles. First, they are fundamental in the sense that they apply to all people at all times and in all circumstances. Any society that did not attempt to embody these principles in its laws would be regarded by all decent people as degenerate and inhuman. Second, these principles are not capable of being *proved*. If anyone is so base as to assert that some people are entitled to greater dignity than others (contra Article 1), or that there is nothing wrong with arbitrarily depriving some people of their life or liberty (contra Article 3), there is no way in the world that you can prove him wrong. If he professes not to believe such a principle, the best that you can hope for is that he will consider it more carefully and by so doing come to see that it is true.

Unprovable though these principles are, however, they can be known by man because they are *self-evident*. They are, so to speak, laws that nature has inscribed upon the heart of man. We *know* that every human being has a right to life, liberty, and security of person—whether he be an American, a Russian, an Indian, or some other nationality, and whether or not that right is actually guaranteed by the laws of his own country. "We hold these truths to be self-evident," said the authors of the American Declaration of Independence; the advocates of the natural-law theory take this to be the status of all of the fundamental principles of right and justice.

In saying, then, that laws have the force and authority of law insofar as they are derivable from these principles, I am saying, quite simply, that laws are valid and worthy of obedience insofar as they embody these principles. As St. Thomas Aquinas said, "Every human law has just so much of the nature of law as it is derived from the law of nature. But if in any point it departs from the law of nature, it is no longer a law but a perversion of law." [1] The basic principles of right and justice contained in the natural law are principles to which every person ought to be subject. The "oughtness" of the laws of any society derives from this source. Government is, so to speak, nature's surrogate in ordering the affairs of men according to nature's laws.

In asserting that valid laws are derivable from natural law I do not mean to be asserting that every particular valid law can be rigorously deduced from natural law by a series of valid syllogisms. The principle that every person has a right to security of his person, for example, justifies in general the limiting of the speed of automobiles in populated areas, but you cannot strictly conclude from this (and other relevant propositions) that the maximum allowable speed on Third Avenue between Apple Street and Cherry Boulevard should be exactly twenty-five miles per hour. Whoever is responsible for establishing speed limits has to exercise judgment in a matter such as this; he might reasonably settle on any of several speeds as the one to be regarded as the "legal limit." Such a law, nonetheless, "embodies the principles" of natural law and is therefore a valid law.

This, then, is the natural-law theory with respect to the justification of society's curtailment of the freedom of the individual citizen. Let us turn

---

[1] St. Thomas Aquinas, *Summa Theologica*, I–II, ques. 95, art. 2, in Anton C. Pegis (ed.), *Basic Writings of St. Thomas Aquinas* (New York: Random House, 1945), vol. II, p. 784.

now to a consideration of the principal arguments that may be given in support of this theory.

Just and Unjust Laws

Consider, in the first place, that if there were no natural law, it would follow that there would be no criterion for distinguishing between just laws and unjust laws. As Plato said, "What is to be the standard of just and unjust is the point at issue." [2] Were it not for the natural law written in the heart of man, human beings would be without any moral basis for opposing tyranny. Legislators could enact laws to further their own interests and those of their friends, and the hapless citizens whose interests were violated by these laws would have no recourse to a higher tribunal. They could not appeal to the conscience of mankind and would be powerless victims whose only hope for redress would be in overthrowing those in power.

But in fact we *do* distinguish between just and unjust laws. We recognize, for example, that the federal Fugitive Slave Law of 1793, which allowed slave "owners" to capture and retrieve slaves who had sought freedom in another state, was a profoundly unjust law because it violated the basic principle that every human being has a right to his personal freedom, that compulsory servitude—slavery—is morally wrong. The Fugitive Slave Law, though it was for many years the law of the land, did not have the force of law because it was inconsistent with the natural law and was therefore repugnant to the moral sense of good people everywhere. Were it not for our common awareness of such a "higher law" we could not make such a judgment.

We recognize, then, that laws subjecting people to arbitrary arrest, or arbitrary seizure of their property, or unnecessary limitations on their freedom, are unjust laws. They are unjust whether or not they are consistent with the constitution (if there is one) of the country in which they hold sway and notwithstanding the fact that they may have the majority or even unanimous approval of the lawmaking agency or of the population of that country. And the principle on which we pronounce them unjust is that they are inconsistent with the unwritten natural law that binds the consciences of all people everywhere.

The Treatment of Aliens

A second argument that may be adduced in support of the natural-law theory is that aliens are held to be punishable if they break a just law of a country other than their own, even though the lawmaking agency of that country has no legal mandate to control their behavior. The British

---

[2] Plato, *Laws*, IV, in *The Dialogues of Plato*, tr. B. Jowett (New York: Random House, 1937), vol. II, p. 485.

Parliament, for example, has no power to make laws governing the behavior of anyone except citizens of Great Britain. Yet we freely grant that an American citizen who commits, say, theft or murder in Great Britain is rightly punished for his crime according to British law. It is as if nature had assigned to each sovereign state the task of enforcing the natural law on all who happen in the course of their lives to come within the geographical borders of this or that state. It is, in the last analysis, the conscience of mankind that renders a verdict when a judge or a jury decides a case. Were it not for the universal applicability of the natural law, individuals would leave the reign of law whenever they left the country whose laws they are, as citizens, legally bound to obey.

Moral Legislation

The natural-law theory is supported by yet another line of reasoning—that natural law provides the only justification for many laws of the civilized nations of the world. Consider, for example, laws governing the distribution of pornographic material. It is hard to make a convincing case for the view that a substantial public interest is involved in this matter. If some people want to pay money to look at lewd pictures or to read about the sexual exploits of others, the rest of society is not at all affected. Why, then, does society pass antipornography laws? On what basis can it justify this restriction of the freedom of those who would produce and sell pornography? On the basis that the proliferation of smut and the encouragement of lust are contrary to what most human beings perceive as good and right—contrary, in other words, to natural law.

Consider another example. Suppose that some individual, contrary to the practice of all civilized people, chose to go about in public (weather permitting) without any clothes. Such a person would most certainly be arrested for indecent exposure and either jailed or committed to a mental institution. On what grounds? On the grounds that such behavior is contrary to what civilized people regard as decent and right. Take away natural law and you must take away much of the moral legislation that governs the everyday life of all of us.

Our Knowledge of Natural Law

In appealing to natural law as the ultimate source of the authority of the actual laws under which human beings live, I do not mean to be implying that our knowledge of natural law is either complete or infallible. The training of the conscience of mankind is clearly a long and laborious process, and I would be the first to admit that we undoubtedly have a long way to go before we can plausibly claim that we have fully comprehended the content of the natural law. Our knowledge of the natural law, like our knowledge of the laws governing the physical universe, is incomplete and subject to error. But in neither case is our partial ignorance a reasonable excuse for ignoring or denying that portion of the whole that we clearly understand. Our legislators must legislate according to their understanding of what is good and right, just as our engineers must design our transportation and communication systems on the basis of their present understanding of the relevant physical and chemical laws.

A legislator, then, is not free to enact as law anything that might happen to suit his fancy or his private interest. In a constitutional democracy he is, of course, bound by the constitution. But even in a country where there is no constitution defining the limits of a legislator's authority, a legislator is bound by the authority of an unalterable natural law to which all people are subject. When he is considering a piece of proposed legislation, he must continually ask, Is this right? Is it just? Does it protect the inalienable rights of our citizens? Does it promote the common good? And to answer these questions he must look not to the constitution, for that is at best an incomplete summary of the basic principles of right and justice, but to the natural law itself. The law that he enacts will have the force of law and will be binding upon the behavior of the citizens only on the condition that it is grounded in the principles of natural law. To the extent that this is achieved the law will commend itself to good people everywhere.

The Need for Written Law

But why, it might be asked, is written law even necessary if, as you say, the natural law is known to all? It is necessary, first, because although the natural law is *knowable* by all human beings, it is not equally *known* to all because not all have the interest or the patience or the time to attend to it. The patient consideration of the dictates of natural law, that is, the conceptualization of the truly good society, requires a concentrated effort for which few individuals have either the leisure or the sustained interest. Written law is necessary, therefore, in order that people may nonetheless be taught to live according to the precepts of the natural law.

Written law is necessary, second, in order to counterbalance the tendency of each individual, even though he may acknowledge what justice requires, to make an exception in his own case whenever the requirements of natural law come into conflict with his own self-interest. I may agree, for example, that citizens ought to pay taxes in proportion to their ability to pay, but I may selfishly desire that an exception be made in my own case because I would rather use my money to purchase something for myself. The written law, therefore, not only prescribes in detail how much a person in my circumstances must pay but it prescribes penalties for nonpayment that are sufficiently severe to make it in my self-interest to do what the law requires. The natural law tells me, in general, what I ought to do; the written law, through its system of penalties, makes reasonably sure that I will do what the natural law requires.

In a world of perfectly reasonable and perfectly good human beings, no written law would be required. In such a world everyone would know the natural law and would willingly do what it requires. But we must deal with the world as it is, accepting the fact that people are neither perfectly reasonable nor perfectly good. Hence there is a need for written law notwithstanding the fact that the natural law is knowable by all.

STUDY QUESTIONS

1. List the three propositions that Natural-Law Theorist (NLT) says constitute the theory he is attempting to defend. Restate them in such a way as to demonstrate that you understand them.
2. Judging by the examples given in this chapter, what do you take to be the defining characteristics of a "natural law"? Can you produce additional examples that fit the definition?
3. "Were it not for the natural law written in the heart of man, human beings would be without any moral basis for opposing tyranny." Attack or defend this statement.
4. What arguments does NLT use to support his theory? What is your opinion of the soundness of each?
5. Objection: If the natural law is "written in the heart of man," there should be no need for written law. What is NLT's answer to this?

51

THE SOCIAL CONTRACT

It seems to me that Natural-Law Theorist (hereafter NLT) has not provided a satisfactory answer to the question concerning the justification for society's exercise of authority over its citizens. NLT's answer is that the laws through which society exercises this authority have the force of law insofar as they embody the principles of natural law, and that government is a kind of "surrogate for nature" in enforcing these laws. This view is then supported by a series of arguments, and NLT concludes by explaining why (according to his view) written law is necessary in spite of the fact that the natural law is theoretically knowable by all.

I now want to show what is wrong with NLT's position and then expound what I believe to be the correct solution to this problem, namely, the social-contract theory.

Critique of the Natural-Law Theory

The crux of the difficulty with the natural-law theory is that even granting that there is a natural law knowable by all men, and that the mandates of written law derive their authority from natural law, the question as to why some individuals should have the right to enforce compliance with the law upon some other individuals remains unanswered. From the fact that some particular written law embodies the relevant principles of natural law, NLT simply assumes that whoever enforces that law upon his fellow-men has the right to do so. But this surely will not do. The question is not, Ought everyone to obey the natural law? The question is, By what right does any group of people have the authority to compel others to act or refrain from acting in some particular way? Let it be granted that you and I and all individuals ought to obey the natural law. Whence comes the authority of policemen and judges and juries to compel us to such obedience? Why is not each of us responsible for his own behavior?

Consider, for example, the matter of penalties. They are necessary, NLT tells us, in order to counterbalance the tendency of man to act in his own self-interest even when he knows that such action is contrary to the requirements of natural law. I agree. But the legislator invents these penalties on the assumption that he has the right to force compliance with the law. Whence comes this right? NLT has no answer.

It is interesting to note that NLT's arguments in support of his position are really arguments in support only of the proposition that there is a natural law. NLT is guilty of a *non sequitur*. From the arguments put forward by him it does indeed follow that there is a natural law, but it does not follow that anyone in particular has the right to enforce that law upon his fellow-men. The fundamental question with which we are dealing remains to be answered.

The State of Nature

Let us imagine, now, a state of affairs in which no person or group of persons has assumed or been delegated the authority to enforce the natural law upon his fellow-men. Each individual, then, is responsible for his own behavior according to the natural law as he understands it. If he breaks the natural law, he is answerable only to his own conscience— with one important exception: if his behavior results or threatens to result in injury to some other person or his property, that person has a right to defend himself and to demand reparation from the offender. Each individual, in this state of affairs, is judge and jury in any case in which his own interest is involved, and each must seek to enforce justice as best he can when he finds it necessary to render a judgment. Let us call this the state of nature, since it is the state in which nature places man pending some action on the part of man himself to create a different state of affairs.

What would it be like to live in this state of nature? It must be apparent in the first place that in such a state no one could be really secure, no one could ever be certain that some person or combination of persons stronger than himself would not endanger his life and property. If there is law (natural law) but no one to enforce the law, then the situation is almost as bad as if there were no law at all. Every person in the state of nature is potentially at war with every other person, and life is likely to be (as Hobbes once said) "nasty, brutish, and short."

Second, human beings living in the state of nature could not fail to observe that justice is rarely achieved, for self-interest will cause individuals always to favor their own side of the matter whenever they find it necessary to resolve a dispute. If I am judge and jury in any case in which my interest is involved, I am most assuredly going to make sure (if I can) that I get at least what is coming to me, and perhaps a little more. Since my opponent will be just as careful to watch out for his private interest, we shall in all probability end up fighting, and the decision will favor not the one having the greater justice but the one who is able to muster a superior force.

The question facing mankind in the state of nature, then, is this: How shall we put an end to this war of all against all? How shall we obtain a state of affairs in which there may be security of person and where our disputes may be resolved not by force but according to the canons of justice?

The Social Contract

Government is mankind's solution to the problems inherent in the state of nature. It is as if the inhabitants of a certain region came together and—in exchange for the greater security and the increase in justice that would thereby result—agreed to delegate to some of their number the right to articulate and enforce the law. The right of each individual in the state of nature to enforce the natural law (as best he can) in any case in which his own interest is involved is thus given over to government when this contract to put an end to the state of nature is entered into. Every legitimate government is, at root, founded on such a social contract.

In saying that all government derives its authority from a certain authority originally held by the individual, I am not, of course, suggesting that as a matter of historical fact all existing governments came about in just this way. We are discussing political philosophy, not governmental history. I am saying that the theoretical basis for the authority of government lies in the will of the governed to avoid the insecurity and injustice of the state of nature. Whether as a matter of historical fact such a state ever existed is not at issue, nor is it relevant to our discussion.

Every individual who accepts the benefits of government—the protection of its laws, the greater security that results from government under law—gives his tacit consent to the social contract upon which that government rests. When someone is born into a situation in which people live under law (as all of us are), then his allegiance to the government (that is, his consent to the social contract) is simply taken for granted unless he declares otherwise. If he emigrates to a foreign country he must formally swear allegiance to this new land: he must, so to speak, explicitly affirm that he wishes to become a party to the social contract that binds together the people whom he is adopting as his countrymen.

Supporting Arguments

The first argument that I would put forward in support of this theory is that it provides an inherently plausible account of why some individuals (those who govern) have the authority to enforce the law upon others (those who are governed). The social-contract theory, unlike the natural-law theory, does not side-step the central issue in this dispute. To the question, What is the justification for society's exercise of authority over its citizens? the social-contract theory replies: This authority is derived from the antecedent right of each individual to enforce the natural law in defense of his own interests. The social contract is the theoretical precondition of the authority of society, through its legally constituted government, to enforce the law equally upon all.

I would argue, second, that this theory is consistent with the widely held view that the right to govern derives from the consent of the governed. The Universal Declaration of Human Rights explicitly states, as a matter of fact, that "the will of the people shall be the basis of the authority of government" and that "this will shall be expressed in periodic and genuine elections which shall be by universal and equal suffrage and shall be held by secret vote or by equivalent free voting procedures" (Article 21 [3]). Through the voting process the people are reaffirming the contract by which they are constituted a body politic and are deciding who shall exercise the authority they have delegated to the holders of various offices.

Third, the social-contract theory is consistent with the general view that the responsibility of government is to resolve internal disputes, to protect from external danger, and to promote the common good. It is consistent with the views of most civilized people regarding both the *scope* and the *limits* of the authority of government.

What is the scope of government's authority according to the social contract theory? Answer: Its authority must be exactly sufficient to solve the problems inherent in the state of nature. It must, therefore, resolve disputes among individuals. This it does by (*a*) developing a body of law clarifying the rights and duties of each individual (the legislative function), (*b*) enforcing those laws (the executive function), and (*c*) adjudicating cases in which some individual is alleged to have broken one of those laws (the judicial function). It must, further, promote the realization of true justice by passing and enforcing laws designed to assist the poor, the weak, and the helpless to achieve a decent life in a world in which they would otherwise be overwhelmed by those stronger and more richly blessed than they.

There are, however, definite limits to the authority of government. It has only such power as has been delegated to it in order to put an end to the perpetual conflict and injustice of the state of nature. The right to enforce the natural law is given over to government by the social contract; all other rights that are man's natural heritage remain in full force and may not be abrogated by government. Hence government cannot legitimately subject the individual to arbitrary arrest, invade his privacy, confiscate his property, or do any of a long series of things that would constitute a breaking rather than an enforcing of the natural law.

We should not minimize the risk involved in handing over to a group of designated individuals the authority originally vested by nature in each individual. Government—any government—is a desperate solution to a desperate problem, and the risk involved is enormous. History is replete with horrible examples of men who have used the power of government for their own selfish gain and who have squandered the lives and properties of their helpless subjects in the process. Unjust laws have been decreed, senseless and immoral wars have been fought, police powers have been exercised beyond all reasonable measure, and justice has been perverted in a thousand ways. Yet men cling to the necessity for government under law and seek a world in which "liberty and justice for all" shall become a reality. Why? Because they cannot tolerate a return to the certain injustice of the state of nature. The social contract is the bargain human beings must make with one another if they are to live together in a world where the interests of each individual are in potential conflict with those of all his fellows. Man's quest for a form of government that will make this a good bargain—his agonizing search for a government that will fulfill his longing for security and justice without itself becoming tyrannical—is one of the most poignant stories to be read in the pages of human history.

STUDY QUESTIONS

1. What is Social-Contract Theorist's (SCT's) main objection to the natural-law theory? Is he right on this point?
2. What exactly does SCT mean by "the state of nature"? Does he seem to you to be describing an actual state of affairs that existed at some time in the past, or is the state of nature merely a logical construct?
3. What arguments does SCT use to support his theory? Do you find his arguments convincing?
4. "The social contract is the bargain human beings must make with one another if they are to live together in a world where the interests of each individual are in potential conflict with those of all his fellows." Does this imply that one might at some point conclude that it was a bad bargain, and revoke the contract? If so, under what circumstances?

52

SOCIAL UTILITARIANISM

Strictly speaking, the authors of the two preceding chapters have given but one answer to the question, What is the justification for society's exercise of authority over its citizens? That answer, precisely stated, is (a) the function of government, as the agent of society, is to enforce the "natural law" and (b) the authority to do this derives from a "social contract" by which the antecedent right of each individual to enforce the natural law, whenever his own interests are at stake, is given over to the governing body. Natural-Law Theorist (NLT) devotes his efforts to demonstrating that there is in fact such a thing as "natural law," which is a logical precondition of the theory. Social-Contract Theorist (SCT), building further on this foundation, argues in support of the "social contract" part of the theory. I think that this theory is wrong on all major points, and I am therefore compelled to attack the main thesis of both NLT and SCT.

No Natural Law

First of all, the assertion that there is a natural law is, in my opinion, nothing but a holdover from the ancient view that there is "in the mind of God" a kind of plan for the government of His creation, an "eternal law" that is "natural" insofar as it is knowable by human reason unaided by divine revelation. St. Thomas Aquinas, whom NLT quotes with approbation, defines natural law in precisely this way. St. Thomas writes:

> The whole community of the universe is governed by the divine reason. Therefore the very notion of the government of things in God, the ruler of the universe, has the nature of a law. And since the divine reason's

conception of things . . . is eternal, . . . this kind of law must be called
eternal . . .

. . .

The rational creature . . . has a share of the eternal reason, whereby it
has a natural inclination to its proper act and end; and this participation of
the eternal law in the rational creature is called the natural law . . . It is
therefore evident that the natural law is nothing else than the rational
creature's participation of the eternal law.[1]

That the natural-law theory is an offspring of a theological view of
ancient origin is not, of course, an argument against its validity. I would
argue, however, that the theory loses much of its plausibility when
divorced from that context. The natural affinity of natural-law theory is
not with the social-contract theorists of the seventeenth and eighteenth
centuries but with the divine-right theorists of an earlier day. It is
understandable that NLT, as a son of the twentieth century, does not
endorse the divine-right theory. It is even understandable that SCT, in an
attempt to salvage the remnants of the medieval view, would appeal to a
mythical "social contract" to fill the void left by the collapse of the view
that the authority to rule is derived by appointment from the antecedent
authority of God. But let us leave these historical considerations and
consider the arguments by which NLT attempts to convince us that
there is in fact a natural law.

NLT has argued, in the first place, that if there were no natural law,
there would be no criterion for distinguishing between just and unjust
laws. His argument is, then, an attempted *reductio ad absurdum* of the
view that there is no natural law. My answer to this is that the alleged
consequence does not follow. All that is required for individuals to
distinguish between just and unjust laws is that they arrive at some
common agreement on what is to count as just. Their opinions as to
what is just and what is unjust are, in fact, constantly changing. To say
that the current opinions regarding justice and injustice constitute a
kind of reading of an immutable "natural law" is merely superfluous.
"Just" is a word we use to describe laws that are to our liking, "unjust" a
word to describe laws we do not like. The appeal to "natural law" in
support of the view that a given law is just or unjust is nothing more
than an attempt to invoke the pale shadow of a vanished deity to support
an opinion that we hold on other grounds.

NLT's argument about the punishment of aliens, which was originally
put forward by Locke,[2] is a puzzling one, and I am not at all clear about
how it supports his position. In any case, I think he is simply mistaken in
asserting that the legislative body in a given country has authority only

---

[1] St. Thomas Aquinas, *Summa Theologica*, I–II, ques. 91, art. 1, and ques. 91, art. 2, in
Anton C. Pegis (ed.), *Basic Writings of St. Thomas Aquinas* (New York: Random House,
1945), vol. II, pp. 748, 750.

[2] John Locke, *Two Treatises of Government*, ed. Peter Laslett, 2d ed. (Cambridge, Eng.:
Cambridge University Press, 1967), pp. 290–291.

with respect to the citizens of that country. A legislature's authority has, I should say, both a geographical and a citizen domain: it covers the relevant behavior of all people within a given geographical area (regardless of their citizenship) and the relevant behavior of its citizens (whether they are at home or abroad). We have yet to say how it comes by this authority, but the fact that legislatures and other governmental agencies do exercise such authority does not seem to me to support the natural-law theory in any way.

NLT's third argument—that without natural law a good deal of "moral legislation" would be found to be without justification—is correct as a simple assertion, but the assertion does not in fact support the natural-law theory: rather, it supports the view that many laws now on the books have no justification and ought to be repealed. In short, I accept the consequence of this attempted *reductio*, but I deny that it is absurd. Laws of this type, in my opinion, are unjustified attempts to meddle in the private affairs of individuals. They are all in the same category as the notorious "blue laws" of colonial New England, which forbade Sunday indulgence not only in drinking and dancing but even in honest work. The view that there is a theoretical justification for governmental authority does not necessarily commit one to the defense of everything that governments do and have done under the guise of legitimate authority. NLT, in my opinion, is not sufficiently sensitive to the need for assigning definite limits to the authority of government over the lives of individual citizens.

There is, moreover, a decisive consideration that may be urged against the idea of natural law, namely, that there are no criteria for determining when an assertion is or is not a "part" of the natural law. NLT concludes from this that the natural law is known directly; I conclude that it is not known at all, for the very good reason that it does not exist. To decide whether a piece of proposed legislation ought to be enacted, the legislator must look, not to some mysterious natural law written, presumably, in heaven, but to the probable consequences of that legislation. I shall return to this point later in this essay.

No Social Contract

The idea of a social contract is no less a fiction than that of natural law. Indeed, SCT seems almost to recognize this when he tells us that he is not suggesting that "as a matter of historical fact" actual governments were created in just this way. What SCT seems to be arguing, then, is that the idea of a social contract is a *useful* fiction: it is a vivid way of stating what he considers to be the correct theory about the ultimate ground of the authority of government. I do not wish to quarrel with his use of the concept "social contract" as a merely literary device, however; my quarrel is with the theory itself.

What the social-contract theory comes down to, once isolated from the twin fictions of an imaginary "state of nature" terminated by an imaginary "social contract," is the idea that individuals have an antecedent natural right to enforce the natural law whenever their own interests are at stake and the idea that they voluntarily hand this right over to the government they create in order to secure certain benefits such as greater security, justice, and so forth.

This theory is wrong, first of all, because it presupposes the existence of natural law, which is either nonexistent or unknowable. It is wrong, second, because it presupposes the existence of "rights" prior to the enactment of any law, which is a contradiction in terms. SCT would, I think, accept the definition of "right" given in Chapter 49: "an opportunity to act (or to refrain from acting) in some specified way, which opportunity is guaranteed by law or by the general consent of the community." He thinks he can talk about "natural rights" because he thinks the opportunities pertaining to those rights are guaranteed by natural law. But without natural law there are no natural rights; hence there is nothing for the individual to hand over to the government that he creates. Rights are created by the enactment of law, which presupposes the existence of a lawmaking agency that, according to the social-contract theory, comes into being only as a result of the social contract. Without natural law, the social-contract theory collapses.

An Alternative Proposal

In dealing with the question of the justification of the authority of society to limit the freedom of individual citizens, it is important that we be very clear about precisely what question we are asking, for it is not (as my opponents appear to have assumed) equivalent to the question, Who originally had the authority that we now see being exercised by government and how did government get this authority from them? The authority of government, insofar as it can be justified, is justified not by its *origin* but by its *ends*. Government is a creature of society, a social institution. Like any social institution it is good insofar as it accomplishes the purposes for which it was created.

Why do people create governments? Chiefly, in my opinion, for purposes of self-protection. What everyone desires is an opportunity to live his own life, to do as he pleases, without interference from anyone else—in short, to be perfectly free. The trouble is that in a world where everyone is free to do as he pleases, to pursue his own self-interest without regard for the interests of anyone else, everyone would be involved in perpetual conflict with everyone else. We need government, therefore, to protect ourselves against our fellows. In order to secure a situation in which all of us—the weak as well as the strong—shall have an opportunity to live our lives without the constant fear of attack by our fellows, we need a system of restraints which each of us accepts on the condition that everyone else accept those same restraints. It is the business of government to make those rules and to enforce them in such a way that it becomes in the self-interest of everyone to obey them. The exercise of governmental authority is justified insofar as it protects each individual member of society from the evils that might be inflicted on him by his fellows were they not restrained by law.

Two important corollaries of this theory should be noted. The first is that the scope of government's authority is limited to those areas in which unregulated behavior is likely to do harm to someone else. Government has no business meddling in the private affairs of individuals, or restraining them in any way, except when such action is necessary to protect the rest of society from some probable harm. If a man wishes to drive sixty miles an hour through a heavily populated area, government has a right to restrain him; if he wishes to wear his hair at shoulder length, that is his own private business—however much the majority may disapprove.

The second corollary is that no particular type of government is a priori better than any other type. In one situation a monarchical type may be best; in another a democracy may be best; and in yet another a military dictatorship may be most effective. The "best" in each case is defined as that type that is most effective in accomplishing the purpose for which government exists, that is, the protection of the members of society from the harm that would result if everyone were permitted to do as he pleases.

I would suggest that an appropriate name for this theory of the authority of government is social utilitarianism. It finds the justification of governmental authority in government's securing the social ends that make it desirable that there be some government rather than none at all.

Supporting Arguments

In support of this position I would argue, first, that it justifies the exercise of governmental authority in the only way that any social institution can be justified, namely, by reference to its consequences. How do we judge whether an educational system is good? Clearly, we judge it by its consequences: we observe the quality of its graduates. How do we judge the practice of medicine? By the consequences: we observe the degree of success physicians have in restoring to health those who are ill. So with government: its "justification" lies in its consequences, by which I mean that it justifies its existence to the degree that it succeeds in creating a situation in which every citizen is able to pursue his own interests so long as those interests do not impose harm on others.

I would suggest, second, that this defense of the authority of government is exactly consistent with the way in which individual pieces of proposed legislation are justified by their supporters. It is absurd to suggest that legislators "look to the natural law" in trying to decide whether a given piece of proposed legislation ought to be enacted. Legislators should not waste their time gazing into the empty lawbook of nature—nor do they. They should, and do, attempt to assess the probable consequences of the law they are proposing to enact. All argument about the wisdom or unwisdom of a proposed law is concerned with its probable consequences, and that is exactly what we should expect given the account of the authority of government I am proposing here.

Last, the utilitarian account of the authority of government provides a usable criterion for determining when government is and when it is not exercising its authority in a defensible way. When the intent of legislation is to eliminate some actual or potential evil, the exercise of governmental authority is justified. When, however, the intent is to impose on an unwilling minority the private preferences of the majority, or even of the lawmakers themselves, the exercise of the power of government has no justification whatsoever. Insofar as the behavior of an individual, however unconventional or unusual it may be, imposes no harm on others, government has no legitimate reason to interfere. The "rights" of the individual, properly understood, mean just this: the presumed freedom of every man to do as he pleases so long as his actions do not inflict harm on others. Government preserves such rights not by passing laws but by refraining from passing laws in areas where it has no legitimate authority.

STUDY QUESTIONS

1. "All that is required for individuals to distinguish between just and unjust laws is that they arrive at some common agreement on what is to count as just." Is this correct? Defend your answer.
2. Why, according to Social Utilitarian (SU), is it a contradiction in terms to assert that men have rights prior to the enactment of any law?
3. What does SU say is the scope of the authority of government? Do you agree?
4. What arguments does SU offer in support of his theory about the authority of government? Do you find these arguments convincing?

53

THEORETICAL
ANARCHISM

I want to distinguish *theoretical anarchism*, the position that I represent, from two other positions with which it is easily confused. The first, *militant anarchism*, is not so much a theory as a political posture: to be a militant anarchist is to be committed to the overthrow of existing government without regard to the practical consequences and with no intention of supporting some new government that might be established in its place. A militant anarchist may admit, for example, that in the absence of all government there would be widespread chaos, but he would say, "Nonetheless, I prefer that situation to the present one in which all of these bureaucrats presume to tell me what I can and cannot do. I am willing to live in the midst of chaos in order to be truly free."

The second position, which I shall call *naïve anarchism*, holds that in the absence of governmental authority not only would chaos not result but on the contrary there would be a greater realization of both freedom and order than there is under any form of government. Naïve anarchism takes an extremely optimistic view of human nature, for it maintains that in a society without governmental authority people would in fact limit their own desires in such a way that they would not be in perpetual conflict with one another.

In contrast to these two positions, theoretical anarchism is simply the view that although society may exercise authority over its citizens as a matter of practical necessity, there is no theoretical justification for such authority. I cannot, of course, be expected to bring forward affirmative arguments in support of this position. Theoretical anarchism is not a theory about the justification of the authority of government: it is, rather, the dilemma in which you find yourself when you discover that none of the theories on this question really answer the question. The only arguments available in support of theoretical anarchism are the

373

arguments demonstrating the inadequacy of all attempts to justify governmental authority.

Social Utilitarianism

I am almost inclined to argue that Social Utilitarian (SU) is on my side in this dispute, since he does not in fact offer a theoretical justification for governmental authority. What he offers instead is a *practical* justification: governmental authority is desirable, he tells us, because it is a necessary means to the desirable end of protecting society from the evils that would result if everyone were free to do as he pleases. And since it seems clear to anyone except a naïve anarchist that society would be in even more serious trouble than it is were it not for the restraining hand of government, SU appears to win an easy victory without even entering into the intellectual puzzles that seem to me to be so insoluble.

Let me say forthrightly that in my opinion SU has not offered a wrong answer: he has simply answered the wrong question. The question to which NLT and SCT addressed themselves—the one to which I wish I could find an answer but cannot—is this: *By what right* do some people (governors, legislators, police, judges, etc.) exercise coercive authority over the rest of society? I know as well as SU that certain goods are achieved through the agency of governmental authority. Indeed, NLT and SCT are equally clear about this. But the question still remains: Where does government get the authority to do what needs to be done in order to secure these goods? How is authority constituted in a world in which nature appears originally to have made us political equals? To this question SU gives us no answer at all.

The Social-Contract Theory

The social-contract theory at least has the merit of being an honest effort to solve the problem with which we are dealing. In many ways it is very attractive. Indeed, I think the theory can be stated in a more persuasive form than SCT has offered and in a way, moreover, that completely escapes SU's criticisms of the theory as put by SCT. I want to present this restatement, because I think it provides the best hope we have of finding a solution to this vexing problem. I shall then give my own reasons for rejecting the theory even in this purified form, as a consequence of which I find myself compelled to be an "agnostic" in political philosophy—a theoretical anarchist.

The form of the social-contract theory that I have in mind is this: Quite apart from any theory about natural law, which SU rightly criticizes, it seems evident that in the absence of any civil authority each individual would constantly have to defend himself against the aggressive behavior of his fellow-men. We could imagine, then, a group of individuals in this "natural condition" getting together and saying, "Let's put an end to all this fighting among ourselves. Let's draw up some rules—we'll call them 'laws'—and let's appoint somebody to make sure that we all behave the way the laws say we should." This, I am suggesting, would be a kind of social contract—without the cumbersome doctrine of natural law that renders the whole theory suspect. Each subsequent individual, as in SCT's account, tacitly enters into the contract by accepting the benefits that are secured by government: no natural law, no natural rights, nothing but a "deal" made by a group of human beings who mutually agree to stop making war so that they can get on with other, more interesting, pursuits. Does this not give us the justification we have been seeking? Unfortunately, no. Let me explain why.

First, it assumes the explicit assent of each and every individual who is to be subject to the authority thus created—an impossible condition to realize in actuality. If some individual says, "I choose not to enter into the contract; I prefer to do as I please and defend myself as necessary," he is precisely the individual who would be singled out (if he does what he says) for punishment under the law. If the whole human population consisted of only ten persons, it would require the consent of all ten to establish the state. If one dissents, the question remains: *By what right* do the other nine presume to coerce him against his will? A cynical answer suggests itself: Not by right but by power.

There is a second difficulty. Suppose that, after a time, one of the original parties to the agreement decides that it was a bad bargain and announces that he is pulling out. What is to prevent him from doing this? Must we say that his original decision to enter into the contract is irrevocable? That is not convincing. If he entered into the contract on grounds of self-intererst, then on those same grounds he should be able to terminate it. But this means, in actuality, that any individual who considers that his self-interest would be best served by breaking the law should be free to do so—and by so doing to terminate his participation in the social contract—in which case the civil authorities would cease to have any right to take action against him. In other words, the social contract establishes the authority of government *except when it is really needed*. In precisely the cases where it would like to exercise legitimate authority, all it has is naked power.

Then there is the problem of the second and subsequent generations, who *ex hypothesi* were not original parties to the contract but are, so to speak, born into it by virtue of being descendants of the original covenanters. Their theoretical case is even stronger than that of the founding father who decides he wants to terminate the contract, since they have never explicitly assented to the bargain and cannot with any degree of plausibility be said to have made an "irrevocable" commitment. By what right does the government established by their parents presume to govern them? Why should they obey a government in whose founding they had no part, and to whose authority they have never explicitly assented?

The social-contract theory justifies the authority of government only insofar as the governed consent to that authority. Those who do not consent become merely the victims of superior power. It may be prudent for them to do what the law requires, but the *right* of government to restrict their freedom has in no way been established.

The Power of Government

The truth of the matter seems to me to be this. Wherever the human species has appeared, some members have succeeded in gaining the power to compel obedience, to rule. Their wishes have been the law, their decisions the decrees of justice, their arms the means of enforcing compliance. They have been obeyed not because they had any right to be but simply because they had the power to ensure that they were. What is called "the duty of obedience" to one who exercises "legitimate authority" is nothing but the habit of bowing to the superior power of one who has assumed the role of ruler. The ruler may, in time, be compelled to share his power with some other powerful individuals (resulting in an oligarchy), or even with the people themselves (producing some form of democracy); yet the power of government, by whomever it is exercised, remains what it was in the beginning: naked power. The difference between a judge and the leader of a band of thieves is just this: the judge has more constituents.

I do not conclude from this that government is in general a bad thing, or that society would be better off in the absence of government. I think those theorists are right who say that in the absence of government man's aggressive and acquisitive tendencies would create a situation of danger and chaos—a "state of nature," as SCT calls it—in which none of us would willingly choose to live. Even bad government is better than no government at all. The practical challenge, as I see it, is to achieve the security and order that we expect our civil authority to provide without creating a monster that seeks to dominate every aspect of our lives. Having said this, however, I do not pretend that I have solved the theoretical problem of the rationale for the authority of government. That problem, in my opinion, has no solution. The authority of government has no higher sanction than the will of some to impose upon all some particular kind of order. If we accede to such authority, as most of us do, it is not because we think its claim to legitimacy has been established. It is simply because as a practical matter we acknowledge the need for civil authority in a society that consists of people like us.

STUDY QUESTIONS

1. Theoretical Anarchist (TA) distinguishes three types of anarchism. Are the distinctions clear? Is it logically possible to be both a theoretical anarchist and

a militant anarchist? both a theoretical anarchist and a naïve anarchist? Explain.

2. "SU has not offered a wrong answer: he has simply answered the wrong question." Is this correct?

3. How does TA's formulation of the social-contract theory differ from that contained in Chapter 51?

4. Summarize TA's objections to the social-contract theory. Do they seem to you to be convincing? Can you defend the theory against these objections?

Aquinas, St. Thomas. *Summa Theologica* II-I, Questions 90–97. See Pegis, Anton C. (ed.). *Basic Writings of St. Thomas Aquinas.* New York: Random House, 1945, pp. 742–805. (The opening chapters of St. Thomas' famous Treatise on Law.)

Aristotle. *Politics.* Many editions. See especially Book VII.

Barry, Brian. *Political Argument.* New York: Humanities Press, 1965.

————. *The Liberal Theory of Justice: A Critical Examination of the Principal Doctrines in "A Theory of Justice" by John Rawls.* New York: Oxford University Press, 1973.

Berlin, Isaiah. *Four Essays on Liberty.* New York: Oxford University Press, 1969 (paperbound).

Bosanquet, Bernard. *Philosophical Theory of the State.* London: Macmillan, 1920.

Brown, D. G. "Mill on Liberty and Morality," *The Philosophical Review,* 81 (1972), 133–158.

Cohen, Carl. *Democracy.* Athens, Ga.: University of Georgia Press, 1971. A comprehensive analysis.

Crocker, L. G. *Rousseau's Social Contract.* Cleveland, Ohio: Cleveland Press of Case Western Reserve University, 1968.

d'Entreves, A. P. *Natural Law.* London: Hutchinson, 1951.

Feinberg, Joel. *Social Philosophy.* Englewood Cliffs, N.J.: Prentice-Hall, 1973 (paperbound).

Fuller, Lon L. *The Morality of Law.* New Haven, Conn.: Yale University Press, 1964. Deals with the status of law and its relation to moral rules.

Gierke, Otto. *Natural Law and the Theory of Society.* New York: Cambridge University Press, 1934.

Gilson, Etienne. *Medieval Universalism and Its Present Value.* New York: Sheed and Ward, 1937.

Gough, J. W. *The Social Contract,* 2nd ed. Oxford: Clarendon Press, 1957.

Grimsley, Ronald. *The Philosophy of Rousseau.* London: Oxford University Press, 1973 (paperbound). Includes an examination of social-contract theory.

Hart, H. L. A. *The Concept of Law.* New York: Oxford University Press, 1961.

————. *Law, Liberty and Morality.* New York: Random House, 1963. Three lectures regarding "the proper scope of criminal law."

Hobbes, Thomas. *Leviathan.* Many editions. Originally published in 1651. See especially Part I, Chapters 13–15.

Hutchins, Robert M., et al. *Natural Law and Modern Society.* Cleveland, Ohio: World, 1963.

Kaplan, Abraham (ed.). *Individuality and the New Society.* Seattle, Wash.: University of Washington Press, 1970.

Locke, John. *Two Treatises of Government.* Many editions.

McPherson, Thomas. *Political Obligation.* London: Routledge and Kegan Paul, 1967. Reviews and criticizes several theories as to the basis for civil authority.

Maritain, Jacques. *The Rights of Man and Natural Law.* New York: Scribner, 1945.

Melden, A. I. (ed.). *Human Rights.* Belmont, Calif.: Wadsworth, 1970 (paperbound). Contains classical and contemporary selections as well as such documents as the Universal Declaration of Human Rights.

Mill, John Stuart. *On Liberty.* Many editions. Originally published in 1859. See especially Chapters 1 and 2.

Montesquieu, Charles de. *Spirit of the Laws,* tr. by Thomas Nugent. New York: Hafner, 1949.

Nagel, Thomas. "Rawls on Justice," *The Philosophical Review*, 82 (1973), 220–234.

Negley, Glenn. *Political Authority and Moral Judgment*. Durham, N.C.: Duke University Press, 1965. Critique of several theories regarding the basis of civil authority.

Nozick, Robert. *Anarchy, State and Utopia*. New York: Basic Books, 1974.

Popper, Karl R. *The Open Society and Its Enemies*. Princeton, N.J.: Princeton University Press, 1950.

Rawls, John. *A Theory of Justice*. Cambridge, Mass.: Harvard University Press, 1971 (paperbound). A contemporary classic. Draws from social-contract tradition.

Rousseau, Jean Jacques. *The Social Contract*. Many editions. Originally published in 1762.

Russell, Bertrand. *Authority and the Individual*. New York: Simon and Schuster, 1949.

Taylor, Richard. *Freedom, Anarchy, and the Law: An Introduction to Political Philosophy*. Englewood Cliffs, N.J.: Prentice-Hall, 1973 (paperbound).

Weil, Simone. *Oppression and Liberty*, tr. by Arthur Wills and John Petrie. Amherst, Mass.: University of Massachusetts Press, 1973.

Wild, John. *Plato's Modern Enemies and the Theory of Natural Law*. Chicago: University of Chicago Press, 1953.

Wolff, Robert Paul. *In Defense of Anarchism*. New York: Harper & Row, 1970.

PART XII

WORLD-VIEWS

54

THE FUNDAMENTAL PROBLEM

When we first set out on this study of philosophy, we observed that the positive goal of the philosopher is to construct a picture of reality in which every element of human knowledge and experience might find its proper place. Philosophy, we said, is man's quest for the unity of knowledge: it consists in a perpetual struggle to create the concepts in which the universe can be conceived as a *universe*, not a *multiverse*. The history of philosophy, then, is the history of man's search for an adequate world-view. The problems of philosophy are the problems that arise as we pursue this quest.

We can say, therefore, that the fundamental problem of all philosophy, which underlies and in some sense ties together all the problems that we have been considering thus far, is the problem of world-views. Which "total view" of reality is most adequate to the known facts? What are the foundational truths about reality in relation to which everything else that we can know needs to be understood?

The reader who has worked his way through any significant number of the problems dealt with in the preceding pages will surely have become aware of the fact that these problems are interrelated in a variety of ways. The relations that obtain among these various problems are, of course, *logical* relations: if we embrace a given position on one problem, we may be logically prevented from adopting certain positions or logically obliged to adopt a certain position on some other problem. We hope that the positions we hold on various problems are at least consistent with each other: that is a minimum requirement that all of us must seek to satisfy. If we look carefully at the various positions that we have taken on the problems considered, we should be able to discern the outlines of a world-view that might be called "our philosophy."

How Philosophical Problems Are Interrelated

Let us explore by means of a few examples some of the logical interrelationships between and among philosophical problems. Suppose, for example, that on the problem of freedom and authority (Chapters 49–53) I adopt the natural-law theory. Then I cannot—if I am to be consistent—accept empiricism, for this would exclude the possibility of having any knowledge of natural law (in the sense intended by the defenders of the natural-law theory). Hence, I must be a rationalist. And if I am a rationalist, then certain options are open to me on other philosophical problems—intuitionism in metaethics (Chapter 45), a belief in the possibility of proving the existence of God (Chapters 16–21), and so forth—that would not otherwise be open to me. If, on the other hand, I decide that on the rationalist-empiricist question I must take my stand on empiricism, then I am obliged to reject those views on other problems that presuppose a kind of knowledge that as an empiricist I cannot acknowledge to be possible. Every position that we adopt on any particular question implies certain positions and excludes certain positions on countless other questions. This is what we meant in Chapter 3 when we spoke about the systematic character of all philosophical thinking and the multidimensional relevance of all philosophical questions.

To the extent that we engage seriously and honestly in the study of philosophy, we become involved in what might be called a systematic clarification of our world-view and a systematic testing of this world-view by means of a rigorous evaluation of certain of its elements. There is more at stake in the answer that we give to this or that philosophical problem than the resolution of that particular problem. Indeed, as we remarked earlier, every philosophical problem is a kind of test case for an entire world-view. The serious study of philosophy thus requires great intellectual courage.

World-Views

At the center of every world-view is what might be called the "touchstone proposition" of that world-view, a proposition that is held to be *the* fundamental truth about reality and serves as a criterion to determine which other propositions may or may not count as candidates for belief. If a given proposition P is seen to be inconsistent with the touchstone proposition of one's world-view, then so long as one holds that world-view, proposition P must be regarded as false.

One important feature of a world-view, then, is that it serves as an intellectual framework for all attempts at understanding. So long as one experiences nothing that cannot be satisfactorily accounted for within one's world-view, one will presumably continue to hold it without question. If, however, one is confronted with some phenomenon that cannot be thus assimilated—if reality gives the lie to the world-view one has espoused—then one has no honest choice but to modify one's world-view in such a way as to allow for the troublesome new fact.

Suppose, now, that the holder of a certain world-view encounters some fact that he cannot incorporate into it, and suppose further that he is unable to think of any way in which he can modify his world-view to accommodate the new fact. What are his options? He may retain his world-view and acknowledge that he has an unresolved problem on his hands, or he may abandon his world-view altogether in favor of another that appears to him to be more adequate to the facts as he perceives them.

Alternative World-Views

There is, of course, no theoretical limit to the number of world-views that might be developed; the world as we experience it is a sufficiently complicated affair to support (with varying degrees of plausibility) a rather wide variety of them. Therefore, we cannot hope to be exhaustive in our classification of alternative world-views. At best, we can list the types that are regarded as the major options by most educated and informed people at the present time.

Ethical theism is probably the most widely held world-view in the Western world, though it has undoubtedly lost some ground in the modern era. The touchstone proposition of ethical theism might be stated thus: *God, who is infinitely good, wise, and powerful, is the creator and sustainer of everything that exists, and man is the crown of His creation.* One form of this world-view is presented in Chapter 55.

In contrast to ethical theism and in perpetual conflict with it stands *naturalism.* The touchstone proposition of naturalism might be stated as follows: *The primary constituents of reality are material entities whose internal structures and external relations determine absolutely everything that happens in the world.* This world-view is further elaborated and defended in Chapter 56.

Some philosophers who have wrestled with the problem of world-views have found themselves unable to accept either ethical theism or naturalism and have adopted instead a world-view called *transcendentalism.* Its touchstone proposition is difficult to state with precision, but a fair approximation would be as follows: *There are dimensions of reality that are not a part of this spatiotemporal world that we perceive with our five senses* (that is, there are dimensions of reality that "transcend" the natural world), *and these transcendent dimensions of reality impinge upon man and his world in a variety of ways.* A world-view of this type is set forth in Chapter 57.

The fourth and last type of world-view that we shall consider is *humanism,* which differs from the three world-views previously mentioned in that it is, so to speak, less global. The touchstone proposition of humanism might be stated thus: *Whatever may be the whole truth about nature, man, and God (if He exists), man at least is unique and not merely a part of nature.* Humanism says, in effect, "Whatever view of the whole you choose to adopt, I insist that you preserve the dignity of man." Such a view is further elaborated and defended in Chapter 58.

It is evident that these four types of world-views cannot be construed as straightforward alternative answers to a single substantive question, since, as a matter of fact, they are not even mutually exclusive. Humanism, for example, could ally itself with any of the other three world-views, and has in fact done so in the thought of many philosophers. Blaise Pascal, for example, could be described as a theistic humanist, Jean Paul Sartre as a naturalistic humanist, and Paul Tillich as a transcendentalistic humanist. World-views may be more or less comprehensive and may be worked out in greater or lesser detail: what they have in common is that they are organized around some truth claim that the holders of the respective world-views take to be *the* fundamental truth about reality. A world-view is a basic intellectual stance, a way of trying to comprehend the totality of things.

Arguments About World-Views

How can anyone argue for or against—or even think intelligently about—a world-view? What kinds of arguments can reasonably be brought forward to support the claim that this world-view is right, or that one wrong? The answer is that in discussing the preceding problems, we have already been arguing for and against various world-views. Insofar as a given philosophical problem is logically related to the world-views question, any argument that arises in the course of the discussion of that problem is thereby a discussion of world-views as well. Indeed, confrontations between the proponents of conflicting world-views most commonly occur, not in the direct and overt way that we shall observe in the chapters that follow, but rather as disagreements over subordinate issues on which they find themselves obliged to differ by virtue of their basic philosophical commitments.

If, however, the world-views question is explicitly under discussion, several kinds of arguments are open to the disputants. First, the advocate of a given world-view may appeal to certain facts or alleged facts that in his opinion favor his view. The range of facts to which appeal may be made in the discussion of this question is, of course, extremely broad. Second, a participant in this debate may "go on the attack" and attempt to show that the views of his opponents are inadequate. A world-view may be attacked in either of two ways: on grounds of *internal inconsistency* or on grounds of *factual error*. And third, a holder of a particular world-view may present rebuttal arguments (after attack or in recognition of points vulnerable to attack) to show that his view is not internally inconsistent or not guilty of factual error in the ways alleged.

These are the principal ways in which arguments may be employed in discussions about world-views. Let us see what kind of case can be made for each of the world-views enumerated above.

STUDY QUESTIONS

1. List the philosophical problems that you have studied thus far, and the positions that you have been inclined to take on each. Do you see any inconsistencies in the positions you have taken? Do you see any instances where your position on one problem logically compels you to adopt a certain position on some other problem?
2. List the positions that you have adopted on the problems studied thus far in order of decreasing certainty. (At the top of your list will be the position about which you feel most certain, at the bottom the position about which you feel least certain.) Assume that the position you have listed as "most certain" is correct. What implications does this have for the remaining positions on your list?
3. What exactly is a world-view? Does everybody have one?
4. How would you describe the world-view that you were given as a child? What, for example, would you say is the touchstone proposition of that world-view? How, if at all, has that world-view been modified to date?

55

ETHICAL THEISM

Most of my readers are no doubt aware that as an ethical theist I speak for one of the oldest and most widely held world-views. Indeed, ethical theism is more than a world-view: it is an attitude toward life, a sense of man's place in the scheme of things that is felt as well as thought. Many of the values that Western thought prizes most highly—the dignity of man, the sacredness of human life, the significance of the individual, the meaningfulness of history—derive from this world-view and may be incapable of surviving apart from it. The question of the validity of this world-view is therefore of great importance.

The Fuller View

Let me begin by sketching in some of the details of this world-view. God exists. This is the fundamental truth from which all thought about reality should begin. I may or may not be able to prove God's existence—but God exists. My understanding of God's true nature may be ever so fragmentary—but God exists. I may be puzzled about the ontological status of the physical world, or about the nature of the self, or about many other things—but God exists. His existence is the elemental fact, the foundational truth from which thought begins and to which it must return whenever we are driven to inspect once again the foundations of the edifice of truth. God exists.

Everything else that exists—inanimate matter, life in all its forms, consciousness, intelligence, everything—has been created by God and is dependent on Him for its continued existence. I of course do not know the manner of God's creation. I do not know, for example, whether the "big bang" that apparently occurred some ten billion or so years ago should be understood as "the moment of creation," or whether it is even correct to think of the original creation as an event that occurred at some moment in time. My point is simply that everything that we now see existing has its ground and origin in God: if He did not exist, nothing would exist.

God, having created this world that we perceive and of which we are a part, continues to love it and to care for it. The process of evolution, for example, despite the appearance of randomness, is in reality one of the arenas in which the marvelous creative activity of God may be discerned. The course of human history, notwithstanding the suffering and tragedy that are so inextricably a part of it, is not merely the story of man's halting efforts to emerge from the jungle and the cave: it is the story of God gently luring His human children toward a future in which His creation will achieve a richness that we cannot yet imagine.

Man, moreover, is in some sense the most glorious product of God's creation. That there should be anything at all—that matter should exist—is truly marvelous. That there should be life, organisms capable of nourishing and reproducing themselves, is more marvelous still. And that there should evolve out of these materials organisms that are conscious, organisms that are aware that they are, is a wonder almost beyond comprehension. But beyond even this, consider that among these conscious creatures one has emerged with a capacity for rational thought, speech, science, an appreciation for beauty, and a sense of right and wrong. Whatever may be in store for God's creation beyond this point, surely it is clear that it is through man that it will be accomplished.

Philosophical Implications

My theistic commitment provides the basic context within which I approach all philosophical problems. It also gives me a particular bias that makes certain philosophical positions very attractive to me because they fit in so nicely with my theistic world-view. I make no apology for this, however, since those who hold other world-views are biased toward the philosophical opinions that favor their world-views. We cannot avoid looking at the world through world-view–colored glasses.

On the question of freedom and authority, for example, I am persuaded that some form of the natural-law theory is correct. To me it seems virtually self-evident that if man was to rise above the law of the jungle, he had to grasp and cherish the concept of a human community ruled by just and humane laws. It seems altogether natural that God should desire the human species to achieve such a community and should have guided the evolution of man in such a way that man would at length begin to discern the outlines of a law (already conceptualized in the mind of God) by which community might be achieved. The question of freedom and authority must of course be decided on the merits of the arguments for the alternative answers that may be given. My point is merely that within the context of my world-view one of those answers is especially attractive, though I could adopt some other view without in any way violating my basic philosophical commitments.

Since space does not permit me to discuss in detail my position on all the problems raised in preceding sections, I shall have to be content merely to list my preferences. They are as follows:

Philosophical Problem	Preferences of an Ethical Theist
A priori knowledge	Rationalism
Ontological status of the physical world	Direct realism
Existence of God	Endorse cosmological argument
Problem of evil	Exoneration of God
Religious language	Analogical theory
Mind and body	Dualism
Freedom and determinism	Soft determinism
Man's highest good	Theological eudemonism
Language of morals	Intuitionism
Freedom and authority	Natural-law theory

Please note that my theistic world-view in no way obligates me to adopt these positions. Indeed, part of the attraction of theism is that it is an extremely "open" world-view: a theist could, for example, be a hedonist in ethics, an empiricist in epistemology, and a phenomenalist with regard to the ontological status of the physical world. A naturalist, on the other hand, could not hold many of the views included in my list. Thus, far from shackling thought (as some people seem to think it does), theism actually enables consideration of alternatives that other world-views will not allow.

There is, in fact, not a single position among all those surveyed in the preceding pages that I am *compelled* to adopt by virtue of the fact that I am a theist. Furthermore, among all those discussed, the only position that I am *excluded* from adopting by virtue of the fact that I am a theist is the one presented in Chapter 20—and that for the obvious reason that it denies the existence of God.

Why I Am a Theist

That theism maximizes a person's philosophical options does not, of course, constitute any kind of a proof that theism is true. What, then, can be said in support of this world-view? Why am I a theist? In dealing with this question, I do not wish to reopen the discussion of proofs for the existence of God. The question before us now concerns not the grounds for believing that God exists but, rather, the broader question of the reasons why we ought to adopt a theistic world-view.

I hold, of course, that theism is adequate as a world-view in the sense that there are no facts that contradict it, no phenomena that cannot be explained within its context. Thus when I cite certain facts, I am directing attention to them merely because in my opinion they *uniquely* favor the theistic view. I would urge my readers to look very carefully at the accounts that the representatives of other world-views are forced to give of these same facts.

Theism provides the most plausible answer to the question, Why is there something and not nothing? That this particular object exists—a chair, let us say—is satisfactorily accounted for by the statement that it was made by a chair-maker. The existence of the wood out of which the chair was made is in turn explained by the laws governing the growth of trees (osmosis, photosynthesis, etc.) until at length what began as a tiny acorn has developed into a mature oak. But the elements that became a part of the oak (and eventually a part of the chair)—why should these exist? Or, given the fact that they exist in this moment, why do they not cease to exist in the next? Why does anything at all exist? According to theism, God created it and sustains it in being moment by moment. Only in the belief that God exists do I find an adequate answer to this inescapable question.

Consider next the place of man in the scheme of things. When I compare the endowments of man with those of any other creature, I cannot avoid the conclusion that man is not merely a species of animal, not merely a part of nature: by virtue of his capacity for rational thought, for language, for morality, and for the appreciation of beauty, man rises above nature. Say, if you will, that man is merely the winner of the grand prize in the evolutionary sweepstakes: I say that this was no accident and that the aspirations that characterize the spiritual life of this most fortunate creature point toward a destiny that lies beyond the confines of this life. Theism enables us to believe that these hunches about the nature and destiny of man are true, for it depicts man as the favorite of God's creatures, the crown of His creation.

Our intuitive sense of the seriousness of good and evil lends further support to the theistic view. I cannot take absolutely seriously a moral law that is nothing more than an expression of my private tastes, or those of my social subgroup, or of my nation, or even of the majority of mankind. The moral imperative, the injunction to do good and shun evil, is an infinitely serious matter. The seriousness of the moral law is satisfactorily accounted for only on the hypothesis that it is ultimately grounded in the will of God.

Finally, I am convinced that an acceptable philosophy of history cannot be developed apart from a theistic world-view. What is the meaning of the struggles, the suffering, the tragedy with which the pages of human history are so distressingly replete? Toward what eventual goal is the story of mankind tending? How can a person believe that his life, his tiny contribution to the common life, has any significance?

Within the context of some world-views, the answers to these questions are all too obvious: no meaning, no goal, no significance. Ethical theism, on the contrary, asserts that history is a meaningful process through which God is patiently and lovingly working out His purposes for His creation. Every moment of a person's life, every good or evil thought or word or deed, makes some contribution to the totality of events that constitute human history. Where this history is tending, or what will be the next significant milestone on the path toward that unknown goal, we do not know. But theists believe, nonetheless, that history is moving toward some *télos* and that its progress toward that goal is being guided by God, Who will not abandon the creation that He loves.

There is in the heart of every individual, as Alfred North Whitehead once observed, an "insistent craving that zest for existence be refreshed by the ever-present, unfading importance of our immediate actions." [1] In the views that it enables us to take of man, morality, and human history, theism answers to this craving in the heart of man. The facts that most strongly support the theistic world-view are the specifically "human" facts—the facts about man by virtue of which he is able to aspire to a life and a destiny appropriate only for one who is a child of God. Man is most truly man when he understands himself in this way; apart from theism, man is swallowed up in the system of nature and becomes nothing more than the most fortunate of the beasts.

STUDY QUESTIONS

1. Summarize the basic tenets of ethical theism as expounded in this chapter.
2. Can Ethical Theist consistently hold all the positions he lists on page 390? Is he logically compelled to adopt any of these positions simply by virtue of being a theist?
3. Theist claims that the only position presented in the earlier portions of this book that he is *excluded* from adopting by virtue of being a theist is the "naturalistic rejoinder" of Chapter 20. Is he correct about this?
4. Summarize the arguments offered by Theist in support of his world-view. Which do you find most persuasive? Which least persuasive?

---

[1] Alfred North Whitehead, *Process and Reality* (New York: Harper & Row, 1960), p. 533.

56

NATURALISM

A world-view, in order to be judged acceptable, must meet three conditions. First, it must be *logically coherent:* it must be free of internal logical inconsistencies. Second, it must be *relevant:* it must provide a plausible interpretive scheme in terms of which at least some facts of our experience can be understood. And third, it must be *adequate to the known facts:* there must be no single fact or realm of facts that cannot be accounted for within the context of the proposed view. Every time a world-view is put forward for consideration it is implicitly claimed that the proffered view meets these three conditions.

I admit that it is extraordinarily difficult to develop a view that simultaneously meets all three conditions. Theism, for example, despite its attractive (and, to man, highly flattering) account of morality and history, has always had to struggle—unsuccessfully, in my opinion—to maintain some semblance of logical coherence. The most dramatic illustration of this is theism's notorious failure to solve the problem of evil. Anyone who is not an apologist for theism can see that the fact that there is evil in the world is not consistent with the hypothesis that this world is the product of a creator who is perfect in goodness, power, and wisdom (see Chapter 24). Try as they will, the apologists for theism cannot account for the occurrence of evil in a way that is consistent with their world-view. All the theodicies that have been written, all the arguments that have been so laboriously woven, have failed to meet the basic issue: if God is perfect in goodness, knowledge, and power, and is the sole creator of this world, then there cannot be evil in the world; if there is evil in the world (and who can deny it?), then this world is not the product of a God who is perfect in goodness, knowledge, and power.

It is not my intention, however, to develop a systematic critique of theism. I want instead to describe *naturalism* as an alternative world-view and to indicate the most compelling reasons for adopting this view. It has been my observation that on the question of world-views people are seldom persuaded by arguments as such: rather, they become bothered by the problem, wrestle with it for a while, perhaps leave it, and one day return to discover that some place along the way they have abandoned one view for another that is more coherent, relevant, and adequate.

A Brief Description

Naturalism asserts, first of all, that the primary constituents of reality are material entities. By this I do not mean that only material entities exist; I am not denying the reality—the real existence—of such things as hopes, plans, behavior, language, logical inferences, and so on. What I am asserting, however, is that anything that is real is, in the last analysis, explicable as a material entity or as a form or function or action of a material entity. Theism says, "In the beginning, God"; naturalism says, "In the beginning, matter." If the theoretical goal of science—an absolutely exhaustive knowledge of the natural world—were to be achieved, there would remain no reality of any other kind about which we might still be ignorant. The "ultimate realities," according to naturalism, are not the alleged objects of the inquiries of theologians; they are the entities that are the objects of investigation by chemists, physicists, and other scientists. To put the matter very simply: materialism is true.

Naturalism asserts, second, that what happens in the world is theoretically explicable without residue in terms of the internal structures and the external relations of these material entities. The world is, to use a very inadequate metaphor, like a gigantic machine whose parts are so numerous and whose processes are so complex that we have thus far been able to achieve only a very partial and fragmentary understanding of how it works. In principle, however, everything that occurs is ultimately explicable in terms of the properties and relations of the particles of which matter is composed. Once again the point may be stated simply: determinism is true.

It follows from what I have said that the categories of space and time are categories of great importance for naturalism, are, in fact, ontological categories. If you cannot locate something in space and time, or if you cannot understand it as a form or function of some entity or entities located in space and time, then you simply cannot say anything intelligible about it. *To be is to be some place, some time.*

Naturalism, therefore, denies the existence of any real entities corresponding to such concepts as God, angel, devil, spirit, or soul (as these concepts are usually understood), because they are asserted by those who affirm their existence to be nonmaterial subjects of activities such as deciding, regretting, suffering, and so forth. But from the point of view of naturalism, any activity must ultimately be understood as a process involving material entities and occurring within space and time. Since the above concepts cannot be understood in this way, naturalism must regard them as bogus concepts that purport to denote some real entities but in fact denote nothing at all.

Unacceptable Philosophical Theories

From the point of view of naturalism, several of the philosophical theories put forward in earlier sections of this book must be judged unacceptable. This does not mean, of course, that a naturalist simply "rules out" these theories in advance. It means, on the contrary, that he attends with special care to the arguments put forward in support of these theories, for he knows that his world-view is at stake in the argument. Naturalism is secure as a world hypothesis precisely because it has had to defend itself—and has done so successfully—on very many vital points. Anyone who has grasped the "vision of the whole" that naturalism espouses will readily understand that a consistent naturalism must in the end reject the following philosophical positions:

Philosophical Problem	Positions Unacceptable to Naturalism
A priori knowledge	Rationalism
Ontological status of the physical world	Direct realism
Existence of God	Any position implying belief in God's existence
Problem of evil	Exoneration of God
Religious language	Analogical or symbolic theories
Mind and body	Dualism, panpsychism
Freedom and determinism	Libertarianism
Man's highest good	Theological eudemonism
Language of morals	Intuitionism
Freedom and authority	Natural-law or social-contract theories

Anyone who wishes to hold the world-view that I represent must be prepared to refute the arguments put forward in support of these theories. As a naturalist I am of course convinced that every such argument can be convincingly refuted.

Why Naturalism?

Naturalists cannot point to certain facts about the world and say, "These facts *uniquely* favor the naturalist world-view." Our claim is that *all* the known facts support the naturalist account of the world and that no facts warrant our asserting more than this. The evidence justifies our asserting that material entities exist and are involved in numerous processes that together give us the world as we encounter it in ordinary perception and scientific inquiry. But the evidence does not justify the assertion that any entities or processes exist other than material entities and the processes in which they participate. Naturalism is simply the modest claim that a generalized account of the world in terms of material entities and spatiotemporal processes is adequate to the known facts and will be adequate to explain any facts still to be discovered in the future.

Let me illustrate my point with a single example. The question, What causes the noise in the heavens that we call thunder? could lead to any number of explanatory hypotheses. One might be that the gods are angry and are having a fight. Another might be that God is scolding one of His angels. And yet another is that air is expanding rapidly as a result of being heated by a sudden discharge of electricity (lightning). The expansion-of-air hypothesis is, of course, a "naturalistic" explanation. It is more modest than the other two in that it does not require us to posit unobserved entities (God, gods, angels). It is, therefore, the *kind* of explanation that naturalism claims is possible in principle for all phenomena. Naturalism is simply the generalization of this explanatory model. "What can be explained by the assumption of fewer things is vainly explained by the assumption of more things" (William of Ockham).

In order to support the naturalist position, then, it is not necessary to construct independent arguments that supposedly "prove" naturalism to be true. It is necessary only to show that the phenomena that lead some thinkers to posit immaterial entities can be satisfactorily explained in a way that is consistent with naturalism. The only intelligent way to deal with people who make unwarranted assertions is to show that those assertions are indeed unwarranted. Let us look, then, at the considerations that have been advanced in support of a theistic world-view.

It is not true that theism has an answer to the question, Why is there something and not nothing? whereas naturalism does not. The truth is that *no* world-view is able to answer this question. All that theism does is move the question back one stage; to the question, Why does *God* exist? it has no answer. When we are dealing with the question of ultimate origins, we are forced to acknowledge that we have reached one of the boundaries of human knowledge. The only honest answer that we can give to the question, Why is there something and not nothing? is that we do not know. It adds nothing to our knowledge to pretend that by uttering the word "God" we have answered this unanswerable question.

Nor is it the case that naturalism is in any way demeaning to man, as our critics frequently suggest. I am sure that I am no less impressed than is Theist with the marvelous complexity of man and with the immeasurable richness of experience that is possible for him by virtue of his capacity for rational thought, language, morality, and the appreciation of beauty. How does asserting that man "rises above nature" add to this description? Why must I posit a divine "cheater" at the evolutionary gaming table in order to be properly appreciative of man's unique endowments? The evidence warrants the belief that life emerged from lifeless matter on this planet some millions of years ago and that the various forms of life we now observe have evolved from earlier forms by means of processes that we understand reasonably well. The hypothesis of "God's love" or "God's plan" adds no more to this account than the hypothesis of "God's anger" adds to the account of thunder.

All that the evidence warrants us in asserting about man's place in the scheme of things is that human life as we know it is "an episode between two oblivions." [1] Man emerged as one of the products of natural processes operating upon lifeless matter under conditions that made his emergence possible; there is every reason to believe that some day he will cease to exist when these conditions no longer obtain. In the meantime we have the task of making our life together on this planet as rich and meaningful as possible. Although naturalists can offer no divine forgiveness for the acts and omissions born of human frailty, and no future paradise for either the few or the many, we are no less concerned than our nonnaturalist fellows with the quality of life here and now. Indeed, since we know of no paradise apart from such approximations as we are able to achieve by our own efforts, we might even make some claim to being more deeply concerned about the human enterprise than are some who do not share our views. The rejection of a divine plan for man, the refusal to acknowledge eternal values in the affairs of man, in no way prohibits a tender concern for *human* plans, *human* values, and such *human* good as we are able to achieve in a universe that wills us neither good nor ill.

Where, Theist asks, is history tending? The answer is that it is tending ultimately toward the extinction of all life on this planet—not necessarily because of what men may do but because in the long-range evolution of the cosmos it appears inevitable that the conditions necessary for life on this planet will eventually cease to exist. For the next several millions of years, however, the history of the human race will be whatever we make it. We are the masters of our fate, the makers of our own history. The meaning of that history will be whatever meaning we give to it. Nothing is added to our understanding of history by positing a God-ordained *telos* in which all of the problems with which we must contend at present will finally be resolved.

Man is indeed, to use Theist's phrase, "the winner of the grand prize in the evolutionary sweepstakes." His unique endowments have enabled him, in a very short time relative to the life of the planet, to emerge from

[1] Ernest Nagel, *Logic Without Metaphysics* (New York: Free Press of Glencoe, 1956), p. 14.

a beastlike existence into one that is infinitely rich both in its present qualities and in its potential for further improvement. If some choose to turn their backs upon the challenges and the opportunities of this life in quest of an imaginary kingdom of God, that is their privilege. The available evidence warrants only a belief in the reality of this material world of which we are undeniably a part. The tasks that are set for us by our situation in the world are those inherent in the human enterprise. They are tasks of sufficient magnitude and sufficient difficulty to keep us all occupied for many generations to come, and with this we must be content.

STUDY QUESTIONS

1. Naturalist asserts that an acceptable world-view must meet three conditions. What are they? Do you agree that these are the criteria to be used in judging a world-view?
2. Is the problem of evil a serious problem for theists? How might a theist defend his position against Naturalist's charge that this problem represents an internal inconsistency that is fatal theism?
3. Summarize the basic tenets of naturalism as they are presented in this chapter.
4. Naturalist presents a rather formidable list of philosophical positions that he says are inconsistent with naturalism. Identify the positions on this list with which you are acquainted, and explain in each case why that position is unacceptable to a naturalist.
5. "In order to support the naturalist position, then, it is not necessary to construct independent arguments that supposedly 'prove' naturalism to be true. It is necessary only to show that the phenomena that lead some thinkers to posit immaterial entities can be satisfactorily explained in a way that is consistent with naturalism." Is this correct? Could the holder of some other world-view reasonably make a parallel claim?

57

TRANSCENDENTALISM

Many readers of the preceding two chapters will, I suspect, find themselves in the following dilemma. On the one hand, they cannot honestly embrace the naïve supernaturalism offered by Theist as the key to an adequate world-view. On the other hand, they cannot escape the conviction that there is something more to human existence than Naturalist's account will allow. I propose to present an alternative view in which what is valid in both of these views can be retained.

Critique of Naturalism and Supernaturalism

Theist has presented a picture of a two-story universe, one part of which is perceivable by us and the other part of which is not. In the unseen part dwells God, who created the world at some moment in time and who continues to love and care for it. Indeed, He presumably interferes with its orderly operation from time to time (miracles), since He is said to have managed the evolutionary process in such a way that things turned out the way they did and since He is also said to be guiding history toward some télos known only to Him. It is also consistent with this world-view to hold (as does Theist) that this God has made provision for the eternal happiness of at least some of His human children.

It is apparent from Theist's arguments that he is chiefly concerned about what might be called the dignity of man, or better, the seriousness of human life. Theist cannot tolerate the view that man is merely "the most fortunate of the beasts," one species among many that have emerged in the evolutionary process. He seeks, therefore, to dignify man by making him the favorite child of a divine Creator and by placing him into a historical process that is being guided toward some good end by this same Creator.

The chief difficulty with this view, however, is that, as Naturalist would say, the evidence does not warrant these beliefs. Natural processes are not interrupted from time to time by divine tinkering, nor is it credible that somewhere out in space—perhaps beyond our solar system—God, like a rich uncle in Australia, is watching the affairs of the world and doing what must be done to ensure that history moves in the desired direction. If we are required to choose between this view and naturalism, then intellectual honesty requires that we choose the naturalist view.

But naturalism is a bitter pill to swallow precisely because it does not take sufficiently seriously the hunger for meaning and the quest for human dignity that theism at least attempts to satisfy. Naturalism depicts man merely as an exceedingly complex physical organism, a unique animal whose artistic, technological, and cultural creations are as much the products of nature as beaver dams, ant hills, and the nests of birds. The world that Naturalist depicts for us is beautiful in its orderliness and in its potentially perfect intelligibility—but its orderliness and intelligibility are purchased at the high price of banishing from the world those dimensions of reality that give significance to human life. Faced with the human consequences of such a view, we withdraw in horror and consider the possibility that our rejection of theism may have been a bit too hasty.

Nevertheless, no world-view could claim the large number of adherents that both theism and naturalism have won if there were not a very great quantity of truth in each of these views. Theism incorporates within itself some important and profound insights, some genuine truths about man and his world: that is why, despite the onslaught to which it has been subjected in the modern world, it has been able to maintain itself. Naturalism also contains within itself some extremely important elements of truth: that is why, despite the opposition of a firmly entrenched theism (in medieval Europe), it was able to make significant headway. The most important intellectual task of our times is that of creating a new synthesis in which the truth that is implicit in theism and the truth that is implicit in naturalism can be comprehended in one all-embracing vision of the whole. *Transcendentalism* claims to be that synthesis.

The Transcendentalist Vision

The fundamental insight of naturalism, without which no world-view can ever be accounted adequate, is that in the attempt to know reality we must be completely honest in the face of the brute facts. The naturalist world-view was born in a kind of revolt against what was regarded as the "arid intellectualism" of the prevailing world-view (theism). Galileo's opponents could muster all kinds of reasons to show why the world ought to be the way they said it is: Galileo swept these reasons aside not by creating superior *arguments* but by appealing to the *facts*. Respect for the facts has become a part of the mentality of modern man. Insofar as naturalism stands for humility before the facts, it stands for truth.

Where, then, does naturalism go wrong? It goes wrong in assuming—indeed, in defiantly insisting—that these brute facts must be assimilated into a mechanistic, deterministic scheme in which there is no place for values, no place for purposes, and really no place for sentience and rationality. Naturalism appears to be haunted by the ghost of the Inquisition: it cannot forget that men who claimed to be God's representatives forced a man (Galileo), who was trying only to be honest before the facts, to say that he had abandoned the beliefs that he was driven by the facts to adopt. But it is not only God and His angels that are banished from the naturalist universe: human consciousness as an agent in the world is banished as well. The scientist who is also a philosophical naturalist is in the position of claiming to know so much about the world that he knows that his very act of knowing is merely a complex physical process involving the material entities of which his brain happens to be composed—and nothing else.

Transcendentalism affirms, on the contrary, that there is a dimension of *depth* in everything that exists, that the complete reality of the world is not apparent on the surface of things. Consider yourself. You are, of course, a collocation of atoms and molecules—material entities—that are governed by certain laws. Like every physical object, you have a certain weight, a certain size, a certain shape, a certain specific gravity, a certain temperature, and so on. You are also an animal organism: you are capable of nourishing yourself by assimilating nutrients from your environment, you are capable of locomotion, and so on. But you know that you are more than this: you are also a mind, a consciousness. Your being as a physical entity and as an organism is illuminated, so to speak, by the spirit that is within you, by the consciousness that you *are*. Deep within you, at a level of yourself that the objective observer cannot fathom, you are the bearer of hopes, fears, dreams, and aspirations that are as much a part of the reality that is you as your height, your weight, your blood pressure, and whatever other "surface facts" anyone may care to mention. It is not without reason that the technique by which modern physicians of the soul seek to penetrate this dimension of the self is called "depth psychology."

What is true of us individually is true also of our collective life as a human community. There are, to be sure, "surface" elements in the history of any era: there are natural occurrences, fortuitous events, influential personalities, and numerous other kinds of "historical facts" to which historians of any age can point with good empirical consciences. But there is also a depth to history, a dimension of meaning that lies beneath and behind the simple facts. Surely it is significant that we commonly use metaphors of deep water when we speak of history:

we speak of the "currents" of history, the "tides" of history. We know that what appears on the surface is but the troubled water of a deep and lasting movement beneath the surface, in the depth of our common life.

Transcendentalism affirms that there is also a dimension of depth in things and asks us to consider things with regard to that dimension. Everything that exists is more than it appears to be, even as we ourselves and the historical events in which we participate are more than we and they appear to be. Every finite thing points beyond itself to that which is infinite, unconditioned, inexhaustible. That, in a word, is what transcendentalism means.

The depth of our life and of our world is the source and ground of nearly everything that is most meaningful to us. If we believe, for example, in the true dignity and equality of man, if we believe that the struggle toward dignity and equality is one of the deep tides of the history of our times, then we are affirming convictions that have been nurtured not on the surface but in the depth of our souls and in the depth of the history of our times. And if we believe these things so passionately that we are willing to risk our own convenience and perhaps our own safety in order to further this goal, and if in the process we find that our lives are somehow enriched by those very experiences that externally considered must be described as instances of inconvenience or suffering, then we are demonstrating—at least to ourselves—that we are living in the strength of that depth whose very reality naturalism refuses to acknowledge.

The Truth in Theism

Theism knows that there is a depth in life, in history, and in the world, but it attempts to give expression to this by means of a conceptual scheme that has become ludicrous to most of us. "God" is the religious name for this depth: that is what the word "God" really means. But since it is impossible to use "God" without conjuring up the image of a celestial superman who oversees the affairs of the world in some mysterious way, perhaps it is best not to speak of God but to speak instead of this depth to which theism, in its inner meaning, is attempting to point the way.

Theism knows, too, of that union of the self with the deeper self that we experience when we become committed to a cause that transcends our own selfish interests—when we devote our efforts to the achievement of values that emerge from the depth of our selves and of our history. The religious term for this union of the self with the deeper self is "salvation." But since it is impossible to use this term without suggesting an imagined future blissful existence rather than a quality of life here and now, perhaps it is better that we also do not speak of salvation and speak instead about the recovery of meaning, the rediscovery of our depth, or the wholeness that we experience in the act of dedicating ourselves to a cause in which we deeply believe.

Some Philosophical Implications

If we take seriously the dimension of depth in man's life and in the world, certain implications follow with respect to a wide variety of philosophical problems. In the realm of ethics, for example, a transcendentalist holds that moral imperatives emerge from the depths of our souls and of our common life—that they are, in fact, imperatives that stand over us as laws only because and insofar as we are estranged from our own depth. The natural law to which natural-law theorists point and the intuited good to which intuitionists point are not strange entities floating aimlessly about in a kind of metaphysical nonspace, waiting to be "intuited" by the discerning mind: they are the voice of our own depth, the law of our own being, in obedience to which we find the wholeness that forever eludes us on the surface of our lives. There are, indeed, many intrinsic goods, but they are all grounded in that depth without which our lives would be pitifully shallow.

Space does not permit a detailed review of all the problems discussed in earlier sections or of my reasons for adopting certain positions on those problems. Very briefly, then, let me simply state that I am a libertarian with respect to the problem of freedom and determinism, a dualist with respect to the mind-body problem, a rationalist in my epistemology, a direct realist in my view of the ontological status of the physical world, a "sympathetic appraiser" (Chapter 21) in my view of the arguments for the existence of God, and a symbolist (Chapter 29) in my theory of religious language. I do not say that consistency *requires* me as a transcendentalist to hold these particular views on these problems. I do say, however, that on the basis of an independent consideration of the arguments I find these to be the most plausible positions to adopt with respect to these questions, and I say further that they are views that as a transcendentalist I find very attractive. Indeed, the chief considerations that may be offered in support of the transcendentalist world-view are precisely those considerations that tend to establish the views stated above.

Let me conclude by making a terminological proposal. "Transcendentalism" is a generic term: it denotes not only the world-view that I represent but many others more or less similar to mine. In order to distinguish my view from others that might with equal appropriateness be called "transcendentalist," I propose calling the world-view I have presented *depth naturalism*. That name represents my position exactly: I want to take absolutely seriously the important truths for which naturalism stands, but I want also to go beyond this to a recovery of that infinite depth without which life becomes shallow and devoid of meaning.

STUDY QUESTIONS

1. What does Transcendentalist find unacceptable about theism? about naturalism? Do you agree with his objections? How might Theist or Naturalist defend their respective positions against these objections?

2. Transcendentalist presents (p. 401) a theory of the self that is, he says, unacceptable to a naturalist. Is it? And is it, in your view, a plausible theory?

3. "But there is also a depth to history, a dimension of meaning that lies beneath and behind the simple facts." What does this mean? What do you think of this claim?

4. Transcendentalist lists a number of philosophical positions (libertarianism, rationalism, dualism, and so forth) which, he says, are especially attractive to him as a transcendentalist. What connections, if any, do you see between his commitment to transcendentalism and his espousal of each of these positions?

5. Transcendentalist proposes that his particular version of transcendentalism be called "depth naturalism." Does this seem to you to be an appropriate name for the world-view he has described? Defend your answer.

58

HUMANISM

A world-view is a way of trying to comprehend in one all-inclusive concept everything that we know and believe about the universe and man's place in it. There is a wonderful grandeur in the very concept of a world-view. Every such view is a monument to man's hunger for knowledge and security. I agree with the sentiment expressed by W. P. Montague:

> The distinctive glory of the human mind is its power to detach itself, not only from the *here* and *now* but from the *there* and *then* of existence, and bathe its tired memories in ideal waters. So it is that the great visions of philosophy, even if considered merely as visions, are precious and imperishable possessions of our culture.[1]

Theism, naturalism, and transcendentalism are some of the intellectual homes that men have constructed, sanctuaries within which they seek to escape the madness of the endless pluralism of experience. To some people they have not proved to be satisfactory. We who are in this situation and who also have certain positive beliefs in common call ourselves humanists.

The first thing to understand about us humanists is that we are a miscellaneous lot. Some of us find our closest affinities with theists, others with naturalists, and yet others with transcendentalists. What we have in common is a vague dissatisfaction with all such world-views, including whichever one each of us individually may happen to favor, and a firm determination that human values and human potentialities shall not get swallowed up in a system that either takes no account of man or that makes of him something less than he truly is. You may recall

---

[1] William Pepperell Montague, *Great Visions of Philosophy* (LaSalle, Ill.: Open Court, 1950), p. 16.

that Socrates protested when he was on trial for his life, "But the simple truth is, O Athenians, that I have nothing to do with physical speculations." [2] I think Socrates meant that he did not have time to speculate about the "big picture": he was completely absorbed in the effort to understand himself, to understand human existence. That task seemed so important to him that he had to devote his full attention to it.

Socrates' attitude describes rather precisely the situation in which humanists find themselves today. Humanism is not a fourth world-view to set alongside the other three: it is rather a group of insights that must be incorporated into *any* world-view if that world-view is to be regarded as adequate. We stand for the dignity, the rights, and the freedom of man, and we are willing to get along with no world-view at all rather than allow man to be squeezed into the categories of a hypothesis that robs him of his humanity.

A Positive Description

Let me state somewhat more precisely the basic convictions upon which humanists are united in defense of human dignity. First, we believe that man is not completely subject to the physical laws that appear to govern material particles. Therefore, we are libertarians on the problem of freedom and determinism, and we are firm and consistent in our opposition to determinism, whether it be offered in a theistic form (as with Jonathan Edwards) or in a naturalistic form (as with most modern determinists). Man is free in a way that is not compatible with universal determinism.

It follows, therefore, that man is more than matter, more than a complex physical organism. "Mind," "soul," and "consciousness" denote real entities that make a difference in the world. Humanists, in spite of the well-known attendant difficulties, are for the most part dualists in their view of man (though some are panpsychists). The essential point is that man is not *merely* a material entity.

Man, moreover, is fittingly subject to no moral imperatives other than those he prescribes for himself. Man is answerable to man. Any law that man is counseled to obey that is not of his own making enslaves him and robs him of his dignity. For this reason we reject all versions of the natural-law theory and favor the concept of law advocated by social utilitarianism (Chapter 52).

It is important to the humanist view to assert that the future is to some extent open and undetermined, notwithstanding the extent to which the future is determined by natural and historical forces beyond man's control. Man is a maker of history, not merely its helpless victim. What man shall become in the future depends primarily on what man

---

[2] Plato, *Apology,* in *The Dialogues of Plato,* tr. B. Jowett (New York: Random House, 1937), vol. I, p. 403.

chooses to make of himself, not on what God or nature may have "programmed" him to become. William Ernest Henley (1849–1903) spoke for the entire race when he said, "I am the master of my fate, I am captain of my soul." [3]

With these convictions clearly in mind, it should not be difficult to see why humanists are unable to fully embrace any of the world-views presented thus far. Let us review them briefly.

Theism

From the point of view of humanism, the chief danger of theism is its implicit authoritarianism. If man is a creature of God, as theism asserts, then presumably he is as totally subject to the will of the Creator as is a pot to the potter: he has no capacity to stand up to the Power that made him and can as easily destroy him. Surely this is the view of the God-man relationship that we find, for example, in the story of the flood:

> When the Lord saw that man had done much evil on earth and that his thoughts and inclinations were always evil, he was sorry that he had made man on earth, and he was grieved at heart. He said, "This race of men whom I have created, I will wipe them off the face of the earth . . . I am sorry that I ever made them." [4]

That there are humanistic elements in theism is, of course, true. Theism in its Judeo-Christian form, for example, speaks of God not only as a wrathful and jealous deity before whom man must cower in fear, but also as the loving Father who cares deeply for His children and as the Good Shepherd who seeks and rescues lost sheep. But these elements, sad to say, have always been subordinate to the authoritarian elements in the theistic view. Historically, the Good Shepherd has been no match for the Grand Inquisitor.

There can be no doubt that theistic authoritarianism is destructive of man's humanity. In the intellectual sphere, for example, it tends to intimidate man in such a way that he is no longer free to follow an argument wherever it may lead, to seek the truth wherever it may be found. In the moral sphere, theism subjects man to an alien law: it requires ceremonies, rituals, and "good works" of various sorts that may or may not commend themselves to him as morally worthwhile. He is counseled to think of himself as a creature of little worth, a worm, a nothing. John Calvin expresses this exactly:

> We cannot think of ourselves as we ought to think without utterly despising everything that may be supposed an excellence in us. This humility is unfeigned submission of a mind overwhelmed with a weighty

---

[3] William Ernest Henley, "Invictus," in R. B. Inglis et al., *Adventures in English Literature* (New York: Harcourt, Brace, 1945), p. 726.

[4] Genesis 6:5–7.

sense of its own misery and poverty; for such is the uniform description of it in the word of God.[5]

In this view man is nothing, God is everything. Any good that man may hope to achieve he must beg from the Celestial Artisan, who in His sovereignty may or may not respond, as He sees fit. "Humility," "sin," "rebellion," "self-abasement"—these are among the most prominent words in the vocabulary of theism. And it is these words that chiefly define how man is taught to think of himself in the theistic system.

Naturalism

Man fares little better in the naturalistic system, however, than in the theistic. As Bertrand Russell wrote in a famous essay: "Brief and powerless is man's life; on him and all his race the slow, sure doom falls pitiless and dark. Blind to good and evil, reckless of destruction, omnipotent matter rolls on its relentless way."[6] In such a world, as Transcendentalist has rightly discerned, it is impossible to find a place for all those things that are most precious to man. In a world where "omnipotent matter rolls on its relentless way" and where mind is at best an impotent epiphenomenon of material processes, the loftiest ideals and the noblest aspirations of the human spirit appear to dissolve into nothingness. What is the status of honor, courage, and the passion for truth in a world where nothing exists but the elemental particles of which matter is composed? How can man abide a world that makes a mockery of his conviction that he is before everything else a conscious agent in the world, a being capable of doing deeds of worth and nobility?

Nor is it only the materialism of the naturalist view that is offensive to humanism: its determinism is equally unacceptable. Whatever difficulties there may be in understanding man's freedom in relation to the lawlike regularity with which natural processes seem to occur, humanists will not acquiesce in the view that man is simply a part of nature, his actions as much a product of its workings as the ocean tides and the revolutions of the heavenly bodies. Man is free. He can make a difference in the course of events—a difference that is not merely the inevitable product of the physical processes in which "his" atoms will inevitably participate. The future is to a certain extent open and, as yet, undetermined. Man has it within his power to put an end to all war—or to terminate all life by unleashing a holocaust that will engulf every living thing. Man has it within his power to end poverty—or to perpetuate conditions that make it inevitable that millions of fellow human beings will live their entire lives as victims of malnutrition and attendant

---

[5] John Calvin, *Institutes of the Christian Religion* (Presbyterian Board of Christian Education, 1928), p. 681.

[6] Bertrand Russell, "A Free Man's Worship," in *Mysticism and Logic* (New York: Norton, 1929), p. 58.

miseries. Man has it within his power—*really within his power*—to change the course of history, to make a difference in the way the future unfolds. Naturalism, by virtue of its deterministic element, will not allow this.

Transcendentalism

A humanist's chief concern about transcendentalism is that it seems to be continually in danger of merely substituting the tyranny of the depth for the tyranny of God (theism) or the tyranny of physical laws (naturalism). For too long, man has been intimidated by laws that are not of his own making, laws that hold him in subjection, render him guilty, and stifle his humanity. Moral imperatives that arise "out of the depth," even if the depth is the depth of our own selves, are nonetheless "alien laws" with respect to the empirical self that is supposed to obey them. Man in his sovereign freedom has the right not to be subjected to imperatives other than those that he prescribes for himself. Only so can the full freedom and dignity of man be preserved and enhanced.

Conclusion

Where do these considerations leave us with respect to the quest for an adequate world-view? They leave us free to continue the search without the fear that we may be seduced into adopting a view that robs us of our human dignity. In the defiant demand that the "big picture" allow full place to those convictions about man that we hold dear, we are, in effect, demanding that the whole truth, which at present we do not know, be consistent with the partial truth that even in our present state of knowledge we see clearly. The philosophical quest, whose ultimate goal is the achievement of a comprehensive view in which every element of truth and every aspect of experience shall find its proper place, is one of the most stupendous efforts of which man is capable. Humanism's contribution to this quest comes in the last analysis to just this: He who pursues this quest, being man, should pursue it in such a way that he does not lose sight of man.

STUDY QUESTIONS

1. "Humanism is not a fourth world-view to be set alongside the other three." Do you agree? Explain.
2. List the propositions that are offered by Humanist as "the basic convictions upon which [all] humanists are united." Are there any with which you disagree? Would Theist disagree with any? Naturalist? Transcendentalist?
3. What does Humanist find objectionable in theism? in naturalism? in transcendentalism? With which of his criticisms do you agree, and with which do you disagree?
4. Does humanism seem to you to have anything to contribute to the quest for an adequate world-view? Explain.

Boyce Gibson, A. *Theism and Empiricism*. London: SCM Press, 1970.

Britton, Karl. *Philosophy and the Meaning of Life*. Cambridge, Eng.: Cambridge University Press, 1969.

Edman, Irwin. *Four Ways of Philosophy*. New York: Henry Holt, 1947.

Ewing, A. C. *Value and Reality: The Philosophical Case for Theism*. New York: Humanities Press, 1973.

Feigl, Herbert. "Logical Empiricism," in Dagobert D. Runes (ed.). *Twentieth Century Philosophy*. New York: Philosophical Library, 1943. Reviews several philosophical problems from the point of view of a contemporary naturalist.

Flew, Antony. *God and Philosophy*. London: Hutchinson, 1966. Detailed critique of arguments for theism.

Hick, John. *God and the Universe of Faiths: Essays in the Philosophy of Religion*. New York: St. Martin's Press, 1974.

Krikorian, Yervant H. (ed.). *Naturalism and the Human Spirit*. New York: Columbia University Press, 1944.

Kurtz, Paul. *The Fullness of Life*. New York: Horizon Press, 1974. A Humanist reflects on the good life.

Lamprecht, S. P. *The Metaphysics of Naturalism*. New York: Appleton-Century-Crofts, 1967.

Maritain, Jacques. *Existence and the Existent*, tr. by Lewis Galantiere and Gerald B. Phelan. Garden City, N.Y.: Image Books, 1956 (paperbound). See Chapter 5, "Ecce in Pace." Representative of what might be called a "Christian humanist" point of view.

Montague, W. P. *The Chances of Surviving Death*. Cambridge, Mass.: Harvard University Press, 1934.

Nagel, Ernest. "Naturalism Reconsidered," in *Logic Without Metaphysics*. New York: Free Press, 1956, chap. 1.

Niebuhr, Reinhold. *Beyond Tragedy*. New York: Scribner, 1937. A collection of essays by a modern theist.

Otto, M. C. *The Human Enterprise*. New York: Appleton-Century-Crofts, 1940.

Pepper, Stephen C. *World Hypotheses*. Berkeley and Los Angeles: University of California Press, 1942. For patient readers only!

Russell, Bertrand. "A Free Man's Worship," in *Mysticism and Logic*. New York: Norton, 1929, pp. 46–58. A very famous delineation of the naturalist position.

Sartre, Jean Paul. *Existentialism*, tr. by Bernhard Frechtman. New York: Philosophical Library, 1947. Atheistic humanism as expounded by one of its best-known modern spokesmen.

Sorley, W. R. *Moral Values and the Idea of God*, 3rd ed. New York: Macmillan, 1924. See especially Chapters 18 and 19 for an interesting discussion of some of the problems implicit in the theistic view.

Stace, W. T. "Man Against Darkness." First published in the September 1948 issue of *The Atlantic Monthly* and in several anthologies since. A rather despairing account of the naturalist position.

Tillich, Paul. "Realism and Faith," in *The Protestant Era*. Chicago: University of Chicago Press, 1948, pp. 66–82. A very condensed statement of Tillich's form of transcendentalism.

Whitehead, Alfred North. *Process and Reality*. New York: Harper & Row, 1960 (originally published in 1929). See Part I, Chapter 1, "Speculative Philosophy."

PART XIII

PHILOSOPHIES
OF LIFE

59

THE IDEA OF A
PHILOSOPHY OF LIFE

Albert Schweitzer (1875–1965) will undoubtedly be remembered for generations to come as one of the most gifted and remarkable men who has ever lived. A brilliant student of many disciplines (he did significant work in philosophy, theology, music, and medicine), Schweitzer decided at an early age to give up the pleasures of life in his native Germany in order to serve as a medical missionary at Lambarene in French Equatorial Africa (now Gabon). During the half century that he lived and worked in Lambarene, Schweitzer developed a large hospital and clinic where he attempted to serve the needs of thousands who previously were without medical care. He also continued to write on a variety of subjects that were of interest to him, and was the recipient of numerous honors (including the 1952 Nobel peace prize) as a result of his humanitarian and scholarly endeavors.

Let us suppose that at some time during his illustrious life we had had an opportunity to put to Dr. Schweitzer the following question: "Sir, what is your *philosophy of life?*" What, exactly, would we have been asking for? What might the eminent doctor have said that would count as an answer to our question? What *is* a philosophy of life?

"I Believe"

It would certainly have been to the point of our question if Dr. Schweitzer had responded by saying, "I believe that all life is sacred, and that every human being has a duty to preserve life, to promote life, to raise to its highest value life which is capable of development . . ." [1] In

[1] Albert Schweitzer, *Out of My Life and Thought* (New York and Toronto: Mentor Books, orig. pub. 1933), p. 126.

asking someone for his philosophy of life, we are asking him to state his creed, his answers to the most fundamental questions that can be asked about human existence.

The distinguishing feature of a belief that belongs to someone's philosophy of life, then, is that it is perceived by its holder to have significant relevance for the way human life ought to be lived. Given his philosophy of life, it made sense for Albert Schweitzer to spend the greater part of his adult life in a foreign land attempting to serve the medical needs of people who otherwise would have been without such care. From the point of view of someone who has a very different philosophy of life, however—one, for example, in which it is maintained that "in this dog-eat-dog world it's every man for himself"—Schweitzer might very well be regarded as a fool who "threw away his life" and received nothing in return. The beliefs that constitute one's philosophy of life are more than propositions to which one gives intellectual assent: they are propositions to which one assents with one's life—that is, by acting in a way that is consistent with those beliefs. One's philosophy of life consists of those beliefs about life that are exhibited in the pattern of one's life.

Now let us look more closely at those "fundamental questions" about human life that we spoke of just a moment ago, the answers to which constitute one's philosophy of life.

Man's Place in the Universe

One of the questions to which a philosophy of life is addressed is, What is the nature of man? or, What is man's place in the universe? And against the background of our recent discussion of world-views, we can readily identify some of the answers that might be given. Man is a child of God, uniquely loved by Him and as such a candidate for eternal life (ethical theism); man is a product of nature, a high-level animal whose present endowments are the unplanned result of a blind evolutionary process (naturalism); man is a citizen of two worlds—a child of nature who nonetheless transcends nature (transcendentalism); man is a unique being whose uniqueness demands that he resist being swallowed up in any system that threatens to deny his freedom and his responsibility for his own destiny (humanism).

This question about the nature of man, or about man's place in the universe, marks the point where one's philosophy of life is connected to one's world-view. Every philosophy of life presupposes a world-view that is consistent with the beliefs that are constitutive of that philosophy of life. Inevitably, therefore, a significant change in one's world-view has important implications for one's philosophy of life (and vice versa).

It does not appear to be the case, however, that for any world-view there is one and only one philosophy of life that is consistent with that world-view: you cannot simply "deduce" all of the constitutive elements of a philosophy of life from the beliefs that constitute a given world-view. Thus it is quite possible for two naturalists, for example, who by definition share a common world-view (and a common view of the nature of man) to hold quite different philosophies of life.

One important element in a philosophy of life, in any case, is a belief about man's place in the universe, about "human nature." But this is only the beginning of a philosophy of life.

The Meaning of Life

A second question to which a philosophy of life must provide some kind of answer is the question, Does human life have any meaning, and if so, what is that meaning? Now this is admittedly a puzzling question—we normally ask about the meaning of *terms* or of *propositions,* not about the meaning of life—yet it is impossible to escape the feeling that it is getting at something that is very important for us as human beings to understand and to think through to a conclusion. Let us try at least to understand the point of the question.

Suppose that a friend comes to us and says, "I've come to say good-bye. Life has no *meaning* for me any more. I'm going to end it all. Tonight." Now under such circumstances it would be obviously inappropriate for us to quibble with our friend about whether he is using the term "meaning" in the proper way. ("End it all? Golly, I'm sorry to hear that. By the way, it seems to me that in what you just said you used the term 'meaning' in an odd way. According to Webster . . .") No, we clearly have to take our friend seriously at this point, and taking him seriously means in the first instance trying to understand exactly what he means when he says, "Life has no meaning for me any more."

Our first thought upon hearing these ominous words might well be that something traumatic must have happened to our friend that has momentarily shaken him to such an extent that he is seriously contemplating taking his own life. We have all read newspaper accounts of suicides in which it was reported that the victim had been despondent over the loss of a loved one, or worried about mounting debts, or suffering from an incurable illness. Anyone who has ever been subjected to severe emotional stress can perhaps understand how a fellow human being might under certain circumstances become so distraught or so despondent that he would consider taking his own life.

Let us suppose, however, that as we talk with our friend about this momentous decision that he has just announced, we learn that none of the usual circumstances surrounding suicide apply in his case. He has not been disappointed in love, he has no debts, he is in excellent health, and so on. "Why, then," we ask him, "do you want to end your life? What is your reason?" And he replies, "I don't have a reason, and I don't really need one. What I need, but have been unable to find, is *a reason to go on living.* Each of us has the power to choose whether we shall live or die. The living—unjustly, it seems to me—expect those who choose death to explain their choice. I think the burden of proof rests with those who choose life: Why should anyone choose life rather than death? What does life have to offer that is worth the effort? The only thing we can be sure of in this life is that sooner or later each of us must die. Why not sooner rather than later?''

In saying that life has no meaning for him any more, our friend is saying that he can find no reason to go on living, that nothing that he can think of that might occupy his time during whatever span of life might be his seems worth the effort. To him, the choice seems to be between a meaningless existence and nonexistence—and he chooses the latter. His philosophy of life fails to provide him with a reason for living.

The view that human existence is totally and irremediably meaningless, that nothing in all the world is really of value, is called *nihilism* (from the Latin word *nihil*, "nothing"), and a philosophy of life that includes such a view is often termed *nihilistic*. Why one who holds such a view should go on living is obviously a critical question for nihilists, and will be discussed in Chapter 61.

Alternatives to Nihilism

With respect to the question whether human life has any meaning, and if so, what that meaning is, the alternatives are really quite limited. In opposition to nihilism there are at most three alternative ways of attempting to give an affirmative answer. One is what may be called the theory of *cosmic purpose,* the view that everything that occurs in the world is part of a "grand design," and that every individual human life derives its highest meaning from its participation in the whole (Chapter 60). A second affirmative answer is what we shall call the theory of *immanent purpose,* the view that notwithstanding the fact that there is no overarching purpose that we can discern, there are purposes that emerge in the course of our lives that demand our allegiance. Life becomes meaningful, according to this view, insofar as we commit ourselves to the purposes that thus claim our attention (Chapter 62). And finally, there is the view that the only purposes that are available to us are those we posit for ourselves—but that these suffice to make human life meaningful. We shall speak of this view as the theory of *temporal purpose* (Chapter 63).

It is evident that each of these views has a certain affinity for one of the world-views discussed in the preceding section. Thus we shall not be surprised to find nihilism allied with naturalism, cosmic purpose with ethical theism, immanent purpose with transcendentalism, and temporal purpose with humanism. Whether we are dealing here with mere affinity or with rigorous logical implication may become clearer as we proceed with our inquiry.

Principles of Action

The third fundamental question to which a philosophy of life must provide some kind of an answer is, On what basis ought one to decide what to do with one's life? As long as one lives, one has the inescapable task of deciding how one will spend one's time—twenty-four hours a day, seven days a week, fifty-two weeks a year, *n* years in a lifetime. How shall one decide? A philosophy of life should provide some kind of an answer. Indeed, a philosophy of life consists in large part of a set of *value commitments* that yield some basis for preferring a given way of spending one's time to some other way that may be equally possible for us.

Consider once again the case of Albert Schweitzer. In his book *Out of My Life and Thought* Schweitzer provides a brief but fascinating account of the reasoning that led him as a young man to decide to devote his life to the service of his needy fellow-men. Schweitzer writes as follows:

> While at the university and enjoying the happiness of being able to study and even to produce some results in science and art, I could not help thinking continually of others who were denied that happiness by their material circumstances or their health . . . It struck me as incomprehensible that I should be allowed to lead such a happy life, while I saw so many people around me wrestling with care and suffering . . . Then one brilliant summer morning . . . there came to me, as I awoke, the thought that I must not accept this happiness as a matter of course, but must give something in return for it. Proceeding to think the matter out at once with calm deliberation, . . . I settled with myself before I got up, that I would consider myself justified in living till I was thirty for science and art, in order to devote myself from that time forward to the direct service of humanity.[2]

Note that in this account Schweitzer is stating a number of value commitments: he affirms the value of science (by which he means serious scholarship of all kinds) and of art as well as the value of devoting a significant part of one's time and effort to the service of one's fellow-men. Note further that in the set of values that he articulates in this passage, Schweitzer strikes a definite balance between egoistic and altruistic values: he will spend his time until age thirty principally doing the things he loves and enjoys (but also preparing for his life's work), and the time thereafter principally doing things intended to enhance the comfort and the happiness of others. And note finally that Schweitzer is affirming these values not merely in the abstract sense of assenting to the propositions that these things are good (though he surely would assent to those propositions), but in the practical sense that he is committing himself to a pattern of life consistent with such assent. The principal evidence of Schweitzer's commitment to these values is not

---

[2] Schweitzer, *op. cit.*, p. 70.

that he articulated them but that he spent his life working for their realization.

So it is with any philosophy of life: it will contain a set of value commitments that enable one who holds that philosophy to choose among alternative ways of spending his time (his life). It will also provide a basis for answering questions of the sort "Why did you do thus and so?" ("Because I believe such and such").

The number of value commitments that may be a part of a given philosophy of life is indefinitely large, and any statement of a philosophy of life is therefore likely to be more or less incomplete. Most of us, if asked to sum up our philosophy of life, would probably identify some few values that seem especially important to us, hoping that our questioner would realize that there is much more that we have left unsaid because at the moment we are not thinking of situations in which values other than those we have mentioned would be more relevant. To adopt a philosophy of life is (among other things) to commit oneself to certain values without being able to say in advance what all the logical and practical implications of such a commitment are.

Moreover, the possible combinations of values to which human beings may commit themselves are so numerous that there is no practical limit to the number of philosophies of life that may be developed. Perhaps we should say that a philosophy of life is in certain respects unique to the individual who holds that particular philosophy—though in its main outlines, of course, it will usually be very similar to the philosophy of life of many other people whose major value commitments are more or less the same. It is surely evident, in any case, that in the chapters that follow we can expect no more than a few contrasting samples of philosophies of life, since it is impossible in principle to identify and describe all the available variations.

The principal components of a philosophy of life, then, are (a) a view concerning the nature of man (i.e., man's place in the universe), (b) a view concerning the meaning of life, and (c) a set of value commitments consistent with those views. We turn now to a consideration of four representative philosophies of life with which we shall conclude this introduction to philosophy.

STUDY QUESTIONS

1. Assume that each of the following beliefs is held by someone. Which of these beliefs would qualify as a part of that person's philosophy of life?
   a. God has a plan for everyone.
   b. Whatever will be will be.
   c. Man has a natural lust for power.
   d. Human nature is perfectible.
   e. Anything that is worth doing is worth doing well.
   f. Man will some day colonize other planets.
   g. Solar energy will some day supply all of our energy needs.
   h. The best things in life are free.

    i. Every human being who is in need has a legitimate claim on my time and attention.

    j. You only go around once, so you may as well enjoy it while you have the chance.

2. List several theories about "man's place in the universe." Does it seem correct to you to assert that any such theory is "the point where one's philosophy of life is connected to one's world-view"?

3. Try to rephrase the question, What is the meaning of life? What do you understand to be the point of the question?

4. What is nihilism? What are the alternatives to nihilism listed in this chapter? Can you think of any other alternatives?

5. Write a brief summary of your philosophy of life, giving attention to each of the "principal components of a philosophy of life" identified in this chapter.

60

THE PHILOSOPHY
OF COSMIC PURPOSE

I know of no question that could possibly be of more importance to a human being than this: Does my life have any enduring meaning? For if one can answer this question in the affirmative, then one can live with confidence and joy no matter what circumstances he may find himself in at any time. But if he must answer in the negative, then it seems to me that even in the midst of comfort and plenty there must be an awful emptiness in his life, for when all is said and done, it still does not add up to anything.

Basically, in my opinion, there are only three ways of dealing with this question (notwithstanding what was said in the preceding chapter). You can pronounce the joyful "Yes" of religious faith; you can pronounce the despairing "No" of nihilism; or you can try to avoid thinking about the question. The other philosophies that are sometimes offered as alternatives to nihilism are nothing more than fleeting afterimages left upon the mind of Western man by the brilliant light of a profoundly purposeful sense of life upon which his gaze was once securely fixed.

I shall attempt, then, to set forth a philosophy of life that in its main outline is as old as the patriarchs and prophets of the Old Testament. It is a philosophy of life that is shared—with, of course, numerous differences in emphasis and detail—by all who believe that God exists and that He cares about His creation. You may, if you wish, call it the philosophy of cosmic purpose: I prefer to think of it simply as the faith of a believer.

The Nature of Man

My philosophy of life is grounded in the world-view of ethical theism. I hold, therefore, that everything that exists—the physical universe and life in all its forms—is a product of the creative activity of God. I hold, moreover, that the present forms of life that we find upon this planet are not the merely accidental products of a blind evolutionary process but are, rather, the exact forms of life that God intended to exist at this particular stage in the development of His creation. I do not mean by this that God had a plan from the beginning of creation that included every last detail of what was to occur at every moment of time for all time to come, for this would imply that there is no freedom in the world and that everything that occurs (notwithstanding the appearance of human freedom) occurs by necessity. I do mean, however, that God had from the beginning a plan for His creation that in its main features will be and is being carried out through an evolutionary process that is coterminous with the existence of the cosmos. Man appeared in that process at the appointed time, after millions and millions of years of preparation for that event (I am referring to the evolution of man's predecessors as well as the development of a planet suitable as a home for man) and is remarkable not least of all for the fact that he is the first creature (so far as we know) capable of knowing himself as a child of God. *Man is a creature who is capable of knowing himself as a child of God*—that, in my view, is the fundamental truth that must guide our thinking about the nature and destiny of man.

As a creature, man is naturally akin to every other creature, indeed, to everything that exists. The earth is his home, the destiny of the lesser creatures is in his hands, and the "care of the earth" is his special responsibility.

As a child of God, created in His image, man is also akin to the Creator of all things. He is destined for fellowship with God, and he finds his greatest fulfillment in realizing that destiny. Man is most fully man when he perceives himself for what he really is—a finite creature who is loved by God and is called by Him to play a unique role in the working out of His will for His creation.

The Meaning of Life

If one really believes what I have just said about God and His creation, and about the unique status of man in that creation, it follows immediately that the ultimate source of meaning in human life is to be found in the concept of *participation in the divine will.* It was by the will of God that the universe was called into existence out of nothing—*ex nihilo,* as the theologians say. It was by the will of God that this universe that He created was launched on its millenniums-long course toward whatever *télos* He has willed for it. It was by the will of God that life was called into existence—first in the sea, then upon land; first in very simple forms, then in species of greater and greater complexity. At every moment, from the beginning of creation to the present and on into the future, the universe was and is filled and moved and lured by the purposes of its Creator. The meaning of the life of every creature consists in its tiny but unique contribution to the fulfillment of the divine purpose.

Does it really make any difference in one's view of life—does it give "meaning" to life in any intelligible way—to believe that one is playing a tiny part in the realization of a divine plan whose final outcome is unknown to us? Yes! For it means, in effect, that everything of value that I accomplish in my life is preserved when I am no more, that the universe will forever be different from what it would otherwise have been because of the fact that I have lived. As each vote in an election makes its unique contribution to the final outcome, so each individual life contributes its unique achievement to the realization of the divine plan. Like Abraham of old, who set out to find the land of promise that was not in fact to be possessed for many generations, we live our lives in the certainty that the role we have been given to play—though we do not know the entire plot of which it is a part—is unique and important in the eyes of God.

I do not mean to be excessively "homocentric" in my account of the meaning of human existence. It should be apparent from what I have said that I believe that the life of *every* creature has meaning by virtue of its participation in the divine will. Man is unique, however, in that he is the creature who asks whether his life has meaning, and who is capable of *knowing* that his life has meaning (and of fearing that it does not). In the history of the universe as it advances through time, God in His infinite love ensures that everything that is achieved by every creature is preserved forever—even the achievements of those creatures that do not know that He exists. Thus, ironically, even the lives of those who despair because they can find no meaning in life are in fact meaningful (objectively considered) by virtue of their unique contribution to the evolution of the universe.

Things Worth Living For

As I try to analyze the pattern of life that seems to me to grow naturally out of the views that I have just stated, I find that I have four overarching value commitments that enable me to fill my life with a rich variety of meaningful activities.

First, I believe that life is deepened and enriched if one is consciously grateful to God for all the blessings of life. I believe, therefore, that it is a good thing to provide for moments of solitude when one can deliberately and systematically cultivate a sincere sense of gratitude toward God. I do not mean by this that one should spend one's time thanking God for life's latest trinkets, like a child sending "thank you" letters to Santa Claus at Christmas. I mean rather that one should meditate on the great and abiding gifts of God's love: the wondrous variety and beauty of the natural world, the miracle of life, the joy of human friendship and companionship, the opportunity to spend one's energy and one's days doing interesting and worthwhile things. In such moments of meditation it is as if one were immersing oneself in the stream of the divine will that pervades the universe; one returns to one's daily life renewed and strengthened for the tasks at hand.

Second, I believe that one's dealings with one's fellow human beings should be guided by the principle of love, by which I mean a sincere desire for their true welfare. The principle of love requires that I treat other people not as means to serve *my* ends, but as ends in themselves. It requires that I "do unto others as [I] would that others should do unto [me]" (the Golden Rule). It means that I should desire for all human beings those things that I desire for myself because I believe that they are truly good. Thus I think it proper in my dealings with other people to attempt to cultivate in them (as in myself) a deeper sense of gratitude to God, a firmer sense of the meaning of life, a clearer understanding of truth, a more sensitive appreciation of beauty, a greater compassion for others. I believe that anything that can be done to alleviate human suffering and to deepen man's enjoyment of life is worth doing; and I believe that one of the greatest rewards that can be had from one's daily work consists in the realization that one is enhancing the lives of his fellows.

The third basic commitment that serves as a guide for the conduct of my daily life is solicitude for all forms of life, and especially for sentient life. I am enough of a realist to know that one cannot live without being the occasion for the death of other living things, for example, the plants and animals that we use for food. Nonetheless, I take very seriously the view that as the dominant species of life on this planet at this particular time in the history of the universe, man has a special responsibility for the care and protection of those other forms of life that exist together with him. That man must kill to live is a sad fact about human existence—but let us not kill wastefully, or painfully, or unnecessarily. The occurrence of life in all its forms is a miracle of unbelievable proportions, and that miracle is not to be undone except for good and substantial reasons.

Finally, I believe that in the living of our lives it is proper for us to make responsible use of the material resources that are available to us. I believe that the prevailing attitude of modern man toward the natural world is exploitative rather than responsible, and I believe that this is wrong. We have known for many years, for example, that there is a finite quantity of petroleum in the earth, but we have been wasting petroleum as if the supply were inexhaustible. We have known for many years that our present practices with respect to waste disposal are seriously polluting the air we breathe and the water we drink, but we continue year after year to dump thousands of tons of pollutants into the atmosphere and millions of gallons of raw sewage into our rivers and streams. We are wasting the resources of the earth as if we were

Kamikaze pilots out for our final fling, and we seem not to remember that these same resources must suffice to serve the needs of our children and our grandchildren for generations to come.

According to the philosophy of cosmic purpose, we human beings are on this earth as agents of the divine will and as stewards of the earth. The treasures of the earth are not ours to waste: they are ours to use in ways that will enhance the quality of life, not only now but for all time to come. This philosophy is, therefore, implicitly supportive of the ecological concern that has come to the fore in the very recent past, and it provides a deeper rationale for that concern than the considerations of mere expedience that are customarily offered in its support.

A Final Word

You will note that in linking my philosophy of life to a belief in divine purpose, I have at no time claimed to know what that purpose is. It is even possible, so far as I am concerned, that the whole process has no temporal *télos*—that what God has wrought in the creation of the world is an evolutionary process of infinite duration in which an infinite succession of *téloi* are achieved, each succeeding *télos* being enriched by the achievements of the beings that preceded it. Be that as it may, the point I wish to make is that the conviction that the evolution of the universe is governed by the divine will not only fills the present moment with meaning but it enables one to face the future with confidence, for one is assured that whatever the future may hold of pain or sorrow or disappointment, it cannot prevent the ultimate realization of the divine will. Thus one can bear life's adversities with courage and with patience, secure in the knowledge that even one's suffering, bravely endured, will contribute in its own unique way to whatever it is that God in His wisdom is seeking to achieve in the world.

STUDY QUESTIONS

1. Theist argues that there are really only three ways of dealing with the question concerning the meaning of life. What are they? Do you think he is right about this?
2. What does Theist assert to be the "fundamental truth" about the nature and destiny of man?
3. What does Theist mean by the phrase "participation in the divine will"? Who "participates" in the divine will, according to Theist?
4. What "overarching value commitments" does Theist profess? Could one reasonably hold some or all of these value commitments without sharing Theist's theological views?
5. What does Theist have to say about the final *télos* of the divine will?

61

THE PHILOSOPHY
OF NIHILISM

Let me begin this account of the philosophy of nihilism by saying that I sincerely wish that human existence could have the kind of meaning that Theist says it has. For there can be no doubt that the beliefs advocated by Theist—that God has a plan for the world, and that every creature plays a role in the realization of that plan—provide the basis for a philosophy of life that is very satisfying to one who holds those beliefs. Theist's universe, to put the matter very simply, is inherently and totally *friendly* to man: whatever problems or obstacles man may encounter as he makes his way through life, the outcome is never in doubt, for the divine will cannot be thwarted. Such a philosophy of life is "fail-safe"— but alas, it presupposes a world-view that I and many other people today are unable to accept.

If one finds it necessary to conclude on the basis of the evidence that the universe is accurately depicted by the world-view of naturalism, then one's thinking about what one is to make of one's life must be very different from that of a theist. For according to this world-view, the emergence of life, including human life, was an incredible accident that came about solely because of the fortuitous occurrence of the conditions that made it possible. It was not intended or planned by God, for God does not exist. It was not intended or planned by anyone: it just happened. That is the premise from which nihilism begins.

Man's Place in the Universe

Objectively considered, man is simply a highly developed organism that has evolved out of earlier and simpler forms of life as a result of natural processes working upon the matter of which the universe is composed. These same processes evolved countless other species of life that have long since become extinct, and it seems more than likely that in due time the human species, and perhaps all life, will become extinct as well. Nature has no favorites. The evolutionary process is as blind and uncaring as the wind that blows; and the same wind that powers the windmill also wreaks great destruction.

The universe is neither friendly nor hostile to man: it is indifferent.

Strictly speaking, the above statements apply with equal force to other living things as well as man. But there is a difference: man is capable of knowing that this is his situation, and of asking how and for what purpose he is to live his life in such a universe. Thus in the case of man we have to ask what is the subjective meaning of the fact that he knows himself to be an accidental product of a blind process in a universe that neither knows nor cares that he exists.

Subjectively considered, man experiences his own existence as having no given meaning or purpose. He is "thrown" into existence, and he has to make the best of it. The only thing that he can know for certain about his existence is that one day it will end. In the meantime, he has to decide what to do with his life—what to work for, what to live for, how to fill the few or many days (he knows not which) that may be left to him. That is the true situation of man that is revealed once you strip away the mythology and the comforting illusions that for so many centuries have shielded him from the truth about himself.

The Search for Meaning in Life

It is altogether futile to suppose that in a world where God does not exist there is any hope of establishing an enduring meaning for any human life. For to say that my life or any life has meaning is to say that it serves some purpose; and in a universe where there are no enduring purposes, there can be no enduring meaning. One must either accept the conclusion that there is no ultimate meaning in life or one must resurrect the myth of cosmic purpose. Or else, as Theist suggests, one must carefully avoid thinking about the matter.

If we have the courage to think about it, however, and if we also have the intellectual honesty to acknowledge the ultimate meaninglessness of human life, the question posed by the young man to whom reference was made in the introductory chapter (p. 415) is clearly a very urgent one: Why should anyone choose to go on living? Does not the view that life has no ultimate meaning imply that life is not worth living? Is not suicide the logical outcome of a nihilistic philosophy of life? Is not nihilism in the final analysis a philosophy not of life but of death?

I think it is important that this apparent consequence of nihilism be considered forthrightly, for I think it is clear that the trend of our times is toward the world-view of naturalism and the philosophy of nihilism. It would be a very strange situation indeed if the final wisdom that we could reap from all our efforts to find answers to the profoundest

questions about the universe and about man were to be the recommendation to pull the trigger and have done with it. We ought to have a
better reason for living than the mere fact that "we get into the habit of
living before acquiring the habit of thinking." [1]

Does the belief that human life has no enduring meaning imply that
life is not worth living? By no means! For to one who clearly perceives
the awful truth of the ultimate meaninglessness of human life, holding
fast to this truth becomes in itself a reason for living. Never is man more
noble than when he stands before the uncaring universe, naked and
alone, and *refuses to be subdued* by it. Never is he more clear of mind or
pure of heart than in that moment when he stares defiantly into the vast
emptiness of heaven and from his heart declares, "I will not be
defeated!" The logical outcome of nihilism is not the ultimate submission
of suicide, but the ultimate defiance of man against the universe. As
nihilism rejects that subtle intellectual suicide by which many flee from
meaninglessness to a God whose alleged business it is to confer meaning
upon our lives, so it also rejects the cowardly flight from life itself that is
the inner meaning of an act of suicide. From the point of view of a
consistent nihilism it is essential, as Camus says, "to die unreconciled
and not of one's own free will." [2]

Moreover, in thus affirming a defiant will to live in a universe that is
without meaning, one discovers a marvelous sense of freedom that is
quite literally inconceivable in a theistic universe. From the point of view
of nihilism it is suddenly clear that in order to secure the prize of
meaning, theistic man has had to pay the terrible price of becoming a
slave for all eternity to a master who demands of him all that he has, and
to whom he is accountable every moment of his life *and beyond.* For the
nihilist, however, all this is changed. His life has no meaning, but neither
has it ultimate accountability to anyone. If God does not exist to confer
meaning upon his life, neither does He exist to issue commands that
must be obeyed. A nihilist is thus free to be what he wills to be, to do
what he wills to do, to become what he wills to become. To be a nihilist is
to be incredibly free.

Moreover, to be a nihilist is to be totally innocent, as innocent as
prenihilistic man longed to be as he sought the forgiveness of the God by
whose laws he was made to be so terribly guilty. Nihilism, in abolishing
all transcendent values, also abolishes all guilt. The burden of the law,
the burden of the past, the burden of being answerable for one's actions
of last year or yesterday or this morning—all are swept away in each
moment that one holds fast to the insight that there is no perspective
from which anything can finally be declared good or evil. Whatever may
be the opinions or the pronouncements of one's fellows, the nihilist
knows in his heart that he is the most innocent man who ever lived, since
for him the prerequisites of guilt simply do not exist.

---

[1] Albert Camus, *The Myth of Sisyphus and Other Essays* (New York: Knopf, 1969), p. 8.
[2] Camus, *op. cit.*, p. 55.

Finally, to be a nihilist is to savor the present moment (*each* present moment) in a way that is not possible for one who is a slave of cosmic purpose. To be without purpose (which has reference to the future) and without guilt (which has reference to the past) is to be free for the present moment, free to focus the whole of one's attention and one's passion on the experience of this present moment which alone is real. A famous spokesman for the philosophy of cosmic purpose once confessed, "We never live, but we hope to live; and, as we are always preparing to be happy, it is inevitable we should never be so." [3] Nihilism says rather, "We hope for nothing, and so we are never disappointed; we care not for the future, but seek to wrest from each passing moment whatever it will yield to one who gives himself fully to the living of this life."

Freedom, innocence, openness to the present moment: these are the rewards for one who holds fast to the truth that there is no enduring meaning in human life. If nihilism teaches that the quest for meaning must, if we are honest, end in failure, it does not draw from this the melancholy conclusion that life is therefore not worth living. On the contrary, it draws from this initially unsettling insight the elements of a philosophy of life that enables one who holds it to live fully and with joy.

Principles of Action

I assume that it is evident to anyone who has followed my reasoning to this point that I cannot derive a list of "things worth living for" from the convictions that I have just stated. Unlike Theist, I have no "overarching value commitments" to tell me what is and what is not worth doing. My convictions about the ultimate meaninglessness of human life yield no blueprint for the living of one's life. I have to improvise as I go along.

Nonetheless, to an outside observer I suspect that my life looks very much like the lives of many other people who do not share my nihilistic views. The truth is that at the level of observable behavior, I am pretty much of a conformist: I observe the laws and customs of society, I pay my taxes, I am a man of my word, and so on. I once even risked my life to save a child from drowning—and was embarrassed beyond words when I was given an award for my "courage" and my "recognition of the infinite value of a single human life." I knew perfectly well that my act was not courageous, and I had no illusions whatsoever about the value of the life of the child who caused all the excitement. It was purely and simply a matter of being there at that moment, and of being open to live that moment through in a way that at the time seemed more alluring, more exciting, than the alternative of staying on the beach and letting the child drown. Tomorrow, under identical circumstances, I might do just the opposite.

---

[3] Blaise Pascal, *Pensées* (New York: Modern Library, 1941), Fragment 172, p. 61.

The principal difference between me and those who do not share my nihilistic convictions, then, lies not so much in the area of outward behavior as in the differing quality of our inner life. I feel no *obligation* to live the way I do, and no *responsibility* for the way I have lived my life to date. As for the past, I would probably do everything differently if I had it to do over again, and as for the future I will simply have to continue to make it up as I go along. I cherish my freedom, and I will be bound neither by my own past nor by the expectations of others.

Another way of expressing the difference between the inner life of other people and my own would be to say that most people seem to me to take life very seriously, whereas I find the whole spectacle of human life rather comical. The comedy consists in the fantastic disproportion between most people's apparent perceptions of themselves ("I'm important in the scheme of things, I'm doing things that make a real difference in the world," etc.) and the reality of their situation as mere blips on the screen of history who will soon be replaced by other blips, and they by yet others—on and on, generation after generation, century after century. The emergence of life out of lifeless matter was an astonishing occurrence for which nature (if it had a mind) might be very proud; but the occurrence of a living being who thinks he has a *reason* for living, a being who thinks he has a role to play in the fulfillment of some "grand design," is a kind of cosmic joke that nature has played upon itself. Nihilism's counterbalance to the ponderous seriousness with which most people regard the spectacle of human life is a hearty laugh.

Why do I live the way I do rather than some other way? Purely out of habit. Society taught me how to live before it taught me how to think—and lacking any value system in terms of which I might develop a "better" way of life, I simply go along with the crowd. I believe in intellectual honesty; I value my own freedom; I believe in my own innocence; I live for the moment. These fragments of a philosophy of life provide no basis for me to reform the lives of my contemporaries nor to live in an unconventional way myself. You might say that it is simply the law of inertia applied to the sphere of human behavior.

Notwithstanding everything that I have said, however, I want in conclusion to state emphatically that the No that nihilism pronounces with respect to the question of meaning in life is not a *despairing* No. It is true that one's initial reaction to the insight that life is without any enduring meaning is a kind of intellectual shock: one wants to say that it cannot be, or that if it is, one cannot live with such a privation. But this, it must be remembered, is only one's initial reaction. It is the reaction of a child who has just been told that there is no Santa Claus—and who wishes he had not asked. But we cannot be children forever, and it cannot be and in fact is not the case that the only way to say Yes to life is to preserve the illusion of cosmic purpose. Nihilism says No to the question of meaning, but it says a joyful Yes to life. That is a proper stance for honest men who find themselves in circumstances such as ours.

STUDY QUESTIONS

1. What is Nihilist's account of "man's place in the universe"? Is this account implicit in the world-view of naturalism (see Chapter 56)?
2. Nihilist states that in his opinion "it is clear that the trend of our times is toward the world-view of naturalism and the philosophy of nihilism" (p. 426). Do you think he is right on this point?
3. Nihilist states that the view that human life has no enduring meaning does not imply that life is not worth living. Summarize his argument on this point.
4. Nihilist argues that a consistent nihilism yields certain "rewards." What are they, and how do they allegedly follow from the fundamental tenet of nihilism?
5. According to Nihilist, how should one who holds a nihilist philosophy of life order his daily life? How does a nihilist decide to do this rather than that?

62

THE PHILOSOPHY OF IMMANENT PURPOSE

As I sit down to write these words the country is quietly observing another anniversary of the death of President Franklin Delano Roosevelt. The memory of the late FDR in turn calls to mind a number of other men who have left their marks upon the history of our times and are with us no more: Winston Churchill, Dwight D. Eisenhower, John F. Kennedy, Martin Luther King, Jr. Each of these men, as we all know, exerted great influence on the thoughts and lives of his contemporaries. Each had a historic role to play, a mission to fulfill. The world is different because of the way they lived, the decisions they made, the goals they set, the things they achieved or failed to achieve.

Nihilism tells me that the conviction that these men made a permanent mark on the experience of mankind is sheer fantasy, that, in fact, their lives and the lives of all men are totally devoid of any enduring meaning. Every human being, according to nihilism, is but "a blip on the screen of history." The blips come and go, year after year, generation after generation; eventually the last blip will vanish from the screen, and the being who fancies that his life has meaning will be no more.

Is this the final truth about human existence? Is it possible that a serious commitment to "follow the argument wherever it may lead" must lead us ultimately to the views that life has no meaning, that nothing is really worth doing, that there is no better guide for the living of one's life than mere convention? No! Nihilism cannot be the end of the journey, for nihilism contains within itself a contradiction that requires us to go beyond nihilism. The resolution of that contradiction provides the key through which nihilism can and must be transcended.

Nihilism's Internal Contradiction

Nihilism takes its stand on the proposition that one must be brutally honest about the question of meaning—as honest as one would be if the question did not concern us at all. In the name of intellectual honesty nihilism accepts the conclusion of philosophical naturalism that life, including human life, is an accidental occurrence in a universe that neither knows nor cares that life exists, and with admirable tenacity it concludes from this that human life is without purpose and therefore without meaning. Nihilist finds, to be sure, some consolation prizes: freedom, innocence, openness to the present moment. But he leaves us with the lurking suspicion that the "hearty laugh" that he recommends in view of the "comedy" of the human situation is not so much a counterbalance to an unwarranted seriousness as it is an antidote to an unhealed grief. Bereavement affects us in peculiar ways.

But is it not strange that Nihilist never asks *why* it is so important to him to be intellectually honest? Intellectual honesty is so important to Nihilist that he finds a reason for living in the alleged "awful truth" that life has no meaning! But how can anything be that important to one who believes that the universe is devoid of meaning, and that nothing is of "overarching" value? Is not Nihilist's assertion equivalent to the claim that there is one ultimate value in human life, namely intellectual honesty? Clearly it is. And then we have to ask how Nihilist knows that this is the case.

The contradiction that lies at the heart of nihilism is this, that its assertion that nothing is truly of value is established on the assumption that honesty before the facts is of supreme value. In the name of truth, which it values absolutely, nihilism denies that anything is of absolute value. And in the name of truth, to which it clings notwithstanding the unpalatable consequences to which it seems driven, nihilism eludes the despair that would seem to be its inevitable concomitant.

The Key to Meaning

I fully agree with Nihilist that it is good to be intellectually honest, but what I want to know is how *Nihilist* is able to assert this conviction. Surely it is evident that on his own premises he cannot know that honesty is good, for he is committed to the proposition that in this universe where life emerged quite by accident, nothing is really of value. Let me then speak for him: he values intellectual honesty because he recognizes that it is the only pathway to truth, and the intrinsic value of truth is so self-evident to him that in all his talk about the nonreality of values he fails to notice his own valuation of truth. Nihilist is committed to speaking the truth as he sees it—I do not doubt his sincerity—but that very commitment presupposes that he has been so impressed by the value of truth that he cannot do otherwise.

Values certify themselves to us as deserving of our commitment, and when this occurs, we respond with our whole being without stopping to ask by what right this or that value presumes to bind our behavior. I cannot prove to you by any argument that as a rational being you ought to seek and honor the truth wherever it may be found: if the intrinsic value of truth has not grasped you, claimed you, won your loyalty, there is nothing I can do for you. But if truth has gained your allegiance (as it clearly has in Nihilist's case), then you have but to reflect on the characteristics of that claim to understand something about the nature of value and the important role that values play in human life.

Nihilist's account provides yet another example of the self-certifying character of values. He tells us that on one occasion he saved a child from drowning, and that he was embarrassed when he was given an award for courage and for his "recognition of the infinite value of a single human life." The embarrassment, I feel sure, derives from the fact that, fortunately, his behavior on that occasion was not consistent with his theory. Since, according to Nihilist, the life of that child, like everything else, was without value, it was not reasonable for him to risk his life to save the child from drowning. And just how does he attempt to reconcile his theory with the "embarrassing" fact that he did save the child? "It was purely and simply a matter of being there at that moment," he says, "and of being open to live that moment through in a way that at the time seemed more alluring, more exciting, than the alternative of staying on the beach and letting the child drown." Poppycock! Poor Nihilist cannot admit that his courageous behavior (which it was) grew out of his instinctive awareness that the life of that child *was* indeed of value, that the child's predicament placed an obligation upon him to do everything within his power to preserve that life. His *theory* requires him to say, "Tomorrow, under identical circumstances, I might do just the opposite." I am willing to bet that his practice would be better than his theory.

I say that it is a fact of human existence that values do thrust themselves upon us in this direct and overwhelming way, and that much of our behavior can be understood only on the supposition that it is called forth by the values that are served by that behavior. Very little of our time is spent in fulfilling our basic animal needs, which presumably would have to be met even if we were not value-loving creatures. Most of our working hours are spent in the service of things we believe in—values—which could in fact be different from what they are (i.e., we could have different values). Medieval man, for example, valued contemplation in a degree that it clearly is not valued by most people today. We, on the other hand, value scientific knowledge and technology in a degree that would have seemed utterly strange to our more contemplative forebears. The "overarching value commitments" of a society are evident in the ways that that society deploys its human and material resources. It is not only because of technological progress that modern Western man builds superhighways rather than cathedrals.

Every human being is part of a community of human beings—a society—and to a large extent shares the value commitments of that society, frequently without even being explicitly aware of what those commitments are. Some such commitments are shared by virtually everyone, and form the subject matter of ethics. Others are peculiar to a given society or social movement at a given time, and constitute what is called an ideology. Yet others may be more or less peculiar to a given individual, and thus become a part of his personal philosophy of life.

Life is experienced as meaningful insofar as it is lived in the service of values that impress us as being worthy of our efforts. If one is grasped by the terrible spectacle of human suffering caused by disease, and in response devotes one's life to the prevention and cure of disease and its consequences, one finds meaning in so doing. If one is moved to action by an awareness of the awful human consequences of ignorance, and in response spends one's best efforts in the overcoming of ignorance, one experiences a sense of meaning in the process. The idea that life is without meaning is an idea that could be entertained only by one who is merely contemplating life, not by one who is involved in the actual living of life. To live is to encounter values that cry out for our allegiance. To respond to that cry is to be redeemed.

The Source of Value

What is the source of these values that confront us on the pathway of life, demand our allegiance, and confer meaning upon our lives? And precisely how and why are our lives made meaningful in the service of such values?

Values emerge out of the depth of our lives, out of that dimension of ourselves in which we are in touch with the eternal. The reason that Nihilist is driven to the dreadful view that human life is without meaning is that his starting point is the world-view of naturalism, and within that world-view there is no place for the concept of the eternal—nor, as a further consequence, is there any place for transcendent values. Thus it is only by the contradiction of affirming a value that on his own premises he has no right to affirm that Nihilist is able to find life worth living, notwithstanding the fact that it is without ultimate meaning.

That values claiming our allegiance do emerge in the course of our lives is the best evidence we have that naturalism does not contain the whole truth about the human situation. Nihilist starts from naturalism and finds himself forced to conclude that when all is said and done, nothing in this world is really of value. I start from the fact that values *do* confront us in the course of our lives, and conclude from this that naturalism is inadequate. If values, which are not temporal entities, emerge in the world of space and time by means of human consciousness, then man is more than a spatiotemporal being: he is a being who lives in the strength of the eternal, and finds his deepest fulfillment in the service of that which is eternal. Man is, in short, what he is affirmed to be according to the world-view of transcendentalism (see Chapter 57).

The quest for meaning in life is not a search for an answer to the question, What is *the* meaning of life? That is not an intelligible question. The quest for meaning in life is a quest for something worth living for, something that will redeem our lives from the superficiality and point-lessness of mere temporality. That quest is satisfied when we are grasped by the inherent worthwhileness of some task—any task—that engages our efforts and our loyalty. Meaning in life is a dividend that is bestowed upon those who invest some portion of their lives in something they believe to be worthy of that investment.

Things Worth Living For

I noted earlier that in the value commitments of most people it is possible to discern at least three layers of values: those that are shared by virtually everyone, those that are a part of the value system of a given society, and those that are more or less peculiar to a particular individual. In analyzing my own value commitments I find it instructive to sort them out into these three categories.

With respect to the first of these it seems to me that the principal values that deserve to be and to a very large extent are revered by people everywhere are the great triumvirate of truth, beauty, and goodness. I believe that the mind of man has a natural hunger to know the truth, and that the experience of coming to know some truth is one of the great "ecstatic" experiences of life—one of the experiences in which one senses a depth and a fulfillment in life. I believe that the spirit of man has a natural love for beauty, and that the perception of beauty—in nature, in the visual arts, in music—is as essential to the life of the spirit as food is for the body. And I believe that the conscience of man has a natural desire to realize true goodness in human affairs, and that the behavior of most human beings is profoundly influenced by this desire. In professing a love for truth, beauty, and goodness, I feel a kinship with the whole human community, a kinship with literally billions of other human beings from whom I am separated by space, time, and cultural differ-ences—and I rejoice in the knowledge that we are as one in our commitment to those values without which we would cease to be truly human.

With respect to the second category of values, I must, of course, acknowledge that I am a product of modern Western culture, and that I probably hold a large number of unexamined commitments that are simply a part of the assumed outlook of all or most people who live in this cultural epoch. To the extent that I have been able to identify the value commitments of our culture, however, I find that in the process of incorporating them into my own philosophy of life I have had to modify them in several important ways. For example: I recognize the power of the scientific method to acquire a detailed knowledge of the laws governing the natural world, but—contrary, I think, to the prevailing view of my contemporaries—I do not believe that all legitimate knowledge comes to us by way of the scientific method. I value modern technology as a means of lessening human toil and enhancing the quality of human life, but—again contrary to the dominant view of our time—I do not think that a steadily increasing quantity of the products of technology results in a corresponding increase in human happiness. I acknowledge the success of capitalism in making possible a higher average standard of living than has ever been realized heretofore, but I deplore the injustice, the waste, and the pollution that many of my contemporaries seem willing to accept as part of the price of affluence. I value representative democracy as the best method yet devised to make government responsive in some measure to the needs of the governed, but I shudder at the naïveté of those of my contemporaries who think that as long as an elected official is a member of the right political party, he can do no wrong. I am, then, both a product and a critic of modern society, and I like to think that insofar as I find it necessary to be the latter, I am acting in the name of those fundamental commitments that are shared by human beings everywhere.

As far as the third category of commitments is concerned, it is largely a matter of particularizing one's broader commitments in ways that are appropriate to one's interests, skills, and circumstances. None of us can do everything, nor can we make life meaningful merely by revering a set of noble-sounding formulations. It is in the concrete details of our everyday life that we finally must live out our values; otherwise they remain nothing but impotent abstractions. In my own case, for example, several projects have captured my interest: an open-housing campaign in my community, an emergency relief program for famine victims in Africa, a scholarship program for inner-city students. Had I lived in a different community, or at a different time, the particular causes that would have engaged my interest would no doubt have been different. Because I have now had the experience of participating in these projects, however, the values which these projects were designed to serve have undoubtedly come to occupy a more prominent place in my personal philosophy of life than would otherwise have been the case. We are what we do.

My advice to the young man who announced that he was going to end his life because he could not think of any reason to go on living is this: Stop looking for a *reason* to live and try actually *living* for a while. Do whatever you feel *might* be worth doing and see if in the process you are not grasped once again by values that claim your attention and your allegiance. To one who is merely a spectator, human life may seem pointless and trivial and futile; but to one who enters fully into the living of life, values worth living for well up like springs in the desert. What is needed to find meaning in life is not a better theory but a renewed commitment to life itself. When we think, we should think clearly; and when we live, we should live deeply and well.

STUDY QUESTIONS

1. What is the "internal contradiction" that the writer of this chapter claims to find in nihilism? Is this a real contradiction? How might Nihilist reply to this criticism?
2. "Values certify themselves to us as deserving of our commitment." What does this mean? Is this a plausible description of your own perception of values?
3. How does the writer of this chapter deal with the question concerning the meaning of life? What is your opinion of this position?
4. What view of man is held by the writer of this chapter? What is the relationship between this view and his view regarding our apprehension of values?
5. This chapter speaks about "three layers of values." What are they? Does the "three-layer" analysis apply to your own value system?
6. What values are said to be shared by virtually all human beings? Does this strike you as a plausible assertion?
7. What values are identified as the principal value commitments of modern Western culture? At what points do you agree and at what points do you disagree with this analysis?
8. "We are what we do." What does this mean?

63

THE PHILOSOPHY OF TEMPORAL PURPOSE

The starting point for my reflections regarding the meaning of life and other matters having to do with a philosophy of life is the world-view of humanism. As a matter of fact, I normally do not make any distinction in my own thinking between the subject of world-views and the subject of philosophies of life. If I am asked, "What is your world-view?" my answer is, "I am a humanist." And if I am asked, "What is your philosophy of life?" I again reply, "I am a humanist." And I think it is clear from the preceding discussion that theism, naturalism, and transcendentalism are also both world-views and philosophies of life. The theories of cosmic purpose, no purpose (nihilism), and immanent purpose appear to me to be implicit in those other world-views just as the theory of temporal purpose is implicit in the world-view of humanism. I shall do my best to show that this last-mentioned theory is more consistent with our experience of life than any of the theories discussed thus far.

The Myth of Sisyphus

Greek mythology recounts the story of Sisyphus, a legendary king of Corinth whose escapades so offended the gods that he was condemned for all eternity to roll a great boulder to the top of a mountain. The gods, according to the myth, had arranged things in such a way that each time Sisyphus neared the top of the mountain the boulder would roll back down to the bottom, and the poor fellow would have to start all over again. Sisyphus' excruciating labor carried on endlessly and without purpose is the classic image of pointless human effort. It is instructive to note how various philosophies of life would have to alter the story in order to make it fit their respective readings of the human situation.

Nihilism simply accepts the story as it is: all human activity is as futile as the activity of Sisyphus going up and down the mountain for eternity, with nothing ever being accomplished through all of his prodigious effort. Suppose, then, that Sisyphus could thwart the will of the gods by taking his own life. Should he not do so? No, according to nihilism, for in holding fast to the insight that what he is doing is meaningless, Sisyphus finds a strange kind of reason for being. Sisyphus' *consciousness of his own fate* makes his fate endurable. The lesson would appear to be that mankind can find a solace for purposelessness in consciously grasping and accepting the fact that life is without purpose. One is reminded of Pascal:

> Man is but a reed, the most feeble thing in nature; but he is a thinking reed . . . If the universe were to crush him, man would still be more noble than that which killed him, because he knows that he dies and the advantage that the universe has over him; the universe knows nothing of this.[1]

According to theism's reading of the human situation, we must imagine that Sisyphus toils up the mountain with boulders that do not roll back down but are received by the gods to be used in building a beautiful cathedral at the top of the mountain. Sisyphus, to be sure, does not personally set each boulder in place—he never even sees the cathedral—but he is assured that the boulders he brings up one by one are in fact being used to build an edifice that will last forever. Thus it behooves him to work quickly and well, for the quality of his work will have definite consequences for the quality of the final product. In theism's reading of the human situation, Sisyphus' efforts unquestionably count for something.

The philosophy of immanent purpose requires a very interesting emendation of the myth of Sisyphus. According to this view, Sisyphus rolls his boulder up the mountain not because that is his fate (nihilism), and not in order to contribute to the building of a cathedral at the top of the mountain (theism), but in order to contribute to a series of lesser projects that have impressed him as being worthy of his efforts. We might say that for the cathedral at the top of the mountain this philosophy substitutes a series of chapels on the mountainside, and Sisyphus' life and work acquire meaning by virtue of the fact that each of these projects in turn certifies itself to him as being worthy of his efforts. He is beckoned, as it were, by transcendent values that cry out for realization, and in responding to that cry his life is filled with meaning.

We will return to Sisyphus later to develop a humanist version of that ancient and haunting myth. First, however, let us consider directly the problem of meaning and the nature and function of values in human affairs.

---

[1] Blaise Pascal, *Pensées* (New York: Modern Library, 1941), Fragment 347, p. 116.

Meaning and Values

You will recall from the earlier discussion of humanism as a world-view (Chapter 58) that humanism affirms the uniqueness, the dignity, and the essential freedom of man. According to humanism, man is a lonely stranger upon the earth. He stands apart from lifeless matter by virtue of the fact that he lives, and he stands apart from all other forms of life by virtue of the very qualities that constitute his humanity: his freedom, his capacity for abstract thought, his power of imagination, his capacity for language, his appreciation of beauty, his capacity for altruistic love. If you imagine the earth existing just as it does now, with the exception of man's never having existed upon it, you must imagine a world without science, without poetry, without art, without love—and without any being who is capable of caring that these things do not exist. However the fact is to be accounted for, it is remarkable that man occupies a class all by himself in the scale of being. It is this radical uniqueness of man that humanism feels obligated to defend against every attempt that is made to incorporate man into a system that robs him of his distinctness, his humanity.

Consider once again the world without man. Such a world would also be devoid of value. Why? *Because man is the being who creates values by positing future possibilities which he then works to achieve.* Man is an infinitely restless creature who simply cannot be content to leave the world as he finds it. He sees the world as it is, and there flashes into his imagination a picture of what it might be: this lump of clay might be formed into a jug, this piece of marble into a statue, these colored stones into a piece of jewelry, these trees into a building to provide shelter from the elements, these sounds into a tune, these words into a poem, these people into a nation. Man creates because it is his nature to create. Were he to cease creating, he would cease to be man.

Most human effort is expended in the service of ideals, values, posited by man's imagination. Only a tiny fraction of the work that is done by people and machines today would be required if all we aspired to do was to meet our absolutely basic survival requirements. A bit of food, shelter, enough clothing to protect us from the elements, that is about all we would need. But we desire more than this: food that is tasty and varied as well as nourishing, homes that are beautiful as well as functional, clothing that is attractive and comfortable as well as practical, greater mobility than we can get by mere walking, activities more interesting than the gathering of food. And so we create those remarkable monuments to human imagination called *civilizations*, and we devote most of our efforts to the pursuit of those things that are valued in the civilization whose life we happen to share.

It is by his imagination, therefore, that man is saved from purposelessness. Man finds meaning in pursuing goals that he has posited as worth pursuing. The building of a civilization is a gigantic game in which any number can play, and almost everybody wins—provided, of course, that the game does not come to an end. When that happens, a sense of weariness sets in, and philosophers and poets lament the vanity of all man's striving (as in the Book of Ecclesiastes). But ever and again, human imagination comes to the rescue: new ideals are generated, new goals are posited; and filled once again with hope and with purpose, people set about the task of building a new and better civilization.

It is quite true that "the glory that was Greece and the grandeur that was Rome" are no more, except in the minds of individuals who study those vanished civilizations and admire the ideals by which the ancient Greeks and Romans lived. As with all things that die, the hopes and the dreams as well as the sorrows and the fears of those noble men and women have vanished forever. The truth is—and perhaps it is a melancholy truth—that nothing in all the world endures forever: on this point, nihilism is correct. But it is also true that individuals find meaning in striving to bring into being the values, the ideals, the visions that they set before themselves. This is the only kind of meaning that is possible for us—but it is enough.

Returning now to the myth of Sisyphus, it is evident that the humanist account of the human situation requires several important changes in the story. First, the humanist Sisyphus is not condemned to forever roll boulders up the mountain: he is free to do whatever he chooses—to play, to make music, to till the soil, to make usable objects from the wood of the trees, to plan a building, to build a city. Second, if he does choose to roll boulders up the mountain, they do not roll back down again: they are used for whatever purpose he intended. Third, he is not alone: the mountainside is populated with human beings like himself who will join their labor to his, that together they may accomplish goals that would exceed the capacity of any one of them. Thus Sisyphus, in the humanist view, is happy on his mountain. If his project of yesterday is swaying in the wind and about to come crashing down, do not feel sorry for him: the joy was in the doing, not in the result. He has already moved on to a new and more exciting project, and will hardly take note when the product of yesterday's efforts has toppled to the earth.

Life as a Work of Art

Each of my predecessors in this debate has concluded his essay with a brief discussion of "things worth living for" or "principles of action"— that is, an account of how he orders his everyday life in a manner consistent with his general outlook. Theist speaks of four overarching values in the service of which his life, he says, is filled with a rich variety of meaningful activity. Nihilist, for obvious reasons, has a bit of trouble at this point, but finally recommends convention as the only available guide for conduct. Transcendentalist tells us he finds several different levels of values (ethical, cultural, personal), and attempts briefly to sort them out for us. And now it is my turn, and my readers no doubt expect that I will offer yet one more set of values for their consideration.

But I will not do so, for there is nothing that I could say at this point that would not be purely and simply autobiographical—and I cannot imagine that an account of my particular pattern of values could be of interest to anyone else. Could it make any possible difference to you whether or not I happen to like music, or art, or literature? Is it any concern of yours whether I am personally involved in this civic project rather than that one? I have my life to live and you have yours. I have my opportunities and you have yours. If I happen to have chosen the rolling of boulders as my principal project in life, that does not mean that you should do the same.

Every human being is an artist, and the life he lives is a unique work of art. The artist, to be sure, is limited to some extent by the materials with which he has to work: we cannot live at a different time, in a different cultural epoch, or with different natural endowments from those we actually have. But within these limitations, the possibilities for the living of our lives are truly boundless. There are oceans to be crossed, mountains to be climbed, truths to be mastered, dangers to be overcome, civilizations to be built. Each of us must set his own goals, and then pursue them with all possible vigor—not because those goals, once achieved, will last forever, but because as artists we take pride in the quality of our art, which is our life. And if in the course of practicing our art we should happen to encounter Sisyphus upon his mountain, let us look carefully into his face. I think we shall discover that as he struggles with his boulder, Sisyphus is smiling—for he is happy.

STUDY QUESTIONS

1. What is Humanist's view of man? What are the most important facts about man that Humanist urges us to keep in mind as we attempt to develop a philosophy of life?
2. What is Humanist's theory of value? How do values come into being?
3. According to Humanist, how does human life become meaningful? Does this strike you as a plausible suggestion?
4. Humanist does not offer a proposal regarding "things worth living for." Why? What does he offer in its place?
5. Read the Book of Ecclesiastes. Summarize its philosophy of life. Do the same for The Rubáiyát of Omar Khayyám.

Bambrough, Renford. *Reason, Truth and God.* New York: Barnes & Noble, 1969. Includes an exhortation to philosophers to concern themselves with philosophies of life.

————. *Wisdom: Twelve Essays.* Totowa, N.J.: Rowman & Littlefield, 1974.

Camus, Albert. *The Myth of Sisyphus and Other Essays,* tr. by Justin O'Brien. New York: Knopf, 1969.

Capps, Walter H., and Donald E. Capps (eds.). *The Religious Personality.* Belmont, Calif.: Wadsworth, 1970 (paperbound). Centers on the ways religion may orient the personality.

Fried, C. *An Anatomy of Values: Problems of Personal and Social Choice.* Cambridge, Mass.: Harvard University Press, 1970.

Friedman, Maurice. *The Hidden Human Image.* New York: Dell, 1974 (paperbound). Wide-ranging discussion of the condition of contemporary man (and woman).

Hoffer, Eric. *Reflections on the Human Condition.* New York: Harper & Row, 1973. A longshoreman's comments.

Kaufmann, Walter. *Without Guilt and Justice: From Decidophobia to Autonomy.* New York: Peter H. Weyden, 1973. Argues for an emphasis on man's creative autonomy.

Margolis, Joseph. *Negativities: The Limits of Life.* Columbus, Ohio: Charles E. Merrill, 1975. Discusses death, illness, inequality, and related topics.

Mayeroff, Milton. *On Caring.* New York: Harper & Row, 1971. An analysis of what it means to be human.

Nielsen, Kai. *Ethics Without God.* Buffalo, N.Y.: Prometheus Books, 1973 (paperbound).

Pepper, Stephen C. *The Sources of Value.* Berkeley, Calif.: University of California Press, 1970.

Peters, Richard S. *Reason and Compassion.* London: Routledge & Kegan Paul, 1973.

Rowen, Stanley. *Nihilism: A Philosophical Essay.* New Haven, Conn.: Yale University Press, 1969. A defense of a rationally ordered life.

Schacht, Richard. *Alienation.* Garden City, N.Y.: Doubleday, 1971 (paperbound). A history of the concept.

Taylor, Richard. *Good and Evil.* New York: Macmillan, 1970. See especially the last chapter on the meaning of life.

Thielicke, Helmut. *Nihilism: Its Origin and Nature—With a Christian Answer,* tr. by John W. Doberstein. New York: Schocken Books, 1969. A sympathetic but critical study.

Weiss, Paul, and John Weiss. *Right and Wrong: A Philosophical Dialogue Between Father and Son.* Carbondale, Ill.: Southern Illinois University Press, 1974 (paperbound).

GLOSSARY OF PHILOSOPHICAL TERMS

Controversial issues can be fruitfully discussed only insofar as a neutral language—that is, one acceptable to everyone discussing the controversy and understood in the same sense by all—is available for the discussion. Unfortunately, it is uncommonly difficult in philosophy to formulate neutral definitions of many key philosophical terms. The definitions that follow will indicate the usage observed throughout this book, and this in turn reflects the usage of a large number of English-speaking philosophers. The reader should be aware, however, that some philosophers have used and do use some of these terms in slightly different ways, and should accordingly be prepared to modify his understanding of any term which he encounters being used in some other way.

Ambiguous: quality of a term that has different meanings when used in different contexts. (*Ex.:* "line" means one thing to a painter, another to a mathematician, and yet a third to a plumber.)

Analogical predication: a mode of speaking about God, first advocated by St. Thomas Aquinas (1225–1274), which is said to be a kind of mean between *univocal* and *equivocal* predication (see below). The idea is extremely complex, no less than three varieties of analogical predication having been distinguished by followers of St. Thomas.

Analytic: quality of a sentence, statement, or proposition which does not purport to say anything about reality, but simply explicates some part of the meaning of one or more of its terms. (*Ex.:* "All circles are round.") Contrasts with *synthetic* (see below).

Anarchism, militant: the view of one committed to the overthrow of existing government without regard to the practical consequences and with no intention of supporting any new government that might be established in its place.

Anarchism, naïve: the view that government actually hinders rather than enhances the good of society, and that greater good would result if government simply ceased to exist.

Anarchism, theoretical: the view that the authority of government to restrict the freedom of individuals has no theoretical justification.

A posteriori: completely dependent on, and a product of, experience; mode of knowledge in which experience is the source as well as the occasion of knowledge. Contrasts with *a priori* (see below).

A priori: not completely dependent on experience; independent in the sense that experience, although it may be the occasion for one's coming to know, is not the source. Contrasts with *a posteriori* (see above).

Argument: (1) an attempt to show that certain considerations or alleged facts provide evidence in favor of the truth of some proposition. (2) a group of propositions about which it is claimed that the presumed truth of some (the premises) constitutes evidence for the truth of one (the conclusion).

Behaviorism: the view that man is constituted in such a way that every detail of his experience and behavior is the inevitable consequence of causes lying outside himself.

Circumstantial freedom of self-realization: the opportunity to do what one wants to do; a situation in which neither personal limitations nor external restraints prevent one from doing a given thing. (*Ex.:* religious freedom, that is, the opportunity to worship as one wishes.)

Cognition: (1) the act or process of knowing (cognizing). (2) that which is known (cognized).

Commonsense, or *direct, realism:* the view that the world as it really is does not differ in any important respect from the world as it appears to us.

Consciousness: a center of awareness, feeling, and perception; mind.

Contingent: (1) (in logic) quality of a proposition that is not necessarily true, that is, a proposition the denial of which does not involve a self-contradiction. (2) (in metaphysics) quality of a being that does not have the cause of its existence within itself; ontologically dependent. Contrasts with *necessary* (see below).

Contracausal: incompatible with determinism.

Cosmological argument: (1) an argument for the existence of God that takes as its first premise some empirical or quasi-empirical observation about the world. (2) some particular formulation of such an argument.

Cosmology: (1) the study of the origin and general structure of the physical universe. (2) a theory or system regarding the same. Most of the inquiries that once belonged to cosmology have now been taken over by the physical sciences.

Critical realism: any view which affirms that the world as it really is is in some respects similar to, and in some respects different from, the world as it appears to us.

Cultural relativism: a metaethical theory according to which moral utterances are held to be statements about the approval- and disapproval-tendencies of some social group to whom the person making the utterance has reference.

Deduction: the act of drawing a conclusion from a set of premises; the act of inferring. In the case of a correct deduction, the conclusion (inference) must be true if the premises are true. In this respect *deduction* differs from *induction* (see below). Also, that which one deduces from a set of premises.

Defining characteristic: a characteristic that a thing must have in order to be a member of the class of things being defined. (*Ex.:* being unmarried is a defining characteristic of bachelorhood; hence, any person who is to qualify as a bachelor must have the characteristic of being unmarried.)

Determinism: the theory that the universe is constituted in such a way that everything that occurs is the inevitable consequence of antecedent causes; universal determinism; strict determinism. Contrasts with *indeterminism* (see below).

Double-aspect theory: the theory, first advanced by the Dutch philosopher Benedict Spinoza (1632–1677), that mind and body are simply two different aspects of a single underlying reality.

Dualism, mind-body: the theory that body and mind are ontologically distinct, neither being reducible to the other.

Dualism, ontological: the theory that reality consists of two different kinds of being (for example, mind and matter), neither of which is reducible to the other.

Emotivism: a metaethical theory according to which moral utterances are held to be ejaculatory in nature, that is, expressions of the feelings (of approval or disapproval) of the speaker; a form of *noncognitivism* (see below).

Empirical: (1) derived from observation; *a posteriori.* (2) about the real world; capable of being exhibited in sense experience.

Empirical generalization: a general statement about a class of objects made on the basis of observation of some members of that class.

Empiricism: the epistemological theory that all knowledge of reality originates in, and is a product of, sense experience, that is, all knowledge of synthetic truths arises out of experience. Contrasts with *rationalism* (see below).

Epiphenomenalism: the theory that mind or consciousness is a mere by-product ("epiphenomenon") of physiological processes, and that it does not influence those processes in any way; the theory that mind is constituted by physiological processes, and is influenced causally by them, but that it has no causal influence on the body.

Epistemology: (1) a study of the nature and limits of human knowledge. (2) a theory concerning the same. (*Ex.:* "the *epistemology* of Kant.")

Equivocal: quality of a term having different meanings in each of two or more applications.

Ethical pluralism: the view that many things are intrinsically good, and that man's highest good consists in securing a maximum quantity of such goods.

Ethical theism: a world-view, the central claim of which is that everything that exists (except God Himself) is the creation of a good, wise, and powerful Creator.

Ethics: see *normative ethics* and *metaethics.*

Eudemonia: literally, "having a good spirit"; from the Greek word *eudaimonia,* usually translated as "happiness."

Existential: of or pertaining to existence, particularly human existence.

Fallacy: an error in reasoning that makes it impossible to establish the conclusion in question on the given premises; a logical mistake. In the case of a deductive argument, the effect of a fallacy is to render the argument *invalid* (see below).

Formalist ethics: a type of ethical theory in which moral obligatoriness is held to be a characteristic of some acts quite apart from any tendency those acts (or acts of that type) may have or be presumed to have to produce a good result. Deontological ethics.

Freedom: (1) the opportunity to do what one wants to do. (2) the power to enact any of two or more genuinely open alternatives; free will. (3) the state in which "ideal manhood" is realized, in which one has become everything that man ought to be. (Note: This term is highly ambiguous. It is always important to try to determine the precise sense in which a given writer is using the term.) See also *moral freedom; natural freedom of self-determination; circumstantial freedom of self-realization; free will.*

Free will: power of the self to enact any of two or more genuinely open alternatives; contracausal freedom; natural freedom of self-determination.

Hard determinism: the view that determinism is true, and that it is not compatible with moral freedom, and that man is therefore not morally responsible.

Hedonism: (1) (analytic form) the theory that "good" (in the moral sense) means "pleasurable." (2) (synthetic form) the theory that pleasure alone is intrinsically good.

Heuristic principle: a principle that is not judged as to its truth or falsity (it is neither affirmed nor denied), but which is assumed for the purposes of some particular inquiry because of its demonstrated usefulness in raising fruitful questions.

Humanism: the view that man, unlike all other creatures, is in some respects not merely a part of nature.

Hypercritical realism: the view that the world as it really is is highly dissimilar to the world as it appears to us; a radical form of *critical realism* (see above).

Immanent: within; near; not transcendent.

Imperativism: a metaethical theory according to which moral sentences are held to be a species of directive language, that is, implicit commands or recommendations to act in certain ways and not to act in other ways; a form of *noncognitivism* (see below).

Indeterminism: the theory that the universe is constituted in such a way that some events are not the inevitable consequences of antecedent causes.

Induction: the act of affirming a general statement about a class of things on the basis of observation of some members of the class; the act of making an empirical generalization. Also, an empirical generalization affirmed on the basis of observation of some members of the class.

Inference: (1) a proposition that follows as a logical consequence of certain other propositions; that which is inferred; an implication. (2) the act of inferring, that is, of deriving the actual or apparent logical consequences from a set of assumed premises.

Interactionism: the theory that body and mind are ontologically distinct, and that they influence each other causally.

Introspection: the act or process of observing or noting one's own feelings, thoughts, or mental states.

Intuition: according to rationalists, the act whereby the mind discerns nonempirical qualities and grasps a priori truths.

Intuitionism: a metaethical theory according to which "good" (in the moral sense) is held to denote a simple, nonnatural quality; nonnaturalistic objectivism, nonnaturalism.

Invalid: quality of a deductive argument whose conclusion may be false even if all of its premises are true; not valid.

Legalism: an ethical theory according to which it is held that right and wrong are determined by one's adherence or nonadherence to a set of moral rules (laws) which are applicable at all times, in all places, and under any circumstances.

Libertarianism: the view that free will is a necessary condition of moral responsibility, and that man has this freedom, and, consequently, that determination is not the case. Contrasts with *hard determinism* (see above) and *soft determinism* (see below).

Logic: (1) a study of the principles whereby one may distinguish correct from incorrect reasoning. (2) a system or theory regarding the same. (*Ex.:* "The *logic* of John Stuart Mill.")

Materialism: the metaphysical theory that the whole of reality consists of matter and its determinations; a form of *monism* (see below).

Metaethics: a study of the logical structure of ethical reasoning and the logical characteristics of ethical discourse. The main effort of metaethics to date has been directed toward the elucidation of the precise meanings of the key terms of moral appraisal ("good," "bad," "right," "wrong," "duty," "ought," etc.).

Metalanguage: a language used for the purpose of talking about language, that is, a language whose terms denote features of language rather than features of nonverbal reality; a language about language. (The language of grammar, for example, constitutes a metalanguage.)

Metaphysics: (1) the study of the nature and structure of being (ontology) and of the origin and general structure of the universe (cosmology); first philosophy. (2) a theory or system concerning the same. (Some philosophers use this term simply as a synonym for ontology, excluding cosmology. Others use it pejoratively as a synonym for "nonsense.")

Monism: the view that the whole of reality consists of various determinations of some one ultimate substance, or kind of "stuff." The principal forms of monism are *materialism* (all is matter), *idealism* (all is mind), and *neutral monism* (all is some substance that is neither mind nor matter, but is the ground of both). Monism contrasts with *dualism* (see above) and *pluralism* (see below).

Moral evil: anything generally regarded as evil that occurs as a result of a deliberate act by a human being. Contrasts with *natural evil* (see below).

Moral freedom: the freedom (whatever its nature) that is a necessary condition of moral responsibility; the freedom without which man is not, or would not be, morally responsible.

Morally responsible: answerable for one's behavior; a fitting subject of moral appraisal.

Naïve realism: see *commonsense*, or *direct, realism*.

Natural evil: anything generally regarded as evil that occurs as a result of the ordinary working of the laws of nature. Contrasts with *moral evil* (see above).

Natural freedom of self-determination: the power of the self to enact any one of two or more genuinely open alternatives; contracausal freedom; free will. Libertarians affirm that man has such a power, determinists that he does not.

Naturalism: (1) any philosophical system which holds that the whole of reality consists of objects and events occurring in space and time. Contrasts with *transcendentalism* (see below). (2) (in metaethics) the view that "good" (in a moral sense) denotes some empirical quality or qualities; naturalistic objectivism.

Naturalistic fallacy: the mistake, according to the intuitionism of G. E. Moore (1873–1958), of attempting to define "good" (in a moral sense), particularly in terms of some natural (empirically discernible) quality or qualities.

Naturalistic objectivism: a metaethical theory according to which the key moral predicates are held to denote some empirically verifiable quality or qualities; ethical naturalism. A hedonist who affirms that "good" means "pleasurable," for example, would be affirming one very common version of this theory.

Natural law: a fundamental principle of right or justice which, according to some philosophers, human reason can discern merely by attending carefully to the proposition stating that principle.

Necessary: (1) (in logic) quality of a proposition the denial of which involves a self-contradiction. (2) (in metaphysics) quality of a being which has the cause of its existence within itself; not ontologically dependent. Contrasts with *contingent* (see above).

Negative predication: see *via negativa*.

Nihilism: the view that nothing is worth living for, and, therefore, that human existence is without meaning.

Noncognitivism: any metaethical theory which holds that moral sentences are not informative, that is, they assert nothing, and therefore are incapable of being either true or false. *Emotivism* and *imperativism* (see above) are examples of theories of this type.

Nonnaturalistic objectivism: see *intuitionism*.

Non sequitur: an argument containing a fallacy; an argument in which the conclusion does not follow from the premises.

Normative ethics: the quest for general principles of right and wrong; the attempt to determine what things really are good or bad, right or wrong, and to identify the general principles by virtue of which they are so.

Occasionalism: the theory that mind and body are ontologically distinct (therefore a *dualistic* theory), and that each operates according to its own laws, but that they appear to interact because from time to time God does whatever is required to keep them synchronized.

Omnipotence: infinite power; an attribute of God whereby He is said to be able to bring to pass whatever He wills.

Omniscience: infinite knowledge; an attribute of God whereby He is said to know everything there is to know; all-knowingness.

Ontological argument: a famous argument for the existence of God, devised by St. Anselm of Canterbury (1033–1106), in which the attempt is made to show that the denial of the proposition "God exists" is self-contradictory.

Ontologically distinct: belonging to different ontological categories, neither of which is reducible to the other.

Ontological status: kind of being. To disclose the ontological status of something is to put it in some ontological category; it is to state in what precise sense it is true to say that a thing *is.*

Ontology: (1) the study of the nature or structure of being. (Some philosophers use this term as a synonym for *metaphysics;* others use it as the name for one main branch of metaphysics, the other being *cosmology.*) (2) a theory or system put forward as a result of such a study.

Panpsychism: the view that the whole of reality consists of minds ("psyches") of varying degrees of consciousness; one of the classical ways of attempting to overcome ontological dualism.

Paradox: an apparently self-contradictory assertion which is nonetheless made on the ground that to eliminate the apparent contradiction would allegedly involve denying some truth.

Parallelism: the view that mind and body are ontologically distinct (therefore a *dualistic* theory), and that each operates according to its own laws, the appearance of interaction between the two resulting from the fact that God has established a perfect harmony between them. This view was first advocated by the German philosopher Gottfried Wilhelm Leibnitz (1646–1716).

Percept: that which is "before the mind" in the act of perceiving; that which is immediately present to consciousness in perception; sense datum.

Perception: the act or process of taking cognizance of the world by means of the senses.

Phenomenalism: the view that the reality of a material object consists in its being perceived by some perceiver, with the corollary that the physical world does not exist apart from the actual or possible perceptions of some perceiver; cf. *subjective idealism.*

Pluralism: the view that reality is not reducible to one ultimate substance, or kind of "stuff," but that on the contrary there are several. Contrasts with *monism* and *dualism* (see above).

Premise: a proposition which, in conjunction with one or more other propositions, is alleged to provide evidence for some proposition (the conclusion).

Primary quality: according to the critical realism of John Locke (1632–1704), a quality that belongs to an object in such a way that no particle of which the object is composed could be conceived to exist without it. Locke gives extension, shape, size, and mobility as examples of such qualities. Contrasts with *secondary quality* (see below).

Private subjectivism: a metaethical theory according to which moral utterances are held to be statements about the personal likes and dislikes of the person making the utterance.

Proposition: that which is affirmed or denied by a declarative sentence; the meaning of a sentence which affirms or denies that something is the case. Propositions (and the sentences in which they are expressed) have the property of being either true or false.

Rational eudemonism: the view that man's highest good consists in "activity according to reason" (Aristotle).

Rationalism: (1) the view that some truths about reality are knowable in a way that is in some degree independent of experience, that is, some synthetic truths may be known a priori. (2) a European philosophical movement, the most prominent representatives of which were René Descartes (1596–1650), Benedict de Spinoza (1632–1677), Gottfried Wilhelm Leibnitz (1646–1716), Christian Wolff (1679–1754), and Immanuel Kant (1724–1804).

Reality: (1) the totality of the real, everything that is. (2) what truly or in actuality is the case, as over against what may appear to be the case. In this sense, reality is often contrasted with appearance.

Reason: (1) a proposition which, in conjunction with some other propositions, supports a conclusion not deducible from the other propositions alone; a premise. (2) a statement which purportedly justifies a belief or act. (3) the faculty of knowledge. (4) the essential nature of the self.

Reasoning: the act or process of drawing conclusions from premises.

Res cogitans: literally, "thinking thing"; that which, according to René Descartes (1596–1650), man essentially is—in contrast to unthinking, extended being (that is, material objects).

Secondary quality: according to the critical realism of John Locke (1632–1704), the capacity of a material object to produce in a percipient an impression (of color, sound, taste, and so on) unlike anything in the object itself. Such a quality is thus said to be "mind-dependent." Contrasts with *primary quality* (see above).

Self: that which one denotes by the pronoun "I"; consciousness; mind. (Its status has long been a matter of philosophical controversy.)

Self-evident: quality of a proposition that can be seen to be true merely by considering the proposition itself, and that therefore does not need to be proven either by deduction from other more evident propositions or by an appeal to factual evidence.

Sense-data: the immediate, uninterpreted objects of sense experience; the patches of color, geometrical shapes, and so on that one sees when looking at a material object, the varipitched noises which one sometimes hears (which may subsequently be interpreted as a melody on a violin), and so on.

Social contract: a voluntary agreement among a group of individuals whereby, according to some political theorists, the members of society acquire a set of mutual obligations legitimately enforceable by established authority.

Social utilitarianism: the view that the authority of government is justifiable in terms of its capacity to secure the greatest good for the greatest number of people.

Societal subjectivism: see *cultural relativism.*

Soft determinism: the view that determinism is true, but that the conditions of moral responsibility are such that man is nonetheless morally responsible whenever he has the opportunity to do what he wants to do.

Solipsism: the theory that oneself is the only mind or consciousness which exists, and that everything else exists only as a perception of this self.

Sound: quality of an argument which is formally valid and contains only true premises.

Subjective idealism: the view, associated with George Berkeley (1685–1753), that the being of material objects consists in their being perceived by some perceiver ("esse est percipi"), that they have no "independent" existence; phenomenalism. Contrasts with all types of *critical, direct,* and *hypercritical realism* (see above).

Summum bonum: literally, "highest good"; that which is most worthy of being sought for its own sake.

Synthetic: quality of a sentence, statement, or proposition which purports to say something about reality. (*Ex.:* "Some camels have two humps.") Contrasts with *analytic* (see above).

System: a comprehensive set of coherent and interdependent propositions in terms of which one attempts to understand and explain the phenomena within the range of its alleged relevance. An *ethical system,* for example, purports to provide a context for the understanding and explanation of all ethical phenomena. A *philosophical system* purports to provide a context for the understanding and explanation of all phenomena.

Teleological: of or pertaining to ends, goals, purposes (from the Greek *télos,* meaning "end" or "goal"). *Teleological* explanations (explanations in terms of ends), for example, are often contrasted with scientific explanations (explanations in terms of causes). The term is sometimes used to describe a kind of thinking, also to designate a famous argument for the existence of God (see below).

Teleological argument: an argument for the existence of God popularized by William Paley (1743–1805). The argument begins with the allegedly empirical premise that there is order (means subservient to ends) in the universe, and by analogy with human contrivances asserts the necessity of positing a cosmic Intelligence to account for this order.

Teleological ethics: a type of ethical theory in which the moral value of any act is held to consist in the tendency of that act (or of acts of that type) to produce a good or bad result.

Télos: end or goal; that toward the achievement of which some process or activity is directed. (Plural *téloi.*)

Theodicy: an attempt to show that the occurrence of evil in the world is consistent with belief in a God who is perfect in knowledge, power, and goodness.

Touchstone proposition: central truth about reality as perceived in some particular world-view.

Transcendent: (1) (Kant's usage) beyond the categories of human experience. (2) (as commonly used in theology and philosophy of religion) beyond the world of space and time; other. Contrasts with *immanent* (see above).

Transcendentalism: any philosophical system which holds that there are dimensions of reality in addition to objects and to events occurring in space and time. Contrasts with *naturalism* (see above).

Univocal: (applied to terms) having the same meaning in all instances in which it is used, or in all instances being considered. Contrasts with *equivocal* (see above).

Utilitarianism: (1) the theory that the goodness or badness of acts consists in their tendency to promote or hinder the realization of that which is intrinsically good. (2) the particular version of this theory advocated by the English philosophers Jeremy Bentham (1749–1832) and John Stuart Mill (1806–1873). This view is more properly called "hedonistic utilitarianism."

Vague: (applied to terms) imprecise in ordinary usage in such a way that any attempt at precise definition would render the term more exact than ordinary usage will allow. (*Ex.:* "warm" is a vague term; it would be inconsistent with ordinary usage to define it precisely in terms of a definite temperature range.)

Verbal: of or pertaining to words. Often applied to a given philosophical controversy to indicate that there is no "real issue" dividing the parties to the dispute, but simply a confusion or disagreement over the meanings of certain terms.

Via negativa: literally, "negative way." A mode of speaking about God wherein one attempts to say not what God *is* but what He is *not.* Thus "simple" (= non-complex), "incorporeal" (= non-corporeal), and so on, are "negative predicates." Used by several medieval philosophers, including St. Thomas Aquinas.

Volition: (1) the act of exercising choice, of choosing among alternatives. (2) the power to exercise choice.

World-view: a comprehensive view of reality in terms of which one attempts to understand and "place" everything that comes before one's consciousness.

INDEX

ABOUT THE AUTHOR

William H. Halverson, Associate Dean of University College at The Ohio State University, received his M.A. and Ph.D. from Princeton University. He has previously taught at Augsburg College and the University of Minnesota and was a Fellow of the American Council on Education from 1965 to 1966. Professor Halverson has contributed articles to such professional journals as *Mind, Pacific Philosophy Forum,* and the *Journal of Religion.*